Ecuador's "Good Living"

Studies in Critical Social Sciences Book Series

Haymarket Books is proud to be working with Brill Academic Publishers (www.brill.nl) to republish the *Studies in Critical Social Sciences* book series in paperback editions. This peer-reviewed book series offers insights into our current reality by exploring the content and consequences of power relationships under capitalism, and by considering the spaces of opposition and resistance to these changes that have been defining our new age. Our full catalog of *SCSS* volumes can be viewed at https://www.haymarketbooks.org/series_collections/4-studies-in-critical-social-sciences.

Series Editor
David Fasenfest (Wayne State University)

Editorial Board
Eduardo Bonilla-Silva (Duke University)
Chris Chase-Dunn (University of California–Riverside)
William Carroll (University of Victoria)
Raewyn Connell (University of Sydney)
Kimberlé W. Crenshaw (University of California–LA and Columbia University)
Heidi Gottfried (Wayne State University)
Karin Gottschall (University of Bremen)
Alfredo Saad Filho (King's College London)
Chizuko Ueno (University of Tokyo)
Sylvia Walby (Lancaster University)
Raju Das (York University)

Ecuador's "Good Living"

Crises, Discourse and Law

Carlos E. Gallegos-Anda

Haymarket Books
Chicago, IL

First published in 2020 by Brill Academic Publishers, The Netherlands
© 2020 Koninklijke Brill NV, Leiden, The Netherlands

Published in paperback in 2021 by
Haymarket Books
P.O. Box 180165
Chicago, IL 60618
773-583-7884
www.haymarketbooks.org

ISBN: 978-1-64259-617-5

Distributed to the trade in the US through Consortium Book Sales and Distribution (www.cbsd.com) and internationally through Ingram Publisher Services International (www.ingramcontent.com).

This book was published with the generous support of Lannan Foundation and Wallace Action Fund.

Special discounts are available for bulk purchases by organizations and institutions. Please call 773-583-7884 or email info@haymarketbooks.org for more information.

Cover design by Jamie Kerry and Ragina Johnson.

Printed in the United States.

10 9 8 7 6 5 4 3 2 1

Library of Congress Cataloging-in-Publication data is available.

For Piedad and Elías

Contents

List of Figures IX

Introduction 1
1 The Context of Good Living 3
2 Critical Approaches towards Good Living 13
3 Why Good Living? 18
4 On Methodology 20
5 Positioning Critical Good Living: Discourse and Rights 25
6 Book Layout 27

1 The Context of Good Living: Situating Theory and Method 31
1 Method 32
2 Politicised Ethnic Cleavage 38
3 The Retreating State 42
4 Changing Citizenship Regimes 47
5 Wider Theoretical Framing 52
6 Transnational Governmentality 54
7 Social Protest and Discursive Democracy 57
8 Conclusion 66

2 Good Living in the Academic Literature 67
1 Ecuadorian Discussions on Good Living 74
2 Indigenist or Pachamama Good Living 76
3 Developmental or Statist Good Living 88
4 Ecologist and Post-developmental Good Living 98
5 Critical Approaches towards Good Living: Power Not Ontology 102

3 The Critical Juncture 108
1 Theory-guided Process Tracing 112
2 Development Paradigms in Indigenous Communities 114
3 Defining the Theory behind a Theory 116
4 Lead-up to the Critical Juncture: 1960–1979 118
    4.1 *Agrarian Revolts and Reforms* 118
    4.2 *Oil Induced Military Nationalism* 120
5 Economic, Institutional, and Political Breakdown 122
    5.1 *State Retreat* 122
    5.2 *Regionalist Challenges to State Building* 123

		5.3	Economic Turmoil and Reform during the 1980s 124

      5.3   *Economic Turmoil and Reform during the 1980s*   124
      5.4   *The Financial Meltdown of the 1990s*   125
      5.5   *Inter-branch Crises and Ghost Coalitions*   128
  6   Politicised Ethnic Cleavages: Rise and Fall of Indigenous Mobilisation   131
  7   Changing Citizenship Regimes   144
      7.1   *The Quest for Civic Virtue*   148
      7.2   *Constitutional Convergence and Graduated Sovereignty*   153
      7.3   *Diffusion and the Scripts of Modernity*   154
  8   The Inter-American Human Rights System   156
      8.1   *Selected Jurisprudence: Vida Digna*   158
      8.2   *The Graduated Sovereignty of the* GATT   158
  9   Conclusion   160

4 The Polymorphism of Good Living   161
  1   The New Governmentality   166
  2   Transnational Governmentality and the Critical Juncture   168
  3   The Theme of Social Capital   172
  4   Social Capital or the Myth of Ethnodevelopment   178
  5   The Sources of Social Capital   182
  6   The Master Framing of Transgressive Politics   185
  7   The Empty Signifier Is Born   193
  8   Yasuní: a Case Study on the Empty Signifier   199
  9   Yasuni and the Discourse of Good Living   201
  10 Conclusion   208

5 Beyond Living Well   209
  1   Crafting Good Living: from Speaking to Listening   212
  2   Exhaustion of the Rights Discourse   217
  3   The Importation of Law: Local and International Influences   221
  4   From Human Dignity to *Vida Digna*   225
  5   Graduated Sovereignty and the Role of the IACtHR   228
  6   The *Vida Digna* Jurisprudence of the Inter-American Court of Human Rights   234
  7   Convergence of Rights: Domestic Approaches to Economic, Social and Cultural Rights   238
  8   Back to Basics: Recalibrating the "Engine Room of the Constitution"   241
  9   Conclusion   243

Bibliography   245
Index   276

Figures

1 Conventional process tracing   35
2 Proposed theory-guided process tracing   35
3 Theoretical and methodological framing   53
4 Protesters battle security forces in an attempt to storm the Presidential Palace in 1997   138
5 Antonio Vargas, Lucio Gutierrez and Carlos Solorzano seize power in Ecuador's Congress on 22 January 2000   141
6 Good Living as an empty signifier   189

Introduction

On 20th October 2008, after months of heated deliberations amongst Constitutional Assembly members and a national referendum, Ecuador's twentieth constitution entered into force with a backing of almost 65 per cent of the country's population (Torre 2010, 188; Mijeski and Beck 2011, 123). The new constitution was a novel piece of legislation that included a repertoire of rights that departed from Euro-American legal tradition. In his analysis of constitutional reform processes in the Andes, Elkins (2017, 114) points out that Ecuador's 2008 Constitution became the 12th longest constitutional text in the world with some 54,000 words that develop and describe the newly minted rights.

Ecuador's 2008 Constitution, as well as the constitutional projects that preceded it in Brazil (1988), Colombia (1991), Ecuador (1979 and 1998) and Venezuela (1999), is part of a regional recalibration of legal structures. As Latin American nations returned to democratic rule at the end of the 1970s, they soon responded to regional economic conditions by either enacting or rejecting the economic policy measures imposed by the International Monetary Fund and World Bank. The 1980s were a particularly turbulent era for Latin America, as the regional debt crisis was compounded by falling commodity prices, crippled government finances, and the reversal of the modernisation programs that had come into play during the 1960s and 1970s (Szablowski 2007, 29). The convergence of external pressures with a forced reordering of domestic policies, spawned a new constitutional framing that transformed longstanding citizen-state relations (Collier and Collier 2002, 773).

Amongst its various additions, the 2008 constitution unveiled the legal principle called *Buen Vivir* or Good Living.[1] Buen Vivir (Sumak Kawsay or Good Living) as discussed by Cubillo-Guevara and Hidalgo-Capitan (2016, 302) also

---

1 The English translation of Ecuador's 2008 Constitution defines Good Living or Sumak Kawsay as: "(...) a term in the Kichwa language referring to an ancestral Andean concept highlighting the importance of solidarity, community ties, harmony with nature and dignity. It is translated as *buen vivir* in Spanish. To avoid the consumer connotation of "to live well," the "good life," "good living" or "standard of living," the phrase "good way of living" has been coined for the translation into English, inspired by the Chinese concept of Tao and the Japanese concept of Do, both of which literally mean "Way." It is closely related to a similar concept in the Aymara language in Bolivia, *suma qamaña*, which can be translated as "living in plenitude" (...)." For all effects and purposes and do to the contested nature its definition carries, I refer to Good Living as the Spanish translation of Sumak Kawsay. I avoid using the Kichwa language form in an effort to circumvent etymological or ontological controversies relating to Indigenous or *mestizo* interpretations.

relates to the Bolivian precept of Suma Qamaña installed in that country's 2009 Constitution. Both concepts have been widely discussed by Andean, Latin American and European authors who refer to them as a "nude name," "usurped word," "utopia under construction," "invented tradition" or "social phenomenon" (Cubillo-Guevara and Hidalgo-Capitan 2016, 302). However, one of its earliest Ecuadorian proponents, Carlos Viteri Gualinga, encapsulates an indigenous understanding of Buen Vivir that relates to a development model in which Good Living may be achieved by recreating indigenous paradigms influenced by external economic dynamics and exogenous knowledge patterns, effectively adapting them to present and future demands (Gualinga 2002, 4). However, what remains to be explained by Gualinga (2002, 5), is how exactly 'local subsistence' framed under Buen Vivir is to remain unscathed by such a process of continuous adaptation whilst simultaneously consolidating an 'autonomous and interdependent' form of dispute resolution.

This book will employ the concept of Good Living[2] rather than Buen Vivir, Sumak Kawsay or Suma Qamaña. Methodological discrimination is warranted as the existing literature on the subject has emerged from works in sociology, anthropology or philosophy seeking to unravel the ontological origins of the concept (Alonso González and Vázquez 2015, 2).[3] Ontological searches for Sumak Kawsay are best determined by Cubillo-Guevara and Hidalgo-Capitan (2016, 302) as they seek to determine where and what the 'genuine' sumak kawsay originates from. This book however seeks to depart from ontological prescriptions in order to develop political and legal framings that may situate the discussion on Good Living within the contexts from which it emerged. In doing so, this book does not seek to determine the genuine, real or actual origin of the concept in philosophical, sociological or anthropological terms but rather develop the political discourse and legal standing it was awarded in the 2008 Ecuadorian Constitution.

This exercise is relevant as Good Living features in 33 per cent of the 2008 Constitution, covering subject matter as diverse as the environment, food, water, health, education, and housing. The multiple areas associated with Good

---

2 Usage of the term Good Living, rather than Buen Vivir, Suma Qamaña or Sumak Kawsay also relates to a simplification of the diversity of theoretical backdrops it has encountered. Within English speakers the term is associated to scholarly works analyzing Ecuador's usage of the concept, effectively separating it from studies focusing on Bolivia. Usage of Good Living as a working concept rather than its other appellatives may be found in works by: Waldmüller (2014); Cochrane (2014); Quick and Spartz (2018); Gallegos-Anda (2017); Séverine (2012); Ponce León (2016) and Fabricant (2013).

3 See: Estermann (2012); Alonso González and Vázquez (2015); Acosta (2010); Medina (2001); Huanacuni (2010); Gudynas (2009); Houtart (2011), amongst others.

Living in Ecuador's 2008 Constitution, as well as the diverse meanings and interpretations the principle's inclusion has sprouted in academia, legal circles or civil society groups, raises questions regarding its legal origins, political force and subsequent enforceability. Whilst present in multiple spaces of the constitution, questions surrounding Good Living's enforceability in regards to other constitutional principles such as equality,[4] non-discrimination[5] or the presumption of innocence are commonplace.[6] If despite its scattered nature within the constitutional text, Good Living does not carry similar enforceability as the previously described principles, then its constitutional inscription is merely declarative in nature, carrying the same legal strength as the right to pursue happiness inscribed in the Declaration of Independence of the United States.

We address issues of enforceability by reviewing the theoretical framings that explain Good Living's birth. Through a critical lens, this thesis reviews the current literature surrounding Good Living in order to identify suitable theoretical responses that may better develop its origins, as well as its present and future applicability.

1 The Context of Good Living

Good Living as a constitutional principle is the result of decades of civil society mobilisations that sought to contest the wave of privatisations, welfare cuts, environmental degradation, and fiscal discipline enacted throughout Latin America and Ecuador during the 1980s and 1990s. Macroeconomic reform policies engulfed the region, as governments forcefully adopted trade liberalisation, Structural Adjustment Policies (SAP), and sovereign loan conditionalities compounding their financial exposure to international markets. As a response to these previous policy ailments, Article 3 of Ecuador's 2008 Constitution, dictates that the state has a primary duty of care towards its citizens, a responsibility that demands the eradication of poverty, equitable distribution of wealth, and attainment of sustainable development standards. All of which are understood within the constitutional text as the tangible means through which Good Living may be reached via policy enactment. Similarly, Article 12 declares water a fundamental human right; inalienable and exonerated from any form of statutory limitations. Such concerns are further strengthened by

---

4 Constitution of the Republic of Ecuador, Art. 11.
5 Constitution of the Republic of Ecuador, Art. 11 (2).
6 Constitution of the Republic of Ecuador, Art. 76 (2).

the environmental prescriptions incorporated through Article 14, which affirm the population's right to live in an ecologically healthy and balanced environment that guarantees Good Living.

Proponents of Good Living, emphasise the possibility of utilising it as a tool through which subaltern knowledges may defy the idealisation of Euro-American political and legal thought (Cuadra 2015, 3). Good Living, according to such proponents, elevates the struggles of subaltern peoples by giving them a privileged place within the spaces where rights, policies and the aspirational goals of society are decided (Acosta 2011; Shilliam 2015; Szlablowski 2009, 142). As a legal principle, Good Living has received heightened levels of attention from scholars, who have, albeit through differing degrees, stressed that the principle could be a legal tool that overcomes the predominant legal formalism that has historically defined Latin American law (Silva 2008, 112). Fashioned under such perspectives, to some at least, Good Living is shaped as a conceptual bridge that unites Euro-American institutions of law with the transgressive politics of civil society resistance that swept Latin America during the 1990s and early 2000s (Acosta 2011; Bonilla Maldonado 2013, 9).

Following Hidalgo-Capitán and Cubillo-Guevara's classification of Good Living (2014), we can categorise existing literature regarding its theoretical anchoring within what could broadly be summarised as three strains or discourses: socialist/statist, ecologist/post-developmental and Indigenist/Pachamama. Each strain forms a particular discourse around Good Living by either highlighting the relevance of state-led planning, environmental conservation or preservation of indigenous epistemologies. Good Living is here framed under the Foucaultian lens of discourse, where it becomes a strategic tool through which a specific version of reality is constructed (Wickham 2013, 225–26). Strategic discourse formation in turn, generates the signs and communication necessary for power to be exercised upon a population (Foucault 1994, 338; 2007).

When viewed through the Foucaultian lens, Good Living's constitutional inscription and the discourses that shape its contours uncover the systems of communication, coordination, and goal-directed activities that transform law into power through the production of a certain truth (Foucault 1994, 338). As a strategic discourse, proponents of the socialist/statist strain advocate for an interventionist and active public sector that defines the necessary public policies through which Good Living may be attained (Hidalgo-Capitán et al. 2014, 27). With its main focus on social equality through wealth redistribution, this state-led vision of Good Living is part of an urban socio-economic political agenda formulated by the highly technocratic left that came to power in Ecuador from 2006 onwards (Nelms 2015, 111).

In the polar opposite of state-led development lies the ecologist or post-developmental strain. By advocating for the preservation of nature and the construction of a participative and inclusive formulation of Good Living, this discourse fuses the political projects and demands of civil society groups composed by peasants, indigenous, socialists, feminists, and ecologists (Hidalgo-Capitán et al. 2014). The third strain discussed by Hidalgo-Capitán et al. (2014), refers to the Indigenist or Pachamama discourse, which focuses on the demands that surfaced through the identity politics that swept Ecuador during the 1990s. Moreover, construction of Good Living through identity politics, underlines demands for self-determination, territorial autonomy, and the construction of *Sumak Kawsay* rather than Good Living. By converting the urban dwelling Good Living to its indigenous Kichwa language form, a conscious effort is made by its proponents to highlight the importance of indigenous knowledge in its formulation. The most predominant difference between Good Living and *Sumak Kawsay*, according to these authors, are the Andean indigenous traditions that construct the latter in contrast to the urban settings of the former (Oviedo 2014, 139). Sumak Kawsay's main exponents hail from Ecuador's Kichwa and Bolivia's Aymara indigenous populations with some influences associated with *mestizo* intellectuals (Hidalgo-Capitán et al. 2014, 29).

Good Living or *Sumak Kawsay*, and their subsequent theoretical complementarity to the three predominating discourses presented by Hidalgo-Capitán et al. (2014), has been formulated by academics, civil society groups and legal scholars as a constitutional avenue that secures socio-economic demands whilst protecting the collective rights of ethnic minorities.[7] Good Living, understood in this way, cannot and should not, be theorised or explained without analysing the ways in which its constitutional inscription came about. As occurred in other parts of Latin America, constitutional reforms between the late 1970s and early 2000s inscribed international human rights treaties into domestic legislation. This process of fusing the supranational with the local, transformed the human rights discourse of the time into 'the universal linguistic unit' that made the globalisation of law possible throughout Latin America (Gardbaum 2010, 155).

Importation of law, conceptual fluidity and the merging of supranational and national legal systems, or what Watson (1979 in Dupré 2003a, 39) called

---

[7] Collective rights according to Kymlicka (1994, 7): '(...) could refer to the right of a group to limit the liberty of its own individual members in the name of group solidarity or cultural purity (...) or it could refer to the right of a group to limit the economic or political power exercised by the larger society over the group, to ensure that the resources and institutions on which the minority depends are not vulnerable to majority decision (...).'

'legal transplants,' have been utilized on numerous occasions to innovate an existing legal system or create a new one altogether. One such event was the multifarious ways in which post-communist countries borrowed legal concepts from Western European law (Dupré, 2003a, 47). This process, called "cross-fertilization" in the Anglo-Saxon tradition and "mimetic institution building" in European continental law, speaks of the ways in which legal concepts are borrowed, copied, transplanted or enacted in jurisdictions outside their place of birth (Dupré 2003a, 48). For Latin America, the human rights discourse, would be one such legal field that permeated multiple legislations, policy decisions and the language of rights spoken throughout the region. As a universal linguistic unit, it allowed or at the very least facilitated, a regional acquiescence towards political, civil, economic, social and cultural rights.

The region's receptivity to foreign legal theories further accelerated this phenomenon, thereby installing what came to be known as neo-constitutionalism (Gardbaum 2010, 159). Between 1978 and 2008, Ecuador and Latin America experienced a series of social, economic and political events that rattled the institutional foundations on which political and economic power functioned. Importation of law was thus facilitated by the economic shocks experienced regionally and locally, paving the way for what was considered a "more authoritative" legal system to take root (Dupré 2003a, 41). The brand of neo-constitutionalism that took place in Ecuador, relied on supranational human rights institutions to cement the validity and legitimacy of legal concepts and their corresponding institutions. As a theoretical variant, neo-constitutionalism promotes transnational and socially-focused rulings that may, through the process of proportionality and balancing,[8] define the ways in which the rights of those excluded from power may be secured (Gardbaum 2010, 163). In this sense, Ecuadorian neo-constitutionalism demanded and depended upon, a form of transjudicial communication that integrated horizontal and vertical legal institutions to enforce legal applicability (Dupré 2003a, 43). In time, local judicial practice would incorporate decisions from supranational institutions such as the Inter-American Court of Human Rights. Neo-constitutionalism, as an emerging field of Latin American legal thinking, placed Good Living as a conceptual variant in which legal transplants, and the merging of local practices with supranational

---

8 Alexy (2003): '(...) balancing is one part of what is required by a more comprehensive principle (...) This more comprehensive principle is the principle of proportionality (...) The principle of proportionality consists of three sub-principles: the principles of suitability, of necessity, and of proportionality in the narrow sense. All three principles express the idea of optimisation. Constitutional rights as principles are optimisation requirements. As optimisation requirements, principles are norms requiring that something be realized to the greatest extent possible, given the legal and factual possibilities (...)'

institutions, were combined to produce a new form of legal analysis, resulting from the social, economic and political processes experienced by a region or country. Ecuador's constitutional reform of 2008 positions it within wider regional processes in which the convergence of domestic legislation and international human rights treaties, coordinated state behaviour and the domestic processes of constitution making; transplanting concepts and institutions in an effort to answer social, political and economic needs through the "intermediated dialogue" of national courts and their corresponding supranational counterparts (Elkins et al. 2013, 62; Dupré 2003a).

Within Ecuador's political sphere, the converging social, political and economic transformations that occurred during this time, and eventually led to constitutional reform, further challenged the power excised by the state or Ecuador's coastal and Andean elites. More precisely put, these transformations, best exemplified in the effects that came about through the politicisation of previously dormant ethnic cleavages, state retreat and the shifting policy dynamics of changing citizenship regimes, converged to transform Ecuador's political arena. Good Living, as a formal constitutional principle, represents the juridification or legal abstraction of the collective grievances suffered in everyday life between 1979 and 2008. In order to address such demands, constitutional reform during the critical juncture increasingly developed a series of economic, social and cultural rights that adhered to popular demands. Within Chapter II of Title II of Ecuador's 2008 Constitution, all rights related to Good Living fall within the realm of economic, social or cultural rights. Rights associated to adequate and dignified housing, health, work and social security constitute the many welfare rights of modern democracies rather than indigenous forms of subsistence (Corte Constitutional 2017, 45). Good Living, according to Ecuador's Constitutional Court is constituted by a positive and negative dimension to be executed by the state. The positive, obliges public policy to make these rights exercisable and the negative limits actions by the state that may limit them (Corte Constitutional 2017, 46). The housing dimension of Good Living, according to the Court, responds to national and international rights that are to be guaranteed. To this effect, Ecuador's Constitutional Court develops the right to housing in the following manner:

> In this sense, the right to adequate and dignified housing is not limited to having a place where to live but should also coincide with General Comment No. 4 of the Committee on International Economic, Social and Cultural Rights (Ruling No. 146-14-SEP-CC in Corte Constitutional 2017, 47).[9]

---

9   The translation is mine.

Moreover, the emergence of Good Living as a legal principle itself, will be argued later on to be the result of the importation of law and institutions that came about from the human rights discourse of the time. The emergence of this discourse, during the critical juncture of 1978–2008, responds to the economic, social and political transformations that took place during this time, rather than merely the local processes or practices localized within Ecuador. Additionally, Good Living itself, will be argued to be the derivative of other legal institutions utilized first in Germany, then in Hungary and later imported into Ecuadorian legislation through the transjudicial communication of the Inter-American Court of Human Rights towards local and regional courts. This period of time, stretching from 1978 to 2008 is methodologically named as a critical juncture; Capoccia and Kelemen (2007, 342) define junctures as 'critical' because they create schisms within a particular period of study.

Whilst the period of study is considerably long, the schisms that took place during this time have all redefined Ecuador's political sphere, whilst erecting institutions, legal concepts and economic paradigms that reshaped Latin America as a whole. The different institutions, processes and actors that came together in the reshaping of Latin American and Ecuadorian politics is thoroughly covered in Chapter 3. Usage of the critical juncture, allows the reader to place a spatial and temporal framing in which a specific set of events took place. Moreover, the critical juncture serves as a frame from which we may review how a specific set of policy decisions, actors, both local and transnational and institutions reshaped Ecuador's political landscape through consecutive crises.

Convergence of newly constituted social movements, economic melt-down and institutional crises paved the way for new approaches towards legislation. It is unsurprising that as a result of these fluctuating conditions, Ecuador gave birth to three different constitutional projects in 1979, 1998 and 2008. Incorporation of Good Living into Ecuador's 2008 Constitution, reflects the different processes the country lived in the political, economic and social landscape as the country returned to democracy (1979), encountered a regional debt crises (1982), witnessed the rising of indigenous politics and widespread social mobilization (1991–1996), endured drastic economic liberalization and deregulation (1990s), succumbed to institutional crises (1996–2000s) and finally was recomposed by a new form of populist authoritative political governance (2006–2008).

Good Living as a legal institution, came into existence during this time. Analysis of Good Living under this lens, has no intention of contradicting or claiming an authoritative analysis of *Buen Vivir, Vivir Bien* or *Suma Qamaña* stemming from other epistemological fields such as philosophy, sociology or anthropology. Rather, what is sought here is to situate discussions on Good Living within the political, legal and economic events that propelled it to become a constitutional principle. Rural sociology, such as that attributed to Bretón (2001; 2008; 2010), has depicted a meticulous account of life in the rural Andes, whilst rich ethnographic research presented by Sawyer (2004) presents the diverging struggles, grievances and triumphs of indigenous mobilization in Ecuador's Amazon province of Pastaza. In the same sense, authors such as Schavelzon (2015), Medina (2014), Oviedo (2014) or Torres (2012) highlight philosophical approaches towards Good Living that develop what Estermann (2012) coined as a "Pachasofía," which basically elaborates on the 'timeless indigenous wisdom of the Andes, which is depicted in their cosmovision or Pachasofía. The parameters of this philosophical and civilizing paradigm contradict, in its great majority, the principles of Western modernity.' In no way have we attempted to elaborate a new philosophical understanding of Good Living, such an objective would far exceed the political and legal focus pursued. However, we do seek to explain the economic, political and legal transformations suffered by Ecuador and Latin America between 1979 and 2008, and how they reshaped legal frameworks after nearly two decades of civil society mobilization. If warranted, a philosophical development or understanding of Good Living in regards to what Estermann (2012, 23) calls a "Pachasofía," should be undertaken in other epistemological fields that utilize the rich literature that has been produced by ethnographic and sociological research on Ecuador's Buen Vivir or Bolivia's Suma Qamaña.

Returning to Good Living's emergence as a constitutional principle, we recount the rupturing of a path dependency that had relied on antecedent conditions such as a (1) strong central government, (2) limited political participation and (3) weak transnational institutions. During the critical juncture these conditions were altered, abolished or subsided, creating the necessary social, economic and political conditions for new actors and concepts to become agents of change and reform. The receding state, product of the 1982 debt crisis, significantly altered the political arena, allowing new actors to push through (Yashar 2005). This in return, created a newly mobilized civil society which was spearheaded by a galvanized indigenous movement that pursued collective rights and territorial autonomy (Van Cott 1994). Finally, the collapse of the Berlin Wall and consequently Communism as a political option, created a fertile ground for multilateral institutions focused on transnational market-orientated policies and human rights protection to proliferate. The emergence of the World Trade Organization in 1994, the explosion of international investment treaties ceding sovereign jurisdiction in favour of multilateral tribunals or the consolidation of the Inter-American Human Rights system, evidence the consolidation of strong multilateral institutions taking control of policy spaces formerly controlled uniquely by states (Galindo 2012; García-Sayán 2011; GATT 1994). Emerging multinational institutions were deployed through a network of international actors representing both international organizations and civil society through transnational NGOs. Agents of the World Bank and representatives of transnational civil society organizations, would soon descend upon Ecuador's Amazon and Andes, dramatically shifting political needs, creating indigenous elites and altering long-standing social organizations that had allowed, until then, for indigenous mobilization to take place (Bretón 2015; Cepek 2012; Collins 2004; Dávalos 2003; Fine 2001).

Good Living, as a constitutional principle, marks the expansion of formal written law into new social interactions and this process of expansion highlights the meaning of juridification. In this process, laws are passed to secure that certain problems brought about in market-led societies are dealt with on the basis of principles of fairness and equity (Baxter 2015, 55; Deflem 2013, 82). According to one account, juridification in the democratic welfare states of the twentieth century represents a point of influx in which economic, social and cultural rights react and contest the unrestrained functioning of the market (Deflem 2013, 82). Good Living as a form of juridification internalises the many ways in which these converging, opposing and at times mutually reinforcing processes, reshaped Ecuador's political arena between 1979 and 2008. Under this reading, Good Living materializes the demands expressed by a newly mobilized civil society led by a growing indigenous movement. As new actors in Ecuador's political arena, indigenous groups reclaimed policy spaces to which they had previously been denied access (North 2004). In this process, laws and subsequently policy, took new forms as the discourse of human rights and opposition to market-led reform fused with local political agendas.

As a strategic discourse formation, Good Living is a juridical abstraction of the convulsive political arena that engulfed Ecuador between 1979 and 2008. Its impact as a constitutional principle however, requires further theoretical discussion, as its enforceability in securing the economic, social and cultural rights that may alleviate historical grievances are yet to be fully explored. This revision is warranted, as the possible impacts such a principle might have in the present or future must be attentive to the warnings that are brought forth when analysing law through social theory. As Deflem (2013, 82) underlines, legal responses to social ills are more often than not framed in ways that accommodate the economic and administrative interests, thereby endangering that which they have been called on to protect. In a similar vein, legal abstraction of socio-economic demands must overcome four persistent problems: collective demands are usually understood as individual claims; procedural rules limit claims to formal conditions; implementation of rights usually suit the needs of bureaucratic organisations; and social demands are often pacified through monetary compensation (Deflem 2013, 82). Aside from the possible novelty Good Living carries as a legal principle, its origins and future enforceability demand further theoretical construction to overcome such limitations or at the very least question their impact on constitutional adjudication. The unravelling of the political, legal and economic origins that led to Good Living's formalization into written law and as a constitutional principle underlines our theoretical objective. In this analysis, we transcend Ecuador as a place of study, by situating the analysis within the regional and global trends that shifted international relations, politics, laws and institutions. For such a reason, the analysis of Good Living here presented, builds on previous sociological and ethnographic research in an effort to relocate the discussion within political and legal theory. As was mentioned before, the objective is to determine if Good Living as it currently stands within Ecuadorian law is legally applicable. To this effect, the vast literature that has been produced on Good Living until now will serve as a starting point from which political and legal analysis of its crafting may take place.

Good Living presents a legal conundrum, as its inscription into formal law does not have an equivalent counterpart in Euro-American Law. But is this so? Moreover, growing interest and expectations, both local and foreign, seek to develop Good Living into a possible option towards post-development, a new Indigenist philosophy towards development or a validation of state-led development policy. Whichever literature one may choose to explain Good Living's relevance, the impact of its inscription as a constitutional principle has yet to be explored and also exceeded Ecuador's borders, gaining support and publicity in many places around the world. As a 2013 English newspaper article highlights:

> ... Ecuador is building on its indigenous past by incorporating the concept of sumak kawsay into its development approach ... buen vivir ... describes a way of doing things that is community centric, ecologically-balanced and culturally sensitive ... Similar thinking is inspiring other social movements across South America ... such as those of the Aymara peoples of Bolivia, the Quichua of Ecuador and the Mapuche of Chile and Argentina ... (Balch 2013).

Labelled by some as an 'alternative to mainstream development' or a constitutional principle that facilitates the ways in which 'the poor could speak' by displacing debates around rights 'away from metropolitan centers or national elites' (Radcliffe 2013, 241), Good Living has evidently sparked a multitude of debates in academia, law, politics, and social movements. Moreover, debates surrounding its legal relevance are engulfed by the constructivist conceptions of law and society that came about in Latin America during the 1990s. In such iterations, Good Living is often conceived as the bridge that connects facts and norms with the inherent socio-economic and political tensions that playout in the region's highly convulsive political arena (Rodriguez-Garavito 2011, 1678). Additionally, interest surrounding Good Living's recovery of subaltern epistemologies within Euro-American codification has sparked academic debates regarding its legal enforceability. Inclusion of the polymorphous epistemologies that have historically remained excluded in Latin America's legal and political thought, seeks to consolidate a 'trans-modern pluriverse' that makes 'another world possible' (Dussel 2009, 514).

Inclusion of multiple epistemologies into any legal system or the highly convulsive and contested political spheres of Ecuador and Latin America require further analysis. Juridification of social reality 'describes its own components in legal categories and employs these self-thematizations for the purposes of constituting and reproducing legal acts by its own means' (Habermas 1996, 49). In other words, the legal system by its very nature is 'autopoietic,' therefore autonomous to the extent that its components and underlining epistemologies become linked through a systematic capacity (Habermas 1996, 50). Social integration through law's systematic capacity becomes an unintentional coordination in which the legal system may neither perceive nor deal with the problems that burden society as a whole (Habermas 1996, 51).

This 'unintentional' coordination is a by-product of a system that has the ability to reproduce itself by integrating multiple meanings or epistemologies that are themselves identified and perceived to have a fixed meaning depending on the viewpoint of the observer (Habermas 1996, 54). Hence, the legal constructivism to which Ecuador's 2008 Constitution owes a great deal may fall victim to the self-referential closure of the legal system. This closed-circuit reference limits avenues of communication with other 'epistemic worlds,' thereby aborting the 'pluriverse' some seek to construct from Good Living's constitutional inscription. In other words, the very juridification of Good Living could very well constrain the possibilities of integrating subaltern epistemologies or combating the social problems they identify.

Finally, Good Living must be contextualised within the supranational processes that have through the years dealt with economic, social and cultural rights. Such a discussion will inevitably lead us to the important role the Inter-American Court of Human Rights (the Court) has come to play. By enforcing the special judiciary powers awarded to the Court through the American

Convention on Human Rights, a series of rulings have developed a regional approach towards economic, social and cultural rights (Antkowiak 2014; Grijalva 2012, 234). Similar to what occurs in the chambers of the Court, approaches towards Good Living have focused on the complex interrelationship between theoretical formulations of economic, social and cultural rights and the countries and contexts in which they are exercised. Within the Court, this expansive judicial review is best exemplified in the jurisprudential construct of *Vida Digna*. *Vida Digna* or the "Right to a Decent Life" is, according to Antkowiak (2014, 129), a configurative principle of several rights that are interdependent such as water, healthcare, education, housing, and cultural identity; a doctrinal formulation that seeks to establish legal protections regarding sustainable development, non-discrimination, lands, resources, and cultural integrity.

The Court, through its analysis of the judicial controversies pertaining to the citizenry's deprivation of collective rights, water, food, healthcare or education has developed a linkage between economic, social, and cultural rights that must be met if the right to life is to be secured (Antkowiak 2014, 150). Good Living as a constitutional principle, creates a similar theoretical backdrop on which life is best safeguarded by the provision of basic services, protection of communitarian practices, and environmental conservation. Although one stems from the internal processes that defined constitutional reform in Ecuador and the other is the result of jurisprudential development by the Court, both surprisingly share the same focus of protecting economic, social and cultural rights by consolidating a judicial and public policy approach directed at 'ending five centuries of oppression, misery and poverty' (CONAIE 1994).

Whilst Good Living has received attention from a variety of civil society sectors and academic disciplines, its theoretical development has been limited to the three particular discourse formations presented above. The limited theoretical a limited scope by building a new theoretical framing under the name of 'critical Good Living.'

2 Critical Approaches towards Good Living

In addition to the main three discourses already discussed, others have attempted to equate Good Living with theories of wellbeing such as Amartya Sen's *The Idea of Justice* (2009). Within such conceptual efforts, *Buen Vivir* or Good Living has allegedly made Ecuadorian society less unjust by reclaiming communitarian solidarity-based forms of justice (Séverine 2012). Whilst such authors have lauded Good Living, others have been quick to question its significance or relevance by stating that it represents a return to archaic knowledge or a form of populist discourse, which is glossed over with esoteric tones and prophetic intentions (Mansilla 2012, 96). As Ecuadorian legal scholar Fabián Corral (2009) puts it:

> Good Living is not only an imagined political theory that surfaced during the hasty strides of Socialist novelty ... It managed to become the substance of a constitution that was voted for without understanding or reading ... in an act of supreme political ignorance ...

Branding of Good Living as an archaic knowledge that lacks linkages with indigenous epistemologies leads some to label it as a 'concept under construction' (Stefanoni 2012, 12). Such criticisms affirm that Good Living's theoretical emptiness is forcedly filled with the diluted 'wishful thinking,' 'quasi mystical rhetoric,' and 'utopic' makings of an 'alter civilizing project' that rejects modernity (Stefanoni 2012, 12). Whilst the three main currents and above-mentioned criticisms represent vastly different theoretical notions, they do share an underlying discursive thread: all construct Good Living in isolation of the political, social and economic events that came about during the critical juncture. This lacking spatiotemporal linkage circumvents the complex antecedents that created the political, social and economic conditions that led to constitutional reform. Good Living's origins are thus hardly discussed through a critical assessment of the multifaceted and often obscured convulsions that took place in Ecuador for nearly thirty years. Within this contextual void, Good Living is deprived of the necessary analysis that might inform its origins or direction.

The rather limited theoretical and contextual scope that has until now been associated with Good Living has made it susceptible to the ontological interpretations of those who at a given point in time assess the concept in relation to specific moral or political ends. Formulations that ponder what is "good" or "bad," offer a binary approximation to Good Living, thereby disassociating conceptual construction from its origins or intended purposes. Ontologically formulated representations of Good Living fail to analyse the complex sources from which the concept emerged. As González and Vázquez (2015, 16) argue when analysing Good Living and the multiple discourses that have been associated with it:

> ...Thinking relationally involves abandoning quantitative and technocratic notions associated with modernity to account for the multiplicity of the social qualitatively in order to elaborate political alternatives without imposing transcendental and essentialist values ... the debate around

INTRODUCTION 15

> BV [Good Living] has treated indigenous peoples as cultural representations, curiously but significantly ignoring indigenous visions ... urban and rural comunas are neither unspoiled pre-modern havens where relationality, ayllu, and Sumak Kawsay subsist, nor revolutionary subjects, nor worthless places contaminated by modernity. Comunas are entangled in different processes of transformation that tend to fragment community life, such as public policy, urban migration, salaried work, abandonment of common work for private enterprises, etc. Debates are missing about the role and functioning of actually existing comunas beyond the abstractions of BV [Good Living] ...

González and Vázquez address what could be labelled as a "missing piece" within the analysis of Good Living. Rather than formulating essentialist theories that demonise modernity or hail Andean cultures, a more complex and theoretically significant exercise must take place. Such an exercise should by all means address the ways in which policies, agents, institutions, and shifting geopolitical dynamics created the necessary converging forces that fostered Good Living's birth during the critical juncture. Good Living is imprinted by strong ontological undertones that stem from its post-development, state-led or Pachamama strains. This ultimately leaves Good Living entangled within theoretical discussions dependent on the "gut" responses of those proposing this or that idea. As Charles Taylor (1989, 6) once argued in reference to the limitation of ontological formulations within analytical framings:

> ... Ontological accounts offer themselves as correct articulation of our 'gut' reactions of respect. In that they treat these reactions as different from other 'gut' responses, such as our taste for sweets or our nausea at certain smells or objects ... It seems to turn to this: in either case our response is to an object [or idea] with a certain property .... Thus, we argue what and who is a fit object of moral respect, while this doesn't seem to be even possible for a reaction like nausea ...

Similarly, ontological accounts associated with Good Living reflect on the particular accounts of its proponents, their "gut" responses to the complex and convulsive political, social and economic events that took place in Ecuador during the critical juncture. Formulated in such a fashion, Good Living will signify one discourse to an acting public servant, serve a different purpose to an indigenous leader in the Andes or legitimate the activities of an NGO worker in the Amazon. This elusive nature in defining Good Living is evidence of the shifting boundaries and morphing constituent elements that are utilised to fit a particular discursive thread within the state-led, post-development or Indigenist strains of Good Living. As legal scholar, and sitting magistrate at the Constitutional Court of Ecuador at the time of writing, Ramiro Ávila (2017, 13;29–13:59) explained during field research, Good Living is an alternative to capitalism because:

> …The construction of what is communal is Sumak Kawsay [Good Living] … Could I reproduce Sumak Kawsay in the building where I live? Yes. The problem is we are in a system where everyone is competing and working … where time is gold. Could it be different? Could it [Sumak Kawsay] be reproduced? Yes. The problem is that it [Sumak Kawsay] is not hegemonic and we don't have the epistemic condition to see that the alternative is there and it is being lived…

For Ávila, Good Living represents a possible aspirational goal for communal living in an urban apartment complex. For others it becomes a policy prescription of the state or a way in which opposition to the hegemonic dominance of capitalism may be articulated. Fused with the ontological aspirations of those who happen to propose it at a given point in time, counter claims towards its viability or conceptual consistency are quickly dismissed through allegations of missing epistemic clarity. Ávila for example, justifies Good Living's intangibility or lack of theoretical abstraction by pointing to the premature theoretical depth current proponents have brought forth. As stated by Acosta:

> … what Ecuador is doing … is using Good Living as political marketing … at times I find that debates outside Latin America are much more consolidated or responsible and have better intentions … at times there appears to be more academic responsibility [towards Good Living] internationally … at various international seminars … in Berlin for example … however debate [in Ecuador] is still very limited, especially in academic terms … (Acosta quoted in Fernández et al. 2014, 106).[10]

Acosta's comments underline the conflictive nature of Good Living as a discourse, concept or legal principle. Whilst it has received praise for novelty, further theoretical construction is yet limited. As such, Acosta's remarks not only alienate Good Living from its epistemic birthplace but additionally point to the contested nature current discourses have sprouted. This dichotomous nature defines how Good Living simultaneously reaffirms indigenous epistemologies

---

10   The translation is mine.

yet is somehow better constructed within the Eurocentric points of reference it allegedly was meant to contest. This inherent contradiction between proposed ideals and what is taking place in academic, policy or civil society debates is a defining feature of the polymorphous nature of the many discourses that constitute Good Living.

Whilst each stream has attempted to analyse Good Living in light of its particular ontological understanding, it has done so by overlooking the events from which it emerged. If indeed Latin American legal scholars have historically been culpable of ignoring real-life situations when interpreting political institutions and legal frameworks, Good Living theorists seem to endeavour in positioning their arguments outside of the social, economic or political processes that led to it. By dismissing the uses and discussions the concept has received locally, proponents of Good Living abort the possibility of more profound discussions that could construct an endogenous theoretical approach. Influence of outside discussions and theories seems to define the building blocks of Good Living. Although publicised as an effort directed at recovering alternate epistemologies, endogenous representations of the social and the formulation of a political "pluriverse," Good Living has yet to fulfil such aspirations.

Central to the following chapters is the proposition that Good Living, as a concept and strategic discourse, came about as a by-product of the antecedent conditions and events that took place during Ecuador's critical juncture. Firstly, Good Living is a result of the converging economic and political processes that collided in Ecuador's political arena. Secondly, the unexpected political force exercised by an incipient indigenous movement led to unforeseen civil society mobilisations. Thirdly, the policy spaces opened by changing citizenship regimes and a retreating state allowed new forms of the political to flourish. This complex interweaving of actors, institutions and policies are the constitutive elements of what critical Good Living is intent on developing; a theoretical approximation that contests ontological accounts previously associated with Good Living by proposing a better suited theory-orientated event reconstruction. Through this new framing, analysis of Good Living is attentive to and unfolds within Ecuador's political arena during the critical juncture.

As a theoretical point of departure within this complex process, previous ontological explanations are called into question by proposing that Good Living, as a product of the critical juncture, harbours two distinct projects: (1) one led by the historic calls for emancipation of Ecuador's ethnic minorities, and (2) one that positioned the hegemonic discourses of market orthodoxy and social development as its cornerstones. The full breadth of how these two opposing, yet mutually reinforcing processes, shaped Good Living's birth will be covered in the subsequent chapters. Before doing so however the methodological tools selected for unravelling the contested nature of Good Living will be presented.

3 Why Good Living?

Since its inception in 2008, Good Living has been the source of multiple contested interpretations by academics, civil society groups and indigenous leaders. Each discourse presents a different construction of reality through the lens of state developmentalism, recovered indigenous epistemologies or biocentric environmentalism. We have previously argued that such interpretations of Good Living have unfortunately been subjected to the narrow scope of ontological iteration. Furthermore, we have discussed that under such iterations the theoretical voids that currently engulf Good Living will most likely be unsurmountable. Attentive to such limitations, we propose a new theoretical scope must necessarily be constructed if such restraints are to be overcome. For such a reason, critical Good Living is brought forth as a theoretical incision point on which a nuanced approximation to the many discourses that have been constructed in recent years may take place. This shifting in theoretical approximation, seeks to enhance the analysis of Good Living by better understanding the complex dynamics that converged in Ecuador during the critical juncture. Finally, this theoretical exercise is intent on formulating a new approach towards Good Living, so the current ontological bent may be overcome.

The proposed analysis of Good Living offers other theoretical vantage points that have, at least until the time of writing, been unexplored. This theoretical approximation will try to convey some, yet hardly all, of the possible theoretical incision points that such an analysis might be used for. Firstly, constitutional inscription of Good Living, as mentioned earlier, responds to the constitutional processes that took place in Latin America for a period of nearly thirty years. Whilst each jurisdiction must be analysed under the specific circumstances that led to one process or another, more than one academic field has identified how constitutional convergence, policy diffusion and international treaty ratification defined state behaviour in the region during this time (Eaton 2013; Elkins et al. 2013; Elkins and Simmons 2005; Gargarella 2013). The ways in which these uncoordinated state conducts led to similar behaviours is in itself worthy of analytical attention (Elkins and Simmons 2005).

Secondly, regional ratification of human rights treaties, not only fuelled the debates that enshrined Good Living as a constitutional principle but also created the necessary conditions for the jurisprudential development of *Vida*

Digna by the Inter-American Court of Human Rights (IACtHR). This advancement of the human rights discourse signals to other important theoretical points of interest that debate the impact of human rights on the resolution of structural societal ailments such as poverty. As D'Souza argues (2010, 55), 'the rights discourse has exhausted itself' yet it continues to be forced upon the Global South, even when none of its most ardent advocates would argue that the idea of rights 'has the potential to shake the world order.' Part of Good Living's appeal to academic circles or otherwise is the still unexplored potential it harbours to reform the status quo. Rather than wholeheartedly accepting such dormant potential, inquisitive research that dissects the origins and tribulations of Good Living should question whether its inscription as a constitutional right is able to deliver on such promises.

Thirdly, Ecuador, through its complex history, dynamic social processes, convulsive political arena, and shifting economic policies has been an important location of academic query. Its particularities in regard to the rise of identity politics (Yashar 2005) and subsequent consolidation of a "Left turn" government (Eaton 2013), creates spaces of academic and political speculation that have in many ways been unanswered. Ecuador was once home to the region's strongest and most consolidated indigenous movement (Becker 2008). Are we to attribute Good Living to the force, dynamism and strategic political manoeuvring of what was once a crafty indigenous movement (Mijeski and Beck 2011)? Or, to the contrary: is Good Living the result of a technopopulist left turn that consolidated its power through a discourse of social equality and rights materialised in Good Living (Torre 2013)? In the same vein: what can be said about the institutional instability experienced by the judicial, executive or legislative branches during Ecuador's critical juncture (Helmke 2017; Mejía-Acosta 2006)? Were such institutional weaknesses instrumental in opening the necessary policy spaces for new rights to emerge in 2008?

Following the institutional and political queries that have just been discussed, another important point of discussion relates to Good Living's association with other social welfare theories and discourses. As Ecuador and other Latin American states retreated from their natural policy spaces new actors came into play (Andolina et al. 2009; Bedford 2009; Sawyer 2004). Transnational in nature, NGOs, lawyers, international financial institutions, and other bilateral and multilateral organisations soon came to occupy the policy spaces that were once zealously guarded by the developmental Latin American states that came to life between the 1950s and 1980s (Issacs 1993; Lind 2005). Through their incremental occupation of previously sovereign spaces of policy formulation these transnational agents of sustainable development, human rights, ethnodevelopment, social capital, and community-based solidarity networks quickly replaced what had until then been an inward-looking national development agenda.

Finally, yet in no way the final point of inquiry that could be made, a deeper and perhaps more elusive theoretical objective can be identified. Good Living has created expectations amongst a variety of actors due to its privileged position within Ecuador's legal system. As a legal principle that occupies one third of the constitution, its legal enforceability has yet to be tested. One possible reason that shines some light as to why Good Living has suffered enforcement problems can be attributed to its elusive and under-theorised nature. Whilst it does occupy a privileged position within Ecuador's constitution, the multiple discursivities that inform it and the conflicting nature of its diverse theoretical foundations create a legal uncertainty that would make troublesome any initial legal approximation.

We have wrestled with the previously discussed issues in one way or another, however, in no way do we present a final or conclusive argument that formulates what Good Living is or how it should be understood. Avoiding such formulations and the ontological drift they would create, grants the flexibility to address the different events, themes and problems that surfaced during the critical juncture, ultimately leading to Good Living. We seek to unravel how converging and mutually reinforcing processes created the conditions in which a complex and dynamic system of local and international actors and institutions created a new discursive construction of reality. Thus, this research informs current theorisations regarding Good Living by providing a new theoretical frame from which its origins may be reviewed. Recreation of the occurrences and converging factors that came to play in Good Living's inception seeks to leverage on previously constructed theoretical premises to better understand where it came from, as well as where it might go. This process of tracing theoretically relevant events during Ecuador's critical juncture will aid in developing Good Living's origins and its possible enforceability. In order to explain how this will be accomplished we now turn to some brief comments regarding the selected method for such a task.

4   On Methodology

Constitutional reform in Ecuador is a result of the complex convergence of multiple social, political and economic factors. This is not to say that such convergence is unique or particular to Ecuador. Rather, what such a brief yet broad introduction seeks to stress is that academic interest in this process should engage with the object of study from a dynamic and adaptive process that is capable of discerning the multitude of nuances, the causes and factors, that inform a particular outcome of interest. Borrowing from Law's (2004) review of research methods—complex occurrences when reviewed by the social sciences—must be attentive to the porous and extended boundaries research must confront when framing a qualitative or quantitative methodology. With this in mind, methodology and the theoretical framings that inform it must 'recognize and treat the fluidities, leakages and entanglements' of research in ways that are capable of capturing such nuances or factors (Law 2004, 41).

Revising Good Living's constitutional inscription takes into consideration the multiple ways in which such a dynamic, fluid, and complex process came together. As mentioned earlier, our object is to overcome the current ontological bent engulfing discussions around Good Living by constructing a theoretical framing better suited to absorbing the particularities that took place during the critical juncture. This construction of the context that surrounded Good Living's birth is intent on providing new fields of analysis from which current and future theorisation on enforceability may take place.

As a constitutional principle, Good Living harbours a particularly important relationship with the legal field. This close association to legal theory informs the selection of the methodology that will be employed. Correspondingly, academic interest in revising Good Living from a theoretical framing is a result of the underlying need to determine if it is legally enforceable. What follows presents the selected methodology by comparing similar usages within the legal field, as both law and social sciences utilise process tracing to recreate occurrences within a specific timeline of interest. The concept of "tracing" specific events within a legal process is a standard tool of the trade within both common and civil law jurisdictions. Whilst for common law jurisdictions tracing within proprietary remedies signifies 'neither a claim nor a remedy' but rather the process by which a claimant is able to trace assets within a claim (Smith 1997). For civil law jurisdictions the process of tracing identifies the ways in which civil or criminal liability may be proven. The so-called *nexo causal*, is the specific action or omission by which liability criminal, civil or otherwise may be attributed to a specific person (Ferrer Mac-Gregor et al. 2014, 1137). In sum, whether in civil or common law jurisdictions, the process of tracing seeks to identify the specific events, actions or omissions by which a claim, liability or other legal actions may be enacted upon.

Departure from traditional avenues of process tracing within politics, seeks to overcome limited scopes of analysis that frame tracing as an interaction of 'components in one stage placing restrictions on those at a preceding or subsequent stage' (Steel 2008 quoted in Waldner 2012). Such a definition of process tracing would limit its use, as the mechanistic necessity of one event leading to another would signify that each event acts independently, yet somehow leads or constricts the other. Framed in this fashion, process tracing would be a mechanistic process rather than a systemic convergence of multiple observable factors. This would seem to be the mechanistic and linear construction of tracing presented by Waldner (2012), who argues that process tracing constitutes 'longitudinal research designs whose data consist of a sequence of events.' Drawing from the legal field once again, Trampusch and Palier (2016), quoting George and McKeown (1985), argue that process tracing seeks to establish an 'intervening process,' or causal nexus (*nexo causal*), between dependent and independent variables. As a method for 'unpacking causality,' process tracing thus performs a 'systemic qualitative analysis that complements the correlational approach to causation' (Bennett and Checkel 2015 quoted in Trampush and Palier 2016). This systemic approach to causation demands that process tracing determine how a relevant variable affects other variables within an observable process. In other words, through a systemic, rather than mechanistic approach, observable occurrences not only act but are constantly acted upon, creating a systemic convergence that leads to an outcome of interest.

To exemplify this, we once again return to the legal field. Suppose a murder occurs and one needs to determine the murderer. Evidence consists of a gun, fired bullet casing, body, and the suspect (for example a disgruntled employee), meeting the requirement of possible criminal intent. These elements on their own constitute, at least for civil law jurisdictions, the necessary elements to indict a suspect. However, to determine whether criminal liability exists, the famous proving "beyond a reasonable doubt," that is that person A effectively committed murder B, is not a mechanistic approach of: Murder = person + gun + bullet + intent + body. The sort of mechanistic A + B + C = X, that conventional process tracing argues for. Rather, what needs to be determined is if the systemic convergence of all these elements actually led to the murder being committed by the person who is under indictment. This is clarified by the simple reasoning that one may own a gun but not use it, fire the gun but not kill the person, have intent but not act on it, and so forth. Hence, what needs to be determined is if all observable evidence actually converged to produce the outcome of interest. Similarly, conventional approaches to process tracing, such as those proposed by Waldner, favour mechanistic approaches to methodology, failing to create a qualitative systemic analysis that complements correlational approaches to causation. Systemic analysis, borrowed from systems theory, demands that actors, institutions and decisions converge to produce an outcome of interest, a logic that falls far from the mechanistic procedures stated within the interlocked chain of events of conventional tracing (OECD 2018; Quade 1972, 4). Put differently, what one is searching for within a systemic approach to theory-guided process tracing is to identify the "cluster" of actors, institutions, processes, decisions and results that come from analysis of a specific event (Kitschelt 1986, 67).

Amongst the multiple methodologies available within the social sciences this book has selected theory-guided process tracing as its weapon of choice. As a methodology, the theory-guided process tracing proposed seeks to depart from the mechanistic and linear conceptions previously outlined. Having briefly explained the limitations of mechanistic approaches to process tracing in both politics and law, we favour the more inductive style of reasoning proposed by theory-guided process tracing. Theory-guided process tracing is selected for the following reasons. Firstly, it overcomes mechanistic approaches to process tracing by demanding that theory inform the conclusion. In other words, the conclusion is uncertain, and only made credible if there is a theoretical background from which it may be interpreted. Secondly, theory-guided process tracing creates what has been called 'intensive tracing, a variant that contributes to theory building' (Trampusch and Palier 2016, 440). As one of the central objectives in order for a new theoretical cover to explain Good Living's origins and its effects on law and politics, this methodology adequately fits research necessities. Finally, through theory-guided process tracing's systemic approach, a much more robust analysis of the process comes together, effectively showcasing the various ways in which multiple, complex and previously unaccounted for events, converged to create a specific outcome within a specific period of time. On a more conceptual level, usage of an inductive method of reasoning, such as theory-guided process tracing, allows us to substantially depart from current accounts of Good Living which utilise deductive methods to determine its theoretical usefulness. What this reasoning technique selection translates into, is that by using inductive methods, Good Living as it stands is not a given certainty but rather a possibility that depends on the evidence and theories that support it. Until now the methodology favoured by all three predominating currents of Good Living take its existence as a given, a factual point of reference from which analysis departs backwards. This sort of "for granted" reasoning has led to the many misinterpretations Good Living has suffered and which we seek to overcome.

Returning to the selected methodology, Falleti (2016, 457) comments, when reviewing George and McKeown (1985), that theory-guided process tracing:

> ... does not merely consist in the naïve observation of empirical events from which theoretical ideas are derived, but rather forms a theoretically informed analysis (= decomposition) of processes looking for causal chains within the observed events...

This form of process tracing differs from mechanistic approaches, as it does not seek to test a hypothesis with pieces of evidence but rather allows theory to guide the process by which 'the relevant events that constitute the sequence or process of interest' surface (Falleti 2016). Theory-guided process tracing grants the methodological flexibility to construct a temporally sequential critical juncture in which institutions, reforms, policies, political parties, and their ulterior effects towards the outcome of interest may be better scrutinised (Falleti 2016). Utilisation of process tracing also removes the clutter that is currently obscuring the various sources from which Good Living emerges by uncovering the micro-foundations that led to it (Falleti 2010, 22). Thus, this form of theory-guided process tracing departs from the metatheoretical arguments that have been forwarded within ontological discourses of Good Living. Focusing solely on Ecuador's Good Living grants another vantage point from which theoretical analysis may take place. By creating an in-depth case study analysis, the research is liberated from the boundaries and shortcomings faced by process tracing when it is applied in comparative studies. These limitations stem from process tracing's limited ability to uncover generalisable points of reference in comparative studies. For such a reason, the case-specific theory-guided process tracing fashioned here is intent on uncovering the processes, decisions or institutional arrangements that led towards a specific outcome of interest—Good Living.

As its name suggests, theory-guided process tracing constructs a theoretical framing that identifies events of interest within a specific timeframe by utilising previous scholarship on a particular subject. Critical junctures allow us to define a specific period in Ecuador's history by guiding the research towards an outcome of interest. Bias in theoretical frame selection, that is avoiding the methodological peril of choosing those theories that suit a hypothesised outcome, is overcome by the triangulation of primary, secondary and archival sources as well as corroboration through interviews. Furthermore, as the selected methodology utilises previous scholarship to construct the theory-guided tracing, it is confined to previously identified theoretical vantage points. As will be developed in greater detail, changing citizenship regimes, politicised ethnic cleavages, and the effects of a retreating state are significant points of theoretical interest throughout the critical juncture. Additionally, their significance, relevance or aptitude for the task at hand is corroborated by the multiple academic disciplines and scholarship that analyse Ecuador between 1979 and 2008. This triangulation of evidence and theoretical frames across the academic disciplines should ameliorate the perils associated to selection bias.

Constitutional reform and the inclusion of new rights is a complex, fluid and dynamic event in any society. Interdisciplinary in nature, we leverage from anthropology, sociology, law, philosophy, politics, post-colonial theory, post-development theory, international political economy and human geography. Whether the anthropological accounts of Sawyer (2004), Cepek (2012) or Altman (2015), the legal insights of Gargarella (2013), Cepeda-Espinosa (2004) or Elkins et al. (2009), the political analysis of Sartori (2005), Skocpol (2005) or Yashar (2005), the research draws from multiple areas of study to create a theory-guided assemblage for process tracing.

Theory-guided process tracing is the methodological approach utilised within this research project. By engaging with previous scholarship that analyses a specific time period in Ecuador's history an 'organisational reality' is uncovered (Law 2004, 107). One in which a process that is complex, polymorphous and fluid in nature is made tangible and concise. Previous scholarship stemming from multiple theoretical fields creates a methodological and theoretical approach that circumvents predominating ontological accounts associated with Good Living. This circumvention displaces the "dazzle" of such accounts thereby uncovering the pattern of theory-guided events that have until now been ignored (Law 2004, 107). In what follows, a brief layout of how this research will be carried out is explained.

5 Positioning Critical Good Living: Discourse and Rights

Current literature on Good Living has focused on the ontological origins of the concept and will be covered throughout the following sections. Thus, we seek to go beyond such discussions in order to situate Good Living in the realm of politics and law. Current ontological discussions surrounding Good Living place a heavy metaphysical burden when trying to apply legal or political analysis to its origins. Hence, we do not explore the so-called "genuine" origins of the concept but rather its emergence as a political tool of discourse and whether its legal inscription carries subsequent judicial enforceability (Cubillo-Guevara and Hidalgo-Capitan 2016). This task is guided by the theoretical ground laid in political science, anthropology and sociology by authors such as Yashar (2005); Bretón (2014; 2017), Van Cott (1994); Rice (2012), Sawyer (2004) and others.

Framing of Good Living as a discourse allows us to analyse the network of power relations that articulate human beings as subject and object (Frost 2015, 2). Discourse, following Foucaultian understandings, is individualized:

> Not [by] the unity of its object, nor its formal structure; nor the coherence of its conceptual architecture, nor its fundamental philosophical

choices; it is rather the existence of a set of rules of formation for *all* its objects (however scattered they may be), *all* its operations (which can often neither be superposed nor serially connected), *all* its concepts (which may very well be incompatible), *all* its theoretical options (which are often mutually exclusive). There is an individualized discursive formation whenever it is possible to define such a set of rules.
(FOUCAULT 1991, 54)

Analysis of Good Living as first a discourse and second as a legal category, allows us to steer clear from ontological discussions surrounding the concept. Furthermore, this analysis leads us to inevitably question the underlying power relations that came together to craft Good Living as a constitutional principle. We thus borrow from sociological reconstruction and objectivization in order to emphasize the relations that are revealed by agents in order to map Good Living as a highly political yet very malleable concept, once it is presented by agents and notably legal agents (Rask Madsen and Dezalay 2013, 126).

This analysis of course does not disregard current writings on Good Living. In an effort to categorize such writings we follow the categories presented by Cubillo-Guevara and Hidalgo-Capitan (2014). However, from that point on we include a new category defined as "critical Good Living" in order to situate our analysis in contrast to preexisting theoretical propositions. This formation of a new category, does not seek to determine societal or ontological origins of the concept as would be the case for studies in anthropology or philosophy. Rather, the objective here is to re-construct Good Living within a particular period of time in order to highlight the confluence of political processes, actors and legal developments that allowed the 2008 Constitution to include novel rights. For this reason, we do not present a comprehensive analysis of all existing literature on the matter but instead highlight some of its main proponents and the core ideas that have developed around it until this point. From that point on, the book is structured through what is called theory-guided process tracing, that is the usage of existing theoretical premises ranging from a multiplicity of epistemological fields. The state of the art on Good Living has emerged from fields outside law and politics, mostly being covered in circles close to anthropology and sociology. For this reason, we inevitably build on the writings of these academic disciplines to later re-frame discussions about Good Living through a "critical" lens that uncovers political processes, power relations and the transformation of social demands into constitutional law.

6   Book Layout

Theory-guided process tracing allows one to trace and reconstruct the events and occurrences previous scholarship identifies as constitutive elements of Ecuador's critical juncture. These occurrences, which redefined the country's political arena, are a by-product of the antecedent conditions that galvanised a previously dormant citizenry, redefined the roles played by an interventionist state or cracked opened the policy spaces necessary for transnational politics to enter. This process of tracing the theory-guided chain of occurrences that led to Good Living defines the selected methodological approach. By shedding light on the socio-historical origins that harboured Good Living's birth the undiscussed occurrences that defined its constitutional inscription in 2008 are uncovered. Rather than reviewing the current theoretical and ontological themes surrounding Good Living, critical context reconstruction allows us to clarify occurrences that shed light as to how this novel concept came to be.

Chapter 1 presents the theoretical frame and methodology. Central to this chapter is the presentation of the theoretical frameworks that integrate concepts from Dryzek's (2000) discursive democracy and the transnational governmentalities framework, first conceived by Foucault (2007), and later integrated to transnational power discussions in Hale (2002) or Andolina et al. (2009). Additionally, it presents the theoretical foundations on which the three theory-guided occurrences—politicised ethnic cleavages, a retreating state and changing citizenship regimes—became interlinked and ultimately led to Good Living. Each converging occurrence, product of theory-guided process tracing, is identified as a catalyst that led to Good Living. This is done through a detailed revision of a diverse universe of literature on Ecuadorian and Latin American politics. Particularly, the work of Yashar (2005), Andolina et al. (2009), Sawyer (2004), Rice (2012), Mejía-Acosta (2006), Helmke (2017), Soifer (2015) and Bretón (2008, 2010, 2015) serve as the theoretical foundation from which the larger research project unfolds.

Chapter 2 reviews the academic literature that has until very recently discussed the alleged philosophical, social, governmental or ethnic roots from where Good Living emerged. Through a broad literature review, as well as a revised reading of what Good Living has been allegedly interpreted to "be" or come from, three different interpretations of the concept surface and are dissected. However, conceptual flaws, loosely-knit arguments or the alleged mystical roots constantly attached to Good Living, evidence that there is still much to discuss in terms of its contribution to legal or political theory.

This chapter also contests the limited conceptual associations Good Living academics, public servants or community leaders have linked to the concept in previous years. By overcoming discussions that take place in a theoretical or contextual vacuum, the fourth strain of Good Living is presented. Critical in nature, it contests the loosely constructed theoretical propositions currently associated with the predominating discourses of Good Living. Questioning the alleged roots inscribed in the three predominating discourses of Good Living, presents a new theoretical point of reference, one that identifies two opposing socio-political dimensions. This two-dimensional theory of Good Living argues that constitutional inscription in 2008 stems from two distinct yet closely-knit social, political and economic projects.

Chapter 3 presents the overall context of the critical juncture. Before engaging with the particularities of the 1979–2008 period, it briefly positions the corporatist regimes that existed prior to the 1980s. This is paramount for theory-guided process tracing, as antecedent conditions aid in the presentation of how occurrences unfolded during the critical juncture (Little 1998, 197 quoted in Waldner 2012). Revision of Ecuador's pre-democratic era reconstructs the basic circumstances from which the relevant converging occurrences of the critical juncture emerged. Transition to democratic rule, swift reform of corporatist practices, ceding sovereignty by the state and ever-worsening economic conditions, converged to create a critical juncture in Ecuador's history. This is followed by a review of the constitutional changes that were enacted in 1979, the birth of CONAIE in the 1980s, the consolidation of indigenous movements in the 1990s and the political and financial turmoil that compounded the overall retreat of the state during this period.

This chapter also discusses how state retreat, compounded by growing fiscal restraints, foreign loan conditionality and a regional process of constitutional convergence, sought to enact legislative reforms that guaranteed human rights by limiting sovereign power. Once state power had been circumscribed, new policy spaces were gradually forced open allowing transnational actors such as NGOs to occupy the policy spaces previously occupied by the state. This unpredicted junction, between state retreat, NGO policy deployment and regional constitutional convergence, created a paradoxical situation where diminishing socio-economic policies threatened basic human rights, whilst civil society organisations and the expansion of cultural rights demanded new forms of recognition towards ethnic minorities (Becker 2011, 5; Elkins et al. 2013, 68). State retreat would therefore be compensated by the growing influence of multilateral and bilateral development agencies and the escalating interventions of the NGOs that came to occupy these newly opened policy spaces.

Through a dual attack on the state's sovereign prerogatives, as well as the corporatist relationships it fostered, the disciplining mechanisms previously used by the state were disbanded. This forceful opening of political spaces allowed civil society to simultaneously condemn market-orientated socio-economic policy whilst demanding ample rights for ethnic minorities; a political occurrence that is unique in Ecuador's republican history (Gargarella 2013, 179). This dynamic process of imbedding political discourses with the mobilising and counter-mobilising ideas and meanings that led towards collective action is what social movement scholars came to label as 'frames' (Benford and Snow 2000, 613). Collective action frames allow us to view social movement actors as 'signifying agents actively engaged in the production and maintenance of meaning' through a phenomenon that implies agency and contention (Benford and Snow 2000). During Ecuador's critical juncture, framing of political discourses allowed a diverse spectrum of political actors to come together against the common enemy of market liberalism.

Chapter 4 develops a theoretical approximation towards Good Living. By building on the events identified during the critical juncture, analysis of Good Living will be framed through a theoretical revision of Laclau and Mouffe's 'empty signifier' (1985). By shifting the discussion from the vacuum of the political, social or economic contexts from where it emerged, the new approach seeks to consolidate how the occurrences selected through theory-guided process tracing defined Good Living's constitutional inscription. Doing so places discussions pertaining to Good Living within a theoretical frame that is rich in contextual analysis. From this contextual analysis the impact of strategic political manoeuvring by indigenous groups, the politics of NGO-led intervention and the converging forces of politicised ethnic cleavages, changing citizenship regimes and state retreat will present a new formulation of Good Living. One in which the commonly associated discourses that have until now engulfed it in circular ontological debates are displaced. The end result is a new approximation towards Good Living, one that not only affirms its dual dimensionality but also stresses its effect on the transgressive politics it was called to protect.

To finalise, Chapter 5 presents the following core arguments: (1) that rather than a new political alternative, Good Living as it has been constructed until now, epitomises the consolidated efforts to demobilise a once active and powerful civil citizenry; and, (2) ontological approaches towards Good Living have failed to leverage on the rich scholarship that discusses how political, social and economic transformations reshaped politics on a local and regional level. Moreover, this heavy ontological bent has created a limited theoretical space in which Good Living's potential as a legal principle has been unexplored. Furthermore, it will be argued that regional efforts towards securing standards of wellbeing through the *Vida Digna* jurisprudence of the Court, award Good Living a more structured, concise and applicable entry point from which future theorisation may take place. Finally, the chapter highlights the lost opportunities and exhaustion of transgressive politics Good Living brought about through its ontological bent. Thus, the "exhaustion" of Good Living comes hand-in-hand with the exhaustion of the rights discourse throughout the region. Moreover, this exhaustion is compounded by periodic and systemic constitutional and institutional shifts, that in time drained the possibility of harnessing theoretical mechanisms that could power a truly emancipatory project. For this reason, repositioning discussions surrounding Good Living with the theoretical clout necessary for its legal applicability is paramount to the analysis at hand.

Such a repositioning will hopefully frame Good Living as a discourse that questions the predominant power structures that constrain its enforcement. For Good Living to become a viable political project or enforceable legal principle, present and future research must question the various ways in which power and its construction of micro-foundations, define politics in ethnically diverse enclaves. If calls for self-determination and the tackling of structural inequality and racially biased dispossession are to take place, a revision of power and how it shaped and still relates to Good Living is more than warranted. Good Living's birth in 2008 placed it on a collision course with what Gargarella dubbed 'the engine room of the Constitution' or the place where visible and invisible power is constructed (2013). The political project of emancipation that allegedly resides in Good Living is at odds with the ways in which power has historically been exercised by the state, as well as the not so evident forms of power that shape discourses, policy and society in general. We have explored the origins and foundations on which such a project could stand by tracing the political, legal, and social transformations that brought Good Living into existence. In doing so, it wishes to contribute to future discussions regarding endogenous processes of political and legal theory formation in Ecuador and Latin America.

CHAPTER 1

The Context of Good Living: Situating Theory and Method

Novel forms of discussing the political emerged in Ecuador at the end of the twentieth century, as politicised ethnic cleavages, a retreating state and changing citizenship regimes altered the public sphere. Ecuador would enter a critical juncture in its history as it suffered the unexpected consequences of weakened sovereignty, political chaos, social unrest and economic meltdown. Confronted with a new form of transgressive politics, civil society would demand a new framing for the social, economic and political demands that had historically been left unattended. This form of rights-based protest sought to revert the regions historic inequality, as well as its structural racism towards indigenous populations. As della Porta (2015) underlined when reviewing the coordinated actions of multiple social movements against neoliberal globalisation, 'respondents converged on four main concerns: calls for rights, social justice, democracy from below, and the global nature of the action.' Furthermore, all these movements gathered around a 'language of rights' with social issues occupying most of their attention (della Porta 2015, 289).

The advent of such an era was made possible through the unexpected shattering of centuries of legal tradition and the consolidation of the nation-state that supported its disciplining logics. By replacing existing institutional arrangements with market-led policy prescriptions, new spaces of political contention soon consolidated, thereby displacing previous technologies of governance (Yates and Bakker 2013, 81). Developing a theoretical approximation towards these changing dynamics and their overall influence on the constitutional inscription of Good Living as a main driver of the analysis here presented.

Identifying and reconstructing the processes and converging events that led to Ecuador's constitutional inscription of Good Living requires a theoretically-guided revision of the events, actors, institutions and policies that transformed Ecuador's political arena (Bedford 2009; Gargarella 2013). Ecuador's 2008 Constitution, and the multiple rights it harbours, are an end product of years of civil society unrest, economic reform and legal convergence. The culmination of a dynamic shift in politics and social interaction that subverted citizenship regimes by displacing corporatist practices. This changing public sphere abruptly altered the dynamics of social cohesion by favouring, through merit or chance, a plural, politically active and internationally engaged civil society (Elkins et al. 2013; Sawyer 2004; Yashar 2004). Such dramatic changes galvanised previously dormant sectors of the public sphere, unleashing a wave of mobilisations that would come to question the very foundations of the Ecuadorian state and the power structures that held it in place.

The following chapter presents the methodological and theoretical framing approach selected to recreate such processes. Through theory-guided process tracing, the chapter identifies the methodology and theoretical framing selected in order to identify the key events and occurrences that defined Ecuador's critical juncture. This process of identifying theoretically relevant events is supported by previous scholarship that reviews Ecuador from multiple theoretical and epistemological disciplines. From such a revision, and for the theoretical reasons that will be presented shortly, specific occurrences that are theoretically relevant in our analysis of Good Living's origins will soon be discussed. More to the point, politicised ethnic cleavages, a retreating state and changing citizenship regimes are the main theoretical backdrops from which our analysis of Good Living departs from. Theoretical framing of these simultaneously occurring and converging events is bundled within two theoretical scopes. The first discusses governmentalities, or the art of government through a transnational lens (Andolina et al. 2009; Foucault 2007; Hale 2002). And the second presents a discursive revision of deliberative democracy, thereby opening the door for the inclusion of a mobilised citizenry in the process of constitution making (Dryzek 2000). To these aspects we now turn.

1   Method

Good Living is the end result of nearly three decades of social protest, economic reform, constitutional transformation, and a redefining of Ecuador's political arena. Revising and analytically deconstructing the events that unfolded between the country's return to democracy in 1979 until the constitutional referendum of 2008 demands a methodological approach that can retrospectively reconstruct the multiple layers of converging social, political, economic, and legal transformations that reshaped power dynamics in Ecuador during this time. As was mentioned in the introduction, the multidisciplinary nature of the research and the necessity of constructing a method that can respond to the porous nature of the object of study, demands a methodological approach that is itself supported on a dynamic theoretical framing.

Through an in-depth case study of the events and occurrences that led to politicised ethnic cleavages, state retreat, and changing citizenship regimes in Ecuador during the critical juncture of 1979–2008, we seek to further the analysis Good Living has recieved. As such, the selected methodological approach must be suitable for conducting in-depth case studies that are able to review the ways in which converging occurrences acted during an expanded period of time. Retrospective case study analysis is therefore the predominant concern that must be considered when selecting a preferred methodology. Theory-guided process is ideal for such a case study as it allows the reader to identify the causes that led to a specific event (Rohlfing 2012, 40). It harbours methodological adequacy, as it aids in identifying the micro-foundations of the event of interest as well as the concatenated and converging occurrences that led to the object of study (Falleti 2016).

Theory-guided process tracing is also well suited for this task as Ecuador has received considerable academic attention. This is advantageous, as theory-guided process tracing depends on existing theoretical framings to develop the analytical process that corroborates or dismisses an outcome of interest, the difference between inductive and deductive reasoning is once again made evident here. The particular set of events, social conflicts, political turmoil and economic upheavals the country faced during the critical juncture made it a fertile ground for academic inquiry. Following the work of Van Cott (1994, 2005, 2008) on the evolution of ethnic politics, Yashar's (2005) review of changing citizenship regimes in the Andes, Rice's (2012) politics of protest, Mijeski and Beck's (2011) analysis of Ecuador's indigenous movement or Andolina et al.'s (2009) analysis of development policies, Ecuador has sparked multiple points of academic engagement. The Andean nation prominently figures in these analyses, in large part due to the meteoric rise of ethnic politics. This regional point of reference is largely attributable to CONAIE's configuration as the most prominent, well-funded and horizontally organised indigenous movement in Latin America during the 1990s (Yashar 2005, 291).

The force of indigenous political mobilisation in Ecuador during this time are summarised in the words of former indigenous leader Miguel Lluco. After a series of protests that led to the overthrowing of then President Jamil Mahuad, Lluco stated 'we are the government' (quoted in Van Cott 2005, 136). Clearly, what had once been a demobilised or scattered political constituency, with little or no political leverage, blossomed into a structured, organised, and active political organisation. Such a metamorphosis not only defied Ecuador's political history but also previous opinions of academics revising cultural pluralism in the region.

Analysing Good Living's emergence, through case study analysis, seeks to uncover the complex unity of interpretable events—the micro-foundations if you will—of the processes and occurrences that came together at its birth (della Porta 2008, 204; Falleti 2016). By re-examining the economic, social and political conditions that converged to consolidate the newly formed political arena in Ecuador, a temporally defined in-depth analysis of the origins of Good Living is consolidated (della Porta 2008, 204; Ragin 1987 quoted in Collier and Collier, 1991, 14). Once again, the theory-guided process tracing selected is further strengthened by the abundant academic literature that reviews Ecuador during the critical juncture. Identifying the existence of sufficient academic literature on Ecuador constitutes the first methodological issue that this research project overcomes, as the inductive reasoning behind theory-guided process tracing demands theoretical support to uncover the occurrences of interest within a specific process (Seawright and Gerring 2008, 296; Trampusch and Palier 2016).

In order to conduct theory-guided process tracing one must first identify such literature. For the task ahead, the proposed theory-guided process tracing to be conducted, builds on previous scholarship by George and McKewon (1985), Falleti (2010, 2016), Rohlfing (2012), Tarrow (2010), Bennett (2010), Bennett and Checkel (2015), and Collier and Collier (1991). As a research methodology that retraces relevant events within a specific time period, it 'reconstructs the process that leads to an outcome of interest' by revealing evidence that is 'not applicable to cross case analysis' (Rohlfing 2012). In other words, circumscription of research methodology to a specific case study is in accordance with the applicable limits of theory-guided process tracing. More simply put, as the research is confined to the events and occurrences that took place in Ecuador during the critical juncture, the methodological approach of process tracing is adequate for such a purpose.

Theory-guided process tracing, as a methodological tool, must first be appropriate for case study analysis, and secondly, be suitable for the uncovering of case-specific explanations. Analysis of Good Living, as a uniquely Ecuadorian event that is contingent on a particular set of local occurrences, makes repetition of the methodology or findings in other settings or time periods difficult if not impossible. For such a reason, theoretical premises must 'create the boundaries' through which the process of tracing will take place (Waldner 2015, 129). In other words, one must first define the temporal boundaries that define the period under analysis. Following on such requirements, and for reasons that will be developed in subsequent chapters, the defined temporal boundary is contained within the critical juncture. This period in which particular agent decisions and institutional responses led to previously unexpected results is the essence of the critical juncture; a period in which a 'dynamic set of events' changed centuries of legal and political history (Tarrow 2010).

As a methodology, theory-guided process tracing is interested in recreating a chain of occurrences. According to Bennett and Checkel (2015, 10), identifying the temporal contiguity of concatenated occurrences allows us to deconstruct the chain of events into diagnostic pieces of evidence. These newly discovered pieces of evidence, when scrutinised under the selected theoretical frameworks, allows one to identify, catalogue, and explain the sequences that led to the end result (Bennett 2010). Whilst in agreement with the overall result of what process tracing seeks, I disagree with the mechanistic approach previously described. Rather than a process of mechanistically sequential concatenated occurrences in which A leads to B which leads to C, the theory-guided process tracing presented here views the convergence of events during the critical juncture as a fluid, dynamic and interactive process that led to Good Living (see Figures 1 and 2). This methodological approach differs from standard process tracing by viewing the pieces of evidence that are uncovered as constitutive elements of the other.

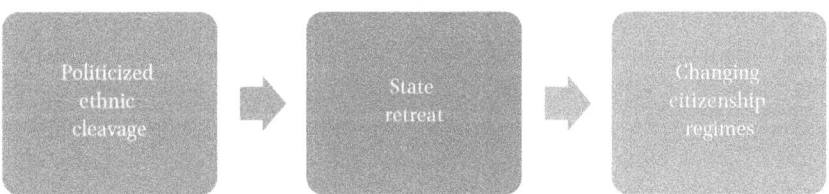

FIGURE 1   Conventional process tracing

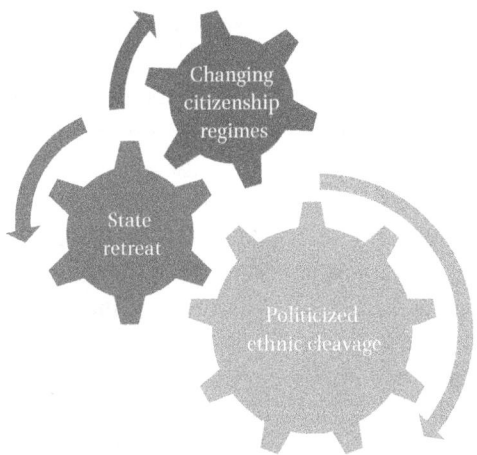

FIGURE 2
Proposed theory-guided process tracing

Equifinality or the possibility that multiple causes can lead to a specific outcome is a peril for many methodologies (Waldner 2012). Usage of theory-guided process tracing however, contains such dangers by utilising theoretical support to determine the importance of selecting politicised ethnic cleavages, state retreat, and changing citizenship regimes as the main occurrences of interest. What this translates into, is that each piece of uncovered evidence, each occurrence, not only has theoretical support to justify its inductive existence, but also, it converges with other occurrences, therefore influencing the outcome of interest. Hence, politicised ethnic cleavages, state retreat and changing citizenship regimes are mutually reinforcing and dependent on each other. The constitutive elements of the perfect storm that defined Ecuador's political arena during the critical juncture.

This methodological clarification is paramount for the task ahead. As was mentioned earlier, the fluidity and complexity of the object of study demands a method that may unravel the multiple occurrences and events under analysis. More importantly, mechanistic approaches towards process tracing would be ill-equipped to analyse the events that took place in Ecuador during the critical juncture as they would fail to uncover how one interacts with the other. Due to the complex nature of the events that unfolded, their interdependability, concatenated nature and mutually reinforcing dynamics, a linear explanation in process tracing is inadequate to grasp the dynamic fluidity of events. For such reasons, what is here proposed is that the process tracing to be conducted, part from the premise that all three relevant events, politicised ethnic cleavages, a retreating state, and changing citizenship regimes, converged to create Good Living. Rather then viewing the occurences that took place during the critical juncture in a sequential and linear logic, these three defining movements are interdependent, expanding or contracting the other but ultimately creating in unison the necessary concurring events that led to Good Living.

Returning to the necessary temporal considerations of any methodological approach we now must develop the concept of the critical juncture. Following the work of Collier and Collier (1991) on Latin America's political arena before the 1980s, Bennett and Checkel's (2015, 26) comments on selecting historical moments of theoretical and explanatory significance, Mahoney's (2000) interest in identifying temporally noteworthy contingent events, and Falleti's (2010, 27) anchoring of a 'comparative sequencing model' on regional macroeconomic shifts that are temporally bound; it is imperative to clearly define the temporal boundaries in which a case study will be executed. To do so, a critical juncture approach is employed and understood by the above-mentioned methodological techniques. In other words, historical moments where a path dependence is broken, abrupted or modified due to the antecedent events that led to it.

Critical junctures are understood as a period of time in which profound changes to agent and institutional dynamics create structural openings that expand the plausible choices of wilful political actors (Capoccia and Kelemen 2007, 343; Mahoney 2000, 513). The critical juncture framework demands identification of 'generative cleavages' that emerge during significant moments of historical change; however the significance of a cleavage depends on the particular contextual setting from which it emerged, that is the antecedent conditions (Collier and Collier 1991, 33). The critical juncture, which spans from 1979 to 2008, represents one such historical moment for Ecuador, as external and internal shocks catalysed the social, political and economic conditions that had for decades been approaching convergence. For Ecuador, the new macroeconomic conditions brought on by the regional debt crisis eliminated the material payoffs that had previously been set in place to create governing coalitions that could simultaneously disarm and defuse social conflict (Collier and Collier 1991, 31; Van Cott 2005; Yashar 2005).

Imposition of SAP and the roll back of state services eliminated negotiating leverages previously utilised on corporatist lobbying groups. This dramatic altering of the public sphere was compounded by the additional pressures enacted by increased economic interdependence, downward pressure on wages, and the re-organisation of global capital away from the Global South (Collier and Collier 1991, 772). The shifting sands of macroeconomic policy would in turn create the social, economic and political conditions that bred social polarisation, economic meltdown, and the subsequent counter-reactions of civil society (Collier and Collier 1991, 37). Hence, the critical juncture and its initial 'generative cleavage' can be traced to the macroeconomic reforms that followed the regional debt crisis. Of course, this initial starting point in no way defines our main points of interest within the critical juncture. Rather, what this represents is the starting point, the catalyst if you will, that made the converging forces of politicised ethnic cleavages, state retreat and changing citizenship regimes converge.

The critical juncture featured here ends with the entry into force of Ecuador's 2008 Constitution. This is an adequate moment on which to anchor our analysis as the historical occurrences that led to the critical juncture are here suddenly reversed. For example, the 2008 constitution created a hyper-presidential system that relied on an expansive state apparatus, a vastly different institutional make-up from that which unfolded during the critical juncture (Gargarella 2013, 154; Torre 2013, 48; Uprimny 2010, 1606). Furthermore, the once fledgling state incrementally began to reconstitute itself through technocratic governance. This rebuilding of an interventionist state brought forth the reinstatement of previous developmental policies through the windfall oil revenues that came with the commodity price hikes that took place between 2006 and 2012[1] (Dávalos and Albuja 2013, 150–53). The reconstitution of a techno-authoritarian central state, newly found fiscal revenues, highly priced commodity exports, and a novel legal framework, erased the various converging factors that had disrupted the ancient régime of Order and Progress. What follows is a theoretical approximation to the selected occurrences that will be traced during the critical juncture. These points of theoretical reference constitute the occurrences that develop the processes which led to Good Living's 2008 constitutional inscription.

2   Politicised Ethnic Cleavage

Usage of the generative cleavage is exemplified in the Collier's (1991) review of Latin America's political arena. As was mentioned in preceding paragraphs, the changing macroeconomic climate that came with the region's debt crisis served as the catalyst from which historical cleavages or institutional weaknesses altered Ecuador's political arena. Once the corporatist policies that had pacified social conflict were erased, new forms of the political consolidated to contest historic inequality and racism. Most prominently, the politicisation of ethnic cleavages unleashed unknown political forces, citizenry mobilisation and coordinated attacks on Ecuador's democratic yet marginalising legal system. Few political occurrences have redefined political life in Ecuador such as the emergence of the indigenous movement during the 1980s. Since the early 1990s, proliferous interdisciplinary studies focusing on Ecuador during the critical juncture have emerged. The rise of identity politics would forever change the political arena of Ecuador and Latin America, sparking multiple points of academic inquiry.

Prominently featuring in this literature is Yashar's (2005) review of indigenous movements during Latin America's neoliberal reform. From her detailed cross-country analysis of Ecuador, Peru and Bolivia we select the politicisation of ethnicity as a primordial element for what unfolds from the generative cleavage of economic reform that came after 1982. Similarly, Van Cott's (1994;

---

[1] Ecuador's petroleum income increased by around 83 per cent between 2000 and 2012. For more, see: Dávalos and Albuja 2013.

2005; 2008) scholarship on radical democracy in the Andes, indigenous peoples, and the consolidation of social movements into political parties, traces the advent of identity politics in Latin America with a particular focus on Ecuador. Becker's (2008, 2009, 2011, 2013) detailed analysis on Ecuador's agrarian and rural politics revises the complex dynamics that led to the consolidation of identity politics by tracing the ways in which agrarian policy in the Andes, rural mobilisation, electoral politics and economic convulsions during the 1980s and 1990s crafted Ecuador's modern indigenous movement.

Yashar (2005, 283) argues that politicisation of ethnic cleavages occurs when policies challenge material and political foundations for community autonomy. Through the generative cleavage of economic reform and the displacement of corporatist policies new forms of citizenship emerged. This shifting of what Gargarella (2013) calls the Order and Progress model of Latin American states, subverted the institutional dynamics that had, until then, contained social conflict (Yashar 2005, 41). Previous corporatist policies had granted indigenous people varying degrees of autonomy and self-governance from the state. Once such policies were erased through the market-led policies of the 1980s and 1990s, indigenous people lost many of the political incentives that had restrained mobilisation against the state (Becker 2008; Yashar 2005, 54).

The uniqueness of how ethnopolitics in Ecuador consolidated is underscored in Gerlach's (2003) historical analysis of indigenous against worsening environmental conditions. Becker (2009) further adds to the consolidation of Ecuador's indigenous movement by reviewing the historical processes that created the institutional arrangements and technologies of governance that allowed a united indigenous movement to surface in Ecuador. Becker's work adds to Yashar's, by creating a detailed study of the circumstances and events that led to a politically engaged ethnomovement. However, it also supports her claim that specific historical conditions and institutional arrangements, allowed its successful emergence in Ecuador, to lesser degrees in Bolivia and with minimal results in Peru.

Strategic alliances, global mobilisation and emerging forms of identity politics define Ecuador's politicisation of ethnic cleavages. This symbiotic relationship, between Ecuador's emerging indigenous movement with international civil society organisations is highlighted in Sawyer's (2004) ethnographic account of indigenous politics, multinational oil, and the market-led reforms of the 1990s. Sawyer (2004, 81) highlights how the politically active indigenous communities of Ecuador's central Amazon province of Pastaza, engaged in local, national and supranational politics by forging alliances with international civil society organisations such as Oxfam. Furthermore, strategic associations with local environmental NGOs like Acción Ecológica,[2] secured a prominent position in domestic politics by granting access to government agencies, international development organisations and other indigenous communities monitoring oil activity (Sawyer 2004, 83; Widener 2011, 85). Sawyer's ethnographic account showcases how a once dormant ethnic cleavage consolidated into a local, national, and emerging supranational political force.

The prominence of indigenous politics in Ecuador and its relevance for regional identity politics is a common point of academic inquiry. Selverston-Scher (2001) for example, highlights that Ecuador's indigenous movement was the most viable social movement the country harboured during the early 1990s. This statement is supported by Van Cott (2005, 99), when she depicts that the form of identity politics that consolidated in Ecuador made it 'Latin America's most effective and internationally renowned indigenous peoples' movement. Securing nationwide support for ethnically based political agendas was a novelty for Ecuadorian politics, as identity had been conspicuously hidden in political discourses. Ethnicity had long been viewed by political parties of all tendencies with suspicion or outright contempt (Albó 2004, 26). Van Cott's (1994, 12; 2005, 110; 2008, 20) analysis highlights how CONAIE's strategic mobilisation lobbied Ecuadorians to recognise indigenous political agendas.

Nationwide ethnopolitics germinated from the creation of a political master frame where indigenous identity became a resource and reservoir for political mobilisation once it was coupled with wider class-based demands (Selverston-Scher 2001, 67). Leveraging on worsening economic conditions, indigenous mobilisation consolidated a national political, cultural and economic agenda that merged class struggle with identity politics (Burt and Mauceri 2004, 3). The rise of identity politics exploited the institutional weakness and myopic policies of elite-controlled party politics, creating the perfect breeding ground for a new form of the political to emerge (Burt and Mauceri 2004, 275; Helmke 2017; Mejía-Acosta 2006).

This political innovation within identity politics forged a political framing where ethnopolitics was successfully coupled with the socio-economic

---

2   In reference to Acción Ecológica's local influence and transnational power base (Widener 2011, 85): "(…) The radical ecologist organizations included the internationally well-known and well-connected Acción Ecológica and its international sister organization Oilwatch. Together, they rejected the pipeline, rejected increased exploration, and eventually called for an oil moratorium in the country. Acción Ecológica served as a local broker for international activist organizations to partner with grassroots community groups, and in this regard Acción Ecológica was the initial key to organizing a transnational network of opposition. Acción Ecológica was also prolific in preparing environmental reports for affected communities (…)"

reclamations of Ecuador's marginalised citizenry. Rice (2012, 25) underlines how the joint pursuit for land and identity created a proto-political master frame to which indigenous people could flock. Framing ethnic political agendas alongside socio-economic demands, crafted a new form of mobilisation, one in which ideas and meanings navigated the drifts of structure and agency that had separated large sways of Ecuador's citizenry.

The economic reforms of the 1980s created the generative cleavage from which ethnicity was politicised but also the necessary conditions from which a wider collective action could take place. By the late 1990s, economic reform and material depravations had left 62.6 per cent of the population under the poverty line (North 2004, 201). CONAIE capitalised on this strategic neglect of the state by creating a political framing that coupled identity politics with broader socio-economic agendas seeking solutions for class-based problematics. With time, indigenous identity became the prime reference point from which to counter neoliberal reforms and the trade liberalisation of the mid-1990s (Rice 2012, 54).

The ability to capitalise on the political incapability of Ecuador's ruling political elites, the strategic absence of the state, and the guarantee of political rights allowed CONAIE to flourish. By 1996 what had started as a social movement in the mid-1980s had secured sufficient political support from which it could branch-off into formal politics through the *Movimiento de Unidad Plurinacional Pachakutik–Nuevo País* (MUPP-NP) or more simply Pachakutik (Yashar 2005, 149). By entering national politics with a degree of organisational and discursive autonomy absent in other political parties, Pachakutik secured a firmly rooted political strength (Rice 2012, 123). Indigenous politics would thus occupy two distinct positions through these organisations. Firstly, as an external actor to formal politics through CONAIE and secondly as a formal power broker through Pachakutik. By 1998 Pachakutik had become an important political player that leveraged on CONAIE-led mobilisations throughout the Andes and Amazon (Mijeski and Beck 2011, 55).

The abundant academic literature on Ecuador's indigenous movement further confirms its theoretical significance for wider academic discussions on social movements, law, sociology, anthropology, and philosophy. In the political arena, the emergence of CONAIE and Pachakutik disrupted centuries of structural racism by granting recognition and voice to those who had been historically silenced. Moreover, the political transformations these actors triggered in Ecuadorian politics would set the agenda for new discussions of the political to emerge, a process that matured for nearly twenty years before it was distilled into the 2008 constitution. The political agendas that consolidated through this form of politics, their influence on wider societal debates regarding the political arena and the galvanised political agency of indigenous people are all relevant factors that must be accounted for when discussing Good Living. Selection of politicised ethnic cleavages as part of the relevant occurrences to be traced within the critical juncture, finds its theoretical justification in the multiple sources of academic reference that have reviewed ethnopolitics in Ecuador. For such reasons, this is our first theoretically-guided occurrence within the reconstructed chain of events that led to Good Living in 2008.

3 The Retreating State

Academic engagement with the effects of the 1980s and 1990s SAP in Latin America has been abundant across the academic disciplines. The transformation of the once developmental states of South America into pro-market competition states has been widely discussed by Harvey (2005), Cerny (1997), McMichael (2000) and Nederveen Pieterse (2009) to name a few. Reshuffling of state powers, limits to its reach and the overall control it exercised on its population came hand-in-hand with a selective absence of the state in key aspects of policy and regulation. The density, extent and reach of economic reforms soon placed many aspects of governmentality outside the orbit of the state. In other words, what had until then, been subjected to the technologies of governance of the state was displaced to civil society organisations and international development agencies. Latin American states redefined their orbits of governance to navigate the perils of economic reform and survive in the newly formed universe of regional market orthodoxy.

Nederveen Pieterse (2009, 187) depicts Latin America's response to neoliberalism through the imposition of neo-structuralism, a framing that sought to overcome state failure through structural reforms that deregulated, privatised and liberalised the economy in order to 'get prices right.' Public choice theories would aid such a purpose by determining that state involvement in the market became an unnecessary impediment, eventually reviewing how government institutions structured the behaviour and interactions of humans. Politics was thus reduced to a competitive game of actors pursuing conflicting interests (Mehmet 1995, 116–17). These new theoretical framings gradually removed state control from the economy, politics and social policy in the hope that a minimal and neutral state would lead to economic growth and social progress (Colin 2008, 280; North 2004, 197).

Whilst central governments slowly loosened their grip on domestic issues they also swiftly reorganised geopolitical power on an upward supranational level. The increased pressures on central governments to delegate responsibilities downward, whilst increasing supranational oversight, was underscored by Anthony Giddens' comments regarding globalisation. In his remarks on the era of market liberalisation Giddens observed how through this process, the 'nation-state [was] too small for the big problems in life and too big for the small problems in life' (quoted in McMichael 2000, 153). Furthermore, decentralisation de-linked governments from the budgetary responsibilities they had once exercised, allowing domestic and international NGOs to occupy and coordinate local development initiatives (McMichael 2000, 153).

During the critical juncture Ecuador suffered from exceedingly high levels of electoral volatility, weak party organisation and low levels of democratic legitimacy, fuelling civil society discontent (Mainwaring and Scully 1995 quoted in Rice 2012, 28). According to Rice (2012, 27), this convergence of factors created the institutional incentives that led social actors to behave in ways that were favourable or inducive towards collective action. Moreover, the newly opened spaces for NGO interaction brought about the development of actor-networks where transnationalised middle-class experts from the North and South disseminated a normalised rationality of development that had significant consequences in the shaping of Good Living as a discourse in later years (Andolina et al. 2009; Bedford 2009; Escobar 2012). The consolidation of transnational advocacy networks further highlighted how the once all-encompassing sovereign powers of the Ecuadorian state succumbed to external forces and the growing participation of civil society. This coordinated, localised, yet global civil society, led to a multiscalar geography that forged network solidarity amongst activists, targeted national and international policy formulations, gradually replacing the policy functions of a retreating state (Scholte 2008, 337).

Re-organisation of state prerogatives was part of the loan conditionalities that were demanded by the World Bank and IMF to assist Latin America through the debt crisis of the 1980s and the ensuing financial difficulties of the 1990s. Hence, the global development architecture that flowed from North to South demanded sovereign governments to accede to supranational pressures in order to maintain economic and political support throughout the age of neoliberalism (Weber 2002, 537). An example of international pressures on governments' sovereign prerogatives is the consolidation of the World Trade Organization (WTO) during the mid-1990s. The WTO's birth, following the Uruguay Round, demanded the Global North and South accept legally binding conditions contained within the General Agreement on Tariffs and Trade (GATT). The Global South was economically compelled to adhere to the GATT if maintenance of preferential market-access conditions to industrialised world markets was to be secured. This globalisation of economic law was quickly met with criticisms that denounced the hegemonic control of the international trade regime by Europe and the United States (Barton et al. 2006, 167).

Another example of yielding sovereign prerogatives in favour of international legal regimes is evidenced in the surge of Bilateral Investment Treaties (BIT) during the 1990s. These international agreements imposed legally binding conditions on national governments, effectively ceding sovereignty in favour of international dispute settlement bodies located in the Global North. Whilst Latin American states had historically rejected the international resolution of investment related disputes, the 1990s saw an international realignment that eventually led to over four hundred BIT ratified throughout the world (Hamilton et al. 2012, 2). Ecuador followed what Elkins et al. (2013) has labelled legal convergence by treaty ratification, eventually becoming party to twenty-three separate investment treaties that sum up to about five per cent of the regions total BIT ratification until 2008 (Galindo 2012, 251). Supranational re-arrangements, such as those brought on by the WTO and BIT, were followed by constitutional reforms that accommodated the changing legal, economic and political environments. Brazil, for example, amended thirty-five of its constitutional articles to facilitate privatisations, whilst similar initiatives were followed by Colombia, Mexico, Peru, and Argentina (Gargarella 2013, 151). Free trade, competition and phobia of the state, demanded a reengineering of Latin American law and the politics it enacted unleashed forces that had been dormant or demobilised until that moment.

State restructuring to accommodate economic liberalisation has been thoroughly documented within academic literature. The formation of the competition state, legal guarantees towards private property, and capital flows are all part of the global realignment that sought freely functioning markets and trade. This new form of the political envisioned competition between individuals, firms, and territorial entities as habilitating factors that lead towards economic development (Harvey 2005, 64).

Economic liberalisation and the new international architecture it fostered would however unleash forces that directly undermined its objectives. Debilitation of the *ancien régime* of Order and Progress distorted predominating notions of a supreme power within a body politic, thereby contesting classic notions of a central unitary sovereignty (Hudson 2008, 23). Unsurprisingly, the absolute sovereignty of the state through territorial unity soon became an obsolete concept as increased decentralisation favoured local, autonomic, developmental governance. Ruptures in sovereign power were further exacerbated by the international human rights discourse of the time. As human rights seeped into domestic jurisdictions, Latin American governments yielded sovereign power in favour of supranational organisations such as the IACtHR or the International Criminal Court (ICC) (Cohen 2012, 182). As a meta-discourse and international regime, human rights outlined the limits of the internal autonomy exercised by states, ultimately defying antiquated notions of sovereign power and the exemptions it had been awarded from external corrections (Cohen 2012, 183).

Additionally, eruption of identity politics in previously depoliticised polities such as Ecuador had unexpected effects, as calls for decentralisation and a minimal state demanded increasing amounts of self-governance, autonomy, individual, and collective rights. Multiculturalism steadily affirmed cultural differences, demanding recognition of multi-ethnic societies in the culturally diverse nations of Latin America (Hale 2002). Securement of new approaches towards the governing regime of multiculturalism was gradually adopted. By the end of the 1990s, ten Latin American states had adopted the International Labour Organization's Indigenous and Tribal Peoples Convention of 1989.

International human rights law further weakened sovereign prerogatives regarding indigenous communities, territory, and public policy. Through regional human rights treaty ratification, the judicial activity of the IACtHR incrementally expanded its jurisdictional reach to matters concerning indigenous collective rights (Hale 2002, 486; Gargarella 2013). With this gained terrain, ethnic politics in Ecuador now shifted its focus on territorial autonomy, bilingual education, and the recognition of legal pluralism (Llasag 2012, 134). Ethnic and cultural demands, constructed upon a platform of territorial autonomy, would define the ways in which identity politics in Ecuador sought self-determination. This political project focused on cultural preservation through territorial autonomy and self-determination created a new form of the political.

Constructing a political framing based on reclamations for autonomy and collective rights set indigenous movements on a collision course with prevailing discourses on competition, free markets, private property, and Euro-American political thought. By contesting the sovereign powers of the state over its people and territories, the basic tenets of Euro-American political and legal thought were simultaneously questioned (Altman 2015, 170; Hudson 2008, 23). Whilst advocating for greater levels of autonomy for indigenous people, social movements highjacked the concepts of decentralisation and local autonomy from neoliberal projects, reshaping them to favour the interests of collective rights (Rajagopal 2003, 263).

Innovative political strategies led by indigenous communities seeking to reaffirm territorial autonomy and self-governance had been previously crystallised in the concept of indigenous nationalities during the late 1970s (Altman 2015, 171). The concept of distinct indigenous nationalities re-imagined Ecuador as a collective subjectivity where indigenous people contested state and elite-controlled nation-building projects, as well as prevailing notions of international law and the development regime (Radcliffe and Westwood 1996, 13; Rajagopal 2003, 264). Exercise of collective rights by multiple indigenous nationalities soon posed a challenge to the extant conceptions of sovereignty and private property rights that had underlined international law and development policy. Contention of such conceptions questioned the unitary notion of the sovereign state housing a homogenous national identity that obediently adhered to liberal market orthodoxy (Rajagopal 2003, 263).

By the late 1980s, governance options for the Ecuadorian Government had been reduced to the policy prescriptions imported from Washington through SAP. Moreover, the inchoate nature of Ecuadorian politics, its weak and fragmented political parties, and the sub-regional tensions between the Andes and coast further exacerbated a complex policy environment (Conaghan 1995 quoted in Burt and Mauceri 2004, 275). Regionalism and atomistic politics in Ecuador date back to the founding moments of the republic, as political cleavages reflected in the country's party system, continuously led to a 'poliarchic' form of governance that exalted regional tensions (Sánchez 2002, 51; Sartori 2005; Soifer 2015).

SAP had limited economic policy manoeuvring whilst fiscal constraints curtailed corporatist practices. Nevertheless, politicians continued to offer social assistance and clientelistic handouts, signing checks no one could ever cash (Segovia 2013, 148). The political miscalculation and economic mismanagement of Ecuador's ruling political classes during the 1990s would surmount to the final blow in the process of state retreat. One striking example of widespread cognitive dissonance between policy and practice can be identified in Ecuador's then National Development Plan (NDP) of 1985–1988. This contradicting piece of policy openly advocated for interventionist state polices whilst government officials enforced market-led reforms. Rhetorical allegory for socially orientated public policy was thus contrasted with the continuous reduction of public spending and the elimination of subsidies throughout the 1980s (Segovia 2013, 159). Political rhetoric favouring a return to the Ecuadorian developmental state of the 1970s was met with the stark reality of a policy universe littered with the stale anti-statist pro-economic liberalisation heralded by Margaret Thatcher (Segovia 2013, 161).

The surmounting incapacity of political actors, the convergence of economic liberalisation, and the human rights regime became converging factors that consolidated the overall retreat of the state. This would in turn inaugurate cycles of civil society unrest that climaxed in a series of coup d'états that levied a total of ten presidents in a time span of less than a decade (Becker 2009). The weakening of state controls opened political spaces for new actors to emerge, thereby creating political opportunities that allowed collective action to form. Substantiation for the importance of state retreat in civil society mobilisation is forwarded within the political process model discussed by McAdam (1982), Tarrow (1994) and Tilly (1978). Social movement scholarship posits that strategic political opportunity is necessary to consolidate the emergence of collective action by civil society. More specifically, the emergence of social movements may be explained by the absence of state repression, tolerance towards dissent, fractiousness of elite groups, cohesion with potential allies, and absence of channels of representation (Rice 2012, 24). During the critical juncture, convergence of these dimensions of political opportunity was made possible through the external and domestic pressures that collided with the previous Order and Progress model.

In sum, state retreat was a by-product of the internal policy reforms that materialised as economic liberalisation and human rights regimes spread. The simultaneous attack of sovereign prerogatives through limitation of economic policy, newly imposed international oversight, and a human rights regime that questioned its coercive power displaced the Order and Progress model. As the Ecuadorian state lost or ceded sovereign prerogatives, its interaction with the citizenry was forever altered, eventually leading to the consolidation of new citizenship regimes.

4 Changing Citizenship Regimes

Latin American states, up until the critical juncture, had designed citizenship regimes through structured identities, defined interests and selective policy preferences. Yashar (2005) outlines how imposition of such citizenship regimes, defined political membership, thereby containing rights within atomistic social or political allegiances. Prior to the critical juncture, citizenship regimes had aided in the process of political intermediation by zealously guarding citizen-state interactions. Citizenship regimes in Latin America were thus historically accompanied by racial projects that straightforwardly excluded, marginalised or compartmentalised racial identities; a process that represented indigenous people as homogenous, poor, spatially circumscribed, and vulnerable (Andolina et al. 2009, 58). Citizenship categories, and the ensuing construction of identities they enacted, concomitantly erected regimes of power which utilised or enforced mechanisms of normalisation. This in turn, forced individual subjects to embody preordained relationships before the powers of the state (Radcliffe and Westwood 1996, 14).

Divergence in citizenship regimes awarded rights to some and none to others, a differentiation highlighted in the voting limitation in force until the 1979 constitution. Furthermore, diverging citizenship regimes and the structural conditions of discrimination they fostered and perpetuated, guaranteed that specific segments of the population remained marginalised. Citizenship regimes in Ecuador had maintained the terms of ethnic, racial, gendered, and sexualised identity construction that flowed from North to South, allowing hegemony to successfully adapt and change national conditions through institutional and individual deployments (Benavides 2004, 180).

Perpetuation of racial marginality was highlighted in a 1999 World Bank report that found 77 per cent of Ecuador's indigenous population purportedly living in poverty and another 42.2 per cent living in extreme poverty (Andolina et al. 2009, 59). A similar 1996 report by the World Bank (1996, 65) estimated that 35 per cent of Ecuador's total population lived in poverty and an additional 17 per cent was vulnerable to it. Thus, more than half of the country's population was either living in or soon to be living in conditions of near extreme poverty. Whilst marginalisation and economic vulnerability affected large segments of Ecuador's population, the racially circumscribed categories of citizenship, enacted through law and institutional dynamics, created binaries of difference that separated the largely rural dwelling indigenous population from urban polities.

Such technologies of governance, defined as 'methodological nationalism,' naturalised territorial boundaries by conflating the nation-state with society, ultimately assuming that a polity who shares borders also shares the same history, language, culture, religion, and adversities (Glick Schiller 2012, 524). Ecuador's citizenship regimes historically reflected the conflations of methodological nationalism by enforcing principles of equality that eliminated difference. Such piecemeal policy, in a country that is home to some fourteen distinct indigenous nationalities, created a cauldron of discontent that erupted throughout the 1990s (SIISE 2016).

The critical juncture challenged methodological nationalism as human rights guarantees loosened restrictions on political participation, augmented electoral participation, and allowed civil society mobilisation to secure recognition of cultural difference. Changing citizenship regimes not only compounded the incremental weakening of Ecuador's political parties but ultimately allowed Pachakutik to participate in formal politics without having to go beyond its natural electorate of the Andes and Amazon (Mijeski and Beck 2011).[3]

---

[3] The Ecuadorian coast is the most demographically dense region of Ecuador. Previous electoral rules demanded that political parties be able to secure minimal representation in all of

Electoral reforms introduced for the 1996 general elections inaugurated a period in Ecuadorian politics where past constitutional requisites that had granted political participation exclusively to existing political parties were removed, opening the floodgates for new independent contenders to emerge (Mijeski and Beck 2011, 49; Sánchez 2002, 47).

The advent of Pachakutik as a new political contender, coupled with the civil society CONAIE-led mobilisations of the time, made identity politics visible. Nationality had been defined by the 1979 constitution through the lens of methodological nationalism. In stark contrast, Ecuador's 1998 text opens avenues of citizenship regimes that are extensive in wording and definition; one such example is Article 83, which includes indigenous peoples, nationalities with ancestral roots, and Afro-Ecuadorians as members of the unitary and indivisible Ecuadorian state. Such ample and inclusive legal wording exemplifies the ways in which citizenship regimes gradually changed during the critical juncture. This shift in citizenship regimes is in fact so profound that Article 7 of the 2008 constitution makes an explicit effort of incorporating nomadic indigenous people that inhabit border areas with Colombia and Peru. This previously inexistent extension of Ecuadorian citizenship to indigenous people exemplifies the complex dynamics that redefined citizenship and society-state relations during the critical juncture; a period in which the state and law was forced to recognise the diversity contained within its borders.

Expansive citizenship regimes elucidated in the 2008 constitution also consider the highly mobile nature of human beings in the age of globalisation. Hence Articles 9 and 416 (6) of the 2008 constitution extend equal rights to foreigners in Ecuadorian territory but also explicitly recognise the principle of universal citizenship and free movement of peoples. Including a concept like universal citizenship responds to Ecuador's traumas with economic migration, as an estimated five hundred thousand to one million Ecuadorians migrated to Spain, Italy and the United States in the early 2000s (Brad 2014; Dávalos and Albuja 2013, 162). Mass economic migration, and the social consequences it brought, was another result of the political, economic and social chaos that engulfed the country throughout the critical juncture (Brad 2014).

However, it also reflects a significant departure from the ways citizenship was understood prior to the critical juncture and how it came to be viewed during and after. When one compares the 1979 text with the 2008 constitution, notions of a transnational citizen permeates the ways in which citizenship

---

Ecuador's regions. The limited indigenous population residing in the coast had been a de facto barrier for indigenous political participation until electoral reforms eliminated this requisite.

came to be understood during the critical juncture. Reconceptualization of citizenship, from geographical spaces divided between Coast, Andes and Amazon into a more fluid, diverse and shifting human mobility scenario. Migration towards the United States and Europe, was accelerated by Ecuador's rampant economic crisis during Jamil Mahuad's failed presidency. According to North (2004, 202), 62.6% of the population during this time lived below the poverty line, forcing some 10% of the country's economically active population to migrate by 2000. Mass migration from economically depressed areas such as Ecuador's southern Andes, would transform inward remittances from migrants into the country's second most important source of foreign currencies (North 2004, 203). By 2008, the social, economic and political effects of migration would be imprinted into the new constitutional text. In more precise terms, article 416 of Ecuador's 2008 Constitution 'advocates the principle of universal citizenship, the free movement of all inhabitants of the planet, and the progressive extinction of the status of alien or foreigner.'

This expansive notion of citizenship to "universal" standards, recognizing inhabitants rather than citizens, drastically contrasts previous immigration policies. Such a sharp contrast is highlighted by previous policies such as the 1899 legislation that prohibited Chinese immigration to Ecuador or the 1939 prohibition of entry towards Jews (Cancillería 2013). Restrictive immigration policy would gradually lead towards more inclusive shifts during the critical juncture with the promulgation of bylaws to enact the Refugee Convention of 1967 or the 2001 creation of the Andean passport (Cancillería 2013). By 2008, international institutions such as the Andean Community or human rights treaties had altered previous immigration policies, ultimately redesigning citizenship regimes. Within the political sphere, relevance of migrant communities would be picked up by articles 63, 109 and 118 of the Constitution as it reshaped voting districts by adding foreign voting districts into the electoral process.

Profound changes to citizen regimes, such as the enactment of universal citizenship, highlight the complex ways in which a new interplay between the local and the transnational converged during the critical juncture. With the overall retreat of the state and the opening of political spaces for NGOs and international development agencies, local communities soon became acquainted with transnational networks of aid workers, volunteers, and other civil society organisations. The deployment of NGOs and their surge in numbers[4] between 1980 and 1995, allowed for new coordinating mechanisms to bypass

---

4 Andolina et al. 2009, 84: 80% of Ecuador's NGOs emerged from 1980 to 1995.

the fledgling institutions of a retreating state, thereby connecting the rural with the local, the local with the national and national with the supranational (Andolina et al. 2009, 225; Bretón 2005). Networks based on transnational civil society engagement highlight the formation of a 'transnational democracy' where deliberative forms of the democratic make-up transcended the formal seats of political power (Dryzek 2000,130–32). Through this process an international public sphere was constructed, one in which the unconstrained and uncoerced interactions between transnational citizens, transcended the particularities of territorial entities. One poignant example is the strategic alliance between Ecuadorian indigenous from the Amazon with Native American activists in an effort to levy demands before the World Bank (Sawyer 2004, 108).

Changing citizenship regimes during the critical juncture are also imbedded in the transformation of citizen-state relations that came with the collapse of corporatism in favour of self-help agency. Both Yashar (2005) and Collier (1991) expose how previous corporatist practices between the state and its citizens were swiftly erased as SAP spread. Furthermore, the sudden and abrupt changes from corporatism to self-help agency, redefined the political arena in Ecuador. During the 1970s the interventionist oil rich developmental state had secured clientelistic practices that defused social conflict. With the dawn of SAP and the elimination of such practices, a new form of stakeholder capitalism quickly ensued. Through this new development agenda, capitalism 'with a human face' would steadily advocate in favour of bridging culture and the market, in an effort to secure economic performance (Nederveen Pieterse 2009, 138). State-centred corporatism thus ceded its reign to the emerging ideas of social capital and stakeholder capitalism allowing citizen-state relations to become increasingly decentralised.

These profound changes to citizenship regimes emerged during the critical juncture, alongside a retreating state, human rights-based development and identity politics. Such changes, underline how the local political community became internationally engaged with transnational democratic networks, crystallised by strategic NGO deployment. This process was further aided by the political manoeuvrings of a strategic indigenous movement that utilised emerging citizenship regimes contained within neoliberal human rights discourse to turn the state rhetoric of methodological nationalism on its head. Through the language of citizenry, multiculturalism, human rights, state efficiency, sovereignty, self-determination, rule of law, and stakeholder capitalism identity politics rallied popular support towards new political framings (Rice 2012; Sawyer 2004, 151). Such strategic actions consolidated a new rallying cry from which civil society could be mobilised. In so doing, what had until then been a political project predominantly concerned with securing territorial autonomy and self-determination soon expanded its political agenda. The ensuing metamorphosis of political projects from autonomy and self-determination to stakeholder capitalism would in time underline the spawning of Good Living as an allegedly indigenous-based project that gradually considered "alternative" forms of economic development. For its impact on the ways the state exercised control over its citizens but also due to the impact transnational engagement defied previous technologies of governance, changing citizenship regimes are the third occurrence of relevance within our theory-guided process tracing.

Up until now, the three main theory-guided occurrences within the process tracing have been identified. Once again, these occurrences have been selected due to the significant academic attention they have received in previous scholarship but also in response to the multiple and complex dynamics they unleashed in Ecuador's political arena. Whilst these theory-guided occurrences inform the process tracing conducted they fail to develop a wider theoretical response that may comprehensively or at the very least minimally account for Good Living's origins.

Although informative in nature the occurrences that are here presented, following the words of Falleti (2016), are nothing more than the micro-foundations from which Good Living emerged. However, this research seeks to develop a wider theoretical understanding that may better inform the complex processes from which Good Living emerged. For such a purpose we now turn to the wider theoretical framings that bundle the selected theory-guided occurrences within a theoretically manageable composite. In so doing, the theory-guided process tracing here presented is informed by a systematic conception of process tracing in which politicised ethnic cleavages, state retreat, and changing citizenship regimes interact within a wider theoretical setting. We now turn to such framings.

5 Wider Theoretical Framing

Preceding paragraphs have been dedicated to laying out the basic methodological approaches that construct the proposed theory-guided process tracing towards Good Living. Through generative cleavages, critical junctures, politicised ethnic cleavages, state retreat and changing citizenship regimes, we have identified the theoretically noteworthy and converging occurrences that surfaced in Ecuador between 1979 and 2008. Through the utilisation of previous academic scholarship on these issues, selection of relevant occurrences within the critical juncture has been informed by the interdisciplinary studies previously highlighted and which will be further developed in Chapter 3.

As was already mentioned, these relevant occurrences and their spatiotemporal demarcation within our theory-guided process tracing only constitutes part of the our objectives. Whilst informative of the events that took place in Ecuador during the critical juncture, they fail to construct a theoretical bridge that delineates how and why their convergence led to Good Living. Having identified this theoretical necessity, we now turn to the selected theoretical framings that bundle these occurrences within the process tracing that leads to Good Living's birth.

Transnational governmentalities and discursive democracy are the two theoretical framings selected for this process. Adding these theoretical framings to our theory-guided process tracing serves two purposes. Firstly, it allows us to theoretically engage with the changing forms of power dynamics that shaped development and political agendas during the critical juncture. Secondly, it illustrates how external pressures and internal conducts redefined the political arena by including previously marginalised sectors of civil society to the process of constitution making. Inclusion of transnational governmentalities and discursive democracy to our theory-guided process tracing completes the theory-guided process tracing through which the origins of Good Living may be traced (see Figure 3).

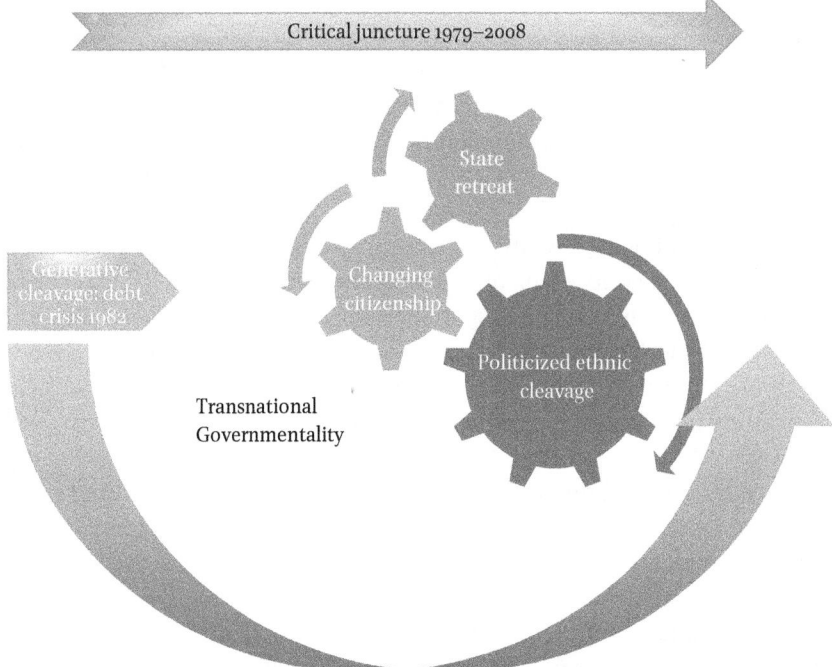

FIGURE 3   Theoretical and methodological framing

6 Transnational Governmentality

Foucault (2007) is credited with introducing the concept of governmentality into academic discussions regarding the state, territory, population and security. He defined governmentality as the technologies of governance that are utilised by the state to discipline a population through decision-making, resources, relationships, and the exercise of control (Foucault 2007, 77; 2008, 124). This perpetual statification or '*étatisation*' exemplifies how the state mobilises governmental rationality through the multiple forms of micro-power that exemplify governmentalities; techniques of control that steer and ultimately guide the population towards a desired outcome of interest (Foucault 2007, 357). To govern is thus not to exercise sovereignty over a given territory but the ability to exercise disciplining power over a specific population towards a convenient end (Gordon 1991, 93).

The management of the population, through the technocratic governance of the state, gives rise to the governmentalities of biopolitics where a population becomes a thing of administration under an all-encompassing power (Foucault 2008, 385). Governmentality is thus understood as an art of government by which human conduct is moulded by calculated means and detailed supervision (Li 2007, 275). What will be proposed in subsequent chapters is that the converging forces that were unleashed during the critical juncture were a form of transnational governmentality. By appealing to the general interests of a diverse citizenry this new form of biopolitics secured the expansion of its activities (Morton 2007, 94). Transnational in nature, this brand of governmentality appealed to an ample social base that was united by the bundling of an intersubjective consciousness that later became Good Living (Morton 2007).

Our process tracing towards Good Living highlights similar actions by a once interventionist government that imposed methodological nationalism in order to control, subdue and demobilise civil society. Furthermore, the concrete actions of the corporatist regimes that came before the critical juncture epitomize governmentality as they intended to control social conflict through clientelistic practices. Once the material means through which these state-led technologies of governance disappeared, new forms of governmentality emerged. This transformation in the technologies of governance during the critical juncture is our main interest when defining the theoretical framings that encompasses our process tracing.

Theory-guided process tracing towards Good Living informs us that a fledgling and debilitated state apparatus lost its grip on the forms of control it had exercised through the previous Order and Progress model. This overall retreat of the state, emerging supranational entities like the WTO and the proliferation of geographically localised NGO-led development projects, highlight the shifting dynamics of state-led governmentality. The surge of transnational civil society organisations exemplify how conduct formation went from the state to the now omnipresent transnationalised forms of governmentality that came with social capitalism and self-help agency. Transnationalised governmentalities replaced state-led forms of governance as NGOs, multilateral, bilateral, and local development agencies began to occupy the once zealously guarded policy spaces of the waning Ecuadorian state (Andolina et al. 2009, 81; Gargarella 2013).

Corporatist practices were thus swiftly replaced by the logics of market-led social policy. Decentralisation and state retreat allowed NGOs to engage with local communities in the search for market-based public goods that could secure economic development (Andolina et al. 2009; Falleti 2010, 26). The rise of multiculturalism during the critical juncture crafted another form of governmentality by installing a discourse or mechanism through which identity politics could be effectively managed (Hale 2002, 495). Thus, the cultural project of social neoliberalism imbedded in liberal multiculturalism was soon paired with the developmental projects commandeered by domestic and foreign NGOs. This unity of the techniques of transnational governmentality with localised transnational agents, consolidated a new form of subject formation that was dependent on a market-orientated understanding of humanity and the social fabric from which it is constituted.

Transnational governmentality formation highlights how technologies of governance migrated from the local to the transnational. This passage from the reign of territorial sovereignty to the dynamic and fluid process of transnational governance, underpins how Ecuadorian civil society changed its response to the state, market, and politics. Transnational governmentalities further examine how these emerging forms of governance, introduced in Ecuador by transnational agents, shifted policy prescriptions, political agendas, and developmental objectives during the critical juncture (Sawyer and Gomez 2012, 7). Materialisation of Good Living is thus the end result of these shifting dynamics by harbouring, through its many associated strains and discourses, the fragmented discursivities of bio-centrism, alter-development, state-led development, market-led social policy, and millenary indigenous ontologies. We will return to each of these discursivities in subsequent chapters, for now what must be retained is the ways in which transnational governmentalities displaced the technologies of governance once utilised by the state.

Multiculturalism, through its liberal lens, aided these new forms of governmentality by merging culture with market (Kymlicka 1994, 108). This strategic combination created a discourse of economic development in which culture could be fused to market principles (Andolina et al. 2009; Bedford 2009; Schild 1998). The advent of economic orientated multiculturalism in time would subvert the political agendas initially forwarded by Ecuador's indigenous movement. This new form of 'managed multiculturalism' became a technology of governance through which subject formation disciplined the citizen-subject to the necessities of the market (Hale 2002; Schild 1998). Of course, this is not to suggest that multiculturalism as a whole has been detrimental to the rights or political projects of indigenous peoples. As Lixinski (2010, 242) argues, Latin American constitutionalism for the last thirty or so years has been predominantly concerned with directing 'all efforts towards constitutional recognition of multiculturalism' as a form of the collective rights of indigenous people.

Rather, what is intended by "managed multiculturalism" is to highlight the complex ways in which ethnicity and economic reform became merged, effectively creating a new technology of governance. Through the shaping of intersubjective forms of consciousness through new forms of governmentality, coercive forms of subject formation were discarded, reaffirming the displaced nature of sovereign power during the critical juncture (Morton 2007, 93). Through managed multiculturalism, transgressive forms of politics soon became subdued and pacified, as articulation of social protest to hegemonic economic development projects became widespread. This process conditioned the flow of economic development resources only to those subjects that adhered to the intersubjective forms of consciousness that were derived from market-led social policy.

Once deployed in the Ecuadorian Andes and Amazon—multiculturalism through the economic lens—a new development approach was crafted. By fusing ethnicity to market-led objectives a nascent form of economic policy emerged. Under the name of ethnodevelopment, neoliberal social inclusion overcame the struggles of cultural knowledge production by steadily integrating indigenous, peasants, and other marginalised social groups to the language of entrepreneurship and property ownership (Bretón 2005, 33; Laurie et al. 2005, 471). Liberal multiculturalism would contain the transgressive political undertones imbedded in Ecuador's indigenous movement through the governmentality of ethnodevelopment (Bretón 2005, 37; Hale 2002, 495). This fusion of ethnicity with economic development, the production of new technologies of governance, and their embodiment in Good Living will be further developed in Chapter 4.

Transnational governmentalities are incorporated as a theoretical frame in order to develop the ways in which social neoliberalism during the critical juncture created a technology of governance that led to economic subject formation. Moreover, its usefulness as a theoretical frame lies in its ability to explain how the ceding sovereignty of the state was soon occupied by a new dynamic form of governance. Through these new forms of subject formation, the transgressive nature of the political demands that flourished within politicised ethnic cleavages were soon silenced. The subjects that emerged during the critical juncture became obedient to the market disciplines that accompanied state retreat and changing citizenship regimes (Wickham 2013, 220).

Transnational governmentalities are a useful theoretical framing for our process tracing, as they frame the geopolitical transformations that descended upon Ecuador's political arena, altering mobilisation, economic agendas, and ultimately the legal framings on which they rest. This process is exemplified in Ecuador's 1998 and 2008 constitutional reforms. Whilst the former adopted market orthodoxy throughout its wording. The 2008 constitutional text reflects a different more elaborate, complex and scattered process, one in which law recoded the disciplines and governmentalities that had descended upon Ecuador during the critical juncture, creating a new discourse that mimicked social reclamations whilst containing them in their disciplining cocoon. This technology of governance, represented in the disciplining cocoon, encapsulates what Good Living came to represent; a strategic discourse formation in which transgressive politics were pacified through the disciplining logics of market-led ethnodevelopment.

We will return to the various ways strategic programs of intervention shifted policy and politics during the critical juncture. Moreover, the technologies of governance that materialised in Ecuador during this time—these floating discursivities of ethnodevelopment—will be the main point of interest in Chapter 4. For now, transnational governmentalities are to be understood as the programs of intervention that shifted the ways in which Ecuador's agents and institutions operated. What follows completes our theoretical framing by introducing the discursive democratic theory proposed by Dryzek (2000). This addition to our theoretical framing will aid our discussion of the importance of social protest and extra-procedural forms of constitution making. To understand Good Living's birth it is paramount that social protest, transgressive politics, and new political actors be taken into account during and after the critical juncture.

7   Social Protest and Discursive Democracy

An intrinsic part of Good Living's birth would be left unattended if civil society mobilisation, and its transgressive form of politics, was unaccounted for. The convergence of newly politicised ethnic cleavages, a retreating state, and changing citizen-state relations created an optimal breeding ground from which civil society could contest historical conditions of inequality, structural racism, and marginality. Emerging forms of protest were carried out in Latin America, as corporatist structures of citizen-state intermediation dissipated unions lost political leverage and left-leaning political parties waivered (Gargarella and Álvarez Ugarte 2016, 103). Marginalisation through market-led objectives created a common discourse through which the unemployed, the socially excluded, ethnic and gendered minorities, indigenous people, and other civil society collectives created a common identity of shared collective action (Holland et al. 2008, 97).

Moreover, the political opportunities that the critical juncture cracked open allowed new forms of the political to emerge. The political process model (PPM) of collective action allows us to argue how a divergent set of actors came together to contest the common cause of market-led reform. Social movement literature defines the PPM as a moment in which collective action materialises due to internal and external forces converging to create a political opportunity in which social mobilisation is made possible (Rice 2012, 24). During the critical juncture, new forms of civil society mobilisation came into play as the state retreated, new policy spaces were occupied by transnational actors, domestic sovereignty ceded to geopolitical interests, local elites imploded, and the absence of institutionalised channels of representation galvanised those who had been marginalised (McAdam et al. 1996, 10 quoted in Rice 2012).

Widespread social protest sought overarching legal reforms throughout Latin America. Collective action came together to denounce and subvert the violence, dispossession, and immiseration that engulfed Latin America throughout the critical juncture. Immiseration, according to such collectives, could be reversed through novel reimaging's of law. Rather than securing immediate material wellbeing, civil society collectives in Ecuador demanded transformations to the legal system by focusing on the ways in which identities had come to be codified (Lemaitre 2009, 36). Thus, social protest during the critical juncture quested for the construction of a legal system where marginalisation and violence could be contained. Citizen mobilisation led by women, students, homosexuals, pacifists, environmentalists, the unemployed, peasants, and indigenous people sought to redefine social reality through law (Lemaitre 2009, 35).

Social protest and transgressive politics during Ecuador's critical juncture was a collective response to the customary unrepresentative forms of government the country had experienced throughout its history. Collective action steadily increased its pressure to demand improvements to material wellbeing conditions and the systematic elimination of racial discrimination (Becker

2009; Rice 2012; Van Cott 2008). This new form of political engagement resorted to road blocks, boycotts, and the restriction of basic commodity provisions to make their demands heard (Gargarella and Álvarez Ugarte, 2016, 104). Civil society mobilisation, and collective action in general, departed from the "traditional" procedural avenues that had been established to secure legal or institutional renewal. Protest tactics during the 1990s sought to subvert the very governmentalities of contained political animosity that had defined the democratic make-up for nearly two hundred years.

Foucault, in his study of governmental rationality, established that counter conducts by civil society are inseparably linked to the formation of the modern state (2007, 357). Politics and governance in Ecuador had historically closed avenues of procedural representation by creating a form of oligarchic rule that favoured elite interests over the general wellbeing of the population (Helmke 2017; Soifer 2015). Counter conducts such as social protest were the only non-procedural avenues that collective action could resort to when particular interests were to be secured. It is in this tension between representation, interest formation, and the general will of the people where our incorporation of discursive democracy becomes most useful.

Ecuador's 2008 Constitution and the articles on Good Living contained therein are the end result of civil society mobilisation during the critical juncture. However, as a product of the civil society mobilisations that took place prior to 2008, the discourses that informed the constitution making process and the birth of good living, fall far from the formal avenues of procedural representation contained in "traditional" notions of democratic theory. Furthermore, the overall crisis affecting Ecuador's party politics, institutions, and systems of representation during the critical juncture develop more precise points of reference as to why collective action consolidated through non-procedural mechanisms.

Diminished or non-existent avenues through which electoral demands could be met fuelled collective action. Institutional failure and lack of representation led Latin American jurists to look beyond local law when attempting to comprehend how social protest could redefine legal structures. In so doing, protest soon became linked to freedom of speech. This novel shift in theoretical approximation allowed collective action demands to be forcibly presented before a judiciary, legislative and executive body (Gargarella 2012). Such formal and procedural locations of power had historically held contempt towards civil society mobilisation. However, 'theoretical revision of the academic debate on democratic theory' (Gargarella and Álvarez Ugarte 2016, 104) had questioned their role and responsibility in widespread processes of collective action, thereby demanding revision to centuries of political authority. More to the point, social protests in Latin America during the critical juncture came to be legally conceived as political expressions that deserved special judicial attention and the highest forms of public protection (Gargarella 2012, 132).

Monolithic systems of representation had led to counter conducts of social protest that rapidly expanded during the critical juncture. The plurality of grievances forwarded through collective action led the Inter-American Special Rapporteur on Freedom of Expression to link freedom of expression with social protest. Protest under such a linkage conceived social mobilisation as a fundamental tool for Latin American citizens to petition public authorities by denouncing the abuses and violations orchestrated through state governmentalities (Gargarella 2012, 136). Regional courts soon echoed this linkage by stating that poverty, exclusion, social protest, and freedom of expression constitute the conditions through which rights may be exercised by exposing the grave responsibilities that derive from the omissions or actions of the state (Gargarella 2012, 144). Freedom of expression opened avenues for deliberation by exposing the responsibility of the state and integrating social protest as an active mechanism in the formation of the democratic make-up of Latin America and Ecuador.

Linkage between protest, deliberation and freedom of expression requires theoretical bridging if we are to explore how the critical juncture led to the crystallisation of Good Living in 2008. Discussions of the democratic make-up, through competitive democracy, elite deliberation, deliberative democracy, and participatory democracy seem ill-equipped to fully grasp the complexity of how democracy was reformed in Ecuador during the critical juncture. Competitive democracy for example focuses on competitive elections that struggle to secure votes in an effort to consolidate peaceful transitions of power (Fishkin 2009, 66). Ultimately, the substance of the public will does not really matter as the system is designed to secure the status quo and preserve a continuous flow of political power.

Elite deliberation follows similar lines, as it emphasises the filtration of the public will by deliberating elites that simply seek to avoid the tyranny of the majority (Fishkin 2009, 70). Hence, the refined public opinion distilled by elite representatives may very well be counterfactual to the desires, expectations or grievances of the entire polity. Contrasting with competitive elite deliberations, participatory democracy seeks to create channels of direct and constant consultation with the people (Fishkin 2009, 76). Missing in this scenario is the fact that one could have mass participation without political equality; consider for a moment the electoral colleges utilised in the US presidential system (Fishkin 2009, 77). Finally, deliberative democracy seeks the will of the people but simultaneously demands a highly active continuously mobile population that is able to allocate its demands (Fishkin 2009, 80). Most criticisms towards this brand of the democratic make-up rest on the procedural restrictiveness that binds how deliberation is to take place, the formal avenues it perpetuates, and the endogamic relationship it generates between the executive, legislative, and judiciary powers (Dryzek 2000, 26).

These four predominant theories on deliberative democracy are ill-equipped to build the theoretical considerations that explain how Ecuador's social protests influence the process of constitution making. The rigidness requiring indirect representation as the source of the public will would overlook the political disenfranchisement that existed and still persists in Ecuador. Furthermore, the political composite of Ecuador during the critical juncture is one of regionally orientated, fragmented, inchoate and squabbling party politics (Helmke 2017; Mejía-Acosta 2006; Van Cott 2005). This crisis of representation that engulfed Ecuador throughout the critical juncture created an insurmountable distance between the will of the people and the imagined ideals of deliberative democracy. Nevertheless, the importance of social protests in Ecuador may not be discarded, as they define the political landscape that led to the 2008 constitution.

Conventional proponents of deliberative democracy, such as Rawls focuses on the institutional ensembles where deliberation may occur such as a Court, Congress or the Executive. In other words, the discussion of meaning and applicability of rules within formal structured settings (Dryzek 2000, 13). Deliberation within such structured settings, allows for constitutional reform solely to take place as a long-term project to be enacted by institutions rather than citizens (Rawls 1995, 152). Rawls and Habermas would thus agree that a 'just constitution cannot be fully realized' as it is a 'project to be carried out' (Rawls 1995, 152).

Dryzek contests this institutional bent towards deliberation by accusing such proponents, and particularly Rawls, of structuring a democracy where discussion on difference is defused and the foundation of the polity resides on material self-interest and partially constructed world views (Dryzek 2000, 15). Such a limited public sphere would be incompatible to the novel constitutional make-up that came to life in 2008. Moreover, discussion of difference would have been defused rather than adopted leaving little room for concepts like the rights of nature, Good Living or universal citizenship to enter constitutional deliberations.

Under such limited forms of deliberation, incorporation of indigenous or Afro-Ecuadorian epistemologies, as well as alternatives to capitalism, which are meant to underline Good Living, would have been impossible. The following comments depict this form of deliberation that existed outside formal institutions of power but ultimately were harnessed into the constitutional text:

> The belief that Good Living is the production of a collective life, one that includes Mother Nature and its life cycles (El Comercio 2010).
>
> There exist at least seven ways to socialize the economy, the centre of which socialism is not statism, as understood in the XXI century but rather the power of society, which is not the State or economic agents, but rather civil society associations that seek to solve societies' problems (Ospina 2017, 40:33)
>
> In the Constitution of 2008 we (Afro descendants) don't speak of Sumak Kawsay or Buen Vivir, you can look at the transcripts and documents (...) We proposed nothing on Good Living, what we did propose was the intercultural state, not even the plurinational state, we envisioned an intercultural state that could guarantee the rights of Afro descendants, amongst which was the right to land[5] (...) We won many things with the 2008 Constitution (...) Article 58 was drafted by us (Afro Ecuadorian descendants), that article was sent to us whilst we were in Chile and it came out as it (...) we won the intercultural State (...) (Anton 2017, 46:31–48:34).

Processes of deliberation in Ecuador during the critical juncture, transcend such limited avenues. Under such procedural or judicial forms of democracy, the power of civil society mobilization that occurred between 1979–2008 would have been subsided by the mechanics of law which, according to Bourdieu (1987, 819):

> Operates like an "apparatus" to the extent that the cohesion of the freely orchestrated *habitus*[6] of legal interpreters is strengthened by the discipline of a hierarchized body of professionals who employ a set of established procedures (...) convincing themselves that the law provides its

---

5 Land in terms of collective rights over specific regions of Ecuador northern coastal province of Esmeraldas and the Andean province of Imbabura.

6 Bourdieu (807) refers to habitus as: 'the practices within the legal universe are strongly patterned by tradition, education, and the daily experience of legal custom and professional usage. They operate as learned yet deep structures of behavior within the juridical field—as what Bourdieu terms habitus. They are significantly unlike the practices of any other social universe. And they are specific to the juridical field; they do not derive in any substantial way from the practices which structure other social activities or realms. Thus, they cannot be understood as simple "reflections" of relations in these other realms. They have a life, and a profound influence, of their own.'

own foundation, that it is based on a fundamental norm, a "norm of norms" such as the Constitution, from which all lower norms are in turn deduced. The communis opinio doctorum (the general opinion of professionals), rooted in the social cohesion of the body of legal interpreters, thus tends to confer the appearance of a transcendental basis on the historical forms of legal reason and on the belief in the ordered vision of the social whole that they produce (...)

Limited forms of deliberation, such as those previously depicted, led Dryzek to further criticize proponents of deliberative democracy that condition democratic engagement to procedurally mediated and legally sanctioned processes of deliberation. Dryzek (2000, 27) denounces the creation of a 'judicial democracy' that is not only a 'naïve version' of deliberation but also negates the impact extra-constitutional agents have on the democratic make-up of the polity. Constructing democracy under the conformity of an unyielding system, such as that proposed by Habermas through his communicative action, constrains deliberation to procedural and judicial rules, leaving little room for participatory deliberation (Dryzek 2000, 27).

Another irreconcilable problem that stems from structuring deliberative democracy under the communicative action theory proposed by Habermas is the Eurocentric conceptions of democracy it perpetuates. Conventional theories on deliberative democracy focus on the primacy of the individual, leaving little room for broader discussions on topics such as the group rights demanded by Ecuador's ethnic minorities (Miller 2006, 359). Habermas for example refers to institutions, states and tribes or peoples as "systems" or vacuous structures that make collectives an artificial construction unable to justify any form of inherent interest in its own will (quoted in Miller 2006, 359). Under this limited conception of deliberative democracy, not only are the demands of ethnic minorities silenced but the widely accepted legal reasoning that collectives are capable of expressing their will and invoking rights is left out of the conversation (Miller 2006, 37). Hence the limitation of Eurocentric deliberative democracy is twofold, its liberal procedural restrictiveness, as well as its unwillingness to incorporate human collectives as legitimate democratic actors. For such reasons, deliberation in democratic settings must consider the impact human collectives have on the conformation, regulation, and transformation of the polity.

The aforementioned limitations of conventional deliberative democracy reaffirm the importance of developing theoretical cover for the social protests that spawned from a variety of collective action points throughout the critical juncture. For this purpose, we utilise Dryzek's discursive democracy (2000, 27).

This critical theory seeks to incorporate alternative forms of deliberation by including critical voices that are determined on constructing a different social reality. Creating a theoretical premise towards social protest and discursive democracy overcomes the limitations Eurocentric deliberative democracy would impose on the collective action that defined Ecuadorian politics during the critical juncture. In so doing, this new participatory form of deliberation creates a conceptual bridging that is dislodged from the restrictive participatory mechanisms of elite-based representation or procedural democracy, as well as the hegemonic discourses they perpetuate (Dryzek 2000, 57).

Discursive democracy overcomes the limitation contained in the conventional forms of deliberative democracy conceptualised by Rawls or Habermas. Thus, discursive democracy gives a deliberative function to social movements by integrating them to the shaping of democracy (Dryzek 2000, 81). Discursive democracy is thus distinct from deliberative democracy in its attracting force of social movements towards the public sphere of democratic deliberation. Rather than stipulating that competitive enlightened elites will somehow filter the public will, discursive democracy demands that wider forms of representation shape the political make-up of a country. For Ecuador, this shaping of the public sphere through social protest and collective action is exemplified in two constitutional texts, one in 1998 and another in 2008.

Discursive democracy however also transcends the local by positioning the concept of transnational democracy. In this variation of discursive democracy, the discourses that flow from civil society are interconnected throughout the globe, thereby creating political interactions that need not worry about the limits imposed by particular territorial entities or endemic forms of governmentality (Dryzek 2000, 129). This transnationalised version of deliberation further aids our process tracing, as it grants theoretical cover to the complex interconnectedness that came from local actors, NGOs, and transnational civil society. Discursive democracy is thus linked to a strong concept of civil society and the idea of an international public sphere that is fluid and made possible by its unconstrained and uncoerced nature (Dryzek 2000, 130). In other words, the lacking coercion that is imposed by the sovereign prerogatives of a state or central mediating authority. Minimal forms of coercion during the critical juncture is best exemplified in the retreating state and the surge of transnational actors that came with NGOs and development agencies.

The introduction of discursive democracy is thus adequate for the following reasons. Firstly, it contests prevailing notions of the democratic make-up that would favour a continuation of the status quo, a proposition that is evidently ill-suited to explain the political reshufflings that occurred during the critical juncture. Secondly, it allows us to vindicate the profound, vast and still to be scrutinised impact social protest had in shaping the 2008 constitution and Good Living. By linking social protest with freedom of speech, a new terrain for democracy is paved whereby the limitations previously imposed by the Order and Progress model once again crumble. Moreover, discursive democracy allows us to transcend the local and interact with the transnational. This is of fundamental importance for us to comprehend how the changing forms of governmentality both opened new forms of democratic experiences but simultaneously reshaped political agendas, as NGOs and international development agencies began to influence social protest in Ecuador.

Finally, insertion of discursive democracy as a theoretical tool allows us to interlink social protest and the constructivist conception of law and society that swept Ecuador and Latin America between 1990 and the early 2000s. This recalibrating of legal rationality included the reclamations levied by social protest, repositioning the nature of law as a medium through which social relations, difference and opposing worldviews could be discussed and subsequently included into the legal domain (Rodríguez-Garavito 2011, 1678). During the critical juncture an ever-growing constructivist interpretation of law sought to remedy historic group inequalities by attending matters pertaining to race and class. Constructivist interpretations towards law materialised in Ecuador's 2008 Constitution through a legal reasoning responsive to the cultural and socio-economic conditions that demanded the forging of a 'living law'; one that is multicultural, pluralistic, and responsive to the context from which it emerges (Gallegos-Anda 2017, 3).

Good Living emerged as a product of social protest and constructivist approaches towards law. By questioning existing legal structures and positioning the expectations, reclamations, and historical grievances of a plethora of social actors, a new form of legal practice was consolidated. Discursive democracy, fuelled by widespread social protests, steadily interconnected local struggles with transnational actors, ultimately reforming Ecuador's political and constitutional order. This process culminated in the forging of new legal principles such as Good Living, a representation of the discourses and power techniques that had surfaced during the critical juncture. The juridification or legal abstract form adopted by these collective action reclamations is what is proposed was distilled into Good Living. By reinstating the role of social protest and its intrinsic importance in Ecuador's 2008 democratic make-up, a form of popular sovereignty was imprinted onto Good Living. In turn, this collective form of popular sovereignty defied previous constructions of deliberative democracy under formal, procedural, and judicial rules, such as those that had been defended by Rawls or Habermas (Sanin Restrepo 2012, 31). Good Living, in addition to being the juridification of social protest, embodies a new form of political engagement, one in which the institutional and procedural mechanisms of democracy collapsed, allowing one and all to enter.

8   Conclusion

This chapter has focused on the methodological premises and theoretical foundations on which the subsequent chapters unfold. It has positioned a theory-guided process tracing that interconnects politicised ethnic cleavages, state retreat, and changing citizenship regimes as the main converging occurrences that led to Good Living. Furthermore, it has introduced the concept of transnational governmentalities to discuss how corporatism ceded to social neoliberalism and, in so doing, altered the prevailing ways in which citizen-state relations functioned. More importantly, this shift transformed the political agendas emerging from social movements defusing their transgressive nature. Such a transformation would later influence the formation of Good Living as a constitutional principle by including a managed form of market-led multiculturalism. Finally, the introduction of discursive democracy reinstates the importance social protest played in shaping the political agendas that led to Good Living. Moreover, social protest and the transnational networks it constructed will later feed into our discussions on transnational governmentalities and the shifting agendas of collective action.

Ultimately, the theoretical discussions emerging from discursive democracy and transnational governmentalities are the subsequent pieces of evidence that surface from our theory-guided process tracing. Good Living under these theoretical covers harbours two distinct and opposing projects. The first of which is based on the emancipatory projects of indigenous people seeking territorial autonomy and self-determination; and a second is influenced by the transnational governmentalities of the social neoliberalism that came to life during the critical juncture. This market-orientated ethnodevelopment would shelter market-orientated social capitalism from collective action throughout the critical juncture. Good Living is thus simultaneously a highly politicised project emerging from transgressive social movements and yet also a project that perpetuates, permeates, and consolidates the underlying tenets of market liberalism.

CHAPTER 2

Good Living in the Academic Literature

Ecuador's 2008 Constitution is part of a continuous process of regional convergence and constitutional reform (Bonilla 2013; Gargarella 2013). According to Tushnet (2017), the process of constitutional reform that occurred in Ecuador falls in line with other regional processes, such as those that led Venezuela (1999) and Bolivia (2009) to change their constitutions. These so-called Bolivarian constitutions are themselves part of constitutional learning processes in Latin America, where new rights were developed and the role of parliamentary sovereignty displaced. This "new-constitutionalism" seeks a stronger form of judicial review where rights may be balanced and weighed according to the contexts in which they are exercised (Goldoni 2012, 927).

Ecuador's constitution was heralded by some as a 'socialist constitution' that 'expanded the powers of President Rafael Correa' whilst forging a 'multinational, intercultural and experimental' societal make-up (Siddique 2008; Uprimny 2010). The dynamics of constitutional reform in Ecuador respond to a complex set of circumstances that have defined the region's legal history. This alleged socialist constitution was birthed during a process of unprecedented legal transformations throughout the region. Stemming from a decade or so of profound macroeconomic policy reforms, state retreat, and ever-changing citizen-state relations, Ecuador's body politic was profoundly transformed, shifting the power structures that had contained political unrest for over a hundred and fifty years.

The critical juncture that came together during this time would unleash unseen political forces, question the very make-up of the Ecuadorian state, and crack open once zealously guarded policy spaces to NGOs, international development agencies, and transnational financial lenders. As economist Pablo Dávalos comments on the processes of intervention that occurred between 1980 and 1990:

> ... the [World] Bank came to change the structure of the state, not only economic policy but political and institutional systems, which in turn fuelled a series of union revolts. These struggles didn't reach the indigenous during the 1980s, they [indigenous] didn't view it [World Bank] as an enemy [yet]. During the 1980s the country was still a largely agrarian

society with the *hacienda* at its core, capitalist relations had yet to reach it ... (2017, 3:38).

The convergence of politicised ethnic cleavages, a weakening of a once interventionist state and shifting dynamics of citizenship regimes, came together in the formation of political, economic, and social agendas that defied previous constitutional models of Order and Progress. Amongst the diverse proposals that came to life during Ecuador's 2007–2008 Constitutional Assembly, the conceptual consolidation of Good Living, as a viable concept or legal principle, is the main focus of this chapter.

In order for us to engage with the multiple interpretations Good Living has brought forth since its 2008 inception we must review the scattered, at times conflicting and overall divergent, literature that emerged since Ecuador's Constitutional Assembly. Due to the contested nature of Good Living, the following chapter will divide the revised literature into three main currents of interpretation. Following Hidalgo-Capitán and Cubillo-Guevara's (2014) classification of Good Living, we are directed towards three overarching currents onto which we can extrapolate our analysis. According to the above-mentioned authors, we may categorise existing literature on Good Living into three opposing currents, the first of which falls under what has been named as the socialist or statist strain, the second labelled as ecologist or post-developmental and a final strain broadly bounded by indigenism or conservation projects that relate to Pachamama (Mother Earth).

The socialist-statist strain advocates for an interventionist and active public sector that defines what policy prescriptions are to configure and enact Good Living in the public sphere (Hidalgo-Capitán and Cubillo-Guevara's 2014, 27). With its main focus on social equity through wealth redistribution, this particular discursive strain is part of an urban and intellectual socio-economic agenda drafted by the populist technocratic Left that came into government in Ecuador's 2006 presidential elections (Schavelzon 2015, 212). Moreover, this strain of Good Living has been dominant in policy discussions in Ecuador since 2008, as the newly minted constitution mandated the drafting of a National Development Plan[1] by the *Secretaría Nacional de Planificación y Desarrollo* (National Secretary for Planning and Development or SENPLADES). This policy paper would however be titled under the politically persuasive name of *National Plan for Good Living*, effectively merging the macroeconomic

---

[1] Constitution of Ecuador, Art 147 (4): it is an attribution and duty of the President of the Republic to present to the National Council for Planning the proposed National Development Plan for its approval.

development policy of the state with the underlying constitutional prescriptions allegedly contained in Good Living.[2]

In sharp contrast, the ecologist or post-developmental strain opposes state-centred economic development as the underlying theoretical justification of Good Living. This strain's building of Good Living as a way towards the preservation of nature and securement of a participative and inclusive formulation of politics, strives to unite the political projects of peasants, indigenous, socialists, feminists, and ecologists (Hidalgo-Capitán and Cubillo-Guevara's 2014, 28). According to Hidalgo-Capitán and Cubillo-Guevara (2014), this particular strain is closely associated with post-modern constructivist theory and stands out for its criticism of neo-extractivist policies in Ecuador. As Ospina points out:

> ...we are discussing an alternative to capitalist society...a project of viable utopias...the different ways we may overcome capitalist society...of socializing the economy and at its center, socialism is not the state, as it was understood in the twentieth century but rather the power of society...the associations of civil society that seek to overcome the problems of the people...voluntary associations...these different associations that are free from the coercive power of the state and capital...if that third sector exists it is what we call society...and what is built on that third axis is what's called Socialism (2017, 41:43).

With its strong inclination towards social movements and citizen participation, this strain seeks to 'open up places and spaces of enunciation' by criticising the inequalities and illegitimate practices that constrain the imagining of other worlds'; one in which the government of the common is made possible (Gonzalez and Vazquez 2015, 2). Finally, indigenism or Pachamama Good Living focuses on broad projects of self-determination by indigenous people, the recovery of Andean cultures and the construction of *Sumak Kawsay*[3] rather than Good Living. However, the debates that led to *Sumak Kawsay*'s constitutional inscription fall short from the novel alternativeness and inclusive political participation that some associate with its birth. As a former indigenous constitutional delegate pointed out:

---

2   Executive Decree 725, Official Registry 433 of 25 April 2011: Dispositions for the Organization of the Executive, Art. 15: The National Secretary for Planning and Development is responsible for integrating and coordinating national planning of sectors and the coherence of national public policies (...); Executive Decree 1372, Official Registry 278 of 20 February 2004: creates the National Secretary for Planning and Development.
3   Sumak Kawsay is the Kichwa language translation of Good Living or Living Well.

> ...The 2008 Constitution included phrases without there being a profound conversation...rather, what was included was the vision of the President and the Government at that time... in order to satisfy demands and avoid political convulsions or protests from indigenous sectors. What this leads to is that nothing has come from the inclusion of *Sumak Kawsay* or plurinationality. Why do I say this? Because the concept of plurinationality is there yet it has failed to change the structure of the state... concepts that were incorporated but don't have much impact, like the rights of nature...a concept that was included but separated from *Sumak Kawsay*... (Chuji 2017, 41:00).

Estermann (2010, 5) however, adheres to a concept of Buen Vivir or Sumak Kawsay that is intent on solving the "Western development derailment" stemming from Judeo-Christian traditions and Greco-Roman Hellenic philosophy. In so doing, Estermann (2010, 24) conceives Good Living to be a "Pachasofía" (a philosophy of nature) that harbours a development formula based on sustainability and harmony with life and nature in order to secure future generations and the entire cosmos '*Vivir Bien, allin kawsay, suma Qamaña, ivi maräei, etc*.' Altmann (2014, 5) echoes previous writings by Carlos Viteri Gualinga (1993, 149 in Altmann 2014) in which a similar stance on Good Living is presented:

> Carlos Viteri Gualinga already published a short but very dense description of indigenous cosmovision, prominently placing Sumak Kawsay and linking it to other aspects of the same cosmovision (...) Viteri already identifies the contradiction between indigenous peoples who employ the concept and non-indigenous, highlighting the need to establish common goals in order to "keep renovating the road towards *sumac allpa*."[4]

However, what Gualinga (1993) fails to disclose in such overarching and sweeping statements is the fact that Ecuador is populated by fourteen different indigenous nationalities that inhabit geographical areas separated by the Andes and Amazon (Yashar 2005, 85). This separation translates into different languages, social structures, political priorities and struggles as has been well documented by Sawyer (2004), Van Cott (1994; 2005) or Selverston-Scher (2001). Accepting the existence of a single unified concept of Buen Vivir, Good Living or Sumak Kawsay, such as the one proposed by Gualinga and echoed throughout existing literature on the matter, would fall into the same homogenising practices that have been utilised previously in Ecuador to construct a single,

---

4 The translation is mine.

unified and homogenous national identity that erases difference amongst indigenous peoples and the *mestizo* population (Radcliffe and Westwood 1996, 11). The ease with which certain authors take, what is allegedly an Andean and Amazonian concept, and export it to far off places such as Costa Rica, Chile, Panama, Colombia, Argentina or New Zealand underlines the perils of conceptual fluidity and emptiness Good Living faces (Broad and Fischer-Mackey 2017, 1327). Although Good Living is heralded as an indigenous concept intent on shifting development priorities in Ecuador and Bolivia, scholarly works recognize the fact that:

> Indeed, the term buen vivir gained renown when both Ecuador and Bolivia incorporated it into their constitutions. Alas, both governments have turned increasingly to neo-extractivism of fossil fuels, even while proclaiming themselves buen vivir proponents (Broad and Fischer-Mackey 2017, 1328).

At the very least, Good Living as a policy alternative has failed to muster the results heralded by many of its supporters. Moreover, conceptualisations of a homogenous *Sumak Kawsay*, such as those proposed by Gualinga or attempted to be reproduced in other countries, recreate an idealised representation of harmonic living conditions within pre-colonial indigenous communities. By exalting self-sufficiency, communitarianism, solidarity, equality, and sustainability *Sumak Kawsay* becomes a tautologically ridden utopia that is reachable only through the untiring stoicism of rural indigenous Andean communities. Ecuadorian anthropologist Sánchez-Parga (2011, 31), would agree with such a framing of Good Living when he states that:

> Recourse to ethnic discursivities (*Pachamama, sumak kawsay*) highlights a *reactionary utopia* that adopts a formula of the past as a project for the future (…) such reactionary utopias are *ideological* and do not have a further objective than resistance and interpellation, political utopias are seen as ethical and bearers of a revolutionary practice towards change.

The alleged alternativeness of *Sumak Kawsay*, as worded by Gualinga and contested by Sánchez-Parga, demands us to refocus our analysis in an effort to include the political, social and economic processes that shaped Good Living during the critical juncture (Hidalgo-Capitán and Cubillo-Guevara's 2014, 29; Oviedo Freire 2014, 139). This effort seeks to situate ongoing debates on the political and legal transformations that occurred during a specific period stretching from 1978 to 2008. This methodological delimitation displaces historical searches intent on finding the ontological origins of millenary indigenous practices. To this effect, indigenous peoples are understood as political actors who steer towards political objectives such as territorial autonomy, collective rights or specific economic reforms (Anaya 2000, 129; Rice 2012, 5).

Good Living does however stem from certain aspects of indigenous epistemology. As former Minister of Foreign Affairs, constitutional magistrate, academic and indigenous leader Nina Pacari explains, Andean conceptions around these subjects are associated with *ayllu* socio-political structures:

> ...The relation between indigenous nationality and its territory is reflected in a traditional socio-political structure that goes from family (ayllu) to wider community (llacta ayllu) and finally to people (mama ayllu), the latter defined by a common language, culture, territory and economic connections. These three levels of social organization correspond with three levels of legislation: family norms (ayllu camachic), social norms (llacta camachic), and legal norms for the whole people (mama ayllu camachic) complete each other harmoniously in the different social entities... Their moral bases are traditional principles, such as 'Don't be lazy, don't lie, don't steal' (ama quilla, ama llula, ama shua) and the "harmonious relation between universe-earth-man (pachamama-allpamama-runa), that resumes the ideological and cultural cosmovision" ... (Pacari 1984, 115 quoted in Altman 2014, 85).

Whilst a rich analysis of Andean cultures and their community experiences are abundant, discussions on *Sumak Kawsay* since 2008 have unfortunately fallen into the hyperreal discussions of Indigenist Good Living. Returning to the roots of *Sumak Kawsay*, we find that its first proponents were mostly of *Kichwa* or *Aymara* indigenous heritage, each of which are respectively from Ecuador or Bolivia, as well as mestizo intellectuals from each country (Hidalgo-Capitán and Cubillo-Guevara's 2014, 29).

Whilst Hidalgo-Capitán and Cubillo-Guevara's (2014) classification of Good Living has been reproduced by Guardiola and García-Quero (2014), Ponce León (2016), Merino (2016), Waldmüller (2014), and Calisto Friant and Langmore (2015), the prevailing literature does not entirely fit into the broad three categories presented above. For this reason, a fourth category is introduced in order to aid the revision of the multiple readings currently surrounding Good Living. Rather than focusing on the ontological analysis of Good Living that emerged within the three predominant discourses, the fourth category opens the theoretical space for critical readings to be introduced (González and Vázquez 2015, 5). Critical analysis circumvents the current focus on 'sources of knowledge production' and the 'accuracy of representation' from which Good Living emerges (González and Vázquez 2015). This fourth category, we shall call "Critical Good Living," grants us the leeway to analyse the concept from the social, political, and economic processes that led to it.

What has been proposed is to refocus analysis on Good Living by staying clear from the ontological discourses that have dominated scholarly discussions regarding its constitutional inscription. We start our analysis by shifting focus towards the conditions of the critical juncture, and the law, practices, institutions, and discourses associated with Good Living during this time (Rask Madsen and Dezalay 2013, 112). Creating this incision point in the analysis of Good Living examines the manifest forms of power embedded therein, revealing the fragmentary practices of domination through which social harmony was achieved in 2008 (Cassidy 2006, 30). Following Foucault's analysis of power, domination is not to be understood as that which is exercised upon a particular class or group but rather as the practices of individuals who simultaneously enact or are acted upon (Cassidy 2006, 31). Examination of power through this lens demands that we revise its points of dispersion, the machinery of institutions, practices, and agents that came to terraform Ecuador's social fabric during the critical juncture (Cassidy 2006).

Moreover, opening this fourth category adds to the theoretical framing presented in Chapter 1 by exploring the points of power dispersion that engulfed Ecuador throughout the critical juncture. Such a shift contests the privileged discourses that have emerged around Good Living once it was codified into the universal object called "the law" (Cassidy 2006, 26). Challenging these privileges situates current proponents of Good Living such as Acosta (2011), Oviedo (2014) or Ramírez (2010), under the necessary scholarly attention that dissects and complements their writings by including the analysis of power in their corresponding discursive formations. Doing so presents the counter-possibility that they, as well as other academics or legal practitioners, are hedged by a variety of occupationally derived norms and power relations, which conceal arbitrariness and subjectivity through positive hermeneutics (Cassidy 2006, 26).

This fourth category also builds on scholarship on Good Living presented by scholars such as Quijano (2011), Recasens (2014), Sánchez Parga (2011), Mansilla (2011), Waldmuëller (2014), González and Vázquez (2015), Radcliffe (2012), Bretón (2001; 2005; 2007; 2008; 2010), Bretón et al. (2014), and Schavelzon (2015). These authors question the viability of discussing Good Living's epistemological or ontological origins whilst disregarding the social, political, and economic processes that led to it. Positioning this fourth level of analysis seeks to further highlight the importance of analysing Good Living through the prism of social, economic and political contexts that led to the 2008 constitutional reform. This revision through "context" is intent on revealing the shifting dynamics of power relations that came to be during the critical juncture. Doing so shifts focus from ontology and normative principles by reviewing the polymorphous ways agents, institutions and practices came together in the crafting of Good Living. Under this new scope, one may unravel the political discourses and legal institutions that came together in shaping what was imprinted into the 2008 Constitution.

Consequently, this additional layer of theoretical discussion helps us situate the ways in which politicised ethnic cleavages, changing citizenship regimes, and a retreating state converged in Ecuador during the 1990s. In so doing, critical Good Living allows us to analyse how transnational governmentalities and international civil society networks came together to build a constitutional project that was heralded as a 'citizens revolution' (Brown 2017). However, before we may discuss the critical engagements that emerge from this additional layer of theoretical analysis, we must review the main discourses that have formed around Good Living. The remainder of this chapter analyses the four proposed currents as follows: first we shall review the indigenism or Pachamama strain, then the socialist and statist formulation, followed by the ecologist or post-developmental branch. The chapter concludes by reviewing and building on the critical strain of Good Living.

1   Ecuadorian Discussions on Good Living

Before engagement with the literature that has dealt with Good Living within the three different existing strains may commence, we must first situate debates surrounding the concept in order to grasp the theoretical dimensions crafted around it. Altmann (2014, 2) for example, situates the political origins of the concept as Buen Vivir in the year 2000 within discussions that took place in Bolivia. Yampara (2001 in Altmann 2014, 2) would later define Buen Vivir within formal logics that equate the concept as 'Suma Qamaña = to live well means to live in harmony and in ecological equilibrium with one and all.'[5] Spedding (2010, 1) however, questions how such an equilibrium may be achieved when she states:

> Within recent national texts about 'buen vivir,' I have not seen elements that may indicate how one may change living practices or one in which

---

5   The translation is mine.

this quotidian cosmovision is attainable, if we were not to abandon capitalist urban employment and become farmers within some rural community, something which its proponents do not seem personally eager to do or propose to their readers (...) Perhaps this has to do with the fact that the philosophy or cosmovision of 'vivir bien' is attributed to members of such communities without empirical evidence that may substantiate what this is and how it is expressed in daily life.

Reservations towards Good Living are also exposed by Ecuadorian academics researching indigenous customs and practices. Anthropologist Fernando García (2017, 31:03) contests the existence of Buen Vivir and Sumak Kawsay altogether when he states:

> What came to the Constitutional Assembly (regarding Good Living) was the result of 30 to 40 years of transformation dating back to the return (Ecuador's) to democracy (...) one of the first things that was done by the Roldos Administration was the bilingual literacy campaign, you have no idea the dimension this had (...) in the final balance many important things have changed in the political but nothing has changed in terms of equality (...) liberal multiculturalism has limited the advancement of interculturality (...)[6]

In accordance to García's understanding of Good Living, what followed the Constitutional Assembly of 2007 is the confluence of longer and more diverse processes of political, economic and legal transformations. As a policy goal, Good Living's ability to shift policy decisions is inherently limited by the liberal multicultural lens through which it has been applied. This inability to materialize Good Living into realizable policy objectives was already mentioned when analysing Gualinga's (2002, 4) proposal of a Buen Vivir that seeks to eliminate the concept of development in order to remedy economic crises, inequality, social chaos and a looming environmental crisis. All of which require transnational and local policy shifts for which the ontological origins of Good Living proposed by Gualinga and others offer no readily available policy proposal. This inability to materialize policy prescriptions is further accentuated by Good Living's distancing from what could be considered an indigenous political project. Separation from indigenous policy objectives is thus highlighted by García (2017, 3:45–7:43) when he states:

---

6 The translation is mine.

> The proposal of the Ecuadorian indigenous movement in the 1980s and early 1990s was the construction of a plurinational and intercultural state which wasn't approved in 1998 but was approved in 2008. That seems to me to be the historical proposal of the movement towards the country. What's behind this? A strong political reform that personally, I believe has only been partially successful. Also, there exists a reckoning with the national state, which I believe calls into question the state that was founded in 1830 (…) I have not found Sumak Kawsay to be a vindication of what the indigenous movement demanded (…) A few weeks ago, this leader that just left CONAIE, Floresmilo Simabaña, who is one of the most interesting indigenous intellectuals of our time told me that *Sumak Kawsay* is just another exercise of rhetoric and *mestizaje*, it's nothing more than that. What it is actually doing is nullifying the original proposal of a plurinational and intercultural state presented by the indigenous movement.[7]

The political usage of Good Living as well as its legal standing defines the main objectives of this book. In order to determine and identify where the legal principle comes from, how it is politically utilised and its legal standing demands that we review the diverse literature produced around it. What follows divides current literature on Good Living in an effort to order its usage and propose a new critical angle. It must however be highlighted that the literature review that follows is not set on completing an exhaustive analysis of all scholarly work on the matter. Rather, what is here proposed is a review of the main theoretical currents that underline the concept in order to define its legal origins and political usage. This revision of theoretical premises surrounding Good Living are also useful for methodological purposes as the theory-guided process tracing that is carried out depends on such revisions to recreate the chain of events that led to the 2008 Constitution.

2   Indigenist or Pachamama Good Living

Whilst some frame Good Living as Ecuador's formulation of the various currents of thought that were discussed above, it can be traced as a derivative discussion of earlier processes that began in Bolivia during the early 1990s. Medina (2014) situates the discursive origins of Bolivia's *Suma Qamaña,* which is broadly an equivalent of Ecuador's Good Living, in workshops that took place

---

7   The translation is mine.

in 1990. These workshops had as their main objective the assessment of development projects financed by NGOs and international development agencies since the 1970s (Medina 2014, 127). Bolivia's *Suma Qamaña,* according to Altman (2014, 85), came to life with the help of the then German Technical Cooperation Agency (GTZ) presently known as GiZ. In the early 2000s, the GTZ harnessed and nurtured meeting spaces where intellectuals and Aymara indigenous could discuss the impacts development projects had brought about to life in the rural Andes. Medina (2014, 128) corroborates Altman by stating that in 2000, the GTZ organised a cooperation program called *Suma Qamaña* within the Global Alliance for Combating Poverty.

Initial conversations in Bolivia surrounding Good Living (Suma Qamaña) during this time are corroborated by Altman (2014, 3), as he situates the emergence of the concept in a series of events sponsored by GTZ throughout Latin America. Altman (2014) also states that the GTZ develops the idea of "Western Good Life" in opposition to "Indigenous Good Life." Product of these meetings and discussions the following provisional concept of Good Living emerged to 'live in austerity, harmony and equilibrium with oneself, the community and the cosmos' (GTZ 2002 in Altman 2014). Such metaphysical qualities carry striking resemblance with the philosophical grounds found in Buddhism and the teachings of the Buddha or "Enlightened One" in which the task of humanity is to "practice morality, mediation, and insight (Scott 2014). Comparison with religious teachings serves to highlight the conceptual openness on which Good Living was originally discussed. Rather than a development paradigm or alternative, initial conversations sought to delineate a metaphysical understanding that defines 'being as such,' 'categories of beings,' 'nature of beings'" and their corresponding 'ontological categories' (van Inwagen and Sullivan 2018). Beyond Buddhism one may also find resemblance with the philosophical reading of Stoicism in which 'the entire cosmos is a living thing' and that 'the only things that are good are the characteristic excellences or virtues of human beings (or of human minds): prudence or wisdom, justice, courage and moderation, and other related qualities' (Baltzly 2019).

These comparisons do not seek to counter or refute the existence of an indigenous knowledge or practice that is endogenous to the fourteen different indigenous groups that populate Ecuador. Rather, what is sought is to highlight the conceptual openness with which discussions on Good Living began which also serves to highlight the highly ontological bent present discussions have taken. Moreover, allegations that Good Living stands as a development alternative to capitalist economies is also wanting of substantiation (Vanhulst and Beling 2016). Whilst metaphysical propositions such as harmony, equilibrium and austerity are well suited for philosophical circles, Good Living as a constitutional principle, requires substantiation in terms of how exactly policy, rights, budgets and legal remedies are to be applied by courts, ministries and local governments. This definition will in turn aid in the usage of Good Living as a political discourse that is clearly defined.

Regardless of the conceptual openness Ecuador's Good Living was nevertheless consolidated as a guideline for policy prescription regarding civil society, representatives of the state, NGOs, academics, and indigenous leaders (Schavelzon 2015, 193). Within these multiple actors, civil society participation in the processes that led to the 2008 constitution was a constant point of reference during Ecuador's Constitutional Assembly. As is evidenced within the transcripts of the Constitutional Assembly, civil society claimed its place in the framing of Ecuador's Constitution in regard to territorial rights, environmental conservation, and the ecological alternatives of a bio-centric development plan:

> ...around 6.400 delegates from communities, neighborhoods, children, women, and peasant organizations, afros, indigenous, municipalities, NGOs, private enterprises, unions, amongst other actors came from 15 provinces, mobilized to present their demands and proposals. All these thesis and proposals were adequately processed... and served as rough draft of the articles here presented... (Majority Report: Constitutional Table No.5, Acta 070, 90).[8]

Moreover, concrete differences between Bolivian understandings of *Suma Qamaña* and Ecuador's Good Living largely stem from the professional backgrounds of those who led the discussions in Bolivia during the 1990s and Ecuador in the early 2000s. Whilst anthropologists, philosophers, and indigenous intellectuals spearheaded Bolivian discussions on *Suma Qamaña*, Ecuador's approach to Good Living was commandeered by left-leaning economists (Schavelzon 2015, 193). Perhaps this economistic approach towards Good Living is what has led authors like Medina (2014, 129) to denounce leftist associations of Good Living to development regimes that have consecutively failed in Latin America.

Schavelzon (2015, 199) credits CONAIE with importing to Ecuador discussions around *Suma Qamaña* during a 2001 congress in which the social movement outlined its political agenda 'for a new social order, a plurinational state and a pluricultural society.' The political project that was presented during this

---

8 The translation is mine.

congress outlined an economic paradigm that focused on ancestral practices, barter, and the fair trade of products as ways through which an ethnically conceptualised market could satisfy socio-economic needs throughout the Ecuadorian Andes (Sanchez 2001 quoted in Schavelzon 2015, 199). Proposals for a new socio-economic paradigm had consolidated in Bolivia throughout the 1990s as discussions regarding development unfolded in multiple spaces. Ultimately, the GTZ would organise, finance, and promote discussions on politics, philosophy, Andean cosmology, and decentralisation throughout the 1990s (Schavelzon 2015, 204). Others however, have pointed to the diverse origins of the concept:

> Good Living is not an invention of the GTZ nor an invention of intellectuals such as Carlos Viteri Gualinga (...) what he (Carlos Viteri Gualinga) does is recollect something of what is used in his community. Another example can be found in Cotacachi (Imbabura Province-Northern Ecuador) where *sumak* is a term that's almost never used. They gave me this example, "when we are dancing the San Juan we are very happy, drinking and dancing and excited in that moment we are in *alli causi* but there is a single moment, that occurs ever so often and which is fleeting, when ecstasy is complete in that moment we are in *sumak*."
> (OSPINA 2017, 31:24)

Merino (2016) has commented that *Suma Qamaña* in Ecuador was transformed into Good Living when indigenous cosmologies and human-nature complementarity was added to the discussions that had been imported from Bolivia. This connection of 'traditional indigenous thinking' with environmental politics would ultimately reconnect Good Living to demands for self-determination, territorial rights, and revitalised environmental politics (Merino 2016, 273). As former constitutional delegate and active indigenous leader Mónica Chuji stated during the Constitutional Assembly:

> ...we must protect human rights from a perspective of different but equal, however we should also protect nature, animals, lakes, highlands, mountains, glaciers. Nature is not for sale. Similarly, nationalities and peoples are not going to be sacrificed once again in the wake of modernity, development and progress. It is not the right of the few against the many, it is not development and progress against barbarism, it is not the position of a few ecologists, indigenous or Leftist's. I call out to you all so we may understand that we are responsible for life on this planet, responsible for the quick transit by which we inhabit...from this Assembly life must be

regulated, planetary conservation must be regulated, to make a Constitution that really harbours hope for the future... (Chuji: Acta 070, 106).[9]

Some clarification is warranted before we continue. When analysing *Sumak Kawsay*, the intention is not to underestimate the power of an indigenous epistemological project that may reshape politics in Ecuador. One would be foolish to deny the impact and sheer relevance ethnic politics had for Ecuador and Latin America during the critical juncture. Moreover, denying indigenous intellectuals, its political leaders or the organisations they represent their rightful place in the formation of Ecuadorian politics and its legal system would reproduce past forms of epistemic violence. That is certainly not here intended. Rather, what is proposed in the analysis of *Sumak Kawsay* that is presented here is that during the Constitutional Assembly and since 2008, this strain of Good Living has been circumscribed to the power dynamics that frame one particular discourse to the detriment of others.

Of course, one cannot deny that a vast and rich scholarship regarding *Sumak Kawsay*, collective rights or interculturality has flourished since 2008 but rather that the discourses that have dominated discussions regarding Good Living's Indigenist strain have been framed around the power dynamics of *Sumak Kawsay*. As indigenous leader Monica Chuji comments when speaking of *Sumak Kawsay's* constitutional inscription:

> What are we speaking of when we speak of *Sumak Kawsay?* We speak of a climax an equilibrated relation with everything around us...We are acting with everything around us. Everything is alive...the rocks are alive... and everyone has a specific function...from these functions is that we achieve equilibrium.... nature is thus integrated to *Sumak Kawsay*...hence when nature is separated from *Sumak Kawsay* a new meaning is given... there was little space during the Constitutional Assembly to discuss these issues further (2017, 43:00).

Similar as to what occurred during Ecuador's Constitutional Assembly, discussion on Good Living or *Sumak Kawsay* has been circumscribed to the power dynamics that framed deliberation at a given point in time. Good Living gradually adopted "new meanings" in order to accommodate the discourses or interests of those who framed it during Ecuador's Constitutional Assembly.

---

9 The translation is mine.

Furthermore, this narrowness of deliberation forged a discourse consolidated on the trinity of Good Living that came to be defined through the state, Indigenist and post-developmental discourses.

When discussing the origins of *Suma Qamaña* in Bolivia, Huanacuni (2010) outlines a project for harmony, equilibrium, and holistic understanding of Pachamama (Mother Earth). Such a project, according to this author, is founded on the teachings of community ancestors as well as Andean cosmology. Additionally, he argues that *Suma Qamaña* is not a political endeavour but rather a project for reconstructing life by eliminating the fictitious divide between man and nature. This reconstruction is thus only made possible if mankind leaves the humanist individuality that separates us from nature. Finally, *Suma Qamaña* according to Huanacuni, is a project through which identity must be reconstituted by strengthening culture, a feat that is only made possible if 'anti-natural dynamics imposed on life forces are eliminated' (2010). The overtly discreet criticism to liberal political thought and capitalist forms of market interactions are abundant in this strain. Moreover, the strengthening of culture as a predominant objective, reminisces on the political search for self-determination and territorial autonomy that has guided indigenous political agendas in Ecuador since the mid-1960s.

Prior to Huanacuni it was Javier Medina (2001), with the financial backing of the GTZ, who first compiled and published an extensive registry of what *Suma Qamaña* had come to represent in the Bolivian Andes. According to this author, *Suma Qamaña* sought to recover a qualitative understanding of life that went beyond Newtonian, Cartesian, Hobbesian, and Smith's rationalist understandings of life and society (Medina 2001, 23). Dismissing Western thought became a crucial part of formulating *Suma Qamaña*, as it was believed reliance on such precepts, imposed the dichotomies of Judeo-Christian beliefs limiting holistic discussions on life and nature (Medina 2001, 24).

Notwithstanding, after dismissal of Western rationalist understandings of life, Medina later goes on to equate Amerindian conceptions of *Suma Qamaña* with notions of quantum physics and earth sciences (Medina 2001, 24). By stating that Amerindian traditions, not only hold similarities to quantum physics but that they are set to become the new paradigm for mankind, Medina perpetuates the universalistic and hegemonic discourses that Good Living or *Suma Qamaña* were meant to contest (Medina 2001, 25). Such a scattered construction of Good Living exposes the contradictory nature of rejecting hegemony and universalism whilst attempting to construct a project for all mankind.

Oviedo (2014, 139–41) constructs a similar conception of Good Living by stating that the Andean system of life called *Sumak Kawsay* is a millenary philosophy of the indigenous people of the Andes, a paradigm that overcomes the marginalising ontologies and epistemological biases of Western thought. Predominant in Oviedo's writing is an ontological debate that seeks to disregard what he calls the 'postmodern theory of Good Living' which was crafted by Ecuador's left (2014, 142). In order to discover and empower discussions on *Sumak Kawsay*, Oviedo denounces attempts at constructing a theory of Good Living, as he believes this is a form of neo-colonialism stemming from the continuation of previously failed development projects (Oviedo 2014, 143). In consequence, rejection of a theoretical construction of Good Living from one of the main discursive strains, further exacerbates the limited conceptual breadth Good Living already faces. Failing to introduce or expose the concept to intellectual inquiry, *Sumak Kawsay* becomes absorbed by pre-emptive fears related to its possible revision.

Oviedo (2014, 144) argues for a framing of *Sumak Kawsay* that is endogenous to Latin America and ultimately distant from mainstream discussions surrounding Good Living. The product of a unique indigenous epistemology, *Sumak Kawsay* has somehow survived "untouched" by Western influence for over five hundred years. Oviedo is also quick to point out that the only "true" conceptualisation of *Sumak Kawsay* remains imbedded in the isolated and uncontacted indigenous peoples of the third world (2014, 144). As a constitutive part of the third world, *Sumak Kawsay* becomes a practice that is shared by indigenous people the world over, transforming it into a universal maxim of which indigenous peoples are the sole proprietors, an intellectual commodity safeguarded by its peripherical location. Such a conceptualisation of Good Living reproduces the dichotomies and binaries of Western thought denounced by Oviedo or Medina and perpetuates the search for an alter hegemonic project that may replace modernity.

Aldano et al. (2015) however, presents *Sumak Kawsay* as a regime through which socio-economic factors may be implemented for an efficient and sustainable utilisation of endogenous resources. For this author, *Sumak Kawsay* is based on the interrelation of various social actors who live and organise themselves within a particular territory, effectively consolidating their local cultures (Aldano et al. 2015, 7). Territorial consolidation will (theoretically) lead to a localised social and economic system based on solidarity, human beings and community (Aldano et al. 2015, 10). Once again, *Sumak Kawsay* becomes laden with rejections to capitalist individualism and transnational interconnectedness. Through the exaltation of local solidarity, *Sumak Kawsay* is intent on constructing a project for communal alterity. This framing of *Sumak Kawsay* through the development of a self-sufficient economic network in Andean villages, which are themselves disembedded from capitalist markets, underscores some of the main tenets proposed by this discursive strain (Aldano et al. 2015, 14).

Torres (2012), however, highlights the spiritual meanings surrounding *Sumak Kawsay* and the holistic connection humans have with animals, vegetables, land, and other beings. For this author, ecology is to be understood as the relationships living beings have amongst each other and the 'eco-biotic' habitat around them (Torres 2012, 42). Within this understanding of *Sumak Kawsay*, physical energy is manifested through Andean territorial deities such as *Wiraxucha* (southern highlands), *Tunupa* (coast and southern highlands), *Illapa* (southern highlands) and *Pachacamac* (central coast) (Torres 2012, 49). Overall, Torres's writings are an effort to highlight Aymara thought and cosmology in relation to communities, agriculture, and cultural expressions (Torres 2012, 176). Whether *Sumak Kawsay* or *Suma Qamaña,* Good Living becomes modelled in reflection to the alleged principles that originate from Andean people, their villages, and historic traditions. Such origins are the 'map towards utopia,' a project for alterity that contests the exclusionary violence inherited from colonial rule by reintegrating man to nature (Oviedo 2014, 146).

Sumak Kawsay according to this discursive strain is a guide for individual or collective equilibrium. Oviedo (2014, 148) stresses the need for equilibrium in one's life by referencing Carl Jung's research on analytical psychology, which (according to him) suggests that human nature is based on long periods of equilibrium and small epochs of crises. However, he fails to mention exactly which of Jung's texts he is referencing to substantiate this or in which ways the twentieth century writings of a Western intellectual coincide with the millenary endogenous roots constantly referenced in *Sumak Kawsay*. This discursive framing of *Sumak Kawsay*, according to Oviedo, represents an epistemological construction that reflects the struggles currently facing a world in crisis (2014, 162). The re-emergence of this form of alternative epistemological *Sumak Kawsay*, should in time, replace the political projects of the Left, effectively recognising the failed projects of Marxists and socialists (Oviedo 2014, 162). One cannot help but question such a totalising remark, as the alleged power *Sumak Kawsay* carries within it is nothing more than the construction of a universal paradigm that is set on replacing all other epistemologies or ontological practices. Moreover, the elimination of the Left seems to be a decisive political objective within *Sumak Kawsay*. Framed in this manner, *Sumak Kawsay* becomes a distant discourse from the solidarity networks evoked elsewhere, as it reminisces on the quarrels that separated indigenous mobilisation from its socialist allies in the 1980s (Becker 2008; Mijeski and Beck 2011).

Medina (2001, 36) shares Oviedo's universalist position, as he states that 'this new paradigm, of millenary roots...is a universal norm, valid for all peoples at all times.' The universal and extemporal validity of *Sumak Kawsay* is apparently justified in the ways in which Andean cultures satisfy needs through love, reciprocity, and connection to cosmic communities (Medina 2001). Whilst universally applicable, *Sumak Kawsay* or the so-called 'Amerindian sweet life,' does not seek to transform the world but rather live harmoniously within it. *Sumak Kawsay* is, according to its proponents, different from Western epistemological constructions that are framed in hegemonic binary classifications. This difference lies in *Sumak Kawsay's* overcoming of the classifications that have labelled peoples, cultures, and ontologies as either good or bad, civilised or savage, modern or primitive.

Good Living under the framing of *Sumak Kawsay* becomes a project for the past, present, and future. Through its extemporal dimensions and Andean roots, *Sumak Kawsay's* origins are framed so as to embed indigenous identity at its core, leading to the fact that negating one would subsequently negate the other. However, this totalising discourse of identity construction, conceals the power relations that are imprinted throughout Andean villages. As Ecuadorian anthropologist Fernando García, who has worked extensively with indigenous communities in the Andes explains:

> When you ask communities in Chimborazo[10] about *Sumak Kawsay* they have no idea what it is. That area is forgotten. Historically it hasn't changed. What has changed, and this I find interesting, is access to local power structures, such as Mayor Curicama…an indigenous elite…one of the effects of Pachakutik's formation as a political party was the creation of an indigenous political elite…only in Otavalo do you find an indigenous bourgeoise…one that has political and economic power…those who have accessed *mestizo* education are those that have best taken advantage of such power structures (García 2017, 25:04).

Many non-indigenous authors have highlighted how Good Living is inspired in the practice of *Sumak Kawsay* and *Suma Qamaña* and how its understanding of 'living a life of fullness' underscores an alternative development model that lives on in the Andes (Unai 2016, 1428). *Sumak Kawsay's* quest to re-link man with nature additionally emphasises wider efforts to construct a plurinational state where Good Living may take place (Dávalos 2014). Such interpretations consequently reinforce certain indigenous understandings of either Good Living or *Sumak Kawsay*. In 2010, former president of CONAIE, Humberto

---

10 Chimborazo is a Province in the Central Ecuadorian Andes with some 38 per cent of its population identifying themselves as indigenous (Andes 2012).

Cholango, stressed similar interpretations by stating that Good Living is to be understood as a new model for life and consequently a proposal that may be applicable throughout the planet (quoted in Houtart 2011, 59). Once again, the underlying universalist nature attached to such interpretations of *Sumak Kawsay* underscore the manifest contradiction of justifying its novelty on endogeneity and the rejection of hegemonic binary discourses yet simultaneously perpetuating them through new representations.

Indigenist or Pachamama interpretations of Good Living are consequently embedded in an exaltation of Andean understandings of life, work, spirituality, and nature. Constant recourse to ethnically charged discursive formulations have led authors to mark this strain of Good Living as a 'reactionary utopia' that seeks to reinstate the past as a project for the future (Parga 2011, 32). Consequently, the reactionary character and exaltation of the past becomes detrimental to the crystallisation of a critical theory that may engage with the struggles facing indigenous people, Ecuador, and mankind in the present (Parga 2011). Such formulations allow authors like Medina or Oviedo to forward a limitless discursivity that is made possible through ontological connotations (Parga 2011, 33). Criticisms against such readings of Good Living have led to the branding of this current with the pejorative label of "pachamamismo,"[11] further questioning why its authors lead the battle to "decolonise" academic discussions through the ambivalence of a totalising discursivity that subsumes or excludes other interpretations (Parga 2014, 47).

Mansilla (2011) adds to such criticisms by stating that the nucleus of Good Living does not stem from the indigenous people of the Andes but rather the complex interweaving of the political projects that came through Liberation Theology, left-of-centre political parties, a domestic and transnational environmental movement, and a fragmented recollection of indigenous practices orientated towards conservation. Criticisms levied against environmentalist organisations' influence on these formulations of Good Living are echoed throughout the academic literature. Rescasens (2014, 62) for example, singles out the ways in which Western environmental groups transformed indigenous territories into bio-centric administered national parks, which in turn reflected transnational conservation projects rather than indigenous interests. Ramos further argues how intervention of indigenous politics and civil society organisations by transnational agents, made 'the NGO very efficient in doing all that, but the flesh and blood Indians [were] edged off stage' (1994, 159).

---

11   "Pachamamismo": in Ecuador this appellative, highlights an alleged, or supposedly environmental, inclination embedded with discourses surrounding Mother Earth or the Gaia hypothesis forwarded by James Lovelock.

Bretón, Cortez, and García (2014, 14) add to this critical revision of *Sumak Kawsay* by incorporating an anthropological lens. When analysing the alleged genealogy of *Sumak Kawsay* they are quick to point out that any such endeavour would require that one be able to trace its oldest sources. The inability of authors like Oviedo or Medina to do so corroborates the inexistence of a millenary *Sumak Kawsay* prior to the conversations that began in Bolivia in the 1990s. Moreover, the lack of any form of registries or records referencing *Sumak Kawsay* in three hundred years of colonial chronicles or present-day ethnographic research highlights the fabricated nature of these discussions (Viola 2011 quoted in Bretón et al. 2014, 14). Bretón et al. (2014) also question why before the year 2000, *Sumak Kawsay* failed to appear in research on indigenous philosophy in the Andes.

Ultimately, these criticisms highlight the essentialised nature of Good Living and how its alleged "alternativeness" masks its intertwinement with the capillary powers of the critical juncture. Those places where the discourses of domination were constructed during the critical juncture, and deployed the intersecting mechanisms, institutions, agents, and policies that conditioned everyday life (Hunt and Wickham 1994, 49). Moreover, it encourages current and future discussions on Good Living to question the complex interweaving of NGO's, international financial institutions, and indigenous political projects that occurred during this time (Andolina et al. 2009; Bretón et al. 2014, 13).

Once viewed through this critical understanding, Good Living or *Sumak Kawsay*, is criticised for 'polariz[ing] separations amongst racial groups' in an effort to create a 'socio-political dualism in which Indians are located outside of history and Western modernity' allowing mestizos to label them as monolithic, static, archaic or primitive (Andolina et al. 2009, 55). Indigenist or Pachamama understandings of Good Living create a mystical representation of indigenous people in the Andes, ignoring urban-rural interlinkages or cultural synchronicity (Andolina et al. 2009, 54). In reference to Said's Orientalism, Andolina et al. (2009) posits that racial projects of assimilation, and in the case of *Sumak Kawsay* marginalisation, once viewed through post-colonial lenses should be denounced as they denaturalise indigenous people's identity by creating a 'cultural stereotype in value laden geographies.'

Moreover, forceful approximations between indigenous cultures and Western conservation efforts created a hybrid "eco-Andeanism" that merged, engulfed, and co-opted the transgressive politics of the critical juncture. Hybridity installed a racial project of alterity that strived to become self-sufficient, socio-environmentally responsible, and de-linked from modernity (Andolina et al. 2009, 56). What we can observe from this process is that Indigenist or

Pachamama discourses of Good Living frame indigenous ethics and culture under essentialised notions. The oversimplified cultural assumptions that engulf this strain of Good Living are equally entrapped in the generalised simulacrum[12] that has led to past and present chastising of Ecuador's urban Indigenist Left. This chastising responds to the Indigenist Left's construction of indigenous culture and identity through essentialised undertones that limit political discussions regarding race, territory or political autonomy (Llasag 2012; Ramos 1994, 164).

Likewise, Indigenist strains of Good Living construct a 'fabrication of the perfect Indian whose virtues, sufferings and untiring stoicism' allow authors like Oviedo or Medina to defend *Sumak Kawsay* on utopian grounds that offer indisputable statements of truth (González and Vázquez 2015, 3; Ramos 1994, 161). This fabrication of an 'Indian that is more real than the real Indian' becomes a dystopian *hyperreal* representation, dislodged from the contextual settings on which Indigenous peoples live and express their cultural heritage (Ramos, 1994). Indigenist *Sumak Kawsay* would thus come to represent a racially essentialised identity category that conflates race with ancestry, custom, civilisation or culture, perpetuating and reproducing an unintended 'grammar of governance' where folk categories secure social and political hierarchies (Harris 2013, 154).

This form of capillary power represents the ways in which a new form of governmentality was consolidated during the critical juncture by repackaging past and present racial projects. Indigenist interpretations of Good Living thus reproduce an essentialised notion of Andean peoples, fabricating a hyperreal indigenous entrapped in 'quietistic'[13] discussions that seek a "true" representation of indigenous cosmology (Andolina et al. 2009; Marcuse 1972, 71; Ramos 1994). Creating and perpetuating such a framing of Good Living detracts from the construction of a political project that may attend to the difficulties

---

12 Ramos (1994) cites Baudillard's (1983, 4) 'simulacrum' as a process in which the signs of the real come to substitute the real itself. An operation in which real processes are deterred by the implantation of pragmatic-operational clones: "a metastable, programmatic, perfect descriptive machine which provides the signs of the real and short-circuits all its vicissitudes. Never again will the real have to be produced."

13 Virvidakis and Vasso, 'Quietism,' *Oxford Bibliographies* (Accessed 9 February 2017) http://www.oxfordbibliographies.com/view/document/obo-9780195396577/obo-9780195396577-0184.xml: Quietism is the view or stance that entails avoidance of substantive philosophical theorizing and is usually associated with certain forms of skepticism, pragmatism, and minimalism about truth. More particularly, it is opposed to putting forth positive theses and developing constructive arguments.

currently faced by indigenous communities. It additionally serves to repackage previous state-led projects of ethnically referenced population control which located indigeneity at the periphery of Ecuador's public sphere.

By supplanting previous demands for territorial autonomy and collective rights, the discourse of *Sumak Kawsay* embodies the culmination of an intervention project that disarticulated the transgressive politics commandeered by indigenous organisations during the 1990s. Containment of this transgressive nature is evidenced in the redirecting of efforts from political demands for territorial autonomy towards the construction of an essentialised *Sumak Kawsay*, Shifting political agendas effectively disarticulated the most transgressive elements of indigenous mobilisation by reframing them to recover a lost millenary culture that had remained hidden somewhere in Ecuador's Andes. Good Living, however, takes on a multiplicity of forms as it embodies different representations of power construction. In sharp contrast to the essentialised notions of *Sumak Kawsay*, state-led Good Living re-centres our discussion around the developmental policies of the state. To this state-centred developmental strain of Good Living we now turn.

3 Developmental or Statist Good Living

This "developmental or statist" strain of Good Living was consolidated in two distinct periods. The first emerged from the Constitutional Assembly of 2008 and the second was forged by the actions of the Ecuadorian Government ever since. Whilst focus on the critical juncture has been predominant, within the time period that spans from 1979 to 2008, it is imperative we review policies enacted beyond this period as they materialise state-led formulations of Good Living. Additionally, citation of Ecuador's Constitution will help situate such discussions, as formal law is the mechanism through which processes of intervention such as Good Living steer institutions, networks, cultural apparatuses, and individual practices towards a desired end (Cassidy 2006, 33).

The prevalent role of Ecuador's SENPLADES during the Correa administration (2006–2017), along with the writings of its former National Secretary René Ramírez, came together in shaping the discursive content of state-led Good Living. Schavelzon (2015) however, states that former National Secretary for the Planning of Good Living, Ana María Larrea, also significantly influenced the content that would ultimately configure this strain. Before we discuss the specific propositions of either of these authors it is imperative we outline the constitutional necessity behind SENPLADES' drafting of Ecuador's national development plans.

As most literature on Good Living has focused on the "novel" constitutional precepts that materialised in the 2008 Constitutional Assembly, a substantial field of inquiry has been left unattended. Most prominently, the lack of attention paid to the other legal frameworks that came together in Ecuador's 2008 Constitution has created a limited analytical framework from which Good Living may be analysed. This necessity of including a broader analysis of Ecuador's Constitution is echoed in the work of legal scholars who question why more scholarly attention has not been paid to other equally significant elements of Ecuador's constitutional make-up. One such element is the hyper-presidential system that was constructed in 2008 alongside the rights of nature or Good Living (Gargarella 2013, 158). The conflicting nature of a reified sovereign power, alongside "progressive" legal projects seeking emancipation, exemplifies some of the questions that Good Living scholarship has left unanswered.

Moreover, enthusiastic comments that label Good Living as 'an indigenous conception of wellbeing that has recently entered Latin American debates on development' are dislodged from the political, social, and economic contexts in which Good Living policies have been deployed since 2008 (Giovannini 2014, 71). To this effect, certain authors have attempted to build theoretical propositions around Good Living but have done so in a contextual void that neglects the conflicting discourses, power dynamics, and interests that respectively shape each discursive strain. Omitting the necessary revision of how Good Living interacts with the rest of Ecuador's Constitution creates a myopic analysis that is blind to the power relations inscribed therein.

Whilst the Ecuadorian Constitution of 2008 enacted a series of groundbreaking legal principles that inaugurated a form of symbolic power,[14] it did so at the expense of other structural areas of legal relevance. This symbolic power, captured in the juridification of social discontent that embodies Good Living, is a form of 'producing new categories of perception and judgement' that install 'a new vision of social divisions and distributions' (Rask Madsen and Dezalay 2013, 119). Revision of novel forms of legal framing such as Good Living are however only a partial element of the analysis. Omitting reference to the power structures reflected in the constitution limits any form of holistic research. Hence, questioning the complex dynamics in which law channels

---

14   Resk Madsen and Dezalay (2013, 119): in line with Bourdieu's Sociology of Law 'symbolic power is the power to transform the world by transforming the words for naming it, by producing new categories of perception and judgment, and by dictating a new vision of social divisions and distributions. More specifically, the emergence of any new field functions both internally and externally as a way of questioning and redefining social hierarchies and power'.

power is paramount if we are to understand the constitutional role Good Living is to play now and in the future. Raising these questions allows present and future scholarship to analyse the ways in which political actors direct their actions through the mechanistic legality of Good Living's constitutional inscription (Nobles and Schiff 2013, 182).

Moreover, the necessary revision of Good Living's constitutional framing and its relationship to other constitutional rights will prove paramount if judicial review is ever to take place. Situating Good Living within a holistic approach, one that is attentive to its legal standing and the underlying power dynamics that encapsulate it, creates a point of analysis through which judicial review may depart. Construction of a new analytical framework for Good Living will thus facilitate how judicial review handles its linkage and articulation to other segments of Ecuador's Constitution. Situating Good Living within the political and legal context from which it emerged will hopefully inform judicial decisions that have to decide on politically crucial cases. Critical analytical frameworks on Good Living seek to enact a theoretical cover from which Ecuadorian courts may be 'selectively assertive' when defining the scope and limits of constitutional law (Kapiszewski 2011, 475). Such assertiveness translates in the judiciary's ability to question if government power, action, inaction or policy, exercised through reference of the 99 Constitutional Articles that frame Good Living, holds up to constitutional scrutiny.

This assertiveness must take into consideration that during the critical juncture a receding state had dislodged itself from the intricacies of public administration. However, the state that materialised after the 2008 constitution is one of a consolidated central power that was mandated to 'plan national development, eradicate poverty, promote sustainable development' and achieve the equitable distribution of resources needed to secure Good Living.[15] These newfound constitutional powers, alongside the rise of 'competitive authoritarianism in the Andes,'[16] gave way to the consolidation of a polarising political discourse premised on state-centred technocratic governance (Levitsky and Loxton 2013, 107). Statist Good Living is thus forged by 'a discourse of experts

---

15 Constitution of Ecuador, Art. 3.5.
16 Competitive authoritarianism was originally coined by Levitsky and Way (2002, 52) to define were 'formal democratic institutions are widely viewed as the principal means of obtaining and exercising political authority. Incumbents violate those rules so often and to such an extent, however, that the regime fails to meet conventional minimum standards for democracy.'; Levitsky and Loxton (2013) would later develop on the idea to define the brand of populism that was cemented in Bolivarian democracies in the Andes, where personalistic outsiders mobilized mass constituencies through anti-establishment appeals, thereby attacking legal procedures and formal institutions.

that seek to transform society for the greater good' (Torre 2013, 39). Public policy was re-routed towards the construction and consolidation of state-led Good Living discursivities. In the words of former Minister of Finance Patricio Rivera, government policy in Ecuador:

> ...is reflected in the National Plan for Good Living, [which] consider[s] all expenditures in education and health as investment. Healthier and better qualified people are more productive. In opposition to orthodox economics. We need to view these expenditures as investment and not simply as expenditures... (El Comercio 2010).

Ecuador's 2008 Constitution was intentionally articulated to overcome the various shortcomings the state experienced during the critical juncture. Through this necessity the post 2008 state was mandated to fulfil its responsibilities, its duty of care if you will, in regard to the enactment, execution, and supervision of national policy. For example, public service outages throughout the critical juncture, created the necessary points of reference from where constitutional drafting departed. Electricity outages were so commonplace during the critical juncture that Presidential Decree No. 285 in force from 28 November 1992 to 5 February 1993, mandated all Ecuadorians forward their watches by one hour in order to take advantage of sunlight (El Comercio 2009). Constitutional drafting reminiscing on these shortages favoured strong state-led policy, further justifying its enactment through the discourses that engulfed the Constitutional Assembly. In the words of former President Correa:

> ...We are living a process of democratic construction at a particular, probably unique, political moment of our Republican history. The state is transformed to defend democracy, liberating it from its previous end of history, prophesized by the ideologists of the "long neoliberal night." These short-lived prophecies, rejected by the majority of the people of *nuestra América* and Ecuador, push us to proactively defeat the neoliberal model, that until recently was unquestionable and hegemonic... (Correa: Acta 016, 5).[17]

Strong state-led development in the 2008 constitution was a response to the staggering socio-economic deprivations that reigned during the critical juncture. During this time some 62.6 per cent of the population lived under the poverty line, facing a form of immiseration that was constantly compounded

---

17   The translation is mine.

by the shrinking services of the state (North 2004, 202). With the vivid memory of past sufferings, the 2008 constitution mandated the state to 'promote the public and private sector'[18] in order to secure free and accessible public education,[19] health,[20] and housing,[21] as well as creating the conditions that will secure labour as an economic right.[22]

The critical juncture is rightfully catalogued as one of 'state dismantling,' a period where interventionist policies ruptured Ecuador's institutional and socio-economic fabrics (North 2004). Post-2008 Ecuador, however, is defined under what North and Grinspun (2016) have labelled as the 'new Latin American Developmentalism'; a post neoliberal order where state capacity was directed at inward-looking economic policy, the improvement of social wellbeing and the overcoming of poverty. This new form of developmentalism is quite an adequate branding, as Article 85 (1) of Ecuador's Constitution mandates the state to 'formulate, execute, evaluate and control public policies and services' in order to guarantee constitutional rights. The same article further stipulates that public services should be orientated at securing Good Living and the fulfilment of constitutional rights. Moreover, what Article 275 defines as the 'Economic Development Regime' is understood as the coordinated enactment of sustainable, economic, political, social, cultural, and environmental regimes set in place to guarantee Good Living. The intertwinement of these spheres and the constitutional construction of a hyper-presidential system further consolidates a discourse of Good Living that is born, developed, and executed from and by the state in order to obtain capitalist economic development.

The constitutional layout that was drafted in 2008, allowed then President Rafael Correa to propose economic policy decisions mimicking the export-oriented initiatives once utilized by South Korea. This industrial development policy steering would see Correa and other ministers visit South Korea on several occasions to tighten bilateral relations (Cancillería 2019). Fascinated by the export policy success experienced in South Korea and other Asian Tigers, Ecuador's industrial policy was directed towards value-added manufacturing in an attempt to consolidate a national development plan or as it was called at the time "The National Plan for Good Living" (Domjahn 2013, 21; SENPLADES 2009). In this sense, industrial export-orientated economic development was

---

18 Constitution of Ecuador, Art. 15.
19 Constitution of Ecuador, Art. 26, 27, 28 and 29.
20 Constitution of Ecuador, Art. 32.
21 Constitution of Ecuador, Art. 30 and 31.
22 Constitution of Ecuador, Art. 33 and 34.

tied to Good Living undertones, such as those described by Bell (2018, 75) when she equates the concept to:

> *Vivir Bien* implies that we are part of a whole, so that we cannot live well if other humans do not, or at the expense of our environment. It urges regulatory mechanisms and community participation in decision making to address environmental issues and eradicate poverty, and it inherently critiques the accepted need for economic growth, emphasizing meeting needs and satisfying rights. Under this ethos, the economy is based, not on the profit motive, but respect and care for humans and the rest of nature in a spirit of solidarity. Hence, Living Well differs from traditional understandings of wellbeing and development in its critique of anthropocentrism; individualization of satisfaction; paternalism; capitalism; perpetual economic growth; material accumulation and the commodification and mercantilization of nature (...).

However, such high hopes for the economic development policy drafted under the Correa administration, utilising the legal regime approved in 2008, would fall along much more "conventional" lines of export-orientated economies. The clearest example of which was the mega project christened as "Yachay City of Knowledge." This economic development project, heralded to become Ecuador's first planned city, under a Master Plan drawn up in imitation of the South Korean Free Economic Zone of Incheon, was designed to harbour a research and manufacturing complex that could utilize natural resources and Ecuador's biodiversity to "transform the country's production matrix" (SENESCYT 2012). Good Living, framed in such a manner, has little to replicate from indigenous knowledges but rather mimics the fascination of accelerated economic development of South East Asia, which has long been the envy of many developing countries seeking capitalist success (Domjahn 2013, 16).

Economic development, enshrined with Good Living undertones, became a constitutional General Duty of the State,[23] as declared in Article 277 of the 2008 Constitution, transforming the attainment of Good Living through economic public policy construction. National development, and the general duty imposed on the state to secure it, is further consolidated through the constitutional authority vested on the presidency. Through Articles 147 and 148 of

---

23 Constitution of Ecuador, Art. 277: "the general duties of the State in order to achieve Good Living shall be: 2) To direct, plan and regulate the development process; 4) To produce goods, create and maintain infrastructure, and to provide public services; 5) To boost development of economic activities (...)".

Ecuador's 2008 Constitution, the president is granted the authority to dissolve the National Assembly if and when it obstructs the fulfilment of the National Development Plan. In other words, national economic development, and the attainment of Good Living it promises, is deemed a sufficient constitutional argument to abolish forms of democratic representation. More importantly, what this reflects is the polar opposite policy framing of what occurred during the critical juncture, a period where institutional weakness made economic policy enactment almost impossible (Helmke 2017; Mejía-Acosta 2006).

Hyper presidential power in post 2008 Ecuador is worthy of study, as the current constitutional regime not only increases presidential authority but allows it to override other points of constitutional power. These new-found legal capabilities allowed the post 2008 executive to implement sweeping regulations as well as amend or reform the constitution to its will (Gargarella 2013, 173). Hence, the advancement of socio-economic rights under the banner of Good Living have come hand-in-hand with an unprecedented expansion of presidential powers. This constitutional imbalance allowed the executive to shape and enact public policy in line with the political promises or necessities of its clientelistic networks (Echeverría 2008 quoted in Gargarella 2013, 174).

Outlining this reordering of executive power, and how it consolidated a technocratic state, is imperative if we are to underscore the foundations of state-led Good Living. Premised on socially-focused market-orientated development models, such as the one outlined in Ecuador's 2008 Constitution, this form of Good Living attempts to mimic public policy executed in Nordic countries. Following this lead, Ecuador's social policy is intent on securing economic equality as a necessary precondition from which broader macroeconomic efficiency goals may be achieved. Hence, expansive social policy, via increased state power and spending, becomes the necessary prerequisites from which a democratic socialist society may flourish (Esping-Andersen 1994, 713 quoted in Nederveen Pieterse 2010, 129).

Similarly, former National Secretary Ramírez (2010, 129) outlines that Good Living is a novel economic perspective as the satisfaction of basic needs are transformed into the new units by which development should be measured. Following Ramírez, Larrea understands Good Living as a mechanism through which the general welfare of the population may be improved via an economic system that redistributes the social and territorial benefits of development (Schavelzon 2015, 202). Under such an understanding, Good Living is reduced to a redistributive mechanism that bestows the benefits of economic development without necessarily altering or rattling the structures of power (Simbaña 2011 quoted in Schavelzon 2015, 202). Developmental or statist discourses on Good Living reify conventional notions of the nation-state and the sovereign power it wields.

As a discourse, state-led Good Living reinstates what has been termed the 'container model of society' a conceptual construction in which societal relations are state-constructed and state-controlled (Rössel 2012, 1152). This conflation of nation-state and society assumes that those who claim origin to some geographical borders share a common history, language, culture, and religion limiting the analysis of identities, networks, social relations, and organisational connections that are interacting around it (Glick Schiller 2012, 524). This revised version of methodological nationalism, where the state is the central unit of measurement for societal relations, raises even more questions regarding state-led Good Living. One such query refers to the suitability of constructing a theoretical premise where the state is the solitary reference point. If for no better reason, this limited analytical scope appears to disregard the transitional processes that have not only displaced the state as an actor but effectively transformed the ways it relates to society. Good Living within this strain is moulded to reify the public administration, turning it into an institutional platform from which the government may implement a 'cultural revolution' that will teach Ecuador's population 'how to live' (Ramírez 2010, 130–31).

Torre (2013) has labelled Ecuadorian policies since 2008 as a form of technopopulism. Such policies are constructed upon instrumental logics of science and technology that mask an irrational populism that confides in the technocratic governance of the masses. More simply put, Good Living under the statist strain, rather than formulating a novel development paradigm, simply recalibrates and endogenises the economic development schemes of ISI, the World Bank, Sweden, Japan or South East Asia. Stemming from concerns relating to poverty reduction, promotion of labour–demanding growth, human capital investment, improved governance, and egalitarian redistribution. Statist Good Living re-enacts the *Advancing Social Development* policies presented during the 1995 Copenhagen Summit (Nederveen Pieterse 2010, 131).

Constructing Good Living under state-centric premises not only un-roots its alleged communitarian indigenous origins but also reinstates the developmental projects that swept Latin America during the 1960s and 1970s. During this period, the implementation of import substitution industrialisation (ISI) was meant to install an independent form of state-led economic development (Harding 2003, 63). Between 2007 and 2012 state involvement in the service and industry sectors exponentially grew thanks to soaring oil revenues that skyrocketed from US$25 billion between 2000 and 2006 to almost US$59 billion by 2013 (Dávalos and Albuja 2013). Indeed, expansive public spending during this time transformed the public administration into a monopolistic utility provider, cementing passé forms of state-led nationalist development that sought modernisation and the consolidation of a 'bio socialist republic' (Lewis 2008, 255; Ramírez 2010).

Developmental Good Living, such as that advocated by Ramírez, strives to install an 'economic, productive, agrarian revolution' that will direct state resources to education, health, roads, housing, R&D, job creation, and the complementarity of urban and rural productive linkages (PND 2009–2013, 9). Good Living in this fashion is built on an economic development project that is fuelled on intensive state spending. Such a paradigm however is 'incapable of coming to terms with the realities of world power' or the neo-colonial projects these forms of industrial modernisation are imbedded in (Nederveen Pieterse 2012, 28).

Methodological nationalism, economic development, and repositioned institutional power underline this strain of Good Living. In it, a so-called 'egalitarian republican socialism' (Ramírez 2010, 131) is set out in order to enact market policies under socialist distributive guidelines. This construction of the state as 'the sole bearer of authority' subsequently authorises it 'to exist in and for itself' (Marcuse 1972, 55). The state is thus transformed into an independent realm, away from individuals or society,' granting it absolute power over the public sphere (Marcuse 1972, 56). This reified institutional undertone is accentuated by Larrea who emphasises that the ultimate objective of the state is to secure Good Living by implementing alternative social and communitarian development models (Schavelzon 2015, 213).

By proposing an alleged alterity project for development, this form of Good Living masks the continuation of previous modernising logics deployed throughout Latin America. State-led Good Living is thus crafted to form a new "*capitalismo criollo*," an endogenous form of capitalism that sets out policy prescriptions that will somehow transform the state into the engine of capitalist economic development (Brana 2016, 48). Good Living, as state-led neo-developmentalism, is what transpires from the writings of Ramírez and Larrea, formulating itself as a state-led form of socially "acceptable" capitalism, one that has been repackaged under a technocratic populist branding to secure its political legitimacy (Brana 2016, 49; Merino 2016, 276).

As was previously mentioned, Good Living as a development strategy is embodied in the Correa administrations flag-ship Yachay project which was executed by Ramírez during his tenure as National Secretary for Higher Education, Science, Technology and Innovation (SENESCYT). In 2012, under Ramírez's leadership, SENESCYT presented a legislative project to inaugurate the new experimental technology university called Yachay–City of Knowledge. Brainchild of Correa and his innovation experts, the project sought to transform

Ecuador from a primary export economy into a service sector provider (Yachay 2012, 1). Emulating the South Korean special province of Jeju, as well as the special economic zone of Incheon,[24] Yachay was set to become a technological hub where petrochemical, engineering and other "hard" sciences were to be developed. With a staggering price tag of around US$20 billion over the next sixteen years, Yachay materialises the modernising logics that engulf statist Good Living (Reuters 2015). Developed in Ramírez's writings, this form of Good Living becomes a state-led policy objective from which the heavy industries needed to modernise Ecuador's agrarian economy will materialise (*The Economist* 2010; Villavicencio 2016). Years after the project was inaugurated, little has changed within Ecuador's primary export economy. Social and economic rights had been advanced on the back of oil revenues fuelling an increasingly ill-advised public expenditure program that became an easy prey for corrupt public official syphoning off state resources (Sosa 2016; El Comercio 2019).

Yachay embodies state-centred Good Living as the materialisation of the 'realist utopia' Ramírez was determined on constructing through public policy (Ramírez 2010, 128). State-led Good Living between 2008 and 2017 was defined by the capitalist developmental models pursued by the Ecuadorian Government; policy efforts that sought industrial development, modernisation, and foreign direct investment as engines of economic growth (Brana 2016, 56). Good Living under this strain required continuous and expansive exploitation of natural resources to fund the so-called 'bio-socialist republic' envisioned by Ramírez (Brana 2016, 72).

Authors like Ramírez or Larrea have repeatedly equated Good Living to ephemeral and unsubstantiated appellatives that label it as a 'utopian republican egalitarianism' or a 'path towards constructing a different World' (Ramírez 2010, 125). Under such framings, statist Good Living becomes the heir to a political project and discourse that was installed to consolidate a form of state-led socialist capitalism. However, its state-centric focus, and the underlying economic priorities that define it, have led the Ecuadorian Government to be heavy-handed in its enactment of development policies. Between 2008 and 2017, civil society protests against corruption, natural resource prospection or

---

24 "Yachay City of Knowledge has a Master Plan drawn up by Korean firm IFEZ (Incheon Free Economic Zone), which submitted all of the studies in November of 2013. The Master Plan defines the fundamental guidelines for the construction of a planned city designed to provide comfort to humans, in harmony with nature and with adequate space for the generation of knowledge" (accessed 22 February 2017) https://www.yachay.gob.ec/empresas/.

the displacement of indigenous peoples, has been met with incarceration, deportation or state-led civil suits.[25]

The alleged novelty of statist Good Living masks the continuation of a capitalist state-led vertical economic development paradigm that was brought to a halt during the macroeconomic reforms of the critical juncture. Unsurprisingly, the resurgence of this form of state-centric developmentalism was only possible once the material resources for state-led policies were once again available and the legal architecture that solidifies sovereign power reinstated in Ecuador's 2008 Constitution. Whilst the state-led strain of Good Living has focused on securing the economic paradigms of the Ecuadorian executive, the ecologist or post-developmental strain has sought to position the demands of a myriad of social groups that came together during the critical juncture. Leaving the state behind, this particular strain of Good Living integrates demands for collective rights, gender, post-development, and environmental conservation.

4   Ecologist and Post-developmental Good Living

Amongst the three discourses that have been branded on Good Living, the ecologist and post-developmental strain is the most disperse and scattered. Through its amalgamation of indigenous, Marxist, environmental, communitarian, humanist, and Aristotelian influences this particular form of Good Living embarked on a worldwide project that could shake the foundations of modernity and liberal politics (Acosta 2010, 13; Deneulin 2012, 15). Attempts of equating Andean cultural traditions with Western environmental ethics has made this strain of Good Living dependent on the conceptual imports of foreign paradigms like the deep ecology movement founded by Arne Naes (Gudynas 2009, 40). This coupling of alleged millenary Andean traditions with the environmental projects of the West transformed this strain of Good Living into an appropriator of Andean cultural paradigms that could aid in the construction of a universal project for deep ecology (Ramachadra 1997, 33). Under the influence of deep ecology Good Living is framed under what Naes described as an 'ecosophy,' an environmental project that takes place in the 'ecosphere' by:

> …Rejecting the man-in-environment image in favour of the relational, total-field image. Organisms as knots in the field of intrinsic relations.

---

25   For more, see: El Universo 2015; Puente 2016; El Comercio 2015; Business and Human Rights Resource Centre 2016; El Comercio 2016; Ecuadorinmediato 2016.

An intrinsic relation between two things ... The total field model dissolves not only the man-in-environment concept, but every compact thing-in-milieu...Biospherical egalitarianism—in principle. The 'in principle' clause is inserted because any realistic praxis necessitates some killing, exploitation, and suppression. The ecological field worker acquires a deep-seated respect, even veneration, for ways and forms of life. He reaches an understanding from within, a kind of understanding that others reserve for fellow men and for a narrow section of ways and forms of life. To the ecological field worker, the equal right to live and blossom is an intuitively clear and obvious value axiom. Its restriction to humans is an anthropocentrism with detrimental effects upon the life quality of humans themselves. This quality depends in part upon the deep pleasure and satisfaction we receive from close partnership with other forms of life. The attempt to ignore our dependence and to establish a master-slave role has contributed to the alienation of man from himself... (1989, 26).

Others however understand this strain of Good Living as a new theory for justice. Deneulin (2012) for example examines Good Living under such a paradigm. In her analysis, Good Living is utilised to re-examine the failures in Rawls theory of justice. Deneulin's (2012, 11) writings, centred on Rawls's inability of accounting for indigenous peoples and their position within the public sphere, proposes that identity concerns or collective action becomes irreconcilable with the dichotomies of liberal politics. Unai (2016, 1428) however distances himself from such Anglo-centric interpretations by underscoring that Good Living is inspired in indigenous practices seeking a life of fullness through community, nature, consensus, and recovered spirituality.

Scholars have also constructed Good Living as a universalising project that stems from indigenous epistemologies (Merino 2016, 271). Through the elaborate fabrication of genealogical "alternativeness," this form of Good Living becomes well suited for structuring a critique of the environmental and developmental policies that have constrained projects of self-determination or the advancement of territorial and cultural rights (Merino 2016). The discursive novelty embedded in this strain of Good Living, makes it *supra* constitutional, as it 'becomes an opportunity to collectively construct a new form of living, one that goes beyond development' a new project for humanity guided by a rediscovered communitarian ethic (Acosta 2011, 51).

Building Good Living as an ethical project also endows it with unlimited capabilities for long-awaited reform. Monni and Pallottino (2016, 50) for example have argued that by piggybacking on Good Living's discursive novelty, a new theory of international development cooperation is slowly emerging in Ecuador. This new ethical paradigm will not only usher in long-awaited institutional reform to the headquarters of international development, but in so doing, will overcome the failures that are currently afflicting international development policy (Monni and Pallottino 2016, 50). Such high hopes rest on Good Living's capability of combating Eurocentric development as well as the hegemonic theories of modernity that fuelled popular discontent during Ecuador's critical juncture (Vanhulst and Beling 2014, 56).

Thus, Good Living's ability to challenge the ruling paradigms of European-inspired development emerge from its alternativeness. Unceta (2014) advocates for this alternativeness when he states that Good Living will allow society to overcome the dualism between man and nature. Creating the bio-centric ecosphere envisioned by Naes makes Good Living a discourse for environmental redemption, one that is legitimised in its communitarian origins and the autonomous environmental management of land (Unceta 2014, 108). Linking territorial conservation with Good Living makes it a master frame of ecospheric environmental politics, a rallying cry that brings together collective action against natural resource extraction and environmental degradation (Barbosa do Santos 2011, 146; Gudynas 2011). Its framing as an alternative to mainstream development makes Good Living a redeeming paradigm that distances itself from "mainstream" development by committing to 'communities, non-humans, and quality of life' (Gudynas 2016, 728).

Good Living is thus not simply an ethical project or development alternative but also a critique of modernity and the social and political theories of the West (Houtart 2011, 63). This all-embarking quality makes Good Living's abilities endless, a discourse destined to construct 'a project for utopia' (Calisto and Langmore 2015, 69). Constantly reinvented and constructed with the help of multiple actors, environmental Good Living becomes a 'collective philosophy of progress,' one that envisions harmony between nature and humans (Calisto and Langmore 2015, 70). Balance between humans and nature is constantly underscored in the writings of Gudynas (2011), who argues for a 'super strong sustainability'; one that is closely linked to the strategies of the 1970s environmental conservation movement. This 'strong bio-centrism' makes the environment a linkage for multicultural conservation efforts, installing and embedding the teachings of the deep ecology movement as an overarching critique of development through 'super strong conservation' (Gudynas 2011).

The environmental shift in this strain of Good Living and the high hopes it has commandeered from conservation groups the world over, is unsurprising if one quickly reviews the wording of Ecuador's Constitution. Whilst the statist strain has consolidated its position by implementing the expansive executive prerogatives anointed on the president, this strain of Good Living utilises the wording of Ecuador's Magna Carta to reaffirm its bio-centrism. This is comprehensible if one reads Article 14, which guarantees the populations' right to live in an ecologically balanced and healthy environment. Or Article 74, which recognises the right to benefit from the environment and the natural resources procured from it. The same article further declares statutory limitations on the exercise of property rights over environmental services.

Beyond the ecological connotations previously described, another strong undercurrent guides this particular strain of Good Living. Efforts directed at constructing an alter-development paradigm from Ecuador's constitutional articles has led many authors to advocate for Good Living as a post-development alternative. Villalba (2016, 1435) for example, states that Good Living is a reclaiming of sovereignty, an opportunity to construct solidarity and economic systems based on citizen's participation. In this way, Good Living becomes an alternative development model that seeks to overcome 'the neoliberal period that led to multiple interconnected global crises' (Villalba 2016, 1438).

Acosta (2011) substantiates Good Living as an alternative to mainstream development on the fact that it has allegedly been practiced and recognised by various peoples throughout human history. According to Acosta, the pressing need to consolidate a new economy stems from the unsustainable production and consumption patterns currently practiced. According to these proponents, Good Living offers a possibility of shifting efforts, resources, and practices towards the fulfilment of societies demands by neutralising the influence of capital in the allocation of resources (Acosta 2011, 54). This project for anti-globalisation depends on the hard work, networks, coordination, and solidarity of self-organised communities, NGOs, and global social movements (Vanhulst and Beling 2014, 56). Additionally, the alter-development project inscribed in this stream of Good Living seeks to overcome the colonial legacy of Spain, as well as the neo-colonial thrust of development modernisation (Barbosa dos Santos 2011, 146).

Post-development Good Living and its addition to the Ecuadorian Constitution is seen by many as a historic moment 'because of [its] pioneering treatment of development' (Escobar 2012). Moreover, Good Living is considered a new historical horizon, one in which indigenous resistance to Eurocentric modernity constructs a new form of endogenous living for the Global South, one that is opposed to capitalistic forms of production (Escobar 2012). Good Living and its power of reform is coupled with economics, environment, society, and culture in an effort to construct the social networks that stem from a pre-colonial millenary communal solidarity (Escobar 2012). Although its roots are set in Andean cultural-political projects, the influence Good Living has received from Western thought grant it a global reach (Escobar 2012). This new paradigm is one of a 'meta-ecological' citizenship, one in which cultural and ecological dimensions protect people and nature by transforming the capitalist self into the ecological self, the self that inhabits Naes' ecosphere (Escobar 2012, xxxvii).

Multiple counter-arguments could be levied against this particular discourse of Good Living. The revision of this discourse will however be completed in the following section. Up to this point we have covered the three overarching currents of Good Living originally forwarded by Hidalgo-Capitán and Cubillo-Guevara. The next section develops the critical strain of Good Living introduced at the beginning of this chapter. This critical analysis of Good Living presents some of the broad criticisms that Good Living's constitutional inscription and academic framing has received since 2008. Adding to this literature, the following section presents a new theoretical cover for the analysis of Good Living. Through this critical framing, ontological or normative arguments are set aside in order to accommodate new points of analysis that reveal the occurrences that led to Good Living. This allows us to revise Good Living by questioning the complex set of power dynamics that led to its constitutional inscription. Through this critical lens, Good Living is understood as an amalgamation of the discourses and power dynamics that came from converging politicised ethnic cleavages, state retreat, changing citizenship regimes, transnational governmentalities, and discursive democracy.

5   Critical Approaches towards Good Living: Power Not Ontology

Good Living's birth was met with overwhelming enthusiasm from social movements, environmental groups, academics, and civil society in general. Indeed, its labelling as an 'alterity to mainstream development' awarded it much praise, as it was meant to inaugurate a new paradigm where 'the poor could speak' and could do so 'away from metropolitan centers or national elites' (Radcliffe 2012, 241). Moreover, its ability to harness the 'alternative thinking' of social movements, peasants, and the urban poor granted it privileged positions in theoretical discussions, as it embodied 'a border thinking' outside of mainstream development paradigms (Radcliffe 2012, 242). However, its proposed novelty conceals substantial deficiencies as a theoretical alternative to hegemonic development practices. This significant weakness is embedded within existing currents of Good Living, as all three appear incapable of taking into consideration the deeply rooted power relations that shaped Good Living during the critical juncture (Recasens 2014, 60).

The euphoria that accompanied Ecuador's 2008 Constitution stated that the newly minted legislation brought about an opportunity to consolidate a post-colonial future. According to such accounts, a new era of post-colonial transformation had been sanctioned by Ecuador's Constitutional Assembly. Once Good Living was made in to law, all that was needed from there on was a strict, in other words formal and literal, application of the newly drafted constitutional mandates (Recasens 2014). For our analysis we will set aside the legal connotations such a formalistic application of constitutional law might have on any project, emancipatory or otherwise. Momentarily bypassing the legal considerations that such an analysis might present leads us to question the ethnic discursiveness that has permeated Good Living since 2008.

Envisioned as a new tool against hegemonic powers, Good Living's Andean roots are sought to construct a project for the future premised on the cultural traditions of a distant past. Through a heavily stereotyped reliance on hyper-real representations of Andean cultures a discourse of alterity is constructed, one in which a new development alternative is allegedly formed (Parga 2011, 31). Recourse to mystical Andean discourses conceals 'a political project that is evasive and reactionary towards memory' (Parga 2011, 32). By decontextualising historical contexts, Good Living has been transformed into a timeless myth, one that has no use for theory or practice as it is legitimated by an endless discursivity void of critical analysis (Parga 2011, 33). Proponents of either strain of Good Living fail to consider the origins of the concept they praise. Mansilla (2011) for example was quick to stress that Good Living's nucleus, its central discursive components, stem from a variety of sources, none of which are indigenous. He weaves his argument by pointing to the influences Good Living received from Liberation Theology,[26] Marxists, Western environmental movements, and the community-orientated development projects promoted by NGOs (Mansilla 2011, 94). All of which converged to create the discursive hybridity that was later framed around Good Living.

Closer research into Ecuador's indigenous politics, or the development regime that was installed in the country during the critical juncture, creates a new point of reference from which Good Living may be analysed. Revision of the close relationship forged between the indigenous movement, religious orders, and the Marxist Left has been well documented by Mijeski and Beck

---

[26] Religions, 'The Case for Liberation Theology,' BBC, 18 July 2011 (Accessed 25 February 2017) http://www.bbc.co.uk/religion/religions/christianity/beliefs/liberationtheology.shtml: "Liberation theology was a radical movement that grew up in South America as a response to the poverty and the ill-treatment of ordinary people. The movement was caricatured in the phrase 'If Jesus Christ were on Earth today, he would be a Marxist revolutionary.'"

(2011, 13), Becker (2008, 146), Bretón (2010), Van Cott (2005, 103), Llasag (2012), Yashar (2005, 58), and Cepek (2012) to name a few.

Furthermore, the intrinsic relationship forged between Western environmental groups and Latin American indigenous political organisations can be traced back to the early 1980s, right at the beginning of the critical juncture. Ramos for example, documents how environmental and indigenous NGOs consolidated in Brazil during the 1980s by fabricating their birth and existence through a discourse where Indians were exploited and 'national society had no proper channels to vent their grievances' (Ramos 1994, 166). This endogamic relationship between Indigenous political agendas and Western environmental concerns was further discussed by Van Cott (1994, 33), who analysed the 'greening of Indian rights'; a process that subordinated political identity to an imposed view of 'Indians as Nature.' Sawyer (2004) showcased this intertwinement in Ecuador through her ethnographic research of Kichwa indigenous politics and their merging with transnational environmental networks. According to Sawyer (2004, 108) these collaborative networks allowed indigenous grievances to be presented before international institutions like the World Bank through the 'building [of] a transnational environmental justice movement' based on subaltern reclamations (Faber 2005, 43).

Finally, the impact of the development regime that was deployed in Ecuador during the critical juncture cannot be understated. Andolina et al. (2009) presents a thorough analysis of the development projects and transnational governmentalities that were deployed in Ecuador during the critical juncture. In their overarching analysis of development projects during the 1990s, Andolina et al. (2009) explains how social capital[27] became intertwined with indigenous identity. Through this process a logic of "uniqueness" created the social glue where 'dispersed ethnic minorities' became the bearers of an 'essentialized social capital' (Andolina et al. 2009, 69). Connection to capitalist markets was made possible through the promotion of the recently discovered commodity of ethnic heritage. Indigenous associational life, and the ability to summon its Andean roots, was quickly forged into the NGO economic development programs that promoted social capital throughout Ecuador. Complicit in the forging of social capital through the ethnic lens, international development agencies and NGOs, positioned their programs of intervention through

---

27   Somers (2005, 235): Social capital is part of a larger ideational regime of market fundamentalism where the appropriate distribution of power among the spheres of market, state and civil society are defined. The ideational and political work of social capital is that of privatization, marketization, anti-statism and the transformation of rights into duties.

the repackaged, yet culturally inclusive, discourse of ethnodevelopment. NGO presence and their interventions of rural communities became legitimised by the social capital narrative of ethnodevelopment that was inaugurated in a period of World Bank modernisation in Ecuador's Andes (Bretón 2005, 24).

The World Bank's ethnodevelopment initiatives served as a discourse of transnational governmentality by providing the necessary framings from which indigenous communities could become integrated to world markets. Social capital or its Andean representation in ethnodevelopment has been criticised under accusations of 'theoretical promiscuity' by Somers (2005).[28] Somers (2005, 233), argues that social capital's floating discursiveness affords it an unprecedented capability of absorbing and appropriating local experience, culture and values in order to legitimise its usage. As has been portrayed elsewhere,[29] social capital has morphed Andean societies into a 'politically manageable, tamed, respectable, domesticated yet bustling community,' a series of horizontal associations and networks set out to increase productivity, cooperation and the securement of wellbeing (Somers 2005, 239). For NGOs and multilateral development agencies, social capital, and its coupling with indigenous culture, anointed it as the 'missing link in the effort to end poverty in the developing world' (Somers 2005, 233).

Convergence of NGOs in Latin America, the rise of social capital, and the "rediscovery" of indigenous culture transformed the transnational governmentalities of development into an 'epistemological public good' (Somers 2005, 237). One that is configured by a multiplicity of de-contextualised ontological abstractions that endow it with 'expansive capacities for appropriation' (Somers 2005). This process of appropriation and intervention within Andean communities culminated in the constitutional inscription of Good Living as a floating discursivity that preserves nature by rediscovering indigenous relationality (Mansilla 2011, 92). Broader criticisms levied against Good Living stress the conceptual merit of proposing that legal reforms, intent on altering current relations of production, will somehow lead to a new society (González

---

28   Somers (2005) outlines that social capital has an inherent contradiction within its conceptual rooting. Social capital according to Bourdieu (1986) was part of the habitus of agency and networks. Once economists took on the concept, the relationality embedded in Bourdieu's analysis was circumcised in order to accommodate the utility maximizing individual that stems from neo-utilitarianism. The theoretical promiscuity of social capital hence resides in its contradictory ontological positions in which it attempts to be 'scientifically positivist' and yet still dependent on anti-positivist explanations of agency, community and networks.

29   For more see: Robert Putnam. 2000. *Bowling Alone: The Collapse and Revival of American Community,* Simon and Schuster, New York.

and Vázquez 2015, 1). Good Living should thus be viewed with suspicion, as it may 'become an epistemological discursive strategy' that conceals hegemonic processes of modernisation (González and Vázquez 2015, 3). This framing of Good Living presents a 'voluntaristic and utopian' representation of society, one that is rendered ambiguous and self-contradictory as it fails to contest the very power structures that abort its realisation (González and Vázquez 2015, 3).

The epistemological and ontological discourses attributed to Good Living frame the discussion in simplistic 'true or false' binaries that seek the most authentic or accurate representation of alterity (González and Vázquez 2015). This unfortunate framing suggests that certain subjects have the ability to move from local knowledge to the world, whilst others move against it. Through this framing, not only are projects of emancipation forgotten but the limited scope it presents differs from the decolonial views it is intent on promoting (González and Vázquez 2015, 7). What is most striking is that through its limited scope and lacking decolonial framing, it reifies the gaps of stratification and differentiated subjectivities that are laden in oppositional value judgements (González and Vázquez 2015, 7).

Critical Good Living, aware of the predominately binary analysis that has been forwarded, proposes a new theoretical cover that may unmask the complex interplay of power and agency that came about in the Andes during the critical juncture. Through transnational governmentalities (Andolina et al. 2009; Foucault 1977; Hale 2000), a retreating state (Cerny 1997; Harvey 2005), changing citizenship regimes (Lijphart 2012; Yashar 2005), politicised ethnic cleavages (Mijeski and Beck 2011; Rice 2012; Yashar 2005), and the emergence of discursive democracy (Dryzek 2000) new theoretical cover seeks to analyse the current theoretical voids afflicting Good Living. Moreover, incorporating these theoretical framings allows for critical engagement with the power dynamics that made post-colonial exclusions possible (Radcliffe 2012, 243). Doing so re-incorporates the identity politics that underscored the critical juncture, a period where indigenous demands regarding territory, identity, agrarian reform, and collective rights ignited civil society mobilisation for nearly a decade. Rather than looking to Ecuador's past, the imports of Nordic environmentalism or state-centred development, this critical revision of Good Living focuses on the power dynamics, historical events, political transformations, and social upheavals that led to the Constitutional Assembly of 2008.

Analysing Good Living through this new lens revises the origins, objectives and possible outcomes of its constitutional inscription. Rather than wholeheartedly accepting Good Living's alterity, the analysis that surfaces unveils the political processes, social transformations, and economic programs of intervention that shaped Ecuador during the critical juncture. Following what was presented in previous chapters, such an analysis unmasks two very distinct currents of Good Living. The first of which emerges from the projects of transnational governmentalities and NGO's that constructed a new development paradigm under the discourse of ethnodevelopment. Rediscovery of culture, networks, and new forms of neo-utilitarian agency in Ecuador's Andes provided the legitimising discourses that made economic intervention possible. The second is premised on the political agendas that shaped indigenous mobilisation and civil society collective action. Both of which forged a political master frame that united a polymorphous body of actors against market-led policy reforms. Predominant in this second current are indigenous demands for self-determination, advancement of socio-economic rights and bio-centric forms of environmental conservation.

Under this critical lens, Good Living contests the predominating currents that have engulfed its analysis since 2008. Advancing a theoretically constructed form of critical Good Living seeks to overcome the 'utopian realism' advocated by Ramírez (2010, 128) or the millenary Andean roots of 'bio-centrism' discussed by Gudynas (2016) and Acosta (2011). Moreover, it contests the sterile discussions of neo-Andeanism forwarded by Medina (2014) or Oviedo (2014), as they create an unsubstantiated analysis that fails to engage with the political projects and social transformations that were spearheaded by what was once Latin America's strongest and most consolidated indigenous movement. The following chapter analyses these complex and multifaceted transformations experienced by Ecuador during the critical juncture, a period plagued by economic turmoil, social upheavals, and political transformations.

CHAPTER 3

The Critical Juncture

This chapter provides an overview of the occurrences and processes that led to a critical juncture in Ecuador between 1979 and 2008. Central to this chapter is the identification of interpretable events that made economic, social, and political conditions shift, thus allowing institutional dynamics to be altered and structural openings to expand (Capoccia and Kelemen 2007, 343; della Porta 2008). In other words, this chapter reviews the multifaceted social, political and economic processes that redefined Ecuador's political arena until Ecuador's 2008 Constitution. The juncture is "critical," due to the unforeseen transformations experienced in the institutional, political, legal, and economic realms, which in time, produced a new legal framing that expanded or innovated approaches to economic, social and economic rights. Widespread economic reform, created the so-called "generative cleavage" from which politicised ethnic cleavages, state retreat, and changing citizenship regimes emerged, utterly redefining political dynamics between 1979 and 2008.

Ecuador's institutional and legal architecture was redefined, creating a juncture in which otherwise implausible policy choices were suddenly made available to political actors who, up until that point, had been barred from the country's political arena (Capoccia and Kelemen 2007; Mahoney 2000). Ecuador's constitutional reform of 2008, and the birth of Good Living therein, are interconnected events that resulted from the converging forces that reshaped Ecuador between 1979 and 2008. Following on from Chapter 1, these contingent and interconnected events have been selected to explain the emergence of Good Living in Ecuador's 2008 Constitution. As such, they point towards the materialisation of a politicised ethnic cleavage, a retreating state, and the changing dynamics imposed by newly defined citizenship regimes. These converging forces are thus instrumental for the analysis of the critical juncture here conducted. These three contingent events, which spawned as a result of the generative cleavage of economic reform, have been selected through theory-guided process tracing (Morgan 2016; Waldner 2012). Building on previous scholarship focusing on Ecuador during the critical juncture, these three converging forces are brought together through a triangulation of primary and secondary sources, as well as archival research and open-ended interviews conducted during field research in Colombia and Ecuador.

This triangulation of research, which is aided by the methodology of theory-guided process tracing, allows us to recreate a sequential period of interest from which to analyse the critical juncture. Through this methodology, previous scholarship, and the theoretical frameworks developed therein, one is able to create a series of interdependent occurrences that theoretically present the most relevant events of the critical juncture (Morgan 2016). Whilst useful in the development of a methodological approach that analyses the internal validity of the occurrences during the critical juncture, it also harbours the potential to construct a 'relatively complete explanation' of the concatenated events that led to Good Living by generating a trade-off between internal and external validity that basically constraints generality (Waldner 2012, 6). Privileging a particular set of events within the critical juncture is done through the methodological tool of theory-guided process tracing, as it identifies the occurrences of interest from past scholarship on Ecuadorian politics. Selecting processes and occurrences based on previous scholarship allows us to construct a theoretical framing that originates from a firm empirical backdrop. The theory-guided process tracing here presented is thus a continuation of past scholarship on ethnic cleavages, state retreat, changing citizenship regimes, discursive democracy, and transnational governmentalities in Ecuador and Latin America.

The present chapter further underscores the validity, relevance and theoretical usefulness of these converging occurrences in the retracing of Good Living's origins. All three of these occurrences have been selected due to their relevance within previous and current scholarship on Ecuadorian and Latin American politics. The theory-guided process tracing presented here is thus a continuation of previous scholarship engaging with the political, social, economic, and legal occurrences that took place in Ecuador during the critical juncture. Central to this chapter is the renewed focus placed on the wider set of conditions and occurrences that came together during the critical juncture as it crafted Good Living (Soifer 2015, 252).

The selected methodology and theoretical framework affirms the significance of these three occurrences and is summarised as follows. Firstly, that the economic reforms that came with Ecuador's return to democracy redefined the roles and capabilities of the state, as well as the relationships of subordination it wielded upon its citizens. These reconfigurations further fed the institutional debacles and inter-branch crises that have historically defined Ecuadorian politics. The continuous, and at times accelerated, retreat of the state from the interests of its constituents, subsequently boosted civil society mobilisation during the 1990s and early 2000s.

Secondly, a systematic retreat by the state, alongside the advent of new political arrangements, created distinct forms of pluralist politics that converged with increasing demands for ethnic recognition. The combination of a retreating state, with emerging forms of pluralist politics, created openings for new political actors to surface. For Ecuador, reconfiguration of the political arena through these events resulted in the emergence of a nascent indigenous movement, which in due time, if only momentarily, seized control of the state. Finally, domestic events that altered pre-existing citizenship regimes were met with a favourable international climate as human rights treaties imposed new limitations to state power. A favourable international human rights arena, alongside Ecuador's expansion of voting rights in the 1979 constitution, had not only swollen the national electoral base but also created new legal avenues from which the disenfranchised could reclaim their place within the public sphere. Expanded suffrage, aborted corporatist practices, and an international human rights regime protective of collective rights, unleashed waves of unexpected ethnonationalism. These new demands focused on radically altering the content of citizenship in multi-ethnic settings by creating a point of rupture in Ecuador's configuration of the public sphere (Yashar 2005).

On a global level, the consolidation of international human rights treaties favouring indigenous autonomy and collective rights consolidated the legal validity of such reclamations. As Shelton (2011, 2) comments:

> The place of international law in domestic legal systems has been especially affected by the post-war emphasis on human rights and democratic governance. Those countries that have experienced dictatorships or foreign occupation generally reveal greater receptivity to international law, often incorporating or referring to specific international texts in their post-repression constitutions. The failures of the domestic legal order appear to have inspired these countries to turn towards an international 'safety net.' This is evident not only in the new constitutions of Central and Eastern Europe, but also in those of Argentina, South Africa, and, from an earlier period, Spain and Portugal. Luxembourg, which owes its creation to a series of treaties, and has been dependent on international co-operation for its economic well-being and even its sovereignty, shows similar respect for international law, giving it primacy in the domestic system.

The impact of international human rights treaties within domestic legal systems is replicated on a regional level. For Latin America, the once dormant Inter-American Court of Human Rights (IACtHR) became evermore engaged with the regions increasing demands for social, economic, and cultural rights. This "awakening" of the IACtHR, was further made possible by the constitutional convergence experienced in the region as international treaty ratification systematically "universalised" the discourses and enforcement of human rights (Elkins et al. 2013, 62). Ultimately, the forging of a unified human rights system, coupled with the constitutional learning of many Latin American jurisdictions, created regional and domestic conditions that questioned the relevance of centralised sovereign state power (Elkins et al. 2013; Tushnet 2017).

The convergence of legal systems with the project of human rights gradually redefined pre-existing citizenship regimes in Ecuador and Latin America, altering centuries of legal tradition, as well as the social and political arrangements they rested upon. New legal framings, regional judicial review, and domestic political reform brought forth a consolidated effort that redefined the contents of citizenship, the role of the state, and the ways in which ethnicity was reclaimed (Yashar 2005). Convergence of domestic and international legal frames would thus challenge the pre-existing conventions regarding the nation-state, uniform constituencies or the constitutional rights that are demanded by the polity. In due time, Ecuador's indigenous movement would become highly mobilised, enhancing their political leverage as they demanded autonomy, territory and collective rights. Consumed by their political momentum, indigenous mobilisation would simultaneously contest neoliberal reforms by accommodating the dispersed interests of a multiplicity of political actors (Becker 2008; Mijeski and Beck 2011; Yashar 2005).

We have proposed that Good Living emerged as a result of these three converging and contingent occurrences; a by-product of the politicised ethnic cleavages, state retreat, and redefinition of citizen-state relations that occurred during the critical juncture. The present chapter develops the detailed theoretical backdrop from which our theory-guided process tracing is conducted. Through the coupling of Foucault's (2007) discussion on power and governmentality with Dryzek's (2000) discursive democracy, a wider framing presents a critical reading of Good Living. This critical lens, focused on the discursive power of Good Living, is further supported in Chapter 4 by reviewing the usages that led to the crafting of Good Living prior to the Constitutional Assembly of 2007–2008.

The current chapter is set out as follows. First, a preface to the critical juncture will be explored. The objective here is to present the basic political, social, and economic conditions that came immediately before the critical juncture. Afterwards, the chapter will examine the different ways in which the state was dismantled due to the economic, social and political crises of the time. Our attention then turns to the emergence of politicised ethnic cleavages in Ecuador, as well as the political triumphs, legal reforms, and demise of what was once Latin America's strongest indigenous movement. The last section of the chapter assesses the domestic, regional and international transformations that made redefined citizenship regimes possible.

1   Theory-guided Process Tracing

By introducing a novel approach towards Good Living, rather than focusing on existing literature focused on the matter, we are positioned to unite various theoretical sources through the methodological approach of theory-guided process tracing. As was explained in previous chapters, this method is most useful when applied to case-specific explanations, which are themselves contingent on a set of local events. As Tarrow (2010) explains, once a specific time period is defined, one may then analyse the 'dynamic set of events' in which agent decisions and institutional responses led to unexpected results. For the case in point, this time period and the occurrences and processes which surfaced therein, led to novel approaches to law and politics, ultimately constituting Good Living in Ecuador's 2008 Constitution. Paramount to our research is uniting often divergent theoretical disciplines such as anthropology, politics, sociology, and political economy in order to constitute a sufficiently robust theoretical framework from which analysis of Good Living may depart. Previous chapters have depicted the sources from which analyses of Good Living have, up until this point, been focused on. The three main analytical frameworks which have been presented are the so-called Indigenist, post-development and state-centered approach. Due to its novel conception, analysis of Good Living is not limited to a specific epistemological field. What has been introduced is a critical assessment of existing literature on Ecuador and Good Living, in order to create an analysis intent on unravelling the legal and political consequences of its emergence. This task requires uniting research that has emerged from multiple fields, for this reason, the theory-guided process tracing which is here proposed defines the relevant literature from which analysis may be constructed. This methodological approach, and its consequence on the theoretical propositions that are forwarded, presents the theoretical boundaries from which literature is either selected or discarded. Analysis of relevant literature is premised on the underlying theoretical need of explaining and understanding Good Living's legal and political depth.

This in itself is a rather cumbersome task as legal inquiry is, more often than not, premised on social, political and economic realities foreign to Latin America, let alone Ecuador. As Bonilla (2013, 12–14) denotes:

(...) the only context for the production of knowledge is the legal academia in the North. The intellectual production of the South is considered to be a weak reproduction of the knowledge generated in the North, a form of diffusion, or a mere local application of the same (...) what I call the assumption of a "protected geographical indications." This indicates that all knowledge produced in the North is worthy of respect and recognition per se, given the context from which it emerges (...)

(...) Many of the legal norms that are issued, the doctrines that interpret them, and the theories they substantiate, evaluate, or contextualize them are a local application of knowledge created in foreign legal communities. Similarly, it is true that legal formalism has controlled part of the Global South's legal conscience and that is a poor concept of law (...) these general arguments ignore the heterogeneity of legal academic communities (...).

Analysis of Good Living, premised on theoretical backdrops that depend on "traditional" or "standard" theoretical approaches succumb to one of two ailments. The first of which may be called "dispersion," or the inability of analyzing Good Living from a theoretically solid stand point. Many of the theoretical analyses forwarded on Good Living in Chapter 2, lack a substantive epistemological approach that allows the reader or researcher to pinpoint where the well of knowledge is located. The second ailment, refers to epistemologically dependent analysis of Good Living, as Latin American scholars often reproduce analytical frameworks from the North, without contextualizing their arguments to the realities where they must be applied. Through theory-guided process tracing, we seek to unravel these issues by framing analysis on Good Living within the locally based theoretical backdrops from which it emerged. Moreover, analysis of Good Living, its constitutional inscription, and later application as a legal and public policy instrument, must be understood in the social phenomena from which it emerged. Constitutional reform in Latin America, occurred only in times of profound political and economic crises, often emerging beyond the traditional political realm, due to the fact that shortsighted interests limited such reforms (Negretto 2015, 289). The theory-guided process tracing that is here presented has therefore been selected as a methodological tool from which multiple epistemological fields come together to explain the social and political phenomenon that in time, led to Good Living's constitutional inscription. Literature utilized to enact this theory-guided process tracing is in no manner random, sparse or selected by chance to "cherry pick" appropriate theoretical backdrops from which to frame one's arguments. Rather, what is here proposed is a leveraging of existing literature in the fields of anthropology, politics, law, political economy or sociology in order to theoretically develop Good Living's relevance as a legal principle. It must be noted that most of the sources that are utilized to do so stem from sociology or anthropology. Material related to politics and political economy, which in its majority is centered on the "niche" fields of indigenous politics and economic structural reform, are also paramount in developing the arguments that are here presented.

The following section presents these theoretical sources, in order to encapsulate and link them to what lays ahead. It must however be pointed out that unlike the academic production that occurs in the Global North, the availability of material, sources, data and relevant literature on matters occurring in the Global South is much more scattered. Therefore, what is here sought is to unite existing academic sources in order to develop a theoretically guided approach towards the emergence of Good Living as a political and legal phenomenon proper to Latin American reality and Ecuador's critical juncture.

2   Development Paradigms in Indigenous Communities

Good Living's post-development and Indigenist strains present opposing paradigms. Indigenist understandings, as was depicted in previous chapters, present an almost millenary form of Good Living, one that has always been present in Ecuador's Andes and Amazon. On the other hand, post-development Good Living frames discussions on the matter as an alternative to standard economic development recipes by envisioning an indigenous inspired alternative to development that reconciles nature, Andean communities and urban-based living. In order to develop a theoretically framed approach on these matters, the work of Victor Bretón Solo de Zaldívar has been identified as a relevant source from which to start our analysis. For example, Bretón's 2001 scholarship analyzing *Development Cooperation and Ethnic Demands in the Ecuadorian Andes* presents a thorough understanding on how new identities and social actors redefined rural development approaches during the time of neoliberal reform. That same year, Bretón (2001) would analyse how social capital, ethnicity and development came together to present a new, uniquely Ecuadorian, approach towards rural development. Following on his research, by 2005 Bretón would debate the "new" rural paradigms of development and how they emerged from within indigenous and Afro-Ecuadorian communities which had become transected by concepts such as social capital and empowerment. The evolution of a uniquely rural and indigenous inspired form of development would be a theoretical focus for Bretón. By 2008, Bretón presents a paper titled "From Agrarian Reform to Ethnodevelopment in the Highlands of Ecuador" in which he traces the multifarious ways in which social capital and self-help agency became fused to present a new concept of development premised on its ethnic origins. Bretón (2008, 585) would question the validity of such mergers as he argued:

> Conspicuous and controversial synergies and reciprocal feedback would develop among these private agencies—especially NGOs—as I will try to show in this article. Thus, while in the 1980s land reform lost momentum as a hegemonic paradigm in favour of integral rural development (IRD), different ways of applying and understanding the notion of development in rural contexts have proliferated ever since. The range extends from 'social capital' to 'ethnodevelopment,' passing through every imaginable version of 'sustainability,' always with a 'gender' focus and a spirit of 'empowerment.' What this collection of buzzwords signals is, in effect, a radical shift in approaches to rural poverty and new peasant movements.

More recent work by Bretón (2015) analyses the complexities that emerged from such synergies or in his own words:

> I draw attention to aspects seldom mentioned in the specialized bibliography, namely a detailed study of how peasant differentiation, the origins of which lay in hacienda hierarchies, and which was upheld in turn by the agrarian distribution, was accelerated by the actions of NGOs, which continued to favour those indigenous peasants with more power and economic resources. Thus, divergences were consolidated and internal fissures opened up in organizations that are at the root of the crisis of representation experienced by ethnic platforms in the Ecuadorian Andes today.

For its comprehensive and continually revised understanding of the dynamics of indigenous rural development paradigms, Bretón's work stands out as a relevant backdrop from which Indigenist and post-development understandings of Good Living may be enacted. His literature proves vital to situate the relevance of social capital as a guiding conceptual framework from which "buzzwords" would later emerge to depict Good Living as either a uniquely indigenous phenomenon or a post development alternative. Moreover, his work is also proven to be invaluable when one seeks to understand how the indigenous movement became infiltrated by the NGO machinery which altered the basis from which it emerged, ultimately leading to its weakening and demise. This of course does not mean that other sources are not utilized but rather that Bretón work offers a privileged starting point from which theory-guided process tracing may begin.

3 Defining the Theory behind a Theory

Much of the academic attention Ecuador has received both at home and abroad, refers to two unique phenomena. The first of which is a niche academic field which relates to the emergence of indigenous politics in Ecuador's Andes and Amazon from 1979 onwards. And a second which is framed around the political, institutional and economic convulsions that unraveled the country between 1979 and 2008. These two fields of interest have sprung a series of literature from different academic fields such as sociology, anthropology, politics and political economy. Rarely, if ever, have these academic fields questioned how political, social, and economic events affected Ecuador's legal system or the policy prescriptions they later inspired. Good Living, is both legal principle and policy prescription. For this reason, we seek to understand its origins and applicability by uniting what at plain sight may seem distant or unrelated studies. Understanding Good Living's legal significance is ever more complex, as no single academic field has, to the moment of writing, troubled itself with explaining the social, political or economic dynamics that led to its birth or empirical applicability. It is with this objective in sight, that the theory-guided process tracing which is here proposed departs. By leveraging on existing literature on Ecuador's politics, indigenous communities, economic processes and institutional dynamics, a more rounded, robust, and theoretically premised understanding of Good Living is offered.

Historical analysis in the fashion offered by Marc Becker (2008; 2009; 2013), presents a rather complete revision of how agrarian reform, social dynamics and political allies formed Ecuador's indigenous movement. Moreover, it presents a retrospective snapshot of the complex relationships indigenous people forged with Left leaning political allies from the 1950s onwards. This historical framing proves invaluable when understanding how Good Living is later framed by Left-of-center urban intellectuals, who are simultaneously committed to indigenous struggles yet frame them from the point of view of an urban political agenda flooded by buzzwords. Complementary to a historical recounting of indigenous politics, Suzana Sawyer (2004) offers a rich ethnographic account in *Crude Chronicles: Indigenous Politics, Multinational Oil, and Neoliberalism in Ecuador.* Most prominent in her work is the snapshot of Amazonian indigenous community dynamics during a rather convulsive time in

Ecuadorian politics. Sawyer's work identifies the complex relationships that emerged in Ecuador during the critical juncture, as economic reform, indigenous rights and NGOs came together to redefine the political arena. Following on this tradition, Michael Cepek (2012) presents a more complex ethnographic approach towards indigenous politics. Cepek's *A Future for Amazonia* presents the reader with the interrelationship that was forged by multinational NGOs, its workers, and indigenous demands. These works are of course further corroborated or enhanced by earlier work by Amalia Pallares (2002) as she framed indigenous resistance and peasant struggles.

The complexity of interrelationships forged by indigenous communities, NGOs and multilateral development agencies is a necessary theoretical backdrop from which Good Living may be understood. In search of a theoretical basis from which analysis may depart two sources are paramount. Andolina, Radcliffe and Laurie's (2002; 2005; 2005; 2009; 2016) on Andean indigenous development, similar to what is proposed by Bretón, unravel the complex political and economic relationships that were forged by indigenous communities, development agencies and the imposition of concepts such as social capital. The myriad of conceptual framings that came from Ecuadorian indigenous communities merging with the development paradigms of multilateral agencies, like the World Bank, is thoroughly covered in Kate Bedford's *Developing Partnerships: Gender, Sexuality and the Reformed World Bank*.

Indigenous politics, the so-called "ethnic cleavage" that emerged from 1979 onwards, has proven to be a source of rich academic debate. The relevance of indigenous politics of course transcends Ecuador, however its magnitude during the 1990s found no better host than this small Andean country. Ecuador would be home to Latin America, and possibly the world's most organized, politically active and relevant indigenous movement. Yashar's (2005) *Contesting Citizenship Regimes in Latin America* proves this much as she analysis the rise of indigenous movements during the region's neoliberal reform. Indigenous politics, powered by natural resource extraction projects within their communal lands or socioeconomic demands, would guide the work of Gerlach's (2003) *Indians, Oil and Politics* or Selverston-Scher's *Ethnopolitics in Ecuador*. Indigenous party politics would however be more acutely understood through Mijeski and Beck's (2011) *Pachakutik and the Rise and Decline of the Ecuadorian Indigenous Movement*, where they propose that electoral preferences amongst indigenous voters are linked to socioeconomic demands rather than an ethnic sense of kinship to the candidate.

The literature that frames the theoretical pursuit at hand defines the boundaries from which two main objectives are set. Firstly, the critical juncture in accordance with the literature that is mentioned above, is necessarily defined between 1979 and 2008. The events that unraveled Ecuador's political arena, ultimately leading to Ecuador's 2008 Constitution began in 1979. Like a crescendo, indigenous demands, power and struggles kicked-off from this point on. Secondly, development paradigms, unleashed during the critical juncture, would be the backdrop from which Good Living emerged. Finally, the theoretical importance of ethnic cleavages, state retreat, and changing citizenship regimes are all identified within the above-mentioned literature, as well as the other multiple sources consulted. The analysis at hand does not seek to cover all possible literature on a given subject, due to the interdisciplinary focus that is proposed, such an endeavor would far exceed the task at hand. What is rather proposed, through theory-guided process tracing, is a leveraging of relevant literature to identify the pattern of interpretable events that makes a case study on Good Living possible.

4   Lead-up to the Critical Juncture: 1960–1979

4.1   *Agrarian Revolts and Reforms*

Ecuador became a cauldron of political discontent and turmoil during the 1960s. The regional and global transformations taking place in far off places like Vietnam, or close neighbours like Cuba, reshaped the contours of domestic policy (Brands 2010). Inspired by the revolutionary triumphs that took place in the Caribbean in the late 1950s, Ecuadorian Marxists and indigenous leaders from the central Andes set out to challenge the structural inequality that plagued the country since its colonial era (Becker and Tutillo 2009, 202). Widespread social discontent towards eschewed patterns of wealth distribution was and still is warranted. To exemplify the source of such discontent, we need only look at the data from Ecuador's first agricultural census from a decade earlier. The 1954 census had determined that 2.1 per cent of all agricultural holdings controlled 64.4 per cent of all arable land (Bretón 2010, 53). Such hyper concentration of land had historically favoured a powerful agro-export elite that acted as the food basket of the country or served as importer of foreign currency reserves through primary exports such as cacao or banana (Guerrero 1994; Soifer 2015, 241). Discontent amongst the urban poor, peasantry and indigenous peoples was further exacerbated by the prevalence of inhumane labour conditions still in place throughout the coast and Andes. These forms of modern-day servitude had been inherited from Ecuador's Inca and colonial past but perpetuated by its Republican forefathers (Alexander 2007, 208).

Social discontent erupted in a major indigenous protest that descended upon Quito on 16 December 1961. The protest was led by twelve thousand indigenous participants that marched on Ecuador's capital demanding land titles for indigenous people and peasants (Becker Tutillo 2009). Social and political unrest during this time had forced then president Velsaco Ibarra from office, effectively ceding executive power to Carlos Julio Arosemena (Becker and Tutillo 2009). Arosemena had publicly supported indigenous demands for land reform, going as far as using his presidential powers to decree the reformation of the servitude institution of *huasipungo* in clear acquiescence of Andean indigenous demands (Alexander 2007, 208). Arosemena would however fall short in the execution and application of any sort of land reform, as mounting opposition from congress led to his early ousting through a military coup (Becker and Tutillo 2009).

The 1960s witnessed the growing influence of the United States-led Alliance for Progress throughout Latin America. The brainchild of the Kennedy administration, this early, yet far-reaching geopolitical development program sought to counter growing communist influences in the Andes by pressuring elites to enact some level of agrarian reforms (Hale 2002; North and Grinspun 2016, 7). Ecuador's recently instituted military regime would ultimately cede to the pressures of the United States, as demands for land reform and growing social discontent gradually increased throughout the 1960s (Yashar 2005, 88). Long-awaited land reform was finally sanctioned by the 1964 *Ley de Reforma Agraria y Colonización*,[1] however this would prove to be a bittersweet victory for civil society groups. Although legal reform had installed mechanisms that could in some way lead to land reform, policies enacted during this time also brought about the continuation and expansion of assimilationist policies targeting indigenous organisations and communities; a symptomatic effect of local elites retaliating to preserve their privileges (Becker 2008; Becker and Tutillo 2009; Breton 2010).

Rather than disrupting the historic patterns of accumulation of wealth in elite hands, the long-awaited land reform shifted land pressures from the Andes to the "abandoned" territories of the Amazon (Llasag 2012,112; Yashar 2005). This shifting of demographic pressures from the Andes to the Amazon ultimately led to conflicts amongst Andean indigenous colonisers and Amazonian indigenous defending their ancestral lands (Becker and Tutillo 2009, 209). The ensuing 1973 reform that took place a decade later reformed the 1964 legislation, enacting evermore dire circumstances on indigenous people. The *Ley de Reforma Agraria y Colonización*[2] of the 1970s would have as its central focus the declaration of protected areas throughout the Amazon. Central to

---

[1] Law of Agrarian Reform and Colonization, 1964.
[2] Reformatory Law of Agrarian Reform and Colonization, 1973.

this reformatory legislation was the safeguarding of large plots of land where oil and precious metals had recently been discovered (Llasag 2012, 111). In sum, the social discontent that had driven the need for overarching reforms had been left unanswered and in some cases the conditions faced by indigenous people had even worsened (Goodwin 2016, 8). The grip of Ecuador's military regime during the 1970s had successfully neutralised any form of social or political confrontation. Fuelled by windfall profits from a bustling oil industry the military regimes of the time were able to defuse social confrontation by expanding social services and reinforcing corporatist practices (Isaacs 1993, 6; Vicuña 2004, 30).

4.2 Oil Induced Military Nationalism

President Velasco Ibarra's fourth term in office (1968–1972) was cut short in 1972 as a new era of military rule spawned in Ecuador (Georgetown University 2009). This new period of de facto governance would coincide with a favourable macroeconomic environment that deepened the prevalent corporatist practices inherited from the colonial administration. In the late 1960s, Texaco began oil explorations in Ecuador's Amazon; however, commercial oil exploitation had been in place since 1925. Although oil had been produced by Ecuador for decades, it wasn't until 1971 that oil exports climbed above the historical trend of 6 per cent per annum growth (El Comercio 2012; Gerlach 2003, 33). Once in office, military rule declared itself as reformist and proclaimed to be 'popular, anti-feudal, anti-oligarchic' and set on creating 'substantial transformations in the socio-economic and judicial orders of the Republic'[3] (El Comercio 1972 quoted in Hurtado 1977, 244). The armed forces' sudden interest in managing the nascent petroleum economy came from a deeply rooted apprehension towards the legal terms through which previous civilian governments had structured oil exploration with foreign capital (Issacs 1993, 25). More importantly, their new interest also stemmed from the 'context of crises' engulfing the region during the 1970s as the Cold War spilled onto multiple aspects of everyday life (Issacs 1993, 28).

Spill over effects from the Cold War, counter-revolutionary efforts throughout the region, and the instalment of the so-called National Security Doctrine in Latin America's armed forces, redefined the military's political responsibilities towards the nation (Issacs 1993, 29). By voicing their concerns in national security terms, the military seized power in February 1972, alleging that the external defence of the country depended on certain domestic conditions within its borders (Hurtado 1977, 246; Issacs 1993, 29). These "conditions" were

---

3 The translation is mine.

a melting pot of social and psychological predefined societal characteristics, that would (in theory) lead to specific economic, cultural and political assemblages that strengthened sovereignty and the process of self-determination (Hurtado 1977).

Consequently, the military regime of the time was vociferous on its intention of radicalising reforms by collaborating with indigenous and peasant groups (Goodwin 2016, 8). Instauration of inward-looking economic development policies, Ecuador's presidency of the Organization of Oil Exporting Countries (OPEC) in 1974, unprecedented economic growth stemming from increased aggregate demand, and rising oil prices throughout the 1970s, created structural conditions that favoured military-led corporatist practices (Hey 1995, 87; Vicuña 2004, 30). The oil "boom" period of the 1970s brought about expanded state spending and considerable improvements to infrastructure and government services. Abundant foreign currency reserves had allowed Ecuador to pay-off the foreign debt that had been backlogged since the country's independence struggles of the nineteenth century, the so-called "English debt" (Vicuña 2004, 32).

The consolidation of OPEC, the economic stagnation of industrialised economies, and the subsequent increases to petrodollar reserves in Western financial institutions supplied easy access to credit for developing nations (Vicuña 2004). Heavily influenced by structuralists' assertion that development problems could be resolved through a state-led "big push forward," Ecuador's military regime took on the role of economic planner and investor (Gerlach 2003; Oatley 2016, 119). In order to do so, foreign debt spiked between 1974 and 1979, as the military regime desperately attempted to contain the worsening macroeconomic environment (Vicuña 2004, 32). Originally intended to consolidate the corporatist regimes installed in Ecuador during the mid-twentieth century, military-led central planning failed in directing education, pensions, subsidies, credit, and health to the peasantry, urban poor or indigenous peoples (North 2004, 196; Yashar 2005, 48). Moreover, the scattered and improvised policies applied throughout the 1970s led to structural deficiencies that culminated in the loss of one hundred thousand jobs in the countryside and a 62 per cent reduction of the agricultural labour force (North 2004, 195).

In addition to its corporatist practices, the inward-looking development sponsored by the military during this time was also part of a broader effort of expanding assimilationist policies that emphasised Ecuador's Indian ancestry as an impediment towards national development. Ecuadorians would "all become white" and modern when they accepted "the objectives of national culture" imposed by militaristic nationalism (Rodriguez Lara in Whitten 1984 quoted in Benavides 2004, 45). Thus, the 1970s ended with a consolidated central state that had successfully stripped power from Ecuador's agro-export elites by instituting or expanding, state-led corporatist practices that benefited a handful of interest groups. Expanded state services and unprecedented economic growth had defused social conflict and allowed inward-orientated economic policies to bolster impressive GDP growth. However, patchy public policy, mismanaged spikes in foreign debt, and contempt towards thoroughly resolving the historic reclamations of the country's indigenous and peasant populations were inaugurated in the 1980s with effervescent social discontent, political crises, and economic turmoil. Ultimately, the snowball effect of inadequate policy management would undo the structural conditions that had, until then, suppressed the country's demands for economic, social, and cultural reform.

5 Economic, Institutional, and Political Breakdown

5.1 State Retreat

First, we must introduce a broad framing of the state to understand the impact its retrocession had on Ecuador's public sphere. Rather than focusing simply on the central state, Helmke's (2017, 20) inter-branch analysis is introduced so the judicial, legislative, and executive downfalls are accounted for. Furthermore, we complement such a conceptualisation by introducing Tilly's concept of state power, here understood as the regulatory, coercive, and extractive dimensions on which the state exercises its sovereign prerogatives (1975 quoted in Soifer 2015, 10). Since independence, many Latin American states, and Ecuador particularly, have faced varying degrees of difficulty when exercising the main tenets of state power. Most commonly, Ecuador had been historically unable to extract taxes from its population, provide reliable public services, impose the rule of law or monopolise the use of violence and coercion (Soifer 2015, 97).

State power is thus understood as the composite summation of coercive, extractive, and regulatory functions performed by any three branches of government. As such, the "elusive or retreating state" refers to the inability faced by either branch of government in the enactment of these sovereign capabilities. Furthermore, a broad conception of the state will be of much use when the institutional instability that plagued Ecuador during the critical juncture is examined. As a result of structural conditions of institutional instability, the elusive state is thus represented by its shortcoming in policy applications that led to multiple judicial, legislative, and presidential convulsions throughout the critical juncture.

5.2 Regionalist Challenges to State Building

Divisive regionalist interests between the coast and Andes have historically aborted state building in Ecuador. Soifer's revision of state building efforts throughout Latin America explains that only if salient regionalism is absent from elite political interests may central state authority be consolidated (2015, 26). Under such absence, regional divergences in public good preferences are subdued, allowing judicial, legislative, and executive power to be asserted (Soifer 2015). However, since local elite administrations have historically supervised state building efforts in Ecuador, public policy has tended to benefit the interests of a small segment of a wealthy creole polity. This has resulted in policy negotiations failing to mediate state-society disputes over scarce resources (Soifer 2015, 61). Such failures underscore the inchoate character of Ecuador's democratic institutions, as political differences cannot be resolved through institutional bargaining or compromise mechanisms (Helmke 2017, 151). Ecuador is a particularly poignant example of such regionalist pressures, as the sharp antagonism of Andes and coast has historically aborted compromise-orientated policymaking. Unsurprisingly, the country has been defined as a "basket-case" that stands out regionally for the institutional crises that have plagued it (Helmke 2017, 42; Soifer 2015).

Regionalist pressures between Ecuador's capital Quito, and its port city of Guayaquil, have historically defined the country's political arena. Guayaquil's economic might has continuously aborted Quito's attempts to extend its influence over the national territory (Soifer 2015, 241). Even when decentralisation policies have been enacted, they have unintentionally created self-reinforcing effects where primary power holders have been able to assert their political dominance in favour of Quito or Guayaquil (Falleti 2010, 16; Llasag 2012, 91; Soifer 2015). Moreover, the predominance of territorial interests within reform coalitions has impeded significant devolution of autonomy to subnational governments in other cities (Falleti 2010, 18). In sum, regionalist interests underpinned the absence of state building efforts in Ecuador for the better part of a century. Even with substantial revenues from oil, cacao, and banana exports, tensions between Quito and Guayaquil continuously trumped development priorities (Gerlach 2003; Soifer 2015, 242).

The advent of Ecuador's oil economy in the 1970s, as was explored earlier in this chapter, allowed the central state to redefine national development priorities. Whilst flamboyant and heavily rhetorical in nature, policies during the country's "military nationalism" were patchy, scattered and ultimately beneficial to an urban middle class. Notwithstanding such shortcomings, the military regimes of the 1970s installed unprecedented reforms that partially allowed a state building effort to consolidate. When Ecuador returned to democratic civilian rule in 1979, it did so with a significantly altered political arena, one in which the state had been able to dominate the national political arena for the better part of a decade.

5.3 Economic Turmoil and Reform during the 1980s

Ecuador's return to civilian rule in the late 1970s kicked-off a decade of precarious economic, political, and social events. The Roldos-Hurtado presidency of 1979 commandeered a fragile democracy and crumbling economy (Hey 1995, 89). By 1980, the country's foreign debt had swollen 55 per cent when compared to 1979 levels (Vicuña 2007, 31). Debilitated democratic governance could be exemplified in Ecuador's weak institutions, lack of judicial accountability or inexistent oversight of government agencies (Jarquin and Echebarria 2007, 6). Institutional shortcomings, compounded by deteriorating economic conditions and plunging oil revenues, were further exacerbated by the haemorrhaging of foreign currency reserves required for the importation of capital goods (Vicuña 2007, 32). Most importantly, the weakening of what had, for the better part of the previous decade, been a highly interventionist and influential state led to unforeseen structural openings that were strategically exploited by emerging political actors (Mijeski and Beck 2011; North 2004; Vicuña 2007, 32). Most of all, Ecuador's heavy dependence on oil exports during the 1970s had set the stage for resource curse patterns to take root (Gamu et al. 2015; Ross 2012, 29). In accordance with resource curse scholarship, such patterns led Ecuador into a situation of economic and institutional underperformance. This situation only worsened as continuous economic shocks, currency fluctuations, and lower levels of democratic governance embattled Ecuador's resource dependent economy (Espinosa 2013, 27; Gamu et al. 2015, 163).

Oil revenues are thus characterised by their exceptionally large size, lack of stability, and crowding out of other sources of state income. Windfall oil revenues had effectively augmented the size of the state as well as the interest groups dependent on their continuous securement (Ross 2012, 33). Unexpectedly, previous inward-looking development policies, championed by the military regimes of the 1970s, had brought about the deleterious effects of Dutch Disease. Rising foreign currency reserves, due to increased oil exports, had effectively hurt or dismantled the nation's agricultural and manufacturing sectors (Ross 2012), thereby worsening the macroeconomic conditions of an already debilitated and underdeveloped economy. In all, resource dependency led to a crippling economic situation as oil prices collapsed in the 1980s, forcing countries from Venezuela to Algeria to submit to pressures from the IMF and World Bank (Escobar 2010, 13; North 2004; Ross 2012).

Between 1982 and 1990, economic conditions had shrunken Ecuador's GDP by 33 per cent, devaluing the national currency from 30 to 767,8 Sucres for every USD, whilst inflation averaged at 48.5 per cent annually (Vicuña 2007, 52). As early as 1983, the Ecuadorian Government had negotiated a series of "letters of intention" with the IMF, as the country's central bank faced dwindling foreign currency reserves, that in 1981 alone had plummeted by about US$300 million (Vicuña 2004, 57). In 1983, collusion between government officials, banking interests, and agro-export elites authorised an unprecedented public buy-out of private debt negotiated in prejudicial terms to the Ecuadorian people (Dávalos 2014). This "welfare for the rich" transferred privately held debt, which had been negotiated in strikingly inept financial conditions, to state coffers (Lind 2005, 40). Collusive government intervention, in the time of *laissez-faire* economics, cost the public treasury an estimated US$1.6 billion (North 2004, 198). By the mid-1980s, the Febres Cordero administration further approved the debt relief of some additional US$1.3 billion in favour of private banks, domestic stakeholders, and foreign corporate interests (North 2004).

IMF demands on the Ecuadorian Governments of the 1980s included tax reform legislation, trade liberalisation, financial sector liberalisation, and the contraction of government spending (North 2004; World Bank 2005, 2). These policy prescriptions would ultimately lead to a GDP per capita growth of 0.37 per cent between 1980 and 1990 (Jarquin and Echberria 2007, 8). Thus, Ecuador entered the 1990s with a sluggish economy, high inflation, price hikes in public service provision, contracted social sector spending, and high foreign debt servicing (Vicuña 2007). However, such conditions were neither unique to Ecuador nor unknown to other parts of the developing world, as many countries in the Global South were soon unable to service the repayment schedules imposed by their guarantors (Hanlon 2000 quoted in Gasper 2004, 20).

5.4 *The Financial Meltdown of the 1990s*

Ecuador's macroeconomic policies during the 1980s may be characterised by the unjustly imposition of publicly funded "welfare for the rich," and the ensuing devastation that was brought forth with foreign debt servicing plans. Following the mismanagement of the previous decade, the 1990s kicked-off a period of financial liberalisation that would ultimately collapse Ecuador's already failing economy. Between 1989 and 1992, Ecuador received some US$730 million in private capital flows a year, or an equivalent of 5 per cent of GDP in 1994 (World Bank 2005). With the approval of the 1994 *Ley General de Instituciones del Sistema Financiero*,[4] banks were granted leeway to determine the costs of

---

4 General Law for Institutions of the Financial System, 1994.

financial transactions, as institutional safeguards were steadily removed (Valencia et al. 2007, 11). In a post-mortem analysis of Ecuador's financial sector, one commentator argued that "the crisis" was due to a grave deficiency in oversight that ultimately led to the embezzlement of financial resources by bank owners (Tibanlombo 2007, 20). Such a situation was worsened by the steady inflows of foreign capital that flooded Ecuador's economy during this time, as contracts were negotiated in speculative tracts that swelled non-FDI[5] flows (World Bank 2005). Moreover, the lack of effective regulatory oversight worsened an already deepened vulnerability to volatile capital outflows (OECD 2008, 14; World Bank 2005, 3).

By 1998, a series of exogenous shocks began to rattle Ecuador's crumbling and highly susceptible economy. Russia's partial debt repudiation brought with it the sudden reversal of capital flows, shifting almost US$2.2 billion of inflows into US$1.3 billion of outflows, or an equivalent to 20 per cent of Ecuador's 1998 GDP (World Bank 2005, 4). Liquidity problems within the financial sector, and the collusion of government officials with banking interests, once again led to a public buy-out of privately held debt (Naranjo 2004, 248). In this second round of "welfare for the rich," the people of Ecuador assumed some US$4 billion in financial sector losses (Naranjo 2004). The IMF quickly stepped in, facilitating an additional US$1.226 billion to Ecuador's financial sector, on the condition that that interest rates on capital lending be raised to 24 per cent (Vicuña 2004, 251). Whilst the IMF had once again helped the Ecuadorian state salvage its financial sector, it had previously warned authorities that state-led "help" to certain banks was excessive and dangerous (Tibanlombo 1997, 22). Warnings that became deafening as some thirty-four banks collapsed by the end of the 1990s (Vistazo 2012, 200).

The new millennia inaugurated Ecuador's loss of its national currency. By adopting the United States Dollar as the country's new legal tender authorities expected to halt looming hyperinflation and the threat of further currency devaluations (Observatorio PyME 2009; Vicuña 2004, 253). As one commentator described it, 'Ecuador entered this currency regime due to the profound crises

---

5   The OECD considers foreign Direct Investment as: "a means for creating direct, stable and long-lasting links between economies. Under the right policy environment, it can serve as an important vehicle for local enterprise development, and it may also help improve the competitive position of both the recipient ("host") and the investing ("home") economy. FDI encourages the transfer of technology and know-how between economies. It also provides an opportunity for the host economy to promote its products more widely in international markets."

it was facing' and its susceptibility to balance of payments deficits, rising interest rates, hyperinflation, and sluggish economic performance (Pozo 2007, 12). In addition to these measures, public panic and the possibility of a "run on the banks," led to a freezing of all bank deposits and a new foreign debt package of some US$2.045 billion in order to salvage the remnants of the country's financial sector (Valencia et al. 2007, 37; Vicuña 2007, 67). Precarious foreign debt negotiations and submission to foreign creditors comprised nearly 50 per cent of all budget expenditures to foreign debt servicing (Grijalva 2008; Vicuña 2004, 303). Dollarisation would partially restore economic performance as the 100 per cent inflation the country faced in 2000 had been successfully reduced to 1.4 per cent by April 2007 (Pozo 2007, 14).

Nevertheless, subsequent administrations would enact measures that further corroded macroeconomic conditions. Between 2000 and 2005, as purchasing power plummeted and subsidies were eliminated, costs of basic services and utilities drastically increased, and indirect taxes hiked (Vicuña 2007, 67). By 2006, foreign debt servicing was once again privileged, leaving a meagre 32 per cent of the national budget to cover constitutionally mandated welfare expenditures (Vicuña 2007, 67). The devastating effects of economic mismanagement, fuelled by the preeminent collusion of private debt and public oversight, deteriorated economic conditions to unprecedented levels.

Ultimately, Ecuador's population would suffer the onslaught caused by the state's incapability to respond to fledgling macroeconomic conditions. Between 1998 and 1999 poverty increased from 39.3 per cent to 52.3 per cent, forcing one million Ecuadorians to migrate between 1999 and 2000 (Valencia et al. 2007, 45). Unprecedented spikes in migration led to remittances flowing into Ecuador's economy. From 2000 to 2004, remittances from Ecuador's migrant populations in Europe and the United States would considerably over pass Ecuadorian agricultural exports, reaching an estimated 10 per cent of GDP, a figure only surpassed by the country's oil exports (Velasco 2007, 41).

By 2004, poverty had stricken 7.4 million Ecuadorians or more than half of its population in this period (Vicuña 2007, 103; World Bank 2017). Hikes in poverty were the subsequent result of spending cuts in education, housing and health (Naranjo 2004, 250). In all, the "elusive state" had once more been unable to mediate social reclamations with policy prescriptions. Policy failure, regulatory collusion, contraction of state spending, and the inability of consecutive administrations in managing macroeconomic turmoil, further contracted a historically weak state. Ecuador's tumultuous economic performance between 1979 and 2008 was thus exacerbated by the institutional breakdowns that prompted a decade of inter-branch crises, social protests, and the continuous disintegration of state power.

5.5 Inter-branch Crises and Ghost Coalitions

Amongst the ten categories outlined by Sartori to define the diverse universe of party systems that can be identified the world over, Ecuador falls into what he labelled as 'atomized pluralism' (2005, 254). This category defines a situation in which political parties are made-up of loose coalitions that morph from one election to the next. Such a category is representative of lacking 'structural consolidation' or 'institutionalisation,' a condition suffered by polities where extreme and polarised pluralism is rampant (Sartori 2005, 253). Ecuador's so-called 'inchoate' or 'collapsing' party system is representative of such a polity, as solidly entrenched party structures throughout the critical juncture were non-existent (Levitsky and Loxton 2013, 112; Sartori 2005, 217; Yashar 2005, 307). Whilst Pachano agrees with implementing Sartori's category when defining Ecuadorian party politics during the critical juncture, he further augments their fragmented atomised nature to Sartori's definition (Pachano 1996 quoted in Sanchez 2008, 54).

Mejía outlines that Ecuador suffers from one of the most fragmented multi-party systems in the region; a situation that is compounded by the institutional volatility that led to the conflicts and crises that riddled the country during the critical juncture (2002 quoted in Sánchez 2008, 54). Ecuadorian politics can thus be identified by its atomised pluralism, factional or fragmented nature, and sporadic cohesiveness. Characteristics that leave political parties exposed to the unexpected effects of inadequate, or in some cases inexistent, structural consolidation (Sartori 2005, 217). During the critical juncture, the lack of consolidated institutional structures that could discipline party performance brought forth a situation of dispersed political allegiances that, more often than not, led to full-scale institutional crises.

By harbouring a fragmented party system throughout the critical juncture, Ecuador compounded the institutional imbalances stemming from its hyper-presidential system, a constitutional make-up that awards the Andean nation the dubious honour of housing Latin America's most powerful presidents (Helmke 2017, 15). Whilst Ecuadorian presidents indeed enjoyed expansive and overly generous *de jure* powers, their de facto powers, which are to be understood as their ability to form, sustain, and nourish legislative coalitions through political party performance, were weak or non-existent (Helmke 2017). Pervading imbalances between *de jure* and de facto powers exposed Ecuadorian presidents to high levels of political volatility, making them susceptible to legislative gridlock and consecutive policy failures (Helmke 2017; Mejía 2006, 69). Moreover, the inability to secure stable coalitions, discipline party performance, or secure sufficient seats in the legislative branch, led to constant bickering and inter-branch crises. Tensions amongst branches would ultimately lead to nine presidents taking office between 1996 and 2006, as well as twenty-one inter-branch[6] crises from 1985 to 2007 (Helmke 2017, 48–49).

Ecuadorian party politics have thus been divided into three chronological sections. The first spanning from 1978 to 1984 and characterised by the country's transition from dictatorship to democracy, via celebration of democratic elections, a period made possible by regime opening and expansive liberalisation (Sánchez 2008, 42). The second, and longest, spans from 1984 to 1996. During this time party politics adhered to electoral rules and a certain degree of stability, which defined the ways in which the country's main political parties competed amongst each other (Sánchez 2008, 42). The third and final stage spans from 1996 to 2006 and has as its defining characteristic the overhaul of the electoral system to favour elite interests. Through electoral reforms, formation of *ad hoc* political alliances soon followed, leading to the apparition of political movements, increased levels of political volatility, and continuous inter-branch crises (Helmke 2017; Sánchez 2008). This third stage of political consolidation, in which elite interests were favoured, presents a counter-image to the inclusive and participatory origins Good Living apparently stems from. Whilst this stage might help explain why political crises in Ecuador were inevitable, it also detracts from the general understanding that Good Living emerged from a unique moment in time, when constitutional drafting was the result of years of multiparty negotiation or inclusive politics.

From Ecuador's 1979 return to democracy to the referendum that approved its 2008 constitution, the country's political parties faced the pressing inability of securing party base adherence to policy reform (Sánchez 2008, 43). Hence, the economic meltdown that was previously described was combined with the 'descending spiral' of continuous and prolonged political crises that occurred during the critical juncture (Helmke 2017; Mijeski and Beck 2011, 127; Sánchez 2008, 48).

Continuous political crises aborted any form of policy reform that could contain worsening macroeconomic conditions. Institutional instability and inexistent political party cooperation further compounded the policy failures that made civil unrest rampant. Moreover, the nature of Ecuadorian politics during the critical juncture enacted a series of "behind the scenes" political dealings between opposing political factions. Mejía (2006, 69) has labelled these reclusive political cohorts 'ghost coalitions' or the establishment of clandestine legislative agreements between political party leaders who exchange,

---

6 Inter-branch crises refer to confrontation between the executive, legislative or judicial branches of the state. All of which are institutions that exercise the coercive, regulatory or extractive prerogatives of the state.

extend, and demand concessions, patronage or monetary payoffs to instrumentally use their voting powers. One such example of ghost coalitions enacting policy reforms between opposing political parties and competing agendas was the approval of Ecuador's 1998 Constitution. Whilst Pachakutik's political performance as the institutional arm of CONAIE is well documented, its complicity with Ecuador's "traditional political parties" is sometimes forgotten.

Although it was part of the scattered political movements that came together to contest market-led reforms, Pachakutik actively participated in the economic reforms that constitutionalised market liberalisation in Ecuador's 1998 Constitution. Pachakutik's instrumental vote during the 1997 Constitutional Assembly allowed the fragmented coalitions of "traditional" parties to secure the necessary support to constitutionalise privatisation efforts that had taken place six years earlier (Llasag 2012, 133). The importance of this participation, and vote, should be reflected upon, as the 1998 text "legitimised" the unconstitutional privatisations that took place between 1992 and 1996, as well as the legislative reforms that created an electoral system that favoured majoritarian features and allowed coordinated efforts that 'assaulted representation in the name of governability' (Ayala Mora quoted in Negretto 2013, 215; Llasag 2013, 133).

Pachakutik's aiding and abetting of atomised fragmented pluralism would in turn demand the party's adherence to the volatile, contradictory, and socially unpopular multiparty coalitions that became defining features of Ecuador's political arena during the critical juncture (Negretto 2013, 221). In exchange for their strategic vote during the 1997 Constitutional Assembly, Pachakutik secured the proclamation of Ecuador as a multi-ethnic and pluricultural state, as well as the ratification of the International Labor Organization's Indigenous and Tribal Peoples Convention of 1989 (Llasag 2012). In their complicity with atomised pluralism, Pachakutik not only defended, but also voted in favour of, the constitutional reforms drafted by the agro-banking elites of the Andes and coast they had opposed six years earlier (Mejía 2006; Negretto 2015). Ghost coalitions and the atomised politics of the time had secured the necessary constitutional reforms that installed creole market socialism, a form of *capitalismo criollo*, that depended on the powers of a hyper-presidential system that could enact the policy reforms that made financial liberalisation possible (Llasag 2012, 133; Mejía 2006, 73).

Whilst it is widely accepted that democratic institutions require political elites to resolve their differences through bargaining and compromise, the peculiar nature of Ecuadorian politics during the critical juncture defies such generalisations. Rather, political processes during the critical juncture were defined by personal patronage, repartition of entire provinces to political parties or unlimited access to the state's coffers (Helmke 2017, 151; Soifer 2015, 242). Ghost coalition performance during this time was hedged on the informal networks supplanting the debilitated or inexistent mechanisms of institutional policy bargaining (Mejía 2006, 70). These informal networks allowed presidents that had in some cases lost forty percentage points in popularity or reached net negative ratings before completing six months in office, to pass policy reforms against popular demands (Araujo 1998 quoted in Mejía 2006, 71). It is thus no wonder that between 1996 and 1997 Ecuadorian political parties and the legislative branch were widely perceived as the least trustworthy institutions in the country (Negretto 2015).

The personalistic nature of political bargaining allowed political capital to be secured through alliances in which votes would be sold-off to the highest bidder (Sánchez 2008, 49). This personalistic and clientelistic nature of policy negotiation led political decisions to be constantly opposed to the demands of civil society. Through the de-coupling of societal preferences from party politics, the 'reasonable consensus' or 'public reason' that theoretically underpins deliberative democracy was disrupted (Rawls 1995, 147). This constant fissuring of the public sphere would gradually undo the basic tenets that justified civilian submission to political coercion (Dryzek 2002). Ecuadorian politics during the critical juncture became engulfed by personal ambitions dominating political decision-making, a shortcoming that is indicative of an inexistent party line or structure, and evidence of a failing deliberative democracy (Dryzek 2002, 13; Mijeski and Beck 2011, 13). By catering to personal needs rather than institutional bargaining mechanisms, party discipline, or the demands of their corresponding electoral circuits Ecuador's political class became estranged from the political reality facing civil society. The weakness of Ecuador's institutional hardware coupled with the personalistic nature of atomised fragmented pluralism led to a systemic failure in the forms in which deliberative democracy functioned. This would ultimately fuel new forms of deliberation to emerge from those excluded or marginalised from the political machinery (Dryzek 2002, 159; Gargarella 2012, 131).

6 Politicised Ethnic Cleavages: Rise and Fall of Indigenous Mobilisation

Prominence of social group categories in political mobilisations became predominant during the critical juncture. Young (1989, 259) for example, underscores the importance of group categories in the consolidation of emancipatory and leftist social movements due to their mobilisation around identity rather than class or economic interests. Thus, a social group, according to Young, is comprised of persons who identify with one another through particular interpretations of history, understanding of social relations, modes of reasoning, values, or the expressive styles that constitute a group's identity. Latin America had, in varying degrees, averted the consolidation of ethnic-based political movements for the better part of the twentieth century. The demobilised nature of identity politics in the region led political scholars to articulate Latin America as an exception within the cultural pluralism literature; a place where ethnic political debates, mobilisation, and conflict seldomly occurred (Yashar 2005, 4).

For Ecuador, the critical juncture unleashed reservoirs of political energy that had been storing up for centuries. The particular concatenation of events that preceded this epoch in the country's history had also fomented the consolidation of a national movement that in its initial stages reclaimed identity as the central political motif of mobilisation. For example, the unsuccessful land reforms of the 1960s and 1970s had unintentionally led to the politicisation of indigenous peoples (Pallares 2002, 52). The inability to access plots of land for subsistence or retail farming, coupled with the instauration of monetised agricultural communities, forced many indigenous from the Andes to become seasonal migrant workers in the plantations of Ecuador's coastal and Amazonian regions (Radcliffe and Pequeño 2010, 997). Bretón (2010, 57) underlines how this re-organisation of labour throughout the central Andes fractured localised notions of identity based on geographical origin. By fracturing geographically based identity constructions indigenous people began to organise around a nationwide social group agenda.

The conformation of a consolidated social group, built on the fluidity of difference, was further accelerated by the structural racism and discrimination faced by indigenous peoples on a countrywide level (Becker 2011, 48; Bretón 2010; Young 1989, 260). Evidentially, racism was not a geographically localised problem or issue affecting a specific indigenous group at a particular moment in history. It was very much an entrenched social problem with lingering political implications which compounded historic trends of economic segregation, exclusion, and marginalisation (Acosta 2009 quoted in Becker 2011, 29). Entrenched forms of discrimination that, according to a United Nations Seminar on the Effects of Racism and Racial Discrimination, 'destroy the material and spiritual conditions' that maintain a particular way of life, but also imbed forms of 'negative discrimination' that isolate indigenous peoples 'from participating in the dominant society' (quoted in Anaya 2000, 98).

State-sponsored neo-colonialisation of the Amazon enacted through the land reforms of the 1960s and 1970s had successfully mobilised indigenous groups who had until then exercised varying degrees of local autonomy (Yashar 2005, 63). Prior to these reforms, areas where the state's reach had been weak or elusive had allowed indigenous communities to exercise varying degrees of political autonomy, customary systems of governance, and control over natural resources (Yashar 2005). As oil exports rose during the 1960s and 1970s, military control over vast sways of land in the Amazonian oil fields was asserted. The restored coercive reach of the state would lead Shuar indigenous people in the Amazon to mobilise against further encroachment of their territories (Van Cott 1994, 9). Ineffective, and in some cases non-existent, political negotiations between indigenous groups and the state were tell-tale signs of a democratic breakdown that impeded confrontation amongst diverse political identities (Mouffe 2005, 124). The lack of institutional mechanisms that could mediate political differences, or navigate through the structural barriers of racial discrimination, created the necessary conditions for an ethnonationalist movement to brew in Ecuador's Amazon (Mouffe 2005; Selverston-Scher 2001, 80; Van Cott 2008, 115).

Ecuador's return to democracy in 1978, and the subsequent entry into force of the 1979 constitution, produced a sudden change in the country's political constituency. By eliminating literacy requirements, the meagre 18 per cent of the national voting base, that had until then exercised the privilege of political rights, was suddenly swollen (Rice 2012, 61). This sudden change to the political arena was capitalised on by the left and centre left through the integration of indigenous cohorts into their ranks (Mijeski and Beck 2011, 13). In 1979, the birth of the Organization of Indigenous Peoples of Pastaza (OPIP) was soon followed by their association to the Shuar Federation and the formation of the Confederation of Indigenous Nationalities of the Ecuadorian Amazon (CONFENAIE), the first transprovincial indigenous organisation in the region (Mijeski and Beck 2011, 13).

Efforts to consolidate mobilisation in the Amazon often differed from the organisational trends of the Andes. As early as the 1940s, government assimilation policies set in place through *Indigenismo* had forced Andean indigenous to organise as peasants (Van Cott 1994, 5). The emergence of the Andean *Federación Ecuatoriana de Indios*[7] (FEI) was a political initiative that brought together socialists, peasants, communists, and indigenous people of the Andes in an effort to unite the scattered political forces of Ecuador's rural communities (Becker and Tutillo 2009, 133). FEI would become Ecuador's first political attempt in constructing a national organisation by and for indigenous (Becker and Tutillo 2009, 133). Unfortunately, FEI's Marxist-inspired horizontal

---

7   Indian Federation of Ecuador

organisation and deeply rooted ties to the Communist Party led to political disappointments, as indigenous were viewed from the class dichotomies of the time, often leading many to label them as 'the peasant arm of the Party' (Becker and Tutillo 2009, 145; Rice 2012, 58; Yashar 2005, 100). The focus was thus not on identity but on the Ecuadorian Communist Party's class-based political agenda, effectively displacing ethnic concerns in favour of rural workers' rights (Becker and Tutillo 2009, 152). FEI would nevertheless be a prominent indigenous organisation in Ecuador's Andes for the next thirty years, up until the birth of ECUARUNARI[8] in 1972 (Yashar 2005, 58).

In sharp contrast to the events that took place in the Andes, Amazonian Indians had exhibited no need to politically mobilise until the 1960s when oil explorations were abruptly accelerated (Mijeski and Beck 2011, 14). CONFENAIE emerged from the distinct processes of oil-induced land colonisation that took place in Ecuador during the 1960s and 1970s. Having enjoyed relative isolation from the violence of colonial expansion that took place in the Andes, Amazonian indigenous now faced the perils of expanding oil frontiers and the social impacts that came with it (Petras and Veltmeyer 2005, 244). Renewed colonisation through state-sponsored land grabbing now placed Amazonian indigenous people, transnational capital, and developmental public policies on a collision course. Transcripts from a 1980 congress that took place in the Amazonian city of Puyo are testament of the demands of the time. Central to the efforts of organised resistance were demands for territorial rights against oil and mining, as well as the recognition of cultural rights that paved the way for the Ecuadorian state to recognise the status of distinct nationalities amongst indigenous communities (CONAIE 1989 quoted in Llasag 2012, 118). The emerging influence of CONFENAIE on Ecuadorian indigenous movements soon renewed the prevailing political agendas of the Andes. Rather than solely focusing on land, the new political agenda steered towards, land, culture, and territory. Political agendas also shifted from securing equality to establishing collective rights that granted autonomy from the central state (Yashar 2005, 109).

By the mid-1980s, Ecuador's indigenous movement would consolidate under a composition of ECUARUNARI and CONFENAIE, which would ultimately lead to the birth of CONAIE (Confederation of Indigenous Nationalities of Ecuador) (Yashar 2005, 24). CONAIE would follow the social movement activism of the time by forwarding questions of identity. This sharp turn in indigenous political agenda setting surpassed the underlining class conflict inherent to the political projects sought by communists, socialists or the marriage of Christian dogmas with the revolutionary agendas underlined in Liberation

---

8   Awakening of the Ecuadorian Indian

Theology (Ibañez Langolis 1984, 29; Mijeski and Beck 2011, 23;). Other important indigenous organisations that consolidated during this time were the National Confederation of Peasant, Indigenous, and Black Organizations (FENOCIN) and the Ecuadorian Evangelical Indigenous Federation (FEINE) (Becker 2013, 50; Lucero 2006, 33). In time, both FENOCIN and FEINE, would shift their earlier sectorial class demands in favour of strong ethnic rights and territorial autonomy (Van Cott 2005,109).

According to Rice (2012), this gradual process of emerging ethnic political demands evidenced the various ways in which indigenous organisations slowly drifted from the class struggles that had been previously forwarded by FEI. This shift now favoured an ethnonationalist agenda constructed by CONFENAIE, and a new political project centred on securing territorial autonomy for the preservation of collective rights (Rice 2012; Selverston-Scher 2001, 80–81). Yashar (2005, 65) attributes the consolidation of an ethnonationalist agenda to the relative isolation enjoyed by Amazonian Indians during and after the colony, a unique occurrence that permeated future political discussions between Amazonian and Andean indigenous peoples. Whilst a certain distance was marked with class-based political demands, Andean upward social mobility politics still managed to merge with Amazonian ethnonationalist agendas, spawning what Rice (2012, 117–18), following della Porta (2009, 84) and Tarrow (2005, 73), called a new 'political master frame'; a successful interweaving of ethnocultural demands with popular resentment towards the socio-economic policies prior to and since the 1980s. New political agendas forwarded by indigenous organisations would leverage on a surging *neo-Indigenismo* that had been brewing since 1972.

Dismissing the assimilationist nature inherent in the *Indigenismo* of the previous thirty years, this new *Indigenismo* had two main objectives. The first was to engage with indigenous as subjects rather than objects and, in so doing, rally respect towards cultural difference (Pallares 2002, 188). As subjects, indigenous could freely associate and participate in the planning of their development, thereby becoming active members of the polity (Pallares 2002). Such a shift would ultimately constitute a significant step in the changing of citizenship regimes that ensued during the critical juncture (Yashar 2005). Secondly, it called for the nation-state to recognise its endorsement of cultural ethnocide, and in so doing, create the policy spaces from which indigenous populations could be plurilingual, pluricultural, and plurinational (Pallares 2002, 188).

Underscoring the importance of CONAIE's consolidation as an ethnically diverse, yet politically unified social group during the 1980s, is paramount to understanding the political upheavals that engulfed Ecuador during the 1990s.

As the new decade began, the political forces that had been brewing throughout the Andes and Amazon reached a boiling point. Alliances that had been weak or inexistent in the past began to consolidate as indigenous organisations rallied support from non-indigenous peasants, urban intellectuals, and international organisations (Sawyer 2004, 163). According to Perreault (2003, 339), indigenous organisations such as CONAIE, CONFENAIE, and OPIP began to shape political debates in Ecuador by challenging official state conceptions of citizenship, the nation, and indigenous claims over territorial rights. Formation of a unified indigenous political agenda led to the 1990 uprising where Quichua, Shiwiar and Achuar indigenous demanded land titles in the Pastaza province (Radcliffe and Westwood 1996, 134). This coordinated political effort of resistance evidenced the different ways in which indigenous political projects were consolidating and slowly becoming active (Benavides 2004, 142).

The 1990 uprising would prove to be a watershed moment in Ecuador's history, as OPIP militants marched from the Amazonian lowlands to the Andean plains of Quito demanding immediate titling of their collective lands (Mijeski and Beck 2011, 17; Van Cott 2005, 111). The magnitude of the uprising swiftly paralysed Ecuador, as road blockades and the suspension of food provisions made "modern" urban centres come to an abrupt halt (Mijeski and Beck 2011). By 1992 Ecuadorian Indians would take part in the hemispheric-wide mobilisations that protested state-sponsored celebrations of the 500th anniversary of Spanish colonial arrival to Latin American shores (Van Cott 2005, 111). Whilst symbolic in nature, boycotting of celebrations reaffirmed widespread sentiments against state-sponsored endorsement of 'the manipulation and utilisation of history' that 'started with the European invasion of our continent'; a process that left 'the history of Indian peoples, of the oppressed peoples' hidden or simply denied (Maldonado 1992 quoted in Benavides 2004, 142).

Following the Zapatista mobilisations in Mexico months earlier, by June 1994 Ecuador's peasant and indigenous organisations, under the leadership of CONAIE, mobilised to counter and protest legislative reforms that sought to privatise communally held land (Becker 2011, 36). Transforming communal land into a marketable commodity would have ended thirty years of partially successful land reform (Becker 2011). More importantly, attacking communal rural land holdings ignited new waves of contention against the state and its economic reform programs.

Neoliberal reforms during the 1990s were aided by the ghost coalitions that defined the executive and legislative dealings of the time (Mejía 2006, 82). Secretive dealings amongst rival political factions, within all levels of government, allowed for widely unpopular policy reforms to be introduced intensifying the estrangement of political power from its electoral constituencies.

Ultimately, mobilisation would pay off, as CONAIE effectively forced the Durán-Ballén government to the negotiating table and successfully demanded that communal lands become immune to further divisions (Llasag 2012, 127; Sawyer 2004, 183). This triumph would cement the indigenous movements political capital, granting it the national profile it required to position its demands and become the umbrella organisation under which collective action could consolidate against the state, economic reform, and worsening socio-economic conditions.

Social mobilisation would become a tool of political predilection throughout the 1990s, as a multiplicity of social groups flocked to CONAIE's leadership to protest salary cuts, welfare shrinkages, electricity outages, and the waves of privatisation that were legitimised by the 1998 constitution (Collins 2004, 40; Mijeski and Beck 2011). Ironically, these market-led measures had been made possible through CONAIE's political arm, as it was Pachakutik's vote during the 1997 Constitutional Assembly that tilted the scale towards privatisation. In any case, citizen mobilisation and collective action made progressive factions within Latin America's legal community conceptualise protest as an expressive component of deliberative democracy; a reshaping of the public sphere where marginalised and excluded groups resort to extra-judicial means to denounce social injustice (Dryzek 2000, 20; Gargarella 2012, 134).

Consolidation of CONAIE's political agenda had allowed it to construct a new political master frame that interweaved ethnocultural demands with historic reclamations for social justice. The economic reforms that were engulfing Latin America and Ecuador during the 1990s, as well as the political chaos that began to sweep through the country as the decade ended, further crystallised CONAIE's political dominance. The new political master frame allowed CONAIE to commandeer nationwide protests throughout the 1990s and early 2000s (Rice 2012, 117–18). (See Figure 4.)

Following the success of organised protests, electoral reforms that had taken place in 1994 allowed CONAIE to foster a political coalition that defeated then president Durán-Ballén's call to referendum. This triumph allowed the harnessing of the necessary political leverage for Pachakutik to become an active political force during the 1996 presidential elections (Mijeski and Beck 2011). Whilst CONAIE and Pachakutik apparently represented the same political agenda, divisions within its ranks began to create fissures that would undo a decade of successful political mobilisations. Pachakutik for example, had been launched against the wishes of the Andean faction of CONAIE. Amazonian indigenous leaders had unilaterally agreed to form a political arm under the name of *Movimiento de Unidad Plurinacional Pachakutik–Nuevo País* or Pachakutik (Gerlach 2003, 128). The newly formed political player rapidly became

FIGURE 4 Protesters battle security forces in an attempt to storm the Presidential Palace in 1997
PHOTO CREDIT: *EL COMERCIO*, 4 OCTOBER 2014 (ACCESSED 22 MAY 2018): HTTP://WWW.ELCOMERCIO.COM/ACTUALIDAD/PROTESTA-CIUDADANA-DESCONTENTO-GOBIERNOS-30S.HTML

the third most successful option in Ecuadorian politics, drawing support towards its horizontal, democratic, and inclusionary nature (Becker 2008,184). Although political support flocked to the new party, this had been achieved by creating serious fissures to the cohesiveness that had previously existed amongst Andean and Amazonian factions. Political timing and favourable circumstances would lead other indigenous organisations to re-brand themselves to attract larger sways of public support. Rival FENOCIN for example, would re-organise itself by 1995 expanding its strictly peasant and unionist discourse in order to position an ethnic political agenda that demanded sustainable development, equality, and democracy through interculturality (FENOCIN 1999 quoted in Altmann 2015, 176).

CONAIE consolidated a political agenda that demanded the preservation of culture through the legal protection of difference. Strategic leveraging on the nationwide mobilisations that it had come to commandeer throughout the 1990s allowed it to position the political agendas of the time. The reconceptualisation of political agendas, based on 'equally weighing legal differences,'[9] sought to guarantee cultural expressions of identity by securing

---

9 The translation is mine.

their affirmation via recognition of difference (Ferrajoli 2013, 159). The need to consider difference sought to denounce the implicit truths nestled within the dictums of liberal democracies, whereby a persons or groups admittance into the public sphere depended on the legal prohibition of any one social group having the ability to claim special rights or elicit differential treatment. This non-difference requirement, and the subsequent assimilationist undertones imbedded therein, were actively denounced during the protests and meetings that were once spearheaded by Ecuador's indigenous movement (Llasag 2012; Sawyer 2004; Young 1989, 251).

Indigenous groups adamantly exalted the forms in which discrimination, particular historical events or each social group's cultural expressions demanded a differentiated treatment before the law (Sawyer 2004, 199; Young 1989, 251). Introduction of a differentiated rights perspective allowed a person or groups' identity to be granted legal value, protecting the differences that makes an individual or social group diverse in relation to others (Ferrajoli 2013). This shift in Ecuador's indigenous political agenda underlines Young's (1989, 251) assertion that social movements of the oppressed, seek to assert pride in group specificity by questioning whether law and policy should enforce equal treatment for all. Social protest denouncing equal treatment before the law laid the groundwork from which differentiated citizenship was later constructed. Through these new forms of differentiated citizenship, centuries of assimilationist policies and the myth of a homogenous national identity was contested, repudiated or reformed.

Political consolidation by 1996 allowed Pachakutik to become the third largest political force in congress. During this same time CONAIE had effectively capitalised on the avenues theorised within the political process model (PPM), whereby civil society mobilisation consolidates political opportunities through newly opened channels of collective action agency (Llasag 2012, 129; Rice 2012). Political opportunity, and collective action's capitalisation of it, is understood as the moment in which absence of institutionalised channels of representation, containment of state repression, fractions amongst political elites, and the presence of newly available allies allows political mobilisation to occur (McAdam et al. 1996 quoted in Rice 2012, 24). The critical juncture's convergence of: (1) a retreating or weak state; (2) the estrangement of political elites with their peers and constituencies; (3) the harnessing of national support through a new political master frame; and (4) the agency mustered by nationwide protests allowed CONAIE to capitalise on the political opportunities that emerged throughout the 1990s.

These political opportunities, however, are not to be understood as compelling determinates that "made" mobilisation occur, but rather as constitutive conditions that in a given point in time—a critical juncture if you will—mobilised a sufficiently large number of people. Collective action was thus only viable once political opportunities and lingering threats to a sufficiently large number of people were enforced, combining the necessary circumstances for nationwide mobilisation to occur (McAdam 1999). During Ecuador's critical juncture, the convergence of draconian economic reforms, state retreat, political party chaos, and the reformulation of pre-existing citizenship regimes paved the way for CONAIE and Pachakutik to commandeer a political master frame that united dispersed social groups. As McAdam states, the 'embedded collaborative meaning-making' that underlines civil society mobilisation considers the relevant local history, culture, and politics to determine the ways in which internal and external forces promote collective action in a specific moment in time (McAdam, 1999, xii).

Pachakutik's first political success would be the 1996 triumph that secured them 10 per cent of all congressional seats, as well as an additional 76 elected positions in various levels of government (Mijeski and Beck 2011, 50). The demise of the Bucaram presidency (1996–1997) opened new political avenues that unified different strains within CONAIE and Pachakutik, particularly the looming constitutional reform that had been recently approved through referendum, forced factions to collaborate with each other (Llasag 2012; Mijeski and Beck 2011, 52). One of CONAIE's central demands to the Constitutional Assembly of 1997 was the recognition of Ecuador as a multicultural and multinational state (Mijeski and Beck 2011, 52). CONAIE was thus able to present its demands through the seven representatives it had secured through popular elections (Van Cott 2005, 125). As they levied their demands for collective rights and territorial autonomy, the ghost coalitions of the time exchanged their support for liberal multiculturalism whilst securing further financial liberalisation and the legitimatisation of state-owned asset privatisation (Llasag 2012; Mijeski and Beck 2011, 53).

The 1998 elections however posed a political problem for Pachakutik. Aware of the relative success indigenous mobilisation had garnished at the voting poles, a conservative controlled congress was quick to pass election law reforms that expanded the size of the legislative body to 121 seats, as well as introduced open list voting (Mijeski and Beck 2011, 55). More significant however, was the fact that seat assignment was now reformed in order to assign positions on the basis of the number of votes individual candidates accumulated; a strategy that secured larger party dominance over congress (Mijeski and Beck 2011). Ultimately, the new electoral rules left Pachakutik with a meagre 6 per cent of all congressional seats (Mijeski and Beck 2011). Legislative manoeuvring to weaken Pachakutik's political success would cost ghost coalitions dearly, as consolidation of further collective action would bring parliamentary processes to a stand-still.

Following the 1997 elections, Jamil Mahuad was inaugurated as president on 10 August 1998. His ill-fated presidency would be defined by the looming economic troubles that had been left unattended during previous years, as well as the collusive policy measures he sanctioned during his term (Gerlach 2003: 123). Mahuad's incompetent management of the financial system, his wilful submission to elite interests, the desperate dollarisation of Ecuador's economy, and growing social discontent eventually led to his ousting from office. CONAIE president Antonio Vargas spearheaded the 2000 coup d'état that ended Mahuad's term as indigenous politics, uniting with Coronel Lucio Gutiérrez and former Supreme Court President Carlos Solórzano to momentarily seize executive power by storming Congress (Becker 2008, 186). (See Figure 5.)

CONAIE had effectively colluded with conservative political parties and mid-level military officers in order to secure the fleeting control of the presidency, a precarious move that was quickly reversed, as high ranking military officials soon replaced Gutiérrez ending the triumvirate's hold on power (Becker 2008). Pachakutik's involvement in the coup weakened its political prominence as former allies now criticised how the party resorted to traditional party practices to secure its presence and political dominance (Van Cott 2005, 131). Pachakutik's allegiance with Coronel Lucio Gutiérrez's anti-system, anti-neoliberal, and anti-political discourse during the 2000 coup would be the beginning of an ill-fated relationship that ended a few years later (Dávalos 2014,

FIGURE 5   Antonio Vargas, Lucio Gutiérrez and Carlos Solórzano (first row from right to left) seize power in Ecuador's Congress on 22 January 2000
PHOTO CREDIT: *EL TELÉGRAFO*, 21 NOVEMBER 2016 (ACCESSED 22 MAY 2018):
HTTPS://WWW.ELTELEGRAFO.COM.EC/NOTICIAS/HISTORIAS/1/
EN-UN-DIA-SE-PRECIPITO-EL-DERROCAMIENTO-PRESIDENCIAL

57). The January 2000 coup closed not only a decade, but also a century, in which indigenous people had successfully reconfigured Ecuador's political arena by redefining political agendas and leveraging on civil society mobilisation to insert their demands (Becker 2008, 188).

After Mahuad's Vice-President Gustavo Noboa ended his term, Coronel Gutiérrez assumed the Ecuadorian presidency in 2003, securing an allegiance with Pachakutik and a wider populist left that rejected IMF policies and promoted racial and class agendas (Becker 2008). However, Mijeski and Beck (2011, 83) have suggested that Gutiérrez would have won without indigenous support, as Pachakutik's internal conflicts and its political dealings with conservative political parties had severely weakened the civil society support they could muster. Whatever influence Pachakutik support had on Gutiérrez's ability of securing the presidency, rifts in the alliance were soon made evident as the president shifted his political discourse towards a market friendly approach that favoured IMF intervention (Mijeski and Beck 2011). The final breaking point was reached in mid-2003 when government handling of strikes and its dealings with the IMF led to Pachakutik's refusal to support a bill that would have modified public sector contracts. Gutiérrez quickly responded by dismissing all cabinet positions assigned to Pachakutik members, effectively ending the crumbling alliance (Zamosc 2009, 280). The rupturing of this weak tit-for-tat alliance brought further divisions within CONAIE and Pachakutik, as Amazonian groups criticised the rupturing and Andean cohorts denounced the delay in breaking with the Gutiérrez administration (El Comercio 2003 quoted in Zamosc 2009, 280). Internal divisions, public bickering, and allegiances with former political rivals, had significantly weakened CONAIE's ability to rally support for civil society mobilisations that could counter Gutiérrez's unpopular policies (Mijeski and Beck 2011, 94). This inability was further compounded as Pachakutik began to create alliances with former enemies to block Gutiérrez in Congress (Mijeski and Beck 2011, 98).

Spontaneous civil society mobilisation through the emerging *"forajido"* movement, came to replace CONAIE's dominance as the gravitational centre of improvised street politics. Without a particular organisation, leader or movement to guide its actions, the alleged seventy thousand strong yet visibly improvised "forajido" movement, denounced Gutiérrez's siding with the IMF (Llasag 2012, 146). Eventually, the *"forajidos"* would lead the coup that ended the Gutiérrez presidency and appointed his Vice President as the new head of state (Llasag 2012, 146). The newly appointed President Alfredo Palacio would nominate a young and politically inexperienced academic as his new Minister of Finance. The new member of cabinet was Minister Rafael Correa who only served four months in office before resigning due to programmatic differences with the Palacio administration's economic policy. CONAIE would openly support Correa for his stance against IMF austerity measures and what he determined was an illegitimate repayment of a dubiously contracted foreign debt (Mijeski and Beck 2011). Correa would respond by offering CONAIE leader Luis Macas the vice-presidential position on the ticket in his run for office.

Once Correa secured the Ecuadorian presidency in 2006, Pachakutik supported his call for a Constitutional Assembly in exchange for the reforms they had worked on since Ecuador's return to democratic governance in 1979. As Mijeski and Beck (2011, 119) underline, Pachakutik got the constitutional reform it wanted at the price of appointing a modern-day caudillo that secured 80 per cent of all votes needed to approve a Constitutional Assembly. Political negotiations by a debilitated indigenous movement granted the newly appointed Constitutional Assembly full legal powers to reform institutions and laws through *mandatos constitutyentes* or constitutional mandates. Through Constitutional Mandate No. 1 for example, the Constitutional Assembly granted itself the legal capabilities to promulgate a vast range of legal documents such as laws, accords, resolutions and all other decisions needed to fulfil its attributions, going so far as to state that:

> The decisions of the Constitutional Assembly are hierarchically superior to any other norm in the legal system and are mandatory to all persons, natural or juridical, as well as all public powers without exception. No decision from the Constitutional Assembly can be submitted to control or impugnation by any of the constitutive powers. Any judge or tribunal that processes a claim against the decisions of the Constitutional Assembly will be removed from office and subjected to the corresponding legal procedures. In the same manner, public servants that are involved or promote, through action or omission, contempt against the decisions of the Constitutional Assembly will be sanctioned (Constitutional Mandate No. 1, Art. 2).[10]

By 2007, Correa had secured 63 per cent of all necessary votes needed to approve the constitution that was drafted by the full powers of the Constitutional Assembly. Meanwhile, Pachakutik gradually witnessed the eclipse of its political might as polling surveys made it clear that what was once a political force to be reckoned with was now barely able to gather a famished 2 per cent of national votes (Mijseki and Beck 2011, 120). Moreover, the widespread belief that indigenous constituencies flock to ethnic parties was subverted. As Mijeski

---

10   The translation is mine.

and Beck (2011, 110) have pointed out, indigenous people are preoccupied with land and material wellbeing rather than multiculturalism. Through the usage of the Ecological Inference Method to analyse individual behaviours from group-level data, Mijeski and Beck (2011, 130) state that Pachakutik's poor performance in voting patterns can be determined from shifts in voting towards class-based demands rather than ethnic agendas.

Analysing the different processes that converged through the critical juncture dissects the trinity of discourses that have been associated with Good Living, questioning not only their substance but their very nature. In all, the politicised ethnic cleavages that had successfully united and mobilised Ecuador's peasants, urban poor, feminists, and intellectuals fell prey to the very ailments that had gutted the country's "traditional" political parties (Becker 2008, 186). Convergence of ghost coalitions, atomistic pluralism, sectarian interests, and the back-alley agenda settings that prioritised ethnonationalist demands over its once successful political master frame of the 1990s, came together to dismantle what had once been Ecuador's and Latin America's, strongest and most organised ethnic movement. By the time the 2008 constitution had been drafted and approved, ethnic politics in Ecuador had fallen prey to the political miscalculations that drained its support base and strained its ability to call on nationwide mobilisations. These now politically defused transgressive subjects ended the critical juncture with their political might thwarted and a new constitution that allegedly met the various political demands levied through the once successful master frame of the 1990s. Of the various "promises" of social justice embedded in the newly approved constitutional text, Good Living prominently stood out as the underlying principle that would (allegedly) reverse decades, if not centuries, of racism, social injustice, and environmental destruction.

7 Changing Citizenship Regimes

Changing citizenship regimes during the critical juncture called into question the basic tenets that had defined "classic" conceptions of state sovereignty. Specifically, the converging forces that gave birth to the critical juncture now defied widely accepted notions of a territorially bounded sovereignty, as well as the policy tools through which the state governs the polity. Longstanding citizenship regimes, and the political structures they perpetuated, crumbled as the forces of economic reform, political chaos, and state dismantling converged to redefine Ecuador's political arena. Moreover, the coming together of universal political rights, differentiated citizenship regimes, the discourse of human rights, and the outsourcing of sovereign decisions via multilayered governance, redefined political participation during Ecuador's critical juncture (McNevin 2011; Wotipka and Ramírez 2008; Yashar 2005; Young 1989). Most significantly, the citizenship regimes that had been enforced through territorially bounded sovereignty were called into question throughout the 1980s and 1990s. The emergence of new citizenship regimes, premised on market principles, as well as the redefinition of the state through graduated sovereignty, allowed transnational civil society, and its institutions, to fill the policy spaces left by Ecuador's retreating state. These new citizenship regimes of transnationally active, market-friendly individuals eventually descended upon Ecuador's indigenous communities, effectively merging ethnic-based political demands with market-led self-development.

The imposition of citizenship regimes upon a territorially bounded population had represented a hallmark of state sovereignty (Kostakopolou 2008, 26). In its most "classic" understanding, sovereignty was the exercise of absolute and indivisible jurisdictional authority over a territory and people (Anghie 2007, 56; Keal 2008, 323). Adding to this understanding, Foucault (2007) argues that state power is best exemplified as a form of 'pastoral governance' that underlines the exercise of sovereign prerogatives by guiding a population towards a desired end, this management of the population in line with policies or objectives encapsulates the concept of biopolitics. Or more clearly put:

> The theme was to have been "biopolitics," by which I meant the attempt, starting from the eighteenth century, to rationalize the problems posed to governmental practice by phenomena characteristic of a set of living beings forming a population: health, hygiene, birth rate, life expectancy, race ...We know the increasing importance of these problems since the nineteenth century, and the political and economic issues they have raised up to the present (Foucault 2008, 317).

Thus, the French philosopher equated the exercise of state sovereignty to a 'shepherds' power' that steered 'the flock of men' (Foucault 2007, 125). Consequently, this so-called pastoral governance depended on techniques that facilitated the 'government of men' and the enforcement of the disciplining powers of the state (Foucault 2007, 383).

Citizenship regimes, and their ability to grant or restrict access to the polity, exemplify these disciplining techniques that Foucault assembled under what he called the 'art of government' (Foucault 2007, 335). More simply put, citizenship regimes can be understood as techniques of government that allow the state to carve out specific domains of power relations that either perpetuate or disrupt the direction of human conduct (Foucault 2007, 388). In pre-critical juncture Ecuador, citizenship regimes had strategically bounded power relations in order to restrict admittance, control mobility or avoid the transformability of the polity. As such, Ecuador's citizenship regimes exemplified Foucault's concept of governmentality by expressing a regime of power that had the population as its target and the state's security apparatuses as its essential technical instrument of enforcement (Foucault 2007, 388).

Citizenship regimes therefore were one of the metaphorical "paintbrushes" through which the art of government was exercised, as it facilitated the government of men by excluding all those who did not fit the idealised conditionalities that granted admittance to the political realm (Yashar 2005, 35). Idealised citizenship regimes were built on the normative beliefs authored by Aristotle or J.S. Mill in the sense that they pre-determined the requisites that allegedly attested to the capability and sufficient reasoning necessary to calculate the general will of the people (Yashar 2005, 36). In Ecuador, these limited notions of citizenship had excluded large percentages of the population from the political sphere. Similar to what happened elsewhere, Ecuador's first constitutional text of 1830 reserved political participation for white, wealthy, male, landowners (Kostakopolou 2008, 24; Yashar 2005, 35).

The return to democratic rule in 1979, and the constitutional provisions that derogated conditional citizenship, redefined Ecuador's political sphere by redefining citizen capabilities. Particularly, the lifting of literacy as a conditioning requirement for the exercise of political rights proved to be a profoundly democratic provision nestled within the 1979 constitution. Universal citizenship thus paved the way for a proportionally larger electoral base to change the political spectrum (Verdesoto 2003, 145). By subverting pre-existing citizenship regimes, Ecuador's 1979 Constitution challenged the racial projects of methodological nationalism that had been in place since the country's independence. Moreover, the 1994 electoral reforms that followed allowed independents to run for office, further corroding the once restricted political participation of idealised citizenship (Becker 2011, 45).

The critical juncture's effect on citizenship regimes in Latin America has been well documented by previous scholarship. Particularly, it was Deborah Yashar's work on indigenous movements during the 1980s and 1990s that brought to light how the imposition of what she called 'neoliberal citizenship regimes' redefined the political arenas of Ecuador, Peru, and Bolivia (2005, 49). Ecuador would figure prominently in her study, as the country housed the region's most organised and mobilised indigenous population during this period. More importantly, the subversion of state-led corporatist practices in favour of pluralist interest group politics, legitimised the universally granted and individually exercised human rights discourse that surged during this time. By creating a multiplicity of small interest groups, a 'free-for-all' competition founded on the premises of liberal political pluralism was inaugurated, creating a political arena set on sectorial agendas and uncoordinated lobbying before the government (Lijphart 2012, 16). This sharp redefining of Ecuador's political sphere reversed the political ensembles that had consolidated throughout Latin America during the first half of the twentieth century (Lijphart 2012, 168; Pallares 2002, 190).

Such a reversal of political arrangements disrupted the tightly knit and largely immobile corporatist structure of medieval bonds that had, until then, defined political association in Ecuador (Pallares 2002; Sartori 2005, 13;). Through the imposition of a 'thoroughgoing individualism,' corporatist citizenship regimes and their co-option by the once interventionist state gave way to neoliberal regimes that threatened the local autonomy of indigenous enclaves (Bretón 2008, 602; Pallares 2002, 190; Sartori 2005). It is precisely this threatening of local autonomy that led Yashar (2005, 34) to argue that 'the erosion of prior citizenship regimes throughout Latin America unwittingly challenged local autonomy, thereby politicising indigenous communities in new ways.'

Changing citizenship regimes effectively mobilised the indigenous communities of the Amazon and Andes, thereby fuelling demands for revised citizenship and the inauguration of a multicultural Ecuador. Moreover, classic notions of sovereignty would now have to accommodate demands for a differentiated citizenship premised on heterogeneous social group demands (Yashar 2005, 32, Young 1989, 258). These newly created political spaces allowed ethnonationalist discourses to emerge, thereby including indigenous demands for a differentiated legal treatment and territorial autonomy to seep into political debates (Becker 2008, 179; Pacari 1984, 115 quoted in Altman 2014, 85). The disruption of corporatist citizenship, and the local autonomy it had previously sponsored, allowed a new neoliberal citizenship to emerge. Loss of local autonomy would lead the once previously demobilised ethnic cleavages to demand a reconfiguration of state sovereignty through differentiated citizenship regimes.

If indeed the mobilisation of indigenous groups inaugurated a new period in Ecuadorian and Latin American politics, their mobilisation only attests to a fraction of the profound changes that defined the emergence of so-called neoliberal citizenship regimes. In this sense, the emergence of a politicised ethnic cleavage, whilst significant in its redefining of Ecuadorian politics, does not fully explain how and why neoliberal citizenship regimes redefined the country's political arena in broader terms. More importantly, it impedes the development of a theoretical premise that may shed light on how changing citizenship regimes, and their concatenation to politicised ethnic cleavages and a retreating state, ultimately led to the inscription of Good Living in Ecuador's 2008 Constitution. It is this theoretical vacuum we address at this time.

By building on Yashar's work on contested citizenship in Latin America, we argue that changing citizenship regimes in Ecuador allowed for a redefining of state sovereignty that ultimately mobilised civil society around a new transnational neoliberal citizenship. This new form of citizenship, premised on the universal dictums of human rights and multilayered governance, effectively linked local demands with a transnational governmentality that made social, economic, and legal reforms possible (Andolina et al. 2009, 80). Once coupled with the policy spaces left by the elusive state and the crumbling of Ecuador's political and economic spheres, a new transnational governmentality redefined how the citizen, state, and international community interacted.

Two main areas of interest will be the focus of the remaining paragraphs. Firstly, how a new form of citizenship was formed, one in which the promises of a 'civic virtue' redefined the aspirations of the now transgressive and mobilised polity. This new civic virtue, premised on market-based conditionalities, effectively disciplined the population to the necessities of liberalisation. This configuration of a market-based citizenship was aided by the deployment of transnational agents and institutions that advocated the need for self-help agency and social capital as the guiding maxims that interconnect communal networks. Secondly, we address how shifting paradigms in international law, the irruption of multilevel governance, and the subsequent adaptation of the region's constitutional regimes, displaced the once interventionist state, ultimately consolidating the emerging transnational governmentalities that redefined citizen-state relationships through the civic virtues of market-based conditionality.

7.1 The Quest for Civic Virtue

Our first point of entry will be the redefining of citizenship regimes during the critical juncture. To aid in this effort we turn to the work of Will Kymlicka who identified two points that help us analyse how citizenship was redefined prior to and during the critical juncture. In his work on citizenship in culturally diverse societies, Kymlicka (2003, 6) underlines that in the 1970s and 1980s the so-called basic structure of society was understood to be formed by constitutional rights, political decision-making procedures, and the functioning of social institutions. However, by the 1990s, political theorists refocused their attention on the identity and conduct of individual citizens, particularly paying attention to how their responsibilities, loyalties, and roles were to be defined

(Kymlicka 2003, 6). Shifts in scholarship presented new theories on how individual citizens should act by reimagining the citizenship regimes of the time.

This "new" theory of citizenship, according to Kymlicka, was to be formed around Robert Putnam's 1993 *Making Democracy Work*. In his revision on democracy in Italy, Putnam states that differences in what he called 'civic virtue' is the casual link that determines the success or failure of regional governments (Kymlicka 2003). The alleged differences in the civic virtue of a given community are thus attributable to the fluctuating social capital nestled within them. Social capital came to be understood as the ability to trust, willingness to participate, and sense of justice that defines a particular social network or community (Kymlicka 2003). Moreover, social capital was defined by the norms of reciprocity and networks of civil engagement that underline the civic virtue that was missing in previous theories regarding the basic structure of society (Burki and Perry 1998, 124 quoted in Bedford 2009, 41). This form of market-orientated social capital would soon become the predominant mantra that legitimised international development interventions by its agents or institutions. The World Bank for example, became increasingly interested in social capital, viewing it as a way of sustaining rural communities and restoring the social fabric that had been dislocated by the economic restructuring of the 1980s and 1990s (Bedford 2009, 41). According to this particular take on civic virtue, the "best" schools of citizenship were the voluntary associations and organisations of civil society, particularly those integrated by ethnic and religious groups (Kymlicka 2003, 8).

Civic virtue was erected upon Putnam's idealisation of social capital and the deployment of international development agencies during the post-Washington consensus era. This new idealisation of civic virtue leads us to Veronica Schild's 1998 revision of *Market Citizenship in New Democracies* (Bedford 2009, 41). In her analysis of Chile's women's movement, Schild addresses how the shifting dynamics of citizenship regimes during the 1990s led to citizenship 'being constructed through an appeal to new selves'; a reimaging of the self, fundamentally premised on autonomy, self-sufficiency, discipline and participation in the market (1998, 233). Schild's critical reading of citizenship regimes correlates to Putnam's understanding of social capital as a concept that is premised on individual agents capitalising on social networks through their investments in the market (Somers 2005, 242). Citizenship regimes during the critical juncture were built on a reimagining of the self, a new civic virtue that demanded individuals capitalise on the social networks that surrounded them. With the introduction of notions such as autonomy, self-sufficiency, and solidarity the welfare policy spaces once occupied by the state were now appropriated by NGOs, religious communities, and civil society in general. The corporatist practices that came with an interventionist state were thus replaced by the actions of individual agents capitalising on the reserve stock of social capital around them.

According to Schild (1998, 233), these cultural transformations paved the way for a new form of citizenship to emerge, one in which neoliberalism and the market subverted subaltern discourses for emancipation and empowerment. This "subversion" is our first point of interest. As will be explored in further detail in subsequent chapters, we propose that the emergence of a new market-based citizenship, founded on the principles of social capital and self-help agency, altered the transgressive political projects forwarded by Ecuador's mobilised citizenry. Specifically, the deployment of agents and institutions like the World Bank, bilateral development agencies, and transnational NGOs legitimised the new social network savvy citizen; an individually framed participant that capitalised on the solidarity of civil society. This new form of empowerment through self-development and social solidarity, constructed a political practice susceptible of appropriation by linking essentialised notions of identity construction with market-based ideals that emphasise autonomy and individuality (Schild 1998).

In Ecuador, changing citizenship regimes were defined by the work of the transnational agents that came to occupy the policy spaces left by the state. In so doing, the technocratic approach of NGOs, intellectuals, bilateral development agencies, and international financial institutions constructed essentialised, and in many cases idealised, representations of the necessities and aspirations of those who they were allegedly representing (Recasens 2014, 63). As will be explored in the next chapter, this particular entanglement of transgressive political projects with the emerging technocratic governmentalities of transnational agents configured the newly formed citizenship regimes under market-based premises. This framing of citizenship regimes through transnational development agents builds on the work of Andolina, Radcliffe and Laurie (2009). In their revision of development projects in the Ecuadorian Andes during the critical juncture, the authors identify the consolidation of a multiethnic transnational community of policymaking institutions, advocacy organisations, and ethnic social movements (Andolina et al. 2009, 223).

This coming together of scattered actors under a transnational political process of market-based development, allowed malleable concepts to affect the issues and networks formed through transgressive civil society mobilisation. In Ecuador, this mobilisation was most invasive as the emerging indigenous movements that flourished during the critical juncture became absorbed by the interventions and development projects of multilateral institutions and its agents. Bretón (2001; 2005) has often highlighted the dynamic of penetration that multilateral donors achieved within indigenous communities. For example, when analyzing the correlation between development NGOs present in indigenous communities, Bretón (2001, 141) states that:

> The obtained results are revealing in that they confirm, with obvious precision, tendencies mentioned earlier. One can, without a doubt, affirm the existence of a direct relation between the spatial concentration of important contingencies of indigenous population and the preference of development NGOs of setting up their development projects within those spaces. It is thus remarkable that out of thirteen shires that have a high presence of development NGOs, ten of them come first in regards to rural populations with indigenous presence: we refer to Riobamba (Chimborazo), Guaranda (Bolívar), Colta (Chimborazo), Otavalo (Imbabura), Cuenca (Azuay), Cayambe (Pichincha), Guamote (Chimborazo), Alausí (Chimborazo), Cañar (Cañar) y Latacunga (Cotopaxi). What this translates into is a correlation of 76.9% (...) those ten shires, represent the maximum concentration of NGO interventions in the rural Andes where more than half of the population living there is predominantly indigenous (51.7% to be exact); an indicator of the importance these organizations assign to indigenous populations when they define them as a priority target population in their pro-development projects in rural settings.[11]

---

11   The translation is mine. Original text (Bretón 2001, 141): Los resultados obtenidos son harto reveladores y vienen a confirmar, obvia- mente con mucha más precisión, las tendencias apuntadas al principio. Se constata fehacientemente, de entrada, la existencia de una relación directa entre la concentración espacial de importantes contingentes de población india y la preferencia por parte de las ONGD para concretar preferentemente allí sus proyectos de desarrollo (mapas 2 y 3). Es remarcable en este sentido el hecho de que, de los trece cantones caracterizados por una alta confluencia de ONGD, diez figuren también entre los trece primeros en cuanto a población rural que habita en API: nos referimos a Riobamba (Chimborazo), Guaranda (Bolívar), Colta (Chimborazo), Otavalo (Imbabura), Cuenca (Azuay), Cayambe (Pichin- cha), Guamote (Chimborazo), Alausí (Chimborazo), Cañar (Cañar) y Latacunga (Cotopaxi). Esto supone una correlación del orden del 76,9%. Debe tenerse en cuenta, por otra parte, que del cuadro 4.5 se desprende que en esos diez cantones –que, insistimos en ello, representan la máxima concentración de intervenciones de organizaciones no gubernamentales en el medio rural andino– se concentra también más de la mitad de la totalidad de la población radicada en zonas predominantemente indígenas (concretamente el 51,7%); un indica- dor más de hasta qué punto es importante para esas organizaciones tomar a la población indígena como sujeto prioritario de sus acciones en pro del desarrollo rural.

Development NGO interventions within indigenous communities would also be analysed by other authors such as Andolina (et al. 2009); Laurie (et al. 2005); Radcliffe (et al. 2004); Cepek (2012) and Sawyer (2004). The complex networks setup by multilateral organizations to enact their development projects, are highlighted by Ben Fine (2001, 142), as he depicts how social capital became the World Bank's go to concept when defining rural initiatives:

> Ethnicity is seen in terms of diversity and difference for which inner organization and bridging spin-offs have to be set against the potential for conflict. The crucial point is that each of the areas covered under each of these last two themes has long, contested and rich intellectual traditions. These are effectively sacrificed in order to import social capital as an organising concept. It is particularly disturbing, in the context of social capital as elsewhere in World Bank literature, how ethnicity has become reduced to a range of stereotypes, either as clever mutually trusting entrepreneurs or, as groups, engaging in conflict with one another.

According to Andolina et al. (2009, 229), development operators viewed indigenous cultures as a bundle of assets that could be harnessed for market-led growth. By coupling the ideals of an emerging neoliberal civic virtue with the relational communitarian models of indigenous communities, a new form of development allegedly emerged; one premised on the social capital networks of Andean rural communities (Andolina et al. 2009, 230).

This emerging neoliberal citizenship regime was thus legitimised when it was coupled with the transgressive political projects of indigenous people. As one of the main receptors of international funds for development during the critical juncture, indigenous communities such as those located in Riobamba, Guaranda, Colta, Otavalo, Cuenca, Cayambe, Guamote, Alausí, Cañar, Latacunga or Pastaza, became the testing ground for new market-led citizenship regimes that coupled ethnicity with entrepreneurship (Bretón 2001, 141; Sawyer 2004, 211). With the formulation of essentialised notions of life in indigenous communities and their merger with the language of social capital, the market-ready citizen was now legitimised. Moreover, it is in this coupling of indigenous identities with neoliberal citizenship regimes that the proto-conceptual discourse formation of Good Living first emerges. Social capital, once deployed in Ecuador's Andes, alluded to the millinery nature of Andean cultures, the inherent civic value of their ethnic organisations, and the market readiness of their social networks. Much like the discourses that formed around Good Living in post-2008 Ecuador, social capital made life in indigenous communities the flagship asset from which a project determined on shaping the future could be achieved by rediscovering idealised notions of the past (Sánchez Parga 2011, 32). The Andean chapter of market-based civic virtue had struck fertile ground in Ecuador's indigenous communities. Through the construction of an idealised representation of life in the Andes, the main tenets of civic virtue theorised by Putnam could be translocated from Italy to Ecuador. Such 'theoretical promiscuity' created a readily available neoliberal citizen that would now capitalise on the millenary social capital that was once forgotten but had remained nestled within the Andean rural communities of Ecuador (Somers 2005, 233).

7.2 Constitutional Convergence and Graduated Sovereignty

The second and final point of interest in the redefining of citizenship regimes is comprised of the many ways in which local, regional, and international legal institutions were transformed during the critical juncture. Evidently it would be foolish, and time consuming, to construct a chronological order of the multiplicity of legal developments that redefined international, regional, and local law in Ecuador and Latin America during the critical juncture. Rather, what is proposed is to pinpoint specific occurrences that redefined how citizenship was exercised, and in so doing, showcase how these changes debilitated the once all-powerful sovereignty of the state. Through treaty imposed graduated sovereignty and domestic acceptance of intervention programs, newly opened policy spaces further corroded citizen-state relations. Our interest in these changes is to underline how the coming together of politicised ethnic cleavages and collective action, was made possible through state retreat. As the state contracted, new policy spaces allowed a transnational community of actors and institutions to challenge the once impregnable space of sovereign authority. These changes are of special importance in the consolidation of Good Living, as they give way to the transnational networks and institutions that redefined domestic law. Redefinition of Ecuador's legal system converged with the newly forming neoliberal citizenship of the time, consolidating a political framework built on human rights, market-led social capital, and transnational institutions. These three converging master narratives of the neoliberal order that came to be during the critical juncture, created the totalising framings of universal truths that were later distilled into the three main discourses of Good Living.

Legal changes pertaining to human rights, citizenship, and the sovereign power of the state created structural openings for transnational actors to occupy the domestic policy spaces left by the retreating state. This "neoliberal civic virtue" was further legitimised by the merger of human rights with economic liberalisation within Andean communities. Adopting the "scripts of modernity" of human rights and economic liberalisation into the economic development programs that legitimised intervention of rural communities, further consolidated civic virtue through the ethnic lens. This initial discourse formation of Good Living not only legitimised intervention of rural communities by transnational actors but also defused the most transgressive features of indigenous political mobilisation in Ecuador. Civic virtue in Ecuador's Andes created a citizen-subject that was tamed by the market-based discourses of entrepreneurship, solidarity, and social capital networks. Ultimately, these processes form the discursive origins of what later came to be distilled into Good Living when it became an abstract legal principle. This critical take on Good Living's origins contests the discursive association it has received regarding the millenary practices of indigenous communities. Indeed, Good Living did emerge from Ecuador's rural communities, it simply did so in ways that vastly diverge from the idealised notions authors like Ramírez, Acosta, Oviedo or Gudynas have been so adamant on defending.

To be clear, what is proposed in this section is that through the distinct changes that occurred in international and domestic law, the once all-powerful state came to be replaced by the predominating "scripts of modernity." With the aid of a new transnational institutional hardware, collective rights and trade liberalisation opened policy spaces that had previously been zealously guarded by the Order and Progress state. This in turn created a new citizen-subject premised on the metanarratives of human rights and economic liberalisation. Intervention of these narratives in Ecuador's rural communities would in time lead to the discursive formation that crystallised as Good Living. To better understand this process, we further develop how these metanarratives led to Good Livings discursive formation.

7.3 Diffusion and the Scripts of Modernity

We begin this section by turning to Wotipka and Ramírez's remarks on sociology's World Society School. We use their analysis to better understand the theoretical landscape on which Ecuador's critical juncture reforms were premised. In their analysis of state interdependence within a world society perspective, the authors outline that nation-states are 'increasingly constructed from and influenced by world models of progress and justice' (Wotipka and Ramírez 2008, 312). Moreover, the horizontal influence these universalistic model's layout is increasingly associated with the defining features which award nation-statehood. As such, adherents to World Society School, 'claim that international human rights norms are scripts of modernity' that legitimate the dominant ideas within a given world system at the particular moment of their creation (Elkins et al. 2013, 64). Adding to these comments we turn to Elkins and Simmons' (2005) and their study on policy diffusion. In their analysis of diffusion as uncoordinated interdependence, they outline that policy reform often leads nation-states to choose similar institutions and policy prescriptions within circumscribed spatial clusters. Diffusion is thus an outcome whereby the actions and choices of one country directly, and indirectly, affect another through uncoordinated policy convergence.

However, the outcome is not attributable to party collaboration or the 'otherwise programmed effort on the part of any actor' (Elkins and Simmons 2005, 6). Rather, governments are independent in making their own decisions without cooperation or coercion, thus they simply factor in the choices of other governments through uncoordinated interdependence (Elkins and Simmons 2005). More importantly, in our search for the origins of Good Living, this uncoordinated interdependence is the result of clustered decisions resulting from economic shock, as well as cultural or institutional similarities (Elkins and Simmons 2005, 3). In other words, during the critical juncture Latin America housed the three necessary conditions that theoretically lead to uncoordinated interdependence through diffusion. As such, not only did domestic and international legal regimes eventually converge but the institutional hardware setup to enforce the new legal landscape was also horizontally integrated through various forms of graduated sovereignty. Ultimately, the scripts of modernity pertaining to human rights and neoliberal citizenship were imprinted throughout Latin America and Ecuador, as a result of the policy and institutional diffusion that came with the critical juncture's economic shocks and the facilitated avenues created by cultural and institutional similarities within the region.

Another way of understanding this event is the coming together of a transnational governmentality that laid out the defining features of policy and institutional reforms during the critical juncture. Human rights, the treaties that made them law, and the institutions set out to enforce their fulfilment, came to life as the political arena was redefined by a convergence of transnational actors and networks. If indeed the safeguarding of human rights redefined state prerogatives before its citizen's, another important occurrence during the critical juncture was the market-led liberalisation of Latin America. In an effort to homogenise and standardise commercial policy on a planetary scale, the birth of the World Trade Organization in 1994 further forced the retraction of state policy by granting supranational actors authority opinions over the future of domestic policy decisions. Rather than scoping the entire landscape of international agreements that came to be during the critical juncture we turn to two different events that illustrate how human rights, trade liberalisation, and their corresponding institutional hardware redefined citizenship regimes through a weakening of the "classic" notions of sovereignty.

The first of these occurrences is the prominent role that began to be occupied by the Inter–American Human Rights System (IAHRS) and how its jurisprudence streamed to the domestic legal realms of the region. The second point reviews how the General Agreement on Tariffs and Trade of 1994 (GATT) redefined state sovereignty in strategic areas of commercial policy. In all, these structural changes to how the state exercised its sovereign prerogatives opened new policy spaces during the critical juncture. These two distinct yet converging forces redefined how policy decisions were to be exercised by the state, and in so doing, reformed the policy spaces and structural openings available to citizens.

8 The Inter-American Human Rights System

As legal scholars Gargarella and Gonzalez-Bertomeu (2016) state, 'any commentary on the state of affairs' regarding human rights adjudication in Latin America would be 'incomplete if it did not acknowledge the impact' exerted by the Inter-American Court of Human Rights (the Court) and the Inter-American Commission of Human Rights. Both of these institutions were spawned from the American Convention on Human Rights or "Pact of San José de Costa Rica" of 22 November 1969 (American Convention). Ecuador became a signatory to the convention on 27 October 1977 but waited until 6 August 1984 to ratify it before the Organization of American States (OAS). For our purposes we zoom in on the supranational jurisdictional capabilities of the Court and the wide jurisdictional scope it was awarded through Articles 62 and 63 of the American Convention. Whilst procedures before the Court depends on a state's acceptance, the Court expansively exercised this contentious jurisdiction during the critical juncture, attesting to the willingness of Latin American governments to yield to the power of the supranational organ.

The Court effectively showcases the 'extraordinary transformation' that took place in Latin America in the past decades as international human rights law seeped into the domestic legal realms (Gargarella 2013, 168). This adherence to international law is apparently motivated by the new political attitude that embraced the 'globalisation of law' during the critical juncture (Gargarella 2013, 169). The Court itself has traversed through different periods. Whilst its first years of practice focused on the transgression of civil and political rights by authoritarian regimes, the Court's interest later swayed towards a multiplicity of subject matters such as economic, social, and cultural rights (Gargarella and González-Bertomeu 2016). Being the final interpreter of the American

Convention, the Court holds, through its binding decisions, the power to shape the contours that make-up the law of the land throughout Latin America (Gargarella and González-Bertomeu 2016). Moreover, during the last decades, the Court has come to finetuning its jurisprudence effectively consolidating the binding nature of its decisions and their compulsory power upon signatories of the American Convention (García-Sayán 2011, 1836).

This monist adherence of supranational human rights treaties with domestic legislation has reshaped legal practice throughout the region. More importantly, it has set new limits and obligations upon Latin American states, effectively reshaping the "classic" notions of sovereignty that had defined state practice for centuries. Latin America's uncoordinated interdependence regarding international human rights throughout the critical juncture was propelled by the binding power of the Court's decisions. This in turn allowed human rights to become the 'exemplary characteristic' of Latin American constitutionalism (Burgorgue-Larsen 2014, 21). Signatories of the American Convention accepted international human rights standards as well as the substantive criteria emanating from the Court (García-Sayán 2011). This process of international and domestic convergence through uncoordinated interdependence harmonised domestic law and constitutions on a regional level (García-Sayán 2011, 1837). Effectively, the Court attained a maturity that allowed it to exercise a developing case-law, which is now 'the juridical patrimony of the countries and peoples of the American continent' (Cançado Trinidade 2003, 2).

Underlining some relevant jurisprudence of the Court regarding economic, social, and cultural rights highlights its relationship to what was later inscribed in Good Living's constitutional birth. Jurisprudential revision highlights some of the main topics that have caught the interest of the Court and the ways in which domestic judicial instances have been mandated to enact them. This process of supranational jurisdiction fusing with domestic legislation exemplifies how the discourse of human rights went from the international sphere to the political agendas that guided civil society mobilisation during the critical juncture. This cascading effect of human rights is of the upmost importance in the origins of Good Living, as it became inevitably tied with the political motivations that shaped it as a constitutional principle set to secure housing, education, healthcare, culture, and the environment. Good Living's constitutional inscription is the culmination of a domestic adaptation of the supranational jurisprudence, policy prescription, and institutional diffusion that took place during the critical juncture. Moreover, Ecuador's 2008 Constitution epitomises the fusion of international human rights law, economic liberalisation, and constitutional convergence on a regional level.

8.1 Selected Jurisprudence: Vida Digna

With regards to cultural rights, the Court's solid jurisprudence has outlined three standards that define indigenous rights throughout Latin America. These standards review indigenous collective property over territory, the securement of prior, free and informed consent, and the obligations member states have in terms of guaranteeing political participation by indigenous people (Ramírez and Maisley 2016, 193). The cascading effect of these standards has effectively obliged Suriname, Nicaragua, and Ecuador (amongst others) to comply with the Court's jurisdictional authority over the American Convention (Ramírez and Maisley 2016, 193). Showcasing the convergence of treaty law with domestic practice, Ecuador's Constitutional Court has effectively upheld the compulsory nature of the Court's standards regarding prior, free, and informed consent.[12]

In regard to economic and social rights, the Court's doctrine on *Vida Digna* is worthy of mention. The strength of this doctrine is its theoretical substantiation on the American Conventions wording regarding the right to life. The Court has built its jurisprudence on economic and social rights, through a theoretical interconnectedness with the right to life nestled in Article 4 of the American Convention. Through this jurisprudence, Latin American states have been obliged to secure the right to life through public policy measures that provide basic public services. Through its 'configurative principle of several rights,' the Court has created an interdependent array of minimum standards that demand procurement of basic services such as water, health care, education, housing, and preservation of cultural identity (Antkowiak 2014, 129). Conjoining the right to life of the American Convention with the doctrinal development of *Vida Digna* has created a series of legal protections regarding social development, non-discrimination, collectively owned territories, resources, and the safeguarding of cultural integrity throughout Latin America (Antkowiak 2014, 114). The Court's jurisprudence on economic, social, and cultural rights has created legal waves that have been felt in Colombia, Peru, Paraguay, Argentina, Costa Rica, and Guatemala, to name a few (Parra Vera 2016).

8.2 The Graduated Sovereignty of the GATT

The waves of economic liberalisation that engulfed Latin America during the critical juncture effectively reshaped the ways in which domestic policy decisions were enacted. The consolidation of the WTO effectively allocated graduated sovereignty upon supranational organs. Once again, the redefinition of

---

12 Ecuador. Corte Constitucional del Ecuador para el Periodo de Transición [Sentencia No. 001-10-SIN-CC] 2010.

state sovereignty had effectively reshaped the ways in which Ecuador's political arena operated. By displacing the state's ability to barter economic policy decisions with domestic lobby groups, the corporatist nature of Ecuador's political arena was once again fractured. This effectively exposed policy decisions to transnational entities that enforced economic liberalisation through the diffusion of institutional and policy networks on a global scale. By 1994, the GATT had been signed and ratified by 128 states, this effectively gave the WTO oversight over a substantial portion of the world's economic output (WTO 2017). In its essence, the GATT is a series of complex multilateral arrangements that expand trade liberalisation by binding state policy to supranational agreements. This effectively limits the possible effects regular elections (the democratic process), which are themselves defined by short-run gains (political favour), may have in disrupting the flow of goods and services (Abbott 1985, 503). Rules governing the WTO are thus drawn from public choice theory, which suggests that 'the metric welfare of each signatory' of the GATT is the domestic political welfare that may be drawn from obeying the rules.

The underlying principle in this "Prisoner's Dilemma" based theory is that, through cooperation, contracting states will enhance the economic welfare of all involved. In theory, what this means is that defection amongst member states is penalised as it would deplete the alleged welfare of all member states. Abbott (1985) suggests that WTO rules give way to a balancing effect between private and public interests by restraining national autonomy in the pursuit of the "greater good" of trade liberalisation. In other words, the WTO system resolves the dominant strategy in the Prisoner's Dilemma scenario by craftily favouring cooperation for the (apparent) economic welfare enhancement of all (Armingeon et al. 2011, 89). Consequently, in theory, GATT regulations should present market efficient solutions that seek the common welfare of WTO member states by limiting national policy autonomy (Abbott 195, 520). An additional feature of the world trade system are the powers awarded to the Dispute Settlement Body (DSB). This supranational entity is effectively entrusted with reviewing domestic policy and assuring its compliance with WTO law (Palmeter et al. 2002, 647; Sebastian 2007, 341).

Once again, the forces that reshaped Ecuador's political arena also altered the ways in which economic policy was to be defined. Stripping the state's ability to formulate inward-directed economic policies allowed the WTO to create a form of graduated sovereignty that displaced governments by favouring the script of modernity that was forwarded by trade liberalisation. Our interest in this occurrence is that it further corroborates the redefinition of citizen-state relations. By implanting a form of graduated sovereignty, with regards to economic policy, the state was effectively displaced. This displacement further underlines the fact that classic notions of sovereignty were indeed disrupted or transformed during the critical juncture. This ceding of sovereign terrain by the once all-powerful Ecuadorian state effectively rattled the political structure and economic policies that had defined citizen-state relations up until this point. This disciplining of rogue states through retaliatory trade measures demonstrates that the institutional and policy diffusion that took place during the critical juncture displaced the centres of sovereign power. By the time Ecuador's 2008 Constitution was enacted, a complex network of actors and institutions had redefined citizen-state relations by subduing them to the transnational governmentalities that came with the scripts of modernity.

9 Conclusion

The focus of this chapter has been on the convergence of apparently dispersed and unrelated occurrences, prior to, and during the critical juncture. The section has presented the three occurrences of politicised ethnic cleavages, a retreating state and changing citizenship regimes to do so. Moreover, theoretical development of these converging occurrences has underscored their importance and prominence during the critical juncture. Developing their empirical relevance to theoretical discussions aids us in constructing a critical lens from which Good Living may be analysed.

As a series of interpretable events, these three converging occurrences substantiate our discussion that the current trinity of Good Living has failed to assess, beyond a superficial level, the complex processes that transpired during the critical juncture and ultimately led to the 2008 constitution. The case study presented here seeks new avenues of theoretical discussion regarding Good Living and its applicability. The next section presents the final layer of analysis that completes our revision of Good Living. Having positioned the relevant events that came with the critical juncture, the next section develops the theoretical umbrella from which Good Living emerges. Through the theoretical premise of floating and empty signifiers, Good Living is presented as a discourse that stems from the scripts of modernity and the converging forces of politicised ethnic cleavages, state retreat, and changing citizenship regimes.

CHAPTER 4

The Polymorphism of Good Living

Previous chapters have presented the overall occurrences that took place during Ecuador's critical juncture and have reviewed the theoretical framings that place Good Living as a by-product of the social, economic, and political events that transpired between 1979 and 2008. They have also developed a critical approach towards Good Living in order to shed new theoretical insights to its study and reframe its understanding and origins. Prior to engaging with the subject matter of the present chapter, let us recapitulate some of the main points covered up until now. Firstly, we analysed a period of Ecuador's history labelled as a critical juncture, a spatiotemporal context in which profound changes to agent preferences and institutional dynamics created structural openings that expanded the plausible choices of political actors. Secondly, we saw that during the critical juncture convergence of politicised ethnic cleavages, a retreating state, and changing citizenship regimes made way for a series of processes that led to an outcome of interest. This "outcome of interest" was the emergence of Good Living as a new legal principle in Ecuador's 2008 Constitution. Thirdly, we saw that Good Living, as a legal principle or better yet a political discourse, stands upon three divergent currents that can broadly be labelled as socialist/statist, Indigenist/Pachamama or ecologist/post-developmental.

All of these processes and their emergence during the critical juncture are bounded by the theoretical framings posited in Foucault's work on governmentality and Dryzek's discursive democracy. Whilst the former constructs governmentality as the technologies of governance utilised to discipline the population by leading it towards a desired end; the latter explains how the convergence of unique processes during the critical juncture, particularly politicised ethnic cleavages, a retreating state and changing citizenship regimes, allowed new forms of politics to emerge through collective action. These forms of collective action, through protest, fall far from the procedural or judicial forms of deliberative democracy theorised by Habermas or Rawls. For this reason, Dryzek's discursive democracy allows us to overcome such limitations by presenting the alternative forms of deliberation that came together in the consolidation of Ecuadorian politics during the critical juncture.

Previous chapters have also traced the processes, actors, and events that converged during the critical juncture, presenting a new contextual form of analysis towards Good Living. Consequently, exploration of the alleged origins and currents that have underlined Good Living allows us to further develop and advance the new theoretical grounds for explaining the points of divergence and convergence that come together in the Indigenist, post-development or statist discourses that emerged since 2008. Consolidating new forms of analysis allows us to engage with the first central point of this chapter.

In an effort to circumvent the competing explanations that have engulfed Good Living until now, the critical approach presented here focuses on an inductive form of reasoning that sidesteps the deductive stances framed by statist, Indigenist or post-developmental strains. Guided by theory, this form of process tracing and its inductive reasoning accepts that Good Living is a constitutional principle; however, it questions whether its existence should be taken for granted. What this translates into is that only through theoretical analysis, premised on the occurrences that led to constitutional inclusion, can Good Living's origins, impact, and future be determined. This form of theoretically premised inductive reasoning is intent on overcoming the deductive form of analysis proposed by writers such as Acosta, Ramírez, Gudynas or Oviedo in regard to Good Living. Whilst divergent in their opinions towards Good Living, all of the previously cited authors in one way or another accept Good Living's *"a priori"* existence, presenting their analysis or interpretations without questioning the process that led to the object of analysis. Theory-guided process tracing has been selected, not only for its inductive power but also because it is a methodology that allows us to consolidate a theory-building process (Trampusch and Palier 2016, 443).

Stated differently, the selected methodology and enacted frames of Good Living analyse the temporal and causal sequence of events that led to its constitutional inclusion. This process is therefore conceptualised both theoretically and operationally with reference to previous theories that allow us to understand an outcome when we are unsure of the causes that led to it (Trampusch and Palier 2016). This methodology therefore capitalises on theories such as Foucault's knowledge–power nexus to state that Good Living is the convergence of a set of practices with a regime of truth; a form of discourse formation that came together to carve out in reality that which did not previously exist (Foucault 2004, 19). In other words, by focusing on the exercise of power during the critical juncture we construct new theoretical approaches towards Good Living.

The critical approach here presented builds on existing theories to explain the origins of Good Living. Large parts of current scholarship on Good Living is bounded by its deductive form of reasoning, failing to provide, or assess, alternate theoretical explanations to Good Living's origins. This oversight in theoretical construction is what this book seeks to overcome. To do so, previous chapters have outlined the various competing theoretical currents that have attempted to create statist, Indigenist or post-development discourses of Good Living. In order to create a counter explanation, the critical strain of Good Living introduced seeks to provide new theoretical explanations. The basic tenet of this critical stance is constructed upon analytical opposition to the totalising and essentialist undertones contained within idealised notions of Good Living. Good Living as a discourse which blends, merges and fuses at times contradicting conceptual levels, promises meagre solutions to the multiple problems affecting indigenous communities, the urban poor or peasants in Ecuador's Andes, coast or Amazon (Parga 2011, 31). In the case of indigenous rights for example, the quest for securing collective rights over territories operating on varying levels of autonomy has been the quest of indigenous groups in Latin America, Australia, Canada, United States and New Zealand (Gallegos-Anda 2009, 358). James Anaya (2000, 78), former United Nations Special Rapporteur on the Rights of Indigenous Peoples, considers this quest in the following terms:

> Although self-determination presumptively benefits all human beings, its linkage with the term peoples in international instruments indicates the collective or group character of the principle. Self-determination is concerned with human beings, not simply as individuals with autonomous will but more as social creatures engaged in the constitution and functioning of communities. In its plain meaning, the term peoples undoubtedly embraces the multitude of indigenous groups like the Maori, the Miskito, and the Navajo, which comprise distinct communities, each with its own social, cultural, and political attributes richly rooted in history (...) The difficulty is in the underlying view that only such units of human aggregation—the whole of the population of an independent state or a colonial territory entitled to independent statehood—are beneficiaries of self-determination. This conception renders self-determination inapplicable to the vast number of substate groups whose claims represent many of the world's most pressing problems in the postcolonial age. And by effectively denying a priori a right of self-determination to groups that in many instances passionately assert it as a basis for their demands, this limited conception may serve to inflame tensions. Moreover, as will be argued, an effectively state-centered conception of self-determination is anachronistic in a world in which state boundaries mean less and less and are by no means coextensive with all relevant spheres of community.

Construction of a critical approach towards Good Living, translates into a new analytical scope on the origins of the concept as a legal principle. This exercise departs from the multiple legal struggles faced by ethnic minorities or the urban and rural poor. As indigenous peoples fought over collective land rights and autonomy, urban populations sought legal remedy to exclusionary policies and laws. As Parra-Varea (2016, 148) argues when analysing the protection of social rights in Latin America, public policy shifted upon a positive dimension that was to guarantee a fundamental right so it could be progressively carried in order to ensure the effective enjoyment of the right that additionally incorporates mechanisms of stakeholder participation. Furthermore, Parra-Varea (2016, 155) determines that Latin American courts gradually prohibited the use of regressive measures that could affect social rights by weighing the prohibition of retrogression against all underlying interests and principles applicable to a specific case.

In this sense, Good Living as a constitutional article is analysed in light of local and international reclamations relating to economic, social and cultural rights. In this manner, the proposed critical lens seeks to depart from the loosely-knit ontological stances that Good Living has been associated with such as Pachasofía (Estermann 2012); deep ecology (Gudynas 2009) and ethnodevelopment (Villalba 2013). Departing from what Somers (2005) called 'theoretically promiscuous' explanations, leveraged on decontextualised historical contexts, grants the theoretical space to construct a critical approach that avoids the transformation of events into timeless myths. These theoretically promiscuous representations of economic, social, legal or political events, according to Parga (2011, 33), have no use for theory or practice, as they legitimate an endless rhetoric of alterity that is wanting of critical analysis.

Agreement with Somers and Parga's comments creates our starting point for this chapter, as it consolidates critical Good Living's proposition that prior to the critical juncture no such concept or discourse existed. Rather, what is proposed by the critical strain constructed throughout this book, is that Good Living came into existence as a by-product of the governmentalities, political processes, legal transformations and social dynamics that surfaced during a specific juncture in Ecuador's history. This critical strain departs from the evolution of domestic legislation and international norms relating to economic, social and cultural rights as well as the converging historical and temporal events that underlined changing citizenship regimes, politicized ethnic cleavages and a retreating state. Analysing how the power dynamics of an increasingly retreating state transformed collective demands, allows us to develop a similar analysis to the one described below for Colombia:

New notions of property rights-such as environmentally-protected areas, collective property for indigenous and Afro-Colombian groups, and informal possession arrangements-have met resistance from formalistic, rigid definitions of property that have remained mostly unchanged since 1887. In both the historical evolution and recent history, the constitutional distributive impulse has been weakened by establishing rigid, time-consuming, and elaborate administrative and judicial procedures (García 2011, 1912).

From a methodological point of view, this critical strain presents a counter explanation to the three predominating theoretical currents engulfing Good Living. Not only does this liberate analysis from the perils of deductive reasoning but it also allows us to explore new avenues that may create a theoretically robust analysis of Good Living, one that overcomes what Acosta (quoted in Fernández et al. 2014) has already pointed out:

> ...in Ecuador, as I have noted, what has existed is the usage of Good Living as a marketing tool, although there have been certain advances on a technocratic level...however for now, I believe that debate is still limited, especially on an academic level...[1]

Once liberated from mystical idealisations or essentialised representation, we may further explore the broader theoretical engagements explained in previous chapters, as well as the new theoretical considerations that will be introduced in the following paragraphs. We are thus left to answer: why did Good Living emerge, as it did, if predominating explanations on its origins are in fact inaccurate?

Finally, analysis of the contextual events and occurrences of the time grants other advantages. Contrary to previous attempts of explaining Good Living's sources through neo-Aristotelian, pre-Columbian or deep ecology frameworks, denying its existence prior to 2008 liberates us from such decontextualised analysis. This is of the upmost importance, as the clear ontological bent currently engulfing Good Living stands in contrast to the lack of anthropological, political, legal or sociological studies engaging with its theoretical analysis (González and Vázquez 2015, 2). Critical approaches towards Good Living introduces power as the main theoretical point of departure. Through its insertion, a new theoretical frame is constructed, one that seeks to understand the

---

[1] The translation is mine.

converging power relations that shaped the discourses that came to be represented in Good Living predominating strains. Power and its formation of the discourses that shaped Ecuador's reality presents a new theoretical analysis of Good Living, one that seeks to uncover the agents, institutions, and forces that pacified transgressive politics during the critical juncture.

Introduction of the power–knowledge nexus and the consolidation of the *dispositif* or general apparatus relocates analysis of Good Living from epistemological current or ontological premise, to the actors, administrative mechanisms, and ultimate objectives that underlined the programs of intervention executed in Ecuador during the critical juncture. This chapter is thus laid out in the following order. The first section reviews how a new form of governmentality surfaced during the critical juncture. Immediately after, we discuss the emergence of a new knowledge–power nexus through Foucault's exploration of biopolitics and the *dispositif*. Thirdly, we shall review the ways in which social capital, as the civic virtue that constructed discourses of intervention, became the new theme for societal governance during the critical juncture. We then move to review how social capital mutated into ethnodevelopment in order to legitimise NGO intervention and market-based logics in the rural Andes, seeping into indigenous communities. The fourth section discusses how the master framing of transgressive politics created ripe conditions for multiple subversive discourses to be bundled under a homogenising discursive construct or "empty signifier." The fifth and final section reviews Good Living's conformation as an empty signifier.

1   The New Governmentality

Previous scholarship has dedicated lengthy and detailed analysis to the utilisation of governmentality as a conceptual bridge that enquires the many ways in which the neoliberal reforms that were deployed in Latin America during the 1990s, redefined the ways in which political agents and structural conditions were interwoven. Examples of this may be found in the work of Hale (2002), Andolina et al. (2009), Bretón (2001; 2005; 2008), Laurie et al. (2005) or Schild (1998). All these authors share, to a greater or lesser extent, Foucault's work on governmentality. Rather than reiterating what has already been covered by these authors, we resituate theoretical analysis within the events that immediately preceded the approval of Ecuador's 2008 Constitution. Through the previously cited authors, analysis of Good Living is framed under new theoretical insights brought from Foucault's work on governmentality and biopolitics. Governmentality and discursive democracy, forge a new theoretical premise that frames analysis of Good Living through power relations and the contextual analysis that is constructed by theoretically-guided process tracing.

Previous chapters have already dealt with the specific contextual settings that defined Ecuador's critical juncture. For this reason, we need only to recapitulate that the critical juncture was defined by the convergence of politicised ethnic cleavages, a retreating state and changing citizenship regimes. Politicised ethnic cleavages effectively inaugurated an arena of contention towards the prevailing political economic arrangements that had, until then, attempted to redesign Ecuador in the image of liberal societies. The politicisation of previously subdued political subjects was made possible by the structural adjustments of the 1980s, as they reshaped or erased the once interventionist state and its corporatist policies. Constraining the role of the state, as mediator of social conflict and ethnic tensions, unleashed a reservoir of political energy. Collective action was commonplace, however the social movement that best capitalised on the effervescent political landscape of the time was the nascent indigenous movement that consolidated in 1986. By fortune or merit, the changing international landscape that consolidated in the late 1980s forged enabling conditions that allowed a newly formed indigenous movement to capitalise on redefined political, economic and social conditions.

Newly defined citizenship regimes in the 1990s further allowed the indigenous movement to capitalise on the weakened sovereignty of the state, strategically utilise the human rights discourse, and present new policy options regarding cultural rights. This process of constitutional convergence towards the protection of economic, social, and cultural rights mimics the processes that took place in other Latin American jurisdictions. The explosion of international NGOs operating in Ecuador between the 1980s and mid-1990s, framed domestic political mobilisation as a response to the transnational interlinkages that came from economic reform and expanding human rights protections. Policy spaces once zealously controlled by the state now became the battlefield of a transnational civil society competing for the resources that flowed from multilateral development institutions like the World Bank or the development agencies of European governments.

Ecuador's critical juncture gave way to a new form of governmental rationality, one that affirmed the displacement of a retreating state by forging a style of biopolitics that was now being formulated through the interventions of international development institutions. These policies of intervention, and the newly developed forms of transnational governmentality they enabled, created a highly active transnational civil society that would in time influence major policy decisions on a domestic level. This new form of transnational policy construction, and its enforcement on a domestic level, consolidates

Good Living as the result of a transnational form of governmentality that was shaped by a knowledge–power nexus that merged economic reforms with ethnic collective action. Contentions between domestic politics and transnational governmentality define Ecuador's critical juncture as a complex web of actors, institutions, transgressive politics and new forms of policy construction. Such processes have been covered in previous sections but may be further scrutinised through the work of Sawyer (2004), Andolina et al. (2009), Dávalos (2003), Yashar (2005) or Cepek (2012).

Theory-guided process tracing, and its theory-building capabilities, affords us the necessary tools to conduct a more profound analysis of Good Living from which this complex interconnection may be better understood. Analysing the convergence and theoretical importance of these forces situates politicised ethnic cleavages, a retreating state, and changing citizenship regimes as the main points of reference when analysing Good Living's origins. Past scholarship by Conaghan et al. (1990), Larrea and North (1997) or Lind (2005) have presented theoretical grounds that explain how neoliberal reforms transformed institutions, fuelled political conflict or redefined policy priorities throughout Latin America. The critical approach towards Good Living here presented, allows us to move beyond the specificity of policies that were carried out in this or that jurisdiction, effectively shifting focus towards the overarching governmental rationality underlining the broader transformations that came together during this time.

Through inductive reasoning, analysis now focuses on the origins of Good Living. The following section answers this central question by further developing Foucault's work on governmentality, biopolitics, and the *dispositif*, as well as Laclau's (1985; 1996) and Mouffe's (1985) construction of the floating and empty signifier. Drawing insights from both theoretical framings allows us to present a new analysis of Good Living that frames it as a form of transnational governmentality that was utilised to pacify transgressive politics in Ecuador.

2 Transnational Governmentality and the Critical Juncture

Foucault (2007, 77; 2008, 124) defined governmentality as a technology of governance that is utilised to discipline the population by knitting a web that interweaves decision making, resources, and relations to grant societal control over a target population. This exercise of power through the network of governmentality has, as its ultimate goal, the control and guidance of a population towards a desired outcome (Foucault 2007, 357). Additionally, according to Foucault (2008, 317), exercise of governmentality is based on the necessity that emerged in liberal societies to rationalise the problems posed to governmental practice by living beings. In the eighteenth and nineteenth centuries, issues pertaining to health, hygiene, death or birth underlined the problems that puzzled and defied political rationality and its policies. These policy problems became the "social questions" that governments focused on wellbeing had to resolve by either limiting, reforming or expanding how its institutions, decisions, and actors confronted them through the web of governmentality.

Foucault argues that during this period the state and its governmental rationality focused on creating the necessary conditions required to provide wellbeing to societies populated by economic man (Foucault 2008, 85). This pursuit of wellbeing became the central work of government institutions who conceived economic man as an interest-driven consumer of freedom, who legitimised governmentalities focused on securing the conditions through which "one could be free" (Foucault 2007, 338; 2008, 63). Wellbeing, and its pursuit by governmental rationality, inaugurated a new horizon of social engineering, one that displaced the need for a disciplinary formulation of society by inserting what Foucault called 'normative mechanisms' (2008, 259). This shifting paradigm, in the exercise of governmental rationality, overcame the 'legal network hemming of individuals' by inserting a theme program of society in which mechanisms of 'general normalisation,' premised on the exclusion of those who cannot be normalised, were dismissed (Foucault 2008, 259). Mechanisms of integration, rather than exclusion, would become the policy tools of governmental rationality. This shift of government policies from coercion or exclusion towards integration and pacification underline the main theoretical inputs that governmentality offers to our analysis of Good Living.

Governmental liberalism and its new way of doing things created a form of governance that was focused on securing economic man's consumption of freedom. This exercise of government power upon a targeted population and towards a specific end is what Foucault labelled "biopolitics," or the rationalisation of problems posed to governmental practice by the actions of economic man. During the early stages of Ecuador's critical juncture, technologies of governance deployed by transnational agents focused on redefining the role of the state. As a result of the debt crises that originated in 1982 multilateral financial institutions such as the World Bank and IMF were granted privileged access to the decision-making processes of multiple Latin American countries. Dávalos (interview 2017) for example, states that during the early stages of this process both institutions often predicated opposing objectives, effectively undermining each other's predominance. However, occasional policy contention was soon corrected and better coordinated creating a regional policy approach led by both international agencies.

In all, the 1980s can be defined as a period in which the deployed technologies of governance focused on the macro by relegating the micro. This disconnect between macro and micro economic objectives is what partially explains why it was not until the early 1990s that politicised ethnic cleavages erupted. As indigenous peoples' political agendas focused on land rather than macroeconomic policy, they would not contest the reforms of the 1980s until they began to redefine land policy, territorial autonomy, and demands for self-determination in the early 1990s (Dávalos interview 2017). The reigning governmentality of macroeconomic reform had, at least until this moment, not directly affected the interests of the emerging social forces that would occupy centre stage throughout the 1990s. Territorial autonomy and collective rights however became the fuel which fed continuous forms of collective action during the 1980s. Construction of collective rights agendas during the 1980s were set on a collision course with the land tenancy reforms and macroeconomic policies of the 1990s. Land reform, economic liberalisation, and new forms of market-led intervention consolidated the new theme program of society, one in which rural communities were to be integrated to world markets through social capital, ethnodevelopment and new forms of living well during the era of neoliberal identity construction.

The new theme for society that was constructed during this time became an exercise of biopolitics that was premised on the interactions that occur on a daily basis between households and firms. Social capital, and its potential as the new theme program of society, exploited the 'radius of trust' that allegedly laid dormant in rural and indigenous communities. Networks, solidarity, and the communal relations they fostered were soon depicted as self-help mechanisms through which the ensuing poverty that had resulted from macroeconomic structural adjustment could be corrected (Collier 1998, 4; Fukuyama 2016, 8; Perreault 2003, 329). Social capital's alleged potential for combating poverty gradually became the preeminent form of transnational governmentality. Moreover, the alleged stocks of social capital that lay dormant in rural communities linked the grass-roots of Ecuador's indigenous movement to the market disciplining logics of the time. This linkage between communal practices and social capital is here understood as the articulatory mechanism that consolidates Foucault's *dispositif*.

In the *Birth of Biopolitics* (2008) and *Security, Territory and Population* (2007), Foucault presents us with the *dispositif* or general apparatus in order 'to account for the system of practices that bring certain social categories and objects into being.' Poverty, as the social question of wellbeing that needed answering, unleashed new forms of societal control that were now deployed by transnational agents such as NGOs and multilateral financial institutions.

Social capital as a form of biopolitics enacted through the *dispositif* will be addressed further along in this chapter. Transformation of Ecuador's political sphere during the 1990s was premised on the emergence of social problems that were disregarded during the previous decade. Political objectification was now a matter of redefining the fields of intervention that could tackle the looming poverty and immiseration that came about throughout the 1990s (Procacci 1991: 167). As occurred in the eighteen and nineteenth centuries, governmental rationality, which was now being defined by transnational actors, shifted its attention towards the securement of wellbeing. Faced with the dire consequences of Latin America's social question, the "market friendly" policies enacted through social capital conspired with broader macroeconomic reforms. Social capital was gradually framed as the remedy that could tackle the unforeseen externalities created by a retreating state. With time, social capital became the discourse from which new forms of knowledge–power was exercised.

The *dispositif* is thus constituted by discursive and non-discursive practices that range from institutions, regulations, administrative measures, philosophical propositions or scientific statements (Hendrik 2011, 118). The *dispositif*, as a form of practical knowledge that encapsulates practices of calculation, vocabulary and techniques, brings together programs of intervention by means of an assemblage, whose component pieces are pulled together from an existing repertoire of options (Li 2007, 276). Envisioning the *dispositif* as the uniting mechanism within the assemblage of government interventions, presents us with a form of power that is polymorphous and adaptable, attracting a range of diverse parties that come together in regulating the conditions in which lives are lived (Foucault 2008, 259; Li 2007, 276). Forging a set of practices with a regime of truth constructs an apparatus or *dispositif* of knowledge–power, which is utilised to shape reality and guide populations towards desired ends that are themselves divided between truth or false (Foucault 2008, 19). Social capital provided the necessary regime of truth from which this shaping of reality could take place. Forging social capital with demands for ethnic rights would in time produce the overarching project of intervention that came to be known as ethnodevelopment; economic development with an ethnic "twist."

What is prevalent during the critical juncture is that the *dispositif*, or the institutions, regulations, administrative measures, philosophical propositions or scientific statements that defined reality were no longer implemented by a monolithic state. Rather, the transnational agents and institutions deployed to enact policies based on social capital are evidence of the many ways in which sovereign power was displaced in the age of liberalisation. As transnational agents and international development agencies penetrated Ecuador's rural communities and policy centres, social capital was moulded as the policy response to public health, welfare, agriculture, conservation, good governance, and 'what we have come to know as development' (Li 2007, 276). Usage of the *dispositif* allows us to account for the societal meaning-making from which social capital was utilised to knit together and articulate the 'conflict-ridden network of social actors, institutional dispositifs and knowledge stocks' that converged during the critical juncture (Keller 2012 quoted in Altman 2015, 162).

From the 1990s onwards, poverty and the social question became the problem or phenomenon to which power had to find a response. Social capital, as an articulatory mechanism within the dispositif, reified a specific technique of power that could secure the continuance of macroeconomic policies whilst disregarding the transgressive demands that came from collective action initiatives (Schöneberg 2017, 605). As an assemblage of interventions whose major function was to respond to an urgent need at a given historical moment in time, social capital articulated a form of knowledge–power that could be deployed through the network of institutions, actors, and policies that converged during the critical juncture (Frost 2015, 9). Social capital provided the theme that articulated conflict-ridden demands, actors, and institutions under the common goal of self-help agency. This articulation would in time disband, pacify, and subvert the transgressive politics that had dawned during the late 1980s and early 1990s.

3 The Theme of Social Capital

During the critical juncture various forms of intervention were executed throughout Latin America. Prominent institutions in the elaboration and execution of these programs were the World Bank and International Monetary Fund. Steering clear from the details or multiple ways in which these programs targeted, executed or ordained new forms of social control throughout the 1990s,[2] we turn our interest towards the transnational institutions and forms of governmentality they promoted. These programs of intervention sought to 'mitigate the effects of structural adjustment among the poor,' through a new "theme program" for the Third World' (Díaz Cayeros and Magaloni 2003, 2; Morely 2003). Underpinning this new theme was social capital as a plausible, market-orientated form of policy construction that could resolve societal problems relating to poverty. Problematisation of Latin America's poverty by

---

[2] For more, see: Andolina et al. 2009; Bedford 2009; Mitchell 2013; Laurie et al. 2005; Radcliffe et al. 2002; Perreault 2003.

multilateral and bilateral development institutions sought to capitalise on active citizen participation as a mechanism through which economic development programs could be consolidated in Bolivia, Venezuela, Peru or Latin America in general (Díaz Cayeros and Magaloni 2003, 2).

Coincidently, the emerging problematisation of poverty by "mainstream" development institutions came about during a time when post-development alternatives heralded that 'poverty could be a resource' (Nederveen Pieterse 2010, 112). Harnessing the agency of the poor was, according to these alternative views, a way of enhancing 'human-scale development' by paying attention to the 'vernacular universes that provide hope and strength' and which allow development to move 'from a statistical universe to a moral universe' (Nederveen Pieterse 2010, 112). Heavily preoccupied with the moral dimensions of poverty, Nederveen Pieterse (2010, 122) argues these alternatives sidestepped issues regarding the actual alleviation or elimination of poverty, as well as the power dynamics that perpetuate them. Poverty's embeddedness into the development industries discourse of alleviation created idealised representations of society by post-development advocates. Similar to what currently occurs in post-developmental understandings of Good Living, this ambivalence towards signifieds allowed market friendly discourses to flood the particular discourses of multiple actors.

Once efforts towards poverty alleviation became coupled with social capital, they were transformed into a simulacrum[3] or an idealised discourse that diluted stronger demands relating to racism, human rights, marginalisation, health, education, and other longstanding problems in Ecuador. As they were sidestepped, first social capital, later ethnodevelopment, and currently Good Living shifted policy focus towards alternative forms of economic development that left more "radical" demands outside of the policy agenda. Framing indigenous and other civil society demands, under the multicultural market-led guise depicted during the critical juncture, led to a reconstitution of political demands that forced groups to cede, effectively constraining future negotiations relating to cultural rights as well as accelerating the disarticulation of indigenous organizations (Hale 2002, 488; Llasag 2012, 133).

Social capital as well as Good Living present a discourse that entangles poverty with alterity, creating idealised representations of indigenous cultures

---

3   Baudillard (1983, 4) identifies 'simulacrum' as a process in which the signs of the real come to substitute the real itself. It is an operation in which real processes are deterred by the implantation of pragmatic-operational clones: "a metastable, programmatic, perfect descriptive machine which provides the signs of the real and short-circuits all its vicissitudes.

that do little to combat the longstanding forms of inequality that are so prevalent in Ecuador. During the critical juncture, ambivalent constructions towards poverty varnished and clouded the policy discussions that were directed at attending economic, social and cultural rights. With certain poignant exceptions, cultural rights such as territorial autonomy and self-determination were granted annunciatory recognition in policy papers and constitutional law, awarding them minimal forms of procedural guarantees.

Social capital and its deployment as a targeted response of societal intervention, can be exemplified in three regional programs that stand out for their respective efforts in containing transgressive political subjects and expanding market friendly responses. Mexico's *Programa Nacional de Solidaridad* (PRONASOL), Chile's *Programa Orígenes*, and Ecuador's *Proyecto de Desarrollo de los Pueblos Indígenas y Negros del Ecuador* (PRODEPINE), were all part of a coordinated and targeted response at containing the subversive politics unleashed by a decade of structural reforms (Bretón 2007; Galindo and Rodriguez 1998; Montalvo 2013; World Bank 2002;). The cited programs shared the common theme of being 'the response to the social and economic adversities' that followed the 1982 crisis, as they were constructed to 'mitigate poverty through social welfare, productivity and regional development' (Escobal and Ponce 2003, 20). Focusing efforts on the procurement of 'water, education, health, agriculture,' primary exports and the improvement of governance capabilities, these theme programs of intervention targeted poverty by 'fostering the necessary social capital of community participation' (Escobal and Ponce 2003a, 20; Morely 2003, 39). In the case of PRODEPEINE, the project was operational from 1998 to 2004, however initial attempts to define it can be traced back to as early as 1995 (Bretón 2007, 98). PRODEPEINE, according to Bretón (2007, 98), exemplifies the political dimension the World Bank granted social capital as it encompassed the development initiatives of the 'neoliberal financial establishment' as it reformed Ecuador's Constitution in order to incorporate cultural demands.

Theoretically, social capital, now an intrinsic part of the assets readily available to the poor and indigenous communities, allowed the different types of income that constitute markets, institutions, politics, and the overall exercise of power to come together (Escobal and Ponceb 2003, 48; Shejtman and Parada 2003, 52). Programs of intervention constructed under the theme of social capital, capitalised on the alleged bundled reciprocity that laid dormant in rural and impoverished households. However, PRODEPEINE has been criticized for being the continuation rather than the innovation of policies directed towards rural and indigenous communities (Bretón 2007, 99). Social capital became the 'strategic reference through which local organisations' could be assessed, as quantification of network asset reservoirs could present plausible ways through which poverty could be tackled through self-help agency (Janvry and Sadoulet 2003, 62). Programs of social intervention in Mexico, Chile and Ecuador were thus orchestrated under the theme of social engineering that sought to combat poverty through market-friendly mechanisms. The deployment of social capital programs in rural and indigenous communities sought to contain the political unrest produced by a retreating state, disappearing corporatist arrangements and the recent politicisation of ethnic cleavages. Dissipation of politically transgressive demands in favour of tamed policy prescriptions that adhered to market logics targeting poverty led to this estimation:

> The results obtained by those agents (NGOs) in reference to the betterment of living conditions in the rural population or the efficiency and efficacy of the proposed projects, presents more questions than answers—one need only observe the brutal persistency of poverty and homelessness within indigenous communities.
> (LARREA 2006 in BRETÓN 2007, 100)

Indeed, a particular interest in all three programs was the ethnic or cultural "turn" needed to consolidate development policy in Latin America. By 'adding culture and stirring' an oversimplification of development began to surface, one in which a blatant reification of culture led to a policy talk that was 'so superficial' that it could only be labelled as 'bogus, absurd and meaningless' (Nederveen Pieterse 2010, 72). Criticisms towards culturally or ethnically based economic development policy argue that through its cultural turn, any and every economic development project could suddenly be legitimised, regardless of the outcome, needs or forces underlining it (Nederveen Pieterse 2010, 72). Economist Pablo Dávalos (Interview 2017) stressed that these three programs were constructed and deployed in countries that had recently experienced a surge in ethnic conflict or anti-market protests. Ecuador's CONAIE had effectively reshaped the domestic political arena, whilst Zapatista revolt against Mexico's 1994 NAFTA brought about a new form of transgressive politics in North America (Prashad 2012, 245). In Chile, Mapuche resistance against neoliberal reform, and the *Decreto Ley* No. 2568, brought about an urgent need to construct a citizen-subject that could respond to the colour-blind social policy that sustains market friendly economies (Briones 2006, 287).

Social capital, once it became consolidated under ethnodevelopment, created a politics of place that idealised emerging forms of stakeholder capitalism. This ethnically orientated form of social capital, through its innovative approach, not only alleviated poverty but would also (somehow) lead to democratic renewal (Nederveen Pieterse 2010, 138). Surprisingly, these forms of 'associative economics' fell in line with the New Left's heralded 'productivism,' which called for 'the popular construction of cooperation through citizenship and authentic participation' (Amin 1997, 316 quoted in Nederveen Pieterse 2010, 138). Revisioning development, through the emerging discourses of idealised social capital that were contained in civic virtue or associative economics, slowly consolidated new forms of societal control. Moreover, social capital's theoretical promiscuity, as stated by Somers (2005), allowed the Right and Left to idealise social capital in diverging points of departure yet surprisingly similar ports of arrival. In their respective ways both sought to 'either outflank the state or combine a strong civil society, state and economy' (Nederveen Pieterse 2010, 138).

Development policy for Latin America's political "hot spots," and Ecuador particularly, was drawn up by the World Bank in an attempt to 'create horizontal networks of social capital' that could mitigate the high indices of poverty and indigence prevalent in the Andes (Bretón 2001, 126; 2007, 97). Strategic development funds were now directed towards the domestic and transnational NGO community operating in Ecuador, allowing them to reconstitute indigenous communities through imposed *Organizaciones de Segundo Grado*–OSG (Second Tier Organisations). These vertically integrated forms of community organisation reformulated the rural Andes by implementing interlocking mechanisms that bounded the recently (re)discovered network of indigenous social capital.

According to Bretón (2001, 129), the prevalence of OSG, as a vertically imposed community organising structure, is directly related to the territorial presence of NGOs utilising development funds. Hungry for the development funds offered by multilateral and bilateral donors, NGO's quickly demanded that indigenous communities re-organise their grass-roots associational structures under the OSG framework. The reasoning behind imposed re-organisation was that it would allegedly grant the institutional and associational hardware necessary for grant proposals to be better structured before international donors. This would in turn allow communities, and the stakeholder capitalism embedded therein, to more easily secure the desperately needed development funds demanded by their communities. Strategic deployment of abundant financial resources in impoverished communities, alongside the "philanthropic" mantra of the transnational non-for-profit community operating in Ecuador, steadily transformed Andean indigenous communities into social capital depositories (Andolina et al. 2009, 11). This re-organisation of indigenous networks and communities not only created a steady dependence on the development funds that began to flow, but gradually disarmed the societal mechanisms that had consolidated indigenous mobilisation during the 1980s and early 1990s.

The transnational governmentality of neoliberalism, enacted through social capital, targeted the so-called dormant reservoirs of social capital that was stored in the rural communities of the Andes. Dependency on transnational development resources created the breeding ground for hegemonic discourses relating to social capital to knit together 'agendas and actors' through a discursive heterodoxy that brought together environmentalists, indigenous people, policy advocates, feminists, peasants, and the remnant of the Ecuadorian state together (Andolina et al. 2009, 42). Social capital came to provide the discursive mantra that in time consolidated into the World Bank's ethnodevelopment guidelines. This new development, with a "human face" and "ethnic turn," established the World Bank's Operational Directive 4.20 and Operational Policy 4.10. These institutional guidelines sought to implant investment projects that could develop indigenous populations by setting up procedural mechanisms that accounted for the bank's recognition of how 'loss of identity, culture and customary livelihoods' are the result of previous development projects (Ingram et al. 2003, 1; World Bank 2013). Loss of culture, due to previous development projects, would somehow be recovered by the newly developed ethnic turn that came with social capital. Ethnicity and social capital became forged into ethnodevelopment, creating the necessary discursive tools through which the 'strong poverty-ethnicity relation' could be tackled (World Bank 2013). Through its recourse to the narrative of social capital, Ecuador's rural development landscape was transformed, as mobile and fluid discursive alliances reshaped the projects and initiatives that were enacted therein. These new initiatives, premised on project autonomy and the harnessing of the hands-on experience allegedly stored within community networks, would come to define social capital's ethnic turn (van Nieuwkoop and Uquillas 2000). Ethnodevelopment would thus consolidate a grass-roots approach to mainstream economic development policies framed around self-help agency.

Once again, assessment of the multiple policies, projects, and targeted populations of these initiatives is by-passed so we may discuss how these contradictory and targeted efforts shaped the discourse of ethnodevelopment. Others have in the past dealt with the specific ways in which these projects of intervention reshaped policy, agency, and domestic institutional structures during the critical juncture.[4] The basis of this previous scholarship, as well as previous comments regarding social capital's thematic construction of society,

---

[4] For more, see: Bedford 2009; Weber 2004; Fine 2001; Anthias and Radcliffe 2013; Laurie et al. 2009; Radcliffe and Pequeño 2010; Bretón 2005.

grants the necessary background from which Good Living may be further assessed. The following section develops social capital's conceptual background, its alleged theoretical pedigree, and the underlying contradictions that plague it. Ailments that in due time became woven into the "mainstream" and "alternative" discourses that flooded Ecuador's 2008 Constitutional Assembly and its shaping of Good Living.

4   Social Capital or the Myth of Ethnodevelopment

The steady increase of NGO presence in Ecuador between 1981 and 1994 shifted policy decisions from the state to civil society organisations. This shift in policy construction transformed NGOs into the agents that deployed neoliberal social policy during Ecuador's critical juncture (Andolina et al. 2009; Breton 2010, 61). Dependent on the development funds provided by multilateral and bilateral development agencies, NGOs swiftly adopted the policy discourses that flowed from North to South. This "NGOisation" of civil society fostered a narrow understanding of the transformative potential that had emerged within Ecuador's social movements during this time. Through a mismatch of development policy and civil society expectations during the critical juncture, a knowledge–power nexus was formed, erasing, subduing or effectively containing the transgressive features of the politics of protest that had surfaced in the early 1990s (Rajagopal 2003, 258). Moreover, NGOs' influence on a multiplicity of Ecuadorian indigenous communities and civil society organisations conflated transnational projects of intervention with emancipatory agendas seeking a new political horizon. This fusion of local politics and transnational agendas gradually subdued the transgressive nature that had initially defined politicised ethnic cleavages. Moreover, dependency on NGOs and the development funds they provided instilled a pressing need for institutionalisation and professionalisation amongst indigenous communities, which in turn constructed a new fabric in civil society, one that was small, privileged, and dependent on the liberal economic agendas of its sponsors (Radcliffe and Laurie 2006, 96; Rajagopal 2003, 261).

NGO policy, and subsequently indigenous politics, now depended or simply adhered to the premises of social capital and ethnodevelopment, a regurgitation of the policy prescriptions that were set out in the Copenhagen Summit of 1995 on Social Development (Bretón 2010, 63). This United Nations sponsored event laid out ambitious goals meant to eradicate the 'profound social problems' troubling the World, 'especially poverty' (United Nations 1995). At the core of the summit's agenda was the recognition that '[g]lobalization also permits countries to share experiences and to learn from one another's achievements and difficulties,' whilst recognising that rapid change and adjustment has intensified poverty and threatened human wellbeing (United Nations 1995, 3). Moreover, recognition of indigenous peoples' pursuit of economic and social development required structured policy responses around 'identity, tradition, forms of social organization and cultural values' (United Nations 1995, 7).

The road to Ecuador's sustainable development was thus necessarily entrapped by the metanarratives that were determined during the Social Development Summit of 1995. Ethnodevelopment and its dependence and promotion of productive investments, technological advancement, scientific knowledge, and the expansion of world trade would thus resolve the social question by bringing global markets to impoverished communities (United Nations 1995, 10). Coincidently, debates during Ecuador's Constitutional Assembly reproduce these metanarratives by linking Good Living to economic development, national growth, and scientific knowledge. As the Economic Development Majority Report from Table No. 7 of Ecuador's 2007 Constitutional Assembly reads:

> .... [the production of scientific knowledge] brings on the need to democratize, adapt and disseminate knowledge, so we may better our quality of life, national production and therefore contribute to the realization of Good Living...a dignified life for all...one in which new levels of information will allow conscientious citizens to decide and collectively work towards Good Living ... (Acta 075, 38–40).

Eradication of poverty, a core principle of the Summit, was to be achieved by attacking hunger and malnutrition through the attainment of full employment, food security, education, health care, and safe drinking water (United Nations 1995, 10). United Nations sponsorship of this human development agenda, according to Des Gasper, did not challenge neoliberalism or competitiveness but blatantly endorsed it by placing structural societal deficiencies as quickly solvable policy problems that could be attended by market mechanisms such as self-help agency and social capital (2004 quoted in Nederveen Pieterse 2010, 135). Innovation in discourse framing allowed the bundling of human development as a more 'inclusive and enabling' form of competitiveness, one that granted a general 'humane aura' to the market mechanisms of the time (Nederveen Pieterse 2010, 135). The addition of an ethnic turn to this aura, legitimised its usage throughout Latin America, as policies of intervention were masked through the deployment of social capital and later ethnodevelopment.

Critical remarks towards NGOisation should not come across as a gross generalisation that conflates the work of a diverse universe of civil society actors. Indeed, many transnational NGOs in Ecuador have led a steady campaign towards the securement of human rights, environmental concerns and economic equity (Cepek 2012; Sawyer 2004). NGOisation, refers to the complex interdependence that stemmed from economic resources flowing from multilateral or bilateral development agencies to civil society organisations during the critical juncture. Resource dependency in a time where development policy prescriptions were dictated in Washington D.C. but executed in the Ecuadorean Andes. Additionally, this dependency demanded that civil society actors, such as Ecuador's emerging indigenous organisations, cede transgressive policy demands or reform their community structures in an effort to secure the development funds they had become so reliant on. This exchange of transgressive politics in favour of market friendly alternatives would ultimately disarm the defining features that had come to consolidate ethnic politics in Ecuador during the late 1980s and early 1990s.

As Ramos argues, NGOs had effectively bureaucratised indigenous resistance, keeping their 'wild otherness' filtered and tamed, thereby relegating the 'real Indian' to a remote source of 'ideological raw material' (1994, 160). This ideological "raw material" would in time seep into the discussions that pervaded rural development in the Andes, a dubious theoretical backdrop that cultivated the essentialised notions of indigeneity that are prevalent in ethnodevelopment and at least two strains of Good Living.

Taming of indigenous resistance was made possible when it was contained within the microcosm of NGO vertical dependency. Starved for development funds, imposition of agendas premised on social capital prospered as communities enacted whatever was needed to keep financial resources flowing. These reform programs of social intervention brought about a complete 'rearrangement of social practices' as different and intersecting logics constructed a new discursive reality for indigenous alterity (Mitchell 2013, 14). Indigenous demands that opposed market logics or liberal politics were now regarded as idiosyncratic beliefs or cultural particularities, whilst construction of indigenous subjects as market friendly entrepreneurs allowed for a 'generic Indian' to surface (Ramos 1994, 162). This generic and tamed representation fed the liberal fantasy of a stoic resistant subaltern whose ideological purity awards her recognition by supporting the status quo (Ramos 1994, 162). Once alterity had been tamed, transgressive political demands were fused with market friendly approaches. For Ecuador, NGO promotion of social development agendas brought about the enshrinement of social capital and ethnodevelopment as the policy alternatives to emancipation, collective rights, and new ways of constructing the public sphere.

Social capital embodies the power of an empty signifier, one that absorbs the concreteness of multiple signifiers by diluting their uniqueness in a sea of conceptual ambivalence. Targeted programs of intervention, which were aided by the agents of transnational development, allowed transgressive politics within Andean communities to be subdued. Revision of the ambitious goals proposed within the Copenhagen Summit of 1995 reveal that social development and the discourse of social capital became the point of reference through which humanity's quest for economic development could be achieved. These all-encompassing goals promoted everything from technological advancement to food security, creating a social development agenda that could subdue, tackle or overcome any and every one of humanity's ailments, whilst promoting market orthodoxy. This process was led by the unbounded discourse of social capital and its strategic "ethnic turn." Through programmatic and discursive amplitude opposing and contradictory logics were forged together. According to Becker (2011, 46), during the critical juncture political alliances cemented under the master frame of neoliberal resistance strategically combined the demands of CONAIE, left-wing unions, and some other fifty rural and urban organisations; a plethora of alterity and resistance. Acosta (2010, 5), further comments that Ecuador's 2008 Constitution distils the political programmes and resistance agendas of workers, teachers, indigenous, peasants, urban dwellers, students, environmentalists, women, senior citizens, children, private business, and other progressive sectors. In sum, the rise of the social development agenda created a steamroller effect that homogenised policy claims by promising redemption to all political expectations. This homogenising effect was further compounded when collective action initiatives were master framed under neoliberal resistance.

Social development agendas were soon constructed under the guiding principle of social capital. Margaret Somers euphemistically describes social capital as the World Bank's 'missing link' in the effort to end poverty (2005, 223). She points out that 'epistemic love' with social capital allowed it to overcome its entrenched 'theoretical promiscuity,' effectively awarding it unlimited powers as it quested for the good of humanity and perpetuated market fundamentalism (Somers 2005, 235). Much like social development, social capital was now a strategic discourse that quested for the good of humanity, offering enthusiastically available solutions to all of humanity's problems, dividing policy and populations under binary classifications. These totalising and dichotomous discourses reminds us of what Charles Taylor once argued when he stated that transforming political issues into questions that ponder "what kind of life is worth living," or that forward 'claims about the good' are readily available strategies to either deny concrete rights or strategically subvert the political opportunity to act (quoted in Orlie 2004, 143).

Through development agendas that relied on the epistemic vogue of social capital and its power to quest for the good of humanity, ethnodevelopment and social capital soon tamed the transgressive political subjects it targeted. Strategic deployment of development resources during the time of a retreating state allowed new policy constructions to create a biopolitics of market fundamentalism; one that strategically utilised the recent politicisation of ethnic cleavages to legitimise its deployment by forging it to social capital. Complicity of a recently constituted indigenous political and intellectual elite further aided in the spreading of these forms of societal control. Social capital and its offspring of ethnodevelopment had created a *dispositif,* a form of knowledge-power that utilised communitarian Andean life to legitimise the market-orientated discourses contained in the self-help agency that reigned throughout the critical juncture. In so doing, a new construction of reality emerged that prophesised that mainstream or alternative economic development was possible, so long as it was framed under the market logics that had come to incorporate ethnicity as its guiding principle.

5   The Sources of Social Capital

Somers (2005) and Portes (1998), respectively agree that Bourdieu originally introduced the concept of social capital by defining it as an:

> aggregate of the actual or potential resources which are linked to possession of a durable network of more or less institutionalised relationships of mutual recognition (Bourdieu 1985, 248 quoted in Portes 1998).

Bourdieu's presentation of social capital as instrumental focused on the benefits that individuals harness from participation in groups that construct sociability (Portes 1998, 3). The so-called "profits" acquired from this critical form of capital came from group membership and the solidarity that makes them possible (Portes 1998). Social connections constructed a network that mobilises the varying volumes of capital that are possessed by an agent or group of agents connected with each other (Bourdieu 1986, 248 quoted in Somers 2005). Bourdieu builds social capital around the 'apparatus of habitus,' which interconnects structure and agency, thereby creating an internalised scheme that guides agent behaviour by the 'sense of reality acquired through one's particular and individual trajectory' (Rask Madsen and Dezalay 2013, 118 quoted in Somers 2005). Bourdieu theorised the dual nature of social capital, transforming it into something one may own but which also possesses you in return (Somers 2005, 246). Thus, social actors simultaneously act and are acted upon.

This reading of social capital was however profoundly changed when it was adopted by economists. Coleman for example borrows the concept from Bourdieu's earlier work, omitting any mention of the French philosopher and creating a derivative of the concept that fails to reflect its original meaning or theoretical construction (Portes 1998, 3). In so doing, Coleman defines social capital through omission of Bourdieu's habitus, leading him to develop a systemic treatment of the concept, which distinguishes possessors, sources, and resources related to the new market asset (Portes 1998, 6). Under this economised version of social capital, bounded solidarity is understood as the accumulation of obligations owed through norms of reciprocity, ultimately making private contracts of trust enforceable without recourse to the state (Portes 1998, 8). Bounded solidarity harnesses the power of social capital by making formal controls unnecessary and eliminating the role of an intermediary state as well as minimising the problem of "free riding" (Portes 1998, 10).

Social capital however, would not reach its full 'charismatic appeal' until political scientist Robert Putnam related social capital to the level of 'civicness in communities and towns' (Portes 1998, 18; Somers 2005). Putnam argued that associational involvement and participatory behaviours in a community could solve everything from violence in South Central L.A. to the nurturing of the shaky democracies that came about with the collapse of the Soviet Union (Putnam 1993, 36 quoted in Portes 1998). Through a simple diagnosis of a country's problems, Putnam seemed capable of fabricating readily available solutions that resonated with the American establishment by invoking a sense of nostalgia that dwelled on the passage of the civic generations of the 1920s and 1930s (Portes 1998, 19). Continuous praise for Putnam's social capital came from many sources. Paul Collier for example developed a 1998 World Bank working paper titled *Social Capital and Poverty*, in which he argues that 'trust building is the main objective of social capital' and that it is sensible to 'work with a concept of civil social capital which excludes the activities of government.' Fukuyama (2016, 8) would follow suite, depicting social capital as 'a private good' that is produced by the cooperation of individuals perusing selfish ends.

Moreover, Fukuyama specifically cites "traditional societies" as 'self-contained social units' that lack the necessary segments or networks which allow 'information, innovation and human resources' to flow (2016, 9). If one were to follow Fukuyama's understanding of social capital it would be difficult to argue that ethnodevelopment could ever be its derivative. However, the body of academic literature on development projects in the Andes and World Bank policy reports during the critical juncture suggest otherwise.

Returning to Putnam's vision of social capital, we must develop how civic responsibility and the virtues it contains, became the answer to the drastic reduction of services provided by national governments during the critical juncture (Skocpol 1996). This conflation of business, market and civil society pitted voluntarism and charity 'in a zero-sum opposition to government' (Skocpol 1996). Through essentialised notions of the institutions and social practices that lived within communities, social capital rose to become the hallmark of 'blaming the state for the breakdown of the social order' (Levi 1996, 48). Once social capital had seeped down to the development discourse, it constructed a new form of intervention commandeered by the World Bank. Evidence of the World Bank's heralding of the new "miracle" concept is the now extinct social capital website that stated that the sources of social capital could be found in families, communities, civil society, the public sector, ethnicity, and gender (Fine 2001, 143). Furthermore, social capital was now the necessary policy component to solve issues relating to migration, violence, economics, trade, crime, education, environment, finance, health, nutrition, population, information technology, poverty economic development, urban development, water supply, and sanitation (Fine 2001, 143). Social capital was thus transformed into a discourse that quested for the good of humanity by serving as the add-in to any policy ailment.

For places like Ecuador, where a new form of transgressive politics had taken shape, social capital was merged with ethnicity creating an imagery of reduced stereotypes, where ethnodevelopment portrayed ethnic minorities as mutually trusting entrepreneurs (Fine 2001, 143). Such a reductionist portrayal strategically deflected the inconvenient moral or political questions that had led to transgressive politics in the first place (Lichterman 2006, 528). Social capital, through its "one size fits all" discursive composition, had successfully legitimised anything resembling neoliberal reform through an ethnic twist (Bretón 2005, 21). Conflation of indigeneity with entrepreneurship tamed transgressive subalterns by integrating them into the global market. Formation of a new social capital discourse reproduced the modernisation theories of the past through strategic deployment of the development funds awarded to NGOs (Bretón 2005, 86). Ethnodevelopment, as the continuation of social capital, had successfully transformed old modernisation theories by appropriating specific characteristics of ancestral cultures which validated the transnational discourses that articulated neoliberal multiculturalism during the critical juncture (Andolina et al. 2005, 678).

Social capital's discursive malleability, alongside its theoretical promiscuity, presents a conceptually riddled product that has been the target of multiple intellectual controversies. Lichterman (2006, 530) for example, adequately states that social capital is a "Trojan horse" that disregards critical thinking about power, civic engagement or structural conditions, ultimately becoming a 'market metaphor.' Social capital, as a Trojan horse, is borrowed from Somers' (2005), who argues that its usage is problematic as the interlinkage it has received between economics and sociology has been inadequate. Social capital's inadequacy, according to Somers (2005, 238), is premised on the misplaced efforts of neoliberal public intellectuals that attempted to consolidate a form of political knowledge that could successfully argue in favour of privatisation through the marketing of the social. Society, through the mutated scope of social capital, created a 'politically manageable, tamed, respectable, domesticated' rationally selfish entity, premised on the ways individual agents invest or exploit new-found capital amongst their community networks (Somers 2005).

Ultimately, social capital became an epistemological public good integrated by various forms of discursivities (Somers 2005). This unique capability of ontological abstraction was then utilised to appropriate the multiple civil society demands levied against the status quo during the critical juncture. However, its merger with ethnicity and ulterior consolidation into ethnodevelopment would grant it a new appeal later utilised to distil a hegemonic discourse, which integrated, disarmed and disbanded Ecuador's transgressive political subjects. Additionally, its conceptual malleability, evidenced in the theoretical shifts that led from Bourdieu to Coleman to Putnam, awarded the theoretical promiscuity needed to consolidate its existence as an empty signifier of hegemonic articulation.

6 The Master Framing of Transgressive Politics

Previous chapters have covered the contextual setting and polymorphous theoretical contours from which Good Living spawned. Additionally, the introduction of social capital as the discursive "mantra" of transnational development during the 1990s, provides a new theoretical avenue from which critical readings of Good Living may be presented. According to Nederveen Pieterse (2010, 137), social capital refers to 'a widely ramifying range of arguments,' which create multiple intersections, 'depending on which angle of social capital one adopts.' Before we assess the similarities between social capital and Good Living we will cover Laclau's (1985; 1996) and Mouffe's (1985) work on the floating and empty signifier. Introduction of the empty signifier as a theoretical tool grants a new avenue of critical engagement from which Good Living may be analysed as a discourse. Discourse framing refers to the ways in which perceived bodies of knowledge are analysed in regard to their implications on the exercise of power, and of course, the ways in which they influence, impede or promote strategic purposes within society (von Groddeck and Schwarz 2013, 31). The empty signifier, for reasons that will be discussed shortly, presents a critical reading of Good Living by forwarding a new theoretical framing in which social capital and later ethnodevelopment become the forbearers of Good Living.

Usage of the empty signifier highlights the advent of a 'theme program of society' during the critical juncture (Foucault 2008). Thematic construction of society, and its articulation of a particular discourse with a set of practices, bounds them together for the production of a new horizon of true or false (Foucault 2008, 18). This thematic construction of society, under market-orientated reforms, redefined the social and political processes that transpired during the critical juncture, effectively transforming the ensemble of institutions, procedures and actors that constitute the knowledge–power nexus (Foucault 1991, 102). Through social capital, its mutation into ethnodevelopment and the inscription of Good Living in Ecuador's 2008 Constitution, an empty signifier was born. Before we engage with the empty signifier, we turn to Levi-Strauss' (1987, 61) work on the floating signifier as a form of 'magical thinking that offers different methods of channelling and containment' by providing symbolic fixation of meaning. The floating signifier becomes an intrinsic part of man's effort to allocate disposable surplus signification. Floating signifiers, according to Mauss, are part of a social phenomenon in which concepts like "manna," adopt a symbolic function which harbours a contradiction between two beliefs or conclusions and is adaptable to the context in which it is being interpreted (Levi-Strauss 1987, 64).

As a floating signifier, specific meaning is inscribed by those who interpret it, depending on the contextual setting where such interpretation takes place. Symbolic functionality within a floating signifier awards it a malleability and polymorphous nature that allows it to take on any content, depending on context. Its malleability forms a discourse which endows observers with multiple points of interpretation, transforming it into a symbol that is both omnipresent and localised, abstract and concrete (Levi-Strauss 1987). In the *Archaeology of Knowledge*, Foucault (1972, 67) describes how the construction of discourse takes shape through the thematic choices that are deployed through non-discursive practices and specific positions of authority. Discursive formation, through the symbolic power of floating signifiers, articulates events and processes through a collage of diverging group concepts such as those ascribed to "manna"[5] by Hebrews, Catholics or Muslims (Foucault 1972, 74; Levi-Strauss 1987).

Floating signifiers become riddled with diverse meanings in multiple settings making them an ambiguous point of symbolic reference that possess many interpretations within differing contexts (Wullweber 2015, 85). Critical Good Living's interest however, lays not in the floating signifier, but its partner concept of the empty signifier, which was critically constructed by Laclau and Mouffe (1985) in their analysis of the usage of discourse in politics. Points of difference between a floating and empty signifier stem from the theoretical purpose each concept respectively serves. Firstly, the floating signifier has altering signification depending on the context where it is utilised, granting it a malleability that allows it to become fully realised when it completes the nexus between signifiers and signified within a given context (Laclau 1996, 37). Secondly, the floating signifier is not ambiguous, as it avoids problems brought on by excess or deficient signification depending on the context of interpretation where it is completed (Laclau 1996). The empty signifier however, emerges under conditions that: (1) create an exclusionary limit that introduces essential ambivalence within a system of differences; (2) constructs a point of reference beyond the signified, thereby creating a threat to the system; and (3) privileges dimensions of equivalence to the point that any differential nature is obliterated and the system comes to signify a totality onto itself (Laclau 1996, 39). The empty signifier therefore absorbs all meanings ascribed to it, effectively homogenising discourses through the ambivalence of differences.

For reasons that will be addressed shortly, social capital and Good Living are both empty signifiers created by a social production of meaning that served the articulatory function of merging transgressive politics with hegemonic discourses (Laclau and Mouffe 1985, 107). Hegemonic discursiveness dominates the various fields of subversive discursivity through the deployment of articulatory mechanisms such as social capital, ethnodevelopment or Good Living. By containing and arresting the flow of difference that comes from partially fixed signifiers, hegemonic articulation consolidates a privileged discourse— in this case social capital or Good Living—by eliminating differences amongst competing discourses. This form of discursive oblivion, and ulterior ambivalence towards difference, consolidates a new form of discursivity, one that

---

5 The Oxford Online Dictionary defines "manna" as: Old English, via late Latin and Greek from Aramaic mannā, from Hebrew mān, corresponding to Arabic mann, denoting a product of the tamarisk Tamarix mannifera. In the Bible the substance miraculously supplied as food to the Israelites in the wilderness (Exodus 16). In Christian contexts a form of spiritual nourishment, especially during the Eucharist. (Accessed 28 June 2017) https://en.oxforddictionaries.com/definition/manna.

overwhelms the signifieds that have become entrapped within mechanistic articulation (Laclau and Mouffe 1985, 112). Discursivity is differentiated from discourse in its permanent changing of meaning relations and signifieds, whilst discourse is permanently attempting to fix meaning within a particular signified. Returning to the example of "manna," its signified holds constant within each particular monotheistic faith, allowing it to consolidate as a floating signifier that has different meanings but nevertheless concrete signifieds within a given context. This however is not the case of Good Living or social capital, which are unable to consolidate a particular meaning within any given context. Inundated by discursivity and the inability to fix meaning within any given context these two concepts define and constitute the empty signifier.

The empty signifier therefore originates from a discourse that has become flooded by waves of discursivity, which have in turn forced it to take on the various meanings from which identities are differentially formed at any given moment (Van Groddeck and Schwarz 2013, 31). Subversive discourses originating from the collective action of feminists, indigenous people, peasants, the urban poor, and so on were merged through opposition to neoliberal reform and the articulatory power of social capital and later Good Living. This consolidation effectively led to a loss of meaning and erosion of identity within each particular struggle. Through the ambivalent discursivity that came to define protests against neoliberal reforms, each particular struggle lost its differential particularity so it could consolidate into a new homogenising totality. The strategic nature of combining multiple collective action initiatives, against neoliberal reform, would create the necessary breeding ground for discursivity to inundate each particular discourse. Focused on the single objective of opposing market-orientated reforms each strain of transgressive politics that flourished during the critical juncture ceded its subversive identity to consolidate into a new master framing. In time, this erosion of transgressive identities and discourses would aid in the consolidation of ethnodevelopment and later Good Living as viable policy options that had no time to deal with the core subject matters that had led to collective action in the first place. Racism, immiseration, social inequality, and other longstanding ailments of Ecuadorian society were displaced as "alternative" forms of economic development began to supersede discussions in policy, academia, and civil society. Social capital, ethnodevelopment, and later Good Living became privileged discursive points that aided in articulating transgressive political forces to hegemonic projects of economic reform.

Privileged discursive points, according to Laclau and Mouffe (1985, 136), are 'nodal points' that articulate antagonistic forces through unstable frontiers. These nodal points partially fix meaning by creating a conceptual openness that is overwhelmed by the constant overflowing of signification (von Groddeck and Schwarz 2013, 32). Social capital, ethnodevelopment, and Good Living embody the nodal points of privileged discourse in which hegemonic articulation and submission of transgressive politics was made possible. Due to its openness, the partially fixed meaning constructed by empty signifiers prevent it from ever reaching closure, an attribute that allows it to engulf multiple signifieds through meaning ambivalence. The empty signifier's inability to be tied to a specific signified allows it to point to all discursive elements and signify them equally (von Groddeck and Schwarz 2013, 32). As illustrated in Figure 6, this unbounded openness, characteristic of the empty signifier, is what differentiates it from a floating signifier which is able to fixate meaning in different contexts.

Laclau and Mouffe's (1985) work on the empty signifier falls into the discourse-theoretical approach in which language is viewed as an active creator and shaper of the world (Von Groddeck and Schwarz 2013, 30). The empty signifier, perceived in the tradition of Antonio Gramsci, is conceived as the articulator of a hegemonic discourse (Wullweber 2015, 80). Articulatory characteristics embedded in the empty signifier allow it to absorb any practice, ultimately modifying its identity so it may fit into a hegemonic project (Laclau and Mouffe 1985, 105). Articulation awards the empty signifier the category of an integrating mechanism of hegemonic dominance, as it alters discourses by impeding the fixation of meaning, thereby allowing discursivity to overwhelm each particular signified (Von Groddeck and Schwarz 2013, 31). Through articulation and the construction of nodal points meaning becomes partially fixed

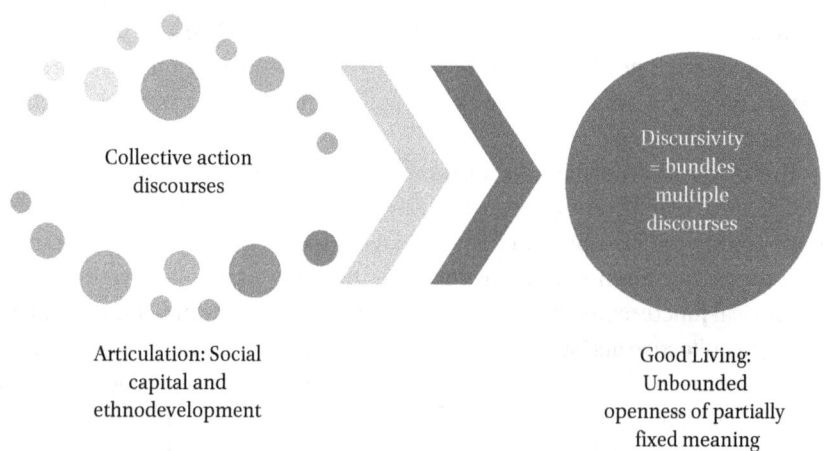

FIGURE 6   Good Living as an empty signifier

constantly overflowing a discourse with multiple discursivities. Articulatory practices thus subvert counter hegemonic projects, as the unique discourses that embody them are diluted into the sea of partially fixed meaning. This dilution of particular meanings in the sea of signified ambivalence is what constitutes an empty signifier within political discourse (Laclau and Mouffe 1985, 136).

Laclau's (1996, 41) reading of Rosa Luxemburg's arguments on the revolutionary mass determines that in a specific historical period, a transgressive political project will establish its identity through the overdetermination of a plurality of separate struggles. The revolutionary moment, or critical juncture, has the ability to fuse multiple subversive struggles by creation of a ruptural point. The implosion of a struggle's primordial meaning, through consolidation of ruptural points, creates a fissure that leads all concrete struggles to be internally divided from the beginning (Laclau 1994). In so doing, the struggle becomes dichotomous, simultaneously confronting uniqueness with bundled unity. In short, any struggle must confront the contradictory movement of asserting singularity by simultaneously abolishing it.

Adding to Laclau's reading of the revolutionary mass, we introduce Rice's (2012) revision of Snow and Benford's (1992) concept of "framing" to account for the 'shared meanings and definitions that legitimate and motivate collective action.' Forging of a political "master frame" allows for the entanglement of the 'ideational dimensions of collective action' which produce a framing that is used to mobilise 'ideas and meaning' by accenting and embellishing the seriousness and injustice of a particular social condition (Rice 2012, 26). Through shared meanings and definitions, collective action is not only motivated but legitimated, as multiple discourses become fused into a single master framing that makes citizenry mobilisation possible (Rice 2012). During Ecuador's critical juncture, formation of a shared collective action master frame, against neoliberal reform, created a ruptural point on which multiple discourses could flock to.

Union of these discourses disrupted the primordial meanings through which particular forms of collective action had originally surfaced. Indigenous mobilisation for example had first originated as a contestation to policies that threatened territorial autonomy, self-determination and collective rights. As the critical juncture progressed, strategic political action by indigenous leaders changed collective action priorities by redirecting efforts against neoliberal reforms. Parallel to these events, NGO intervention of indigenous communities, and the complicity of an indigenous political and intellectual elite created a fertile ground through which social capital and ethnodevelopment could become an articulatory mechanism to the hegemonic project of self-help agency.

Through intervention and articulation transgressive politics in urban and rural Ecuador were tamed, as the promise of solidarity networks, entrepreneurship and the recently discovered asset of social capital created the new discursivity to which collective action could flock.

Emergence of a political master frame, and the processes of intervention and articulation that followed, are to be understood as a point of ideational rupture. This moment in Ecuador's critical juncture fused the multiple subversive struggles and particular revolutionary identities of multiple civil society organisations, bundling their particular discourse identity under the all-embarking discursivity of anti-neoliberal reform, social capital, ethnodevelopment, and finally Good Living. Overwhelmed by the discursivities that presented ethnodevelopment and social capital as a response to neoliberal reforms, collective action identities, and their corresponding discourses, became entrapped within a newly forming empty signifier. Discursive dismemberment of a struggles uniqueness was thus made possible by the numerous ruptural points that fissured the collective action of multiple stakeholders, paving the way for their transgressive agendas to be articulated to the hegemonic discourses of social capital and ethnodevelopment as policy responses that could confront neoliberal reform. Ironically enough, policy responses intended to correct neoliberal market-orientated policy reform actually underlined hegemonic policy responses to transgressive politics during the critical juncture. Social capital or ethnodevelopment had no place for questions of self-determination, collective rights or social equality. Entrepreneurship, solidarity, and communal networks were all assets that could be marketed to correct the failings of a retreating state and attend to rising levels of poverty.

Having lost the defining characters of discourse that came with the merger of multiple points of collective action, transgressive politics became overwhelmed by the unbounded openness of opposition to neoliberal reform and articulated by social capital as ethnodevelopment. As transgressive struggles were forged into an all-encompassing signifier that opposed neoliberal reform the most controversial and market oppositional elements of their political demands were silenced, allowing for self-help agency to take centre stage. Social capital and ethnodevelopment's promise of not only attending to Ecuador's social question, but in so doing, also resolving five hundred years of discrimination, granted social development the discursivity it needed to pacify any form of resistance during the critical juncture.

Returning to the dichotomous nature of the revolutionary mass identity outlined by Luxemburg, we observe how Ecuador's politics of protest traded demands for territorial autonomy and collective rights for the policy prescriptions of social capital and ethnodevelopment. Discourse ambivalence imbedded in the framing of subversive identity during the critical juncture forced different forms of collective action to become overwhelmed by the multiple meanings that came from the articulation created by projects of intervention such as PRODEPINE. Privileged nodal points came to occupy the policy agendas of a plethora of civil society actors, pacifying their transgressive otherness whilst articulating their demands through the empty signifiers of social capital, ethnodevelopment, and finally Good Living (Laclau 1996; Rice 2012, 26).

This framing of a 'revolutionary mass identity' against the common enemy of neoliberal reform created conditions necessary for the partially fixed meaning of multiple subversive discursivities to overwhelm the particular discourses of identity, social equality or broader economic, social and cultural rights (Laclau 1996, 41). As a plurality of separate struggles were interwoven, the political capital at the disposal of a galvanised indigenous movement steadily increased. However, the price paid for this seemingly endless stock of political leverage was rather steep, as the amalgamation of a continuous repertoire of subversive discursivities steadily became punctured by the diffuse meanings they incorporated. In time, this would consolidate the empty signifier of Good Living. The advent of a political master frame effectively articulated demands prompted by multiple subversive discursivities, ultimately bringing together feminists, peasants, ethnic minorities, environmentalists, anarchists, transnational and domestic NGOs, left-leaning political parties, the urban poor, civil servants, families, and so on. The formation of a revolutionary mass identity against the ambivalent concept of neoliberalism created the conceptual breadth from which multiple subversive struggles became articulated to the hegemonic project of social development via the promise of social capital, ethnodevelopment, and Good Living.

Loss of uniqueness in the demands that were levied created ripe conditions for the emergence of an empty signifier, one that could be articulated to a hegemonic project by absorbing 'different particular struggles' (Laclau 1996, 42). Oppositional factions, competing for political prominence, now fell under a common discursive umbrella, forfeiting the transgressive nature of their particular demands as they gradually submitted to hegemonic articulation. The forging of a new interlocking political body under a common framing, made each struggle continuously lose its concreteness, thereby jeopardising its differential self and creating the illusion of a 'communitarian fullness' (Laclau 1996, 42). Such a bundled unity of identities forfeited the presence of any unique signifier, allowing equivalential conceptual spaces to emerge. Throughout the critical juncture this emptying of signifieds was traversed by three processes, the first of which was the consolidation of the political master frame discussed by Rice (2012). Secondly, the emergence of social capital and ethnodevelopment as the market friendly solution to Latin America's "social question." And thirdly, through the birth of Good Living as a constitutional principle premised on the solidarity and communitarian alterity that came from social capital's mutation into ethnodevelopment. These three movements during the critical juncture gave way to the formation of the empty signifier that was born in Ecuador's 2008 Constitutional Assembly.

7   The Empty Signifier Is Born

The present chapter has focused on developing the theoretical framework needed to present Good Living as a derivative of the social capital theme of society that flourished during Ecuador's critical juncture. It has further proposed that Good Living is an empty signifier that came to life as a multiplicity of collective action movements became forged in opposition to neoliberal reform. This forging of diverse political agendas, under a common master framing, was made possible by the converging forces that interacted during the critical juncture. Politicised ethnic cleavages, a retreating state, and changing citizenship regimes came together to redefine Ecuador's political arena. This critical reading of Good Living builds a new understanding of its discursive origins by utilising theory-guided process tracing. By theoretically tracing Good Living and linking its emergence to politicised ethnic cleavages, state retreat, changing citizenship regimes, transnational governmentality, and discursive democracy, broader, yet theoretically bounded insights, frame its discursive origins. This not only presents a new theoretical analysis but further questions why post-developmental, statist or Indigenist strains of Good Living have failed to incorporate more robust theoretical framings to their corresponding readings.

In particular, transnational governmentality and discursive democracy have provided a broader theoretical background from which policy intervention by transnational actors and the transformation of Ecuador's public sphere may be analysed. Insights from both concepts further consolidates the analysis that Good Living is the end result of broader policy transformations that emerged with social capital, continued through ethnodevelopment and were finally consolidated in Ecuador's 2008 Constitution in the form of Good Living. Tracing the origins of Good Living from social capital, as well as discussing ethnodevelopment's articulatory power in the merging of transgressive politics to hegemonic processes of market reform, consolidates a new understanding of a concept that has been widely discussed amongst academic, policy, and civil society sectors. Moreover, the theoretical proposition that Good Living is an empty signifier presents new questions regarding the role collective action played in its forging and the implicit power dynamics that framed it in Ecuador's 2008 Constitution. A product of almost twenty years of civil society unrest, Good Living's framing as an empty signifier must not be viewed in pejorative terms. Rather what is here proposed is that Good Living harbours in its roots the projects of new political agendas that stem from transgressive political subjects.

The point of critique however, is that Good Living, as it currently stands within either strain, fails to attack or question the underlying political demands that led to collective action in the first place. Good Living is thus the end product of collective action, this is simultaneously its biggest strength and its ultimate weakness. Absorbed by the master framing of opposition to neoliberalism, the particularities of each struggle were lost in their convergence towards a common enemy. The loss of collective action identity, within the revolutionary mass, does not automatically translate into Good Living losing its emancipatory potential. More to the point, what is here proposed is that Good Living may still be utilised as a strategic discourse and even as an enforceable right that crystallises the demands of a previously galvanised civil society. Furthermore, the refocusing of Good Living towards the strategic agenda of guaranteeing economic, social, and cultural rights allows it to be shielded from the overwhelming discursivities that flow in and out of statist, Indigenist or post-developmental understandings.

Loss of what Luxemburg called 'the revolutionary mass identity' has been substantiated on the strategic political manoeuvring of Ecuador's indigenous movement, as it consolidated into a national political force during the critical juncture. In an effort to strategically exploit the political support of a nationwide collective action, transgressive political agendas such as territorial autonomy or collective rights were sidestepped in favour of social development agendas regarding solidarity, entrepreneurship, and ethnodevelopment. Complemented by the processes of articulation and intervention that occurred in the multiple geographical locations where indigenous people live, political alterity was pacified in order to accommodate market friendly logics. Through this process, Good Living is here presented as the continuation of a poverty-framed theme program of society in which social capital could remedy the looming effects of widespread poverty that was brought about when neoliberal reform descended upon Latin America. Social capital and later ethnodevelopment, embody the knowledge–power nexus that made transnational governmentalities, biopolitics and the assemblage of *dispositifs* possible throughout Ecuador's critical juncture. The introduction of Laclau and Mouffe's empty signifier further aids in stating that Good Living, as a derivative of social capital, became a constitutional principal due to the events that unfolded during the critical juncture. As traditional political elites crumbled, government institutions collapsed and economic mayhem became widespread, new actors—agents of discursive democracy—came to occupy the policy spaces of a once highly interventionist and elite-controlled state.

These new forms of deliberation, this discursive construction of the public sphere, led to widespread policy reform that was later enacted into law. This juridification of discursive democracy, which is the abstract legal representation of political action during the critical juncture, was imprinted onto Good Living. By conceding small recognitions to all civil society groups, whilst simultaneously articulating them through social capital and ethnodevelopment, Ecuador's 2008 Constitution reflects the contradictory and opposing discursivities that flooded meaning-making during the critical juncture. As such, Good Living through its many constitutional representations, embodies these contradictions, as it simultaneously seeks the local and the transnational, the communal and the global, the rural and the urban, development and post-development, alterity and modernity.

Good Living in its Indigenist, statist or post-development strains is thus understood as an articulatory mechanism utilised to pacify transgressive politics during the critical juncture. The critical reading of Good Living that has been developed in this chapter frames a new theoretical discussion, one that identifies the strategic discursive usages it has embodied as an empty signifier but also highlights the potential of reframing its future under a human rights discourse. This reorientation may very well consolidate the demands for economic, social and cultural rights that led to collective action during the critical juncture. Rather than framing Good Living in its Indigenist, statist or post-development undertones, what is here proposed is that it be reframed under the power of discursive democracy. As was mentioned in previous chapters, social protest during the critical juncture was a widespread phenomenon throughout Latin America. Its elevation to a human right, interlinked with free speech, presents a new form of consolidating the public sphere, one that falls far from the procedural, judicial, and mechanistic forms of deliberation envisioned by Habermas or Rawls. If Good Living is indeed the end product of social protest during Ecuador's critical juncture, then further theoretical development is needed to consolidate it in accordance to the demands that were levied during this time.

The "social question" that emerged in Latin America throughout the critical juncture, and the consolidation of social capital as its solution, embodies the phenomenon and response crafted by the knowledge–power nexus. Faced with multiple political schisms throughout the continent, as well as the rising prominence of indigenous movements, this orchestrated discourse of truth targeted multiple collectives through a network of actors, institutions and decisions. Transnational promotion of a social development agenda, by events like the Copenhagen Summit of 1995, created the metanarrative from which a new regime of truth emerged. Legitimised by its power to solve humanity's ailments, social capital and ethnodevelopment agendas allowed hegemony to respond to subaltern political demands. Integration of subversive discourses, through targeted processes of articulation, crafted a common discursivity, one that blended the necessary discursive elements from which the empty signifier of Good Living could later emerge. Aided by programs of intervention such as PRODEPINE, Ecuador's social question was framed in accordance to market logics. The master framing of political demands under anti-neoliberal reforms dissolved the uniqueness that had come to characterise each particular form of collective action. Through the conformation of a unitary revolutionary mass identity, and the homogenising effects social capital programs of intervention had on local political demands, transgressive political subjects were gradually tamed. Unitary mass identity, targeting neoliberal reform, ironically created the conditions that allowed collective action to be later dismembered. Social capital, and later Good Living are both empty signifiers, waves of discursivities that overwhelm the uniqueness of particular forms of transgressive politics. Usage of Good Living as an empty signifier has received increasing scholarly attention in recent years. Van Teijilingen and Hogenboom (2016) for example carry out a qualitative data analysis through ATLAS.ti software in which they assess and interpret data in order to carry out a critical discourse analysis on Good Living/*Buen Vivir*.

Their findings concur with our analysis of Good Living as a strategic framing of discourses that unite diverse, contradictory and opposing logics (van Teijilingen and Hogenboom 2016, 385). Once again, this absorption effect Good Living has on many discursivities further corroborates its actions as an empty signifier. Struggles over the meaning of Good Living, evidenced in the three predominating strains, further corroborate that as a discursive form of power, *Buen Vivir*, *Sumak Kawsay* or Good Living in its current form, are configured in accordance with the particular social struggle or power politics interpreting them at any given point in time (van Teijilingen and Hogenboom 2016, 387). The scattered discursive nature of Good Living has serious implications for its enforceability as a constitutional principle. Whilst it is imprinted into almost one third of Ecuador's Constitution, Good Living's jurisprudential development has yet to be completed. This lack of judicial review, coupled with the dispersed discursive features we have identified, make it a constitutional principle and public policy guideline that is non-enforceable, as its interpretation will depend on a particular individual at any given time. So long as Good Living remains an empty signifier, flooded by many discursivities, it will be unable to fix meaning onto a particular signified, thus condemning it to remain a non-enforceable constitutional mandate.

This is further substantiated in Van Teijilingen and Hogenboom's (2016) discourse analysis, which highlights how Good Living becomes riddled by its inability to successfully forge a new form of politics. Each discursive strain of Good Living has respectively led to government co-option, essentialised representations of indigenous identity or the enactment of conservation policies that are dislodged from the realities of Ecuador's largely agricultural economic bases. Moreover, Good Living's instrumentalisation within either strain, has further debilitated any possible theoretical construction that transcends its nature as an empty signifier. Borrowing from Van Teijilingen and Hogenboom (2016, 408):

> (...) Buen Vivir has become a term that is interpreted through a variety of meanings, which shift according to the user and the context, and that despite its lack of clear-cut meaning, it is used extensively within a societal debate (...).

This shifting landscape of interpretations, within the same national context, further corroborates its configuration as an empty signifier, one that creates ambivalence within a system of differences, obliterating the particularities of its constitutive parts. Good Living, as a nodal point of hegemonic articulation, allowed it to partially fix any meaning ascribed to it, overwhelming the discourses that were imprinted on to it with the discursivity of signification that came from social capital and ethnodevelopment. For such reasons, Good Living's alleged statist, post-development or Indigenist currents, rather than fixating the meaning they intend, further compound its unbounded conceptual openness, making it utterly impossible for it to adequately construct the universal maxims each strain is so eager to promote.

Not only is Good Living currently an empty signifier that falls far from the idealised strains it promotes, it also forms a knowledge–power nexus constructed on the remains of dismembered collective action. Charles Taylor's comments, presented earlier in this chapter, resonate with this reading, as Good Living in its current forms hides its deficiencies through its self-serving quest for the good of humanity. Such discourse formation serves the strategic purpose of denying, aborting, and dismantling demands for far-reaching rights that could contest the power of the state, transnational capital or the racism that has condemned generations to abject poverty and marginalisation. Through the complex interweaving of agents, institutions, and decisions, programs of intervention disarmed transgressive political subjects during the critical juncture. Social capital's ability to permeate political opposition created the necessary conditions for Good Living to appear in Ecuador's 2008 Constitution. Flooded by the discursivities of social capital, these programs of intervention debilitated subversive politics during the critical juncture by strategically acting upon civil society, rural communities, and forging a bureaucratic indigenous elite dislodged from its roots. When the 2007–2008 Constitutional Assembly was finally materialised the diluted integration of multiple political demands against neoliberal reform successfully contained the most transgressive political agendas that surfaced during the critical juncture.

As had previously occurred with social capital, Good Living served as an articulatory mechanism that satisfied all yet disarmed many. Opened to the demands and conceptual imports of multiple collectives, it failed to embody the political projects of the few transgressive and novel political subjects that had emerged during the critical juncture. Articulation had effectively disarmed political contention by crafting Good Living as an all-encompassing discourse that could contain all political demands in Ecuador's 2008 Constitution. Gratuitous granting of novel rights that lacked procedural guarantees or depended on the will of a hyper-presidential system, exemplifies how the Constitutional Assembly of 2008 was in many ways a missed opportunity for transgressive politics to consolidate its power base. Failing to contest the ingrained forms of power that have historically impeded the consolidation of human rights, Good Living, although inscribed into the constitution is yet to develop its full potential. For example, little or no attention was paid to reforming what Gargarella (2013) called the "engine room of the constitution," the place where power and sovereign prerogatives perpetuate the Order and Progress model that has endured since the birth of the Latin American republics.

This disconnect between the engine room of the constitution and the discursive democracy of social protest was a determinate factor in the reshaping of Ecuador's public sphere. However, what became imprinted onto Ecuador's 2008 Constitution, were the sectarian preferences of Ecuador's historic atomistic pluralism; a series of contentious propositions that interpret rights and constitution making in accordance to personal preference. Once institutionalised within the power dynamics of Ecuador's 2007–2008 Constitutional Assembly, civil society demands, and the protests they fuelled, were overwhelmed by the multiple discursivities that sought to enact particular readings of rights, alterity, and development. This forging of Good Living, through the integration of multiple discursivities, further diluted transgressive political agendas. However, this integration does not ultimately translate into Good Living being bounded by an eternity of empty signification but rather that to overcome such a state, new theoretical angles and grounds must be paved. This task is of the upmost importance if Good Living is ever to reach the level of justiciable constitutional principle.

The following chapter will present the possible pathways that might lead Good Living from its current state of an empty signifier into the realm of enforceable right. A product of decades of social protest, Good Living not only represents an endogenous response to the historic inequality that has plagued Ecuador and Latin America, it also harbours the potential to frame a uniquely regional response towards the consolidation of economic, social, and cultural rights. Good Living, and the regional *corpus iuris* or body of laws it may be linked to, may very well reflect the demands of the many. Therefore, Good Living, as a form of discursive democracy, will be linked to processes that have sought to consolidate economic, social, and cultural rights through broad judicial interpretations that have taken place on a regional level. This framing of Good Living, as the continuation of a human rights discourse that began in the early 1980s, is made possible by its interlinkage to the supranational judicial protections enacted by the *Vida Digna* jurisprudence of the Inter-American Court of Human Rights, as well as similar efforts led by domestic courts.

8 Yasuní: a Case Study on the Empty Signifier

Ecuador gained international praise when it decided to keep vast amounts of oil reserves under ground in the Yasuní National Park located in its rich Amazonian region. As Larrea and Warnars (2009, 219) put it:

> Large petroleum reserves have been recently confirmed in the Yasuni National Park in Ecuador, one of the most biodiverse hotspots in earth, and home of two isolated indigenous cultures. President Correa of Ecuador proposed to the world to indefinitely keep petroleum reserves in the ground, if an international contribution reaches at least half of the opportunity cost of exploiting the petroleum. A trust fund, under international administration with UN participation, will be created for investments in conservation, renewable energy and social development. This innovative Yasuni-ITT Initiative simultaneously mitigates global

warming, protects biodiversity and indigenous cultures, reduces poverty and enhances environmental justice.

International excitement towards this proposal was however short lived, as the Correa administration steered towards what came to be coined as "Plan B" or the extraction of oil located underneath the Yasuní. As Vallejo (et al. 2015, 177) described:

> Plan B is to extract the oil from the ITT fields over a period of 13 years. In this case, we also assume favourable conditions for the state recovery of rent extraction (under the current contractual arrangement with the oil firms that provide services for the exploration and exploitation of hydrocarbons). We assume mitigation and remediation of the environmental damage. However, it is also accepted that the recognition of environmental damage may be incomplete because certain impacts associated with petroleum activities (such as the loss of biodiversity) are unknown and irreparable (no complete catalogue of of endemic species exists).

The Yasuni initiative serves as an example of the contradicting usage Good Living has received as a constitutional principle and public policy objective. Due to the protected status of the Yasuní National Park, the Correa Administration required a Declaration of National Interest from the National Assembly in accordance with article 407 of the Constitution. Immediate public outrage against the possible extraction of oil flooded public opinion and local NGOs. Amongst the most prominent organizations opposing oil prospection was the "Yasunidos" collective who sought to reverse the decision by campaigning for a national referendum that could stop oil extraction within the Yasuní (El Comercio 2015). Through a series of administrative and legal hurdles, Ecuador's Constitutional Court set a series of requirements that made the referendum unviable (Sentencia 001-13DCP-CC). Moreover, Ecuador's National Electoral Council invalidated many of the signatures that were required to move the referendum forward, this ultimately impeded any referendum going ahead in 2013 (Dictamen No.1-19-CP/19).

This matter would remain unresolved until 22 April 2019 when the newly appointed Constitutional Court reversed its existing jurisprudence through Dictamen No. 1-19-CP/19, effectively paving the way for that the referendum regarding Yasuní to go ahead, so long as the administrative procedures before the National Electoral Council were completed. To this effect, the National

Electoral Council of Ecuador would only have to validate the once voided signatures and send the proposed referendum question back to Ecuador's Constitutional Court. This decision would however require a motion to be voted in favour by the Council's Plenary.

9 Yasuni and the Discourse of Good Living

The Yasuni Initiative represents a case study on the plasticity, ambiguous, morphing and ultimately open-ended nature of Good Living as a constitutional principle, policy objective or political discourse. We have highlighted two relevant moments in the initiative's history. The first referring to the declaration of National Interest by Ecuador's National Assembly, and the second, which refers to the required Plenary vote to allow the referendum to go forth by Ecuador's Electoral Council. What is interesting about these two specific moments in the initiative's history are the agents who approved the National Interest Declaration, thereby denying the procedural advancement before the Electoral Council for a national referendum regarding preservation of Yasuní to go forth.

Interest in these events relates to the public servants and their corresponding political origins. When the Declaration of National Interest was approved by Ecuador's Legislative Assembly, it was done so based on the Committee Report prepared by the Permanent Commission of Biodiversity, presided by Carlos Viteri Gualinga (La Republica 2013). Viteri Gualinga has been cited in numerous academic papers relating to Good Living, as his early work in the 1990s and then in the first decade of the XXI century, according to some, developed the tenets of an Amazonian approach towards Sumak Kawsay or Buen Vivir. On 17 September 2013 Viteri Gualinga, alongside other members of the Biodiversity Commission, approved the exploitation of Blocks 31 and 43 within the Yasuni National Park. In order to provide as much detail as possible on the reasoning behind the decision to declare the area of national interest and overturn the protection status of the Yasuní, we present a transcript of the decision:

> *This Specialized Permanent Commission on Biodiversity and Natural Resources has been charged, in light of the Resolution by the Legislative Administrative Council CAL-2013-2015-021 of 29 August 2013, to draft the corresponding reports that will be notified to the Plenary of the National Assembly.*
>
> *The Declaration of National Interest to exploit Blocks 31 and 43 is sustained with the firm purpose of obtaining Buen Vivir or Sumak Kawsay.*

> *The analysis carried out by this Specialized Permanent Commission on Biodiversity and Natural Resources, concludes that the profits that will be obtained from the responsible exploitation of the natural resources that exist within Blocks 31 and 43 of the Yasuni National Park, will be destined to satisfy the right to Good living of the Ecuadorian population in general, due to the enormous investment that will be carried out in health, education, housing, roads and environmental remediation, amongst other important expenditures. As well as the safeguarding of the collective rights recognized in article 57 of the Constitution of the republic and international instruments. Specifically, the collective rights to life and self-determination of the Tagaeri and Taromenane indigenous peoples, the rights of nature and the right to a healthy and ecologically balanced environment, complying with the environmental guarantees that are defined in our Constitution, which holds the highest protection standards on the matter.*
>
> *The exploitation of Blocks 31 and 43 within the Yasuni National Park is a matter of doubtless national interest, due to the valuable and irreplaceable opportunity it represents to accelerate the national development process and guarantee, with the quickest and fastest way, the rights of each and every Ecuadorian, in their own diversity and in harmony with nature, as has been proposed in the planning of Good Living, which is manifested in our legislation and public policies, implemented during the government of the Citizens Revolution.*
>
> *This is exposition of motives presented by the Specialized Permanent Commission on Biodiversity and Natural Resources to the Plenary of the National Assembly in order to sustain the Special Resolution to Declare National Interest, in conformity with article 407 of the Constitution of the Republic, and in compliance with articles 8, 49 and so forth of the Organic Law on the Legislative Function. (National Assembly, 22 October 2013)*[6]

The reasoning behind the Declaration of National Interest, according to Gualinga, is closely tied to Ecuador's need for accelerated development in order to achieve Buen Vivir, or in his own words:

> We must start from the fact that in the last 10 years the Amazon, in line with the Central Government, has significantly changed. For example, we

---

6   The translation is mine.

now privilege the resources provided by oil and mining within the Amazon in order to reinvest those proceeds privileging communities and provinces located in areas where these activites are located. What the law seeks is to enact this vision. (El Comercio 2017)[7]

When we contrast Gualinga's 2017 pro-extractive industry development reasoning, one is immediately steered towards what Vanhulst (et al. 2014) and others label as neo-extractivism or more precisely put:

> In practice, however, the contradictions between Buen Vivir and neo-extractivism discredit the capacity of governments to effectively challenge the omnipotence of markets and their neoliberal foundations. Arguably, Ecuador and Bolivia, the breeding grounds of the Buen Vivir discourse, increasingly resemble textbook illustrations of neo-extractive economic agendas. After having attained office by appealing to the larger and historically underprivileged or marginalized population strata (invoking, i.a., the indigenous heritage of Sumak kawsay and Suma Qamaña), the administrations of President Correa in Ecuador and of President Morales in Bolivia are currently rather following a pathway of economic development that reinforces well-worn (neo)extractivist practices (mainly oil exploitation but also large-scale mining). This contradiction between discourse and practice is increasingly arousing the disappointment and indignation of former supporters in many civil society strands (Vanhulst et al. 2014, 60).

More striking is the author of such comments, as Gualinga's writings on Buen Vivir, as has been previously presented throughout this book, served to legitimate the discursivities that inevitably inundate Good Living's use as an empty signifier within the indigenous and post-development strains. As Gualinga exposed in a 2002 article titled "Indigenous vision of development in the Amazon":

> The author argues that in the beliefs of indigenous societies there is no concept of development, less as something to undertake by people in order to achieve well-being; nor the concepts of wealth and poverty determined by accumulation and lack of material goods. There does exist an

---

7 The translation is mine.

holistic view about what should be the goal or mission of every human effort, which is to find and create material and spiritual conditions for building and maintaining an "harmonious life." This places sustainability under a different paradigm which incorporates transcendence and the spirituality.

(GUALINGA 2002, 6)

The forced correlation between indigenous holistic views regarding human effort and the outright promotion of oil and mining in the Amazon, contest what certain strains of Good Living seek. Gualinga's usage of Good Living represents the contradicting nature of a discourse inundated by discursivities. As an indigenous man from Sarayaku, his representation of one of Ecuador's most well-known indigenous peoples, famous for fighting oil prospection within their territories (Sarayaku v Ecuador, 2012), adds puzzling questions regarding the conceptual origins, usage and power struggles that frame Good Living as a political tool. The unpacking of Good Living's usage, at least within the aforementioned case, further confirms its nature as an empty signifier, capable of adapting its usage to the power context from which it breeds or in the words of Laclau (1996, 15):

> If democracy is possible, it is because the universal has no necessary body and no necessary content; different groups, instead, compete between themselves to temporarily give to their particularisms a function of universal representation. Society generates a whole vocabulary of empty signifiers whose temporary signifieds are the result of a political competition. It is the final failure of society to constitute itself as society —which is the same thing as the failure of constituting difference as difference—which makes the distance between the universal and particular unbridgeable and, as a result, burdens concrete social agents with the impossible task of making democratic interaction achievable.

Laclau's acute conceptual unpackaging of an empty signifier, further corroborates our understanding of Good Living and its corresponding signifieds. Rather than a holistic indigenous worldview, post-development model or state-led development agenda, Good Living embodies the representation of alterity through specific, politically orientated goals. This underlying conceptual power struggle between strains of Good Living, are the result of diverse social movements merging in a given point in time, and ultimately inundating an indigenous discourse that had, in its origins, been framed around land and autonomy, with contestations to neoliberal hegemony (CONAIE 1994). Once fused with these multiple discursivities, Good Living's usage as an empty signifier became commonplace, allowing public servants, academics and civil society to call upon it for their particular struggles. Of course, what this translates to is 'the impossible task of making democratic interaction achievable' (Laclau 1996). Each strain of Good Living, once preoccupied with its universal validity, is subsumed by a trench warfare of the particular, inevitably dismissing points of deliberation or agreement as the struggle is framed by ontology rather than institutions or democratic needs.

Moreover, the linkage of Good Living to an apparent indigenous ontology, strays from the political events that occur in Ecuador on an everyday basis. This derailment of Good Living's political usage is the main focus of this book. As has been covered in previous chapters, Good Living's framing around an indigenous understanding of well-being, seems to assume that all indigenous communities and people have a clear-cut understanding of economic or societal development. Similar to what occurs with Gualinga, one need only observe the political and administrative decisions that are assumed by indigenous leaders and politicians in Ecuador on a daily basis.

In 2019, after years of appeals, the Yasunidos Collective brought before Ecuador's National Electoral Council a petition to give way to a referendum that would allow Ecuadorians to decide whether or not to exploit the Yasuni National Park (El Comercio 2019). This petition was echoed by Council Member Luis Verdesoto before the Plenary of the National Electoral Council. Before we turn to the motion and the subsequent voting process of the Council Members, it must be pointed out that two of the five Council Members are of indigenous descent. The first, Council Member Esthela Acero, is a Kayambi indigenous from Ecuador's north and the second is Council Member Diana Atamaint who also held the presidency of the organism and thus the casting vote of Plenary decisions. Council Member Acero, describes herself as a former juvenile leader within the indigenous movement (Linkedin 2019) whilst Council President Atamaint describes herself as 'an indigenous woman, academic and first congress woman of the Shuar indigenous people' (CNE 2019). Both Council members represent the Andes and Amazonian regions of Ecuador, the breeding gorunds of indigenous moblilization. Moreover, their government positions grant them a great deal of authority in relation to Ecuador's electoral and therefore democratic processes. The Yasuni initiative, aside from leaving oil underground had been orchestrated in order to preserve Ecuador's last remaining indigenous peoples in voluntary isolation the Tagaeri and Taromenane unscathed. Following a 2019 ruling by the Constitutional Court of Ecuador (Dictamen No.1-19-CP/19), the path for a national referendum regarding the Yasuni had been cleared. On 11 July 2019, a motion was brought before the

Plenary Session of the National Electoral Council of Ecuador regarding the Yasuní. However, two days before, President Atamaint was interviewed by the digital media platform *La Posta* in regards to the Yasuní referendum, to which she responded:

> *Vivanco: The Yasuni referendum... you are from the Amazon. What is your political stance?*
>
> *Atamaint: You have seen me in the streets defending my Amazon and my brothers that live in voluntary isolation. My principles and struggles will always go in line with that (...) We must comply with standing legislation and will continue fighting for life and the defence of indigenous peoples.*
>
> *Vivanco: Will there be a referendum?*
>
> *Atamaint: (...) Yasunidos has gone through a process in which the Transient National Electoral Council evaluated everything that happened. I was part of that Council, we audited all administrative procedures. What we were unable to determine was whether or not they had complied with the necessary recollection of signatures. Documents have deteriorated or been lost. What we now must do is to...*
>
> *Vivanco: It was lost? (...) However, rights must be guaranteed. In the end they have a right that's been recognized and our institutions must follow line.*
>
> *Atamaint: I completely agree. The Constitutional Court rule on the constitutional validity of their question.*
>
> *Vivanco: So, there will be a referndum so long as the Constitutional Court qualifies the question.*
>
> *Atamaint: Indeed.*
>
> *Vivanco: If that is so, then Minister of Energy Pérez won't call and suddenly the document will (...) you're not going to put red tape around the matter?*
>
> *Atamaint: No. The Constitutional Courts ruling is mandatory and we must follow the administrative procedure in line with that.*
>
> *Vivanco: I hope so.*
>
> *Atamaint: And don't ask me what I hope the result will be because I can't comment on the matter.*
>
> *Vivanco: But you already said you are defending life and in favour of not touching the Yasuni.*
>
> *Atamaint: Indeed, however we must comply with procedures (...).*[8]

---

8 The translation is mine.

Following the Monday 9 interview by *La Posta*, Council Member Luis Verdesoto presented a motion within Ordinary Plenary Session No. 45-PLE-CNE-2019 (Minute 4:25-15:53):

> *Council Member Verdesoto: I propose that the fourth point on our agenda be changed in order to include my petition regarding a citizen petition to have a consultation process demanded by the Yasunidos collective. As it cannot be postponed due to the legal and constitutional ramifications it carries (...) in which we must adhere to what has been ordered by the Constitutional Court and the Consejo de Participación Ciudadana y Control Social Transitorio. This cannot be postponed and we must adhere to what has been ordered in line with article 35 (5) of Electoral Code (...) I have already asked the President (Atamaint) to include this topic in our agenda in order to have a resolution on the matter, however it has not been included. I would like to highlight why this must be done. First of all, let me remind you that the rulings of the Constitutional Court are compulsory and must be immediately complied with. They are not discretional. It has been at least two months since the publication of the ruling (...) and we, as the National Electoral Council, have not said or done anything (...) Second, by previously having recognized a violation of rights (...) to the Yasuindos Collective, the National Electoral Council must remedy said rights in line with what has been ruled by the Consejo de Participación Ciudadana y Control Social Transitorio (...) We must therefore with all urgency take on this matter today (...) therefore I motion that we alter the agenda of the day (...).*
> *President Atamaint: Does the motion have any support?*
> *Vice-president Pita: It does.*
> *President Atamaint: Proceed to voting Mr. Secretary.*
> *Secretary General: I move to take votes in reference to the motion presented by Dr. Luis Verdesoto to include in the present session as fourth point of the day, the matter relating to the Yasunidos Collective.*
> *Council Member Acero: Abstention.*
> *Council Member Cabrera: Abstention.*
> *Council Member Verdesoto: In favour.*
> *Council Member Pita: In favour.*
> *President Atamaint: Abstention.*
> *Secretary General: With three abstentions and two votes in favour the motion does not pass.*[9]

---

9   The translation is mine.

10   Conclusion

We will not address the legal ramifications of denying a referendum regarding the Yasuni to go forth. However, we must address the clear contradiction that exists between political decisions taken by indigenous leaders at the top of Ecuador's governmental machinery and the underlying presuppositions that engulf the political and academic usage of Good Living. By framing Good Living through the lens of alterity and universal conceptual breadth, the particularisms and corresponding struggles identified by Laclau are ignored. Indeed, neither of the aforementioned Council Members cite Good Living, however their political decisions fall in line with the reasonings guiding Gualinga's earlier comments. That being that like any other political operator, regardless of ethnic origin or descent, political decisions are still premised on opportunity and interest.

Whilst one may never know what led either Council members or even Gualinga, to frame their responses in such a way, it burdens those who interpret Good Living as an indigenous worldview to answer how three different indigenous peoples place their decisions and comments so far from what apparently Good Living seeks. Rather than delving into the ontological possibilities of where these answers lay, this book proposes that Good Living as has been exposed in the decisions and statements analysed previously, responds to political interest and power struggles that are ultimately packaged within an empty signifier. For this very reason, this book also argues that Good Living must stay clear from ontological struggles and instead be positioned within the language and discourse of rights the stem from human dignity that have been imported in Ecuador and Latin America's legal systems.

CHAPTER 5

Beyond Living Well

This book has framed a critical approach towards Good Living in order to revise the dominant strains that have emerged towards its analysis since 2008. Throughout the preceding chapters, the following overarching points have been forwarded in order to present a critical approach that analyses the context, power relations, and events that unfolded between 1979 and 2008. In methodological terms, the approach towards Good Living here presented shifts current forms of analysis from deductive reasoning to an inductive method, which incorporates theoretical guidance to scrutinise the origins and effects it has brought about since 2008. In so doing, the first theoretical development of relevance is that to better comprehend the origins of Good Living, broader theoretical framings were needed. Identifying the necessity of a wider, better suited, theoretical premise from which Buen Vivir may be constructed, demands that present and future discussions move beyond the Buen Vivir-Living Well writings that have so far been discussed by Gudynas, Ramírez, Acosta or Oviedo. In order to trascend the triage of developmental, Indigenist or post-developmental strains of Buen Vivir, that is, the "Living Well" scholarship that has until now proliferated, we shall utilize the critical approach towards Good Living that has been discussed throughout this book. This theoretical addition, allows the reader to move beyond the living well scholarship identified by Hidalgo-Capitan and Cubillo-Guevara (2014), positioning one's self in the critical realm of Good Living that has been crafted. From this point on, our discussion displaces Buen Vivir or Living Well scholarship, centering on Critical Good Living and its legal applicability.

Critical Good Living develops new theoretical grounds by incorporating transnational governmentality and discursive democracy. As new additions, the former discussed the many ways in which the receding sovereignty of the state changed power relations in Ecuador, therefore allowing transnational actors to occupy policy production spaces. Whilst the latter forwarded the theoretical insights from which civil society protest, collective action, and new forms of deliberation that escape liberal forms of deliberative democracy could be integrated into the redefinition of Ecuador's public sphere; these new forms of discursive democracy present novel points of analysis regarding the ways in which politics, policy change, and civil society interact in ethnically diverse spaces such as Ecuador.

As a theoretical backdrop, discursive democracy also presents new pathways through which protest may lead to profound transformations in the realms of policy and law. The significance of this is twofold. Firstly, it opens the door for Latin American academics to question the highly formalistic, legalistic, and procedural forms of policy construction that have engulfed governance since pre-republican times. Development of legal precedent through what has been referred to as "structural cases" constructs legal judicial proceedings in such a way as to:

> (1) affect a large number of people who allege a violation of their rights, either directly or through organizations that litigate the cause; (2) implicate multiple government agencies found to be responsible for pervasive public policy failures that contribute to such rights violations; and (3) involve structural injunctive remedies, i.e., enforcement orders whereby courts instruct various government agencies to take coordinated actions to protect the entire affected population and not just the specific complainants in the case.
>
> (RODRÍGUEZ-GARAVITO 2011, 1671)

Rupturing centuries of formalistic approaches towards law and policy would also counter the judicial and procedural processes forwarded by Habermas or Rawls in their envisioning of a public sphere dominated by legal or policy mechanics. Constitutional reform, fueled by social mobilisation and indigenous political demands, reshaped the language of diversity effectively changing the discourses that permeated legal institutions. As Uprimny (2010, 1590) underlines:

> This trend toward the recognition of diversity and the granting of special rights for indigenous communities is even more radical in the recent Bolivian and Ecuadorian constitutions, both of which suggest the existence of a nation of peoples or a multinational state, and constitutionalize conceptions from indigenous tradition. Furthermore, these constitutions strengthen the recognition of autonomy of indigenous peoples to manage their affairs. According to some analysts, this more radical orientation on the issue of nationality and the recognition of indigenous peoples makes the Bolivian and Ecuadorian constitutions part of a distinct and emerging constitutionalism. These constitutional shifts differ from recent changes in other Latin American countries in that the changes go beyond the scope of liberal constitutionalism-even in its multicultural

and multiethnic form and move toward a different constitutional form that is multinational, intercultural, and experimental.

Discursive democracy sidestepping the judicial or procedural rules proposed by conventional approaches to deliberative democracy, inaugurated new forms of discourse forwarded by marginalised actors (indigenous peoples, African Ecuadorians, women, transgender collectives) and other disenfranchised civil society groups to levy their demands before public authorities. Much like the political schisms that were brought forth by the lifting of literacy requirements in Ecuador's 1979 Constitution or the electoral reforms of the early 1990s, a public sphere that is defined by the right to protest, as a form of freedom of speech creates new and yet to be theorised dynamics in the construction of Ecuador's and possibly Latin America's public spheres.

As a second point of theoretical significance, discursive democracy resituates the relevance of civil society protest in the forging of the political changes that engulfed Ecuador between 1979 and 2008. The impact of this theoretical shifting point is that it comes to contest the predominating interpretations that have, until now, been forwarded by statist, Indigenist or post-developmental strains of Good Living. Primarily, by situating civil society protest and social discontent as the overarching forces that crafted Good Living into the legal construct that was incorporated into Ecuador's Constitution, discursive democracy dismantles the main propositions associated with current predominating strains. Collective action during the critical juncture would therefore be the driving force that led to the policy changes and proposals that ultimately crafted Good Living. In so doing, statist, Indigenist or post-developmental interpretations are left wanting of a theoretical explanation capable of linking their respective analyses to the events that transpired in Ecuador during the critical juncture. This linkage is of the upmost importance if either interpretative strain is to triumph in coinciding their respective interpretations of Good Living with the events, theories, and practices that have analysed Ecuadorian politics for the better part of three decades.

This wanting of theoretical explanation by either strain is further compounded by the theory-guided process tracing that introduced politicised ethnic cleavages, state retreat, and changing citizenship regimes, as the converging occurrences through which Good Living was crafted. Whilst neither of the predominating strains appear to actively include political, legal, sociological, anthropological or international relations theories to develop their overarching interpretations, the critical reading of Good Living here presented has drawn from multiple academic fields to explain its crafting. Interdisciplinary in nature, the inclusion of politicised ethnic cleavages, state retreat, and changing citizenship regimes throughout this book presents a theoretically robust explanation towards the origins of Good Living. In contrast to the ontological interpretations that have engulfed its analysis since 2008, the critical reading here presented brings together a multitude of analytical frameworks, which aid in the analysis of the different processes that converged in Ecuador during the critical juncture. Good Living is thus transformed from an ever-present truth, that is to be deductively reasoned into a contested discourse formation of reality. This inductive questioning of Good Living's origins, which is supported by theory-guided process tracing has presented a new critical reading towards Ecuador's 2008 Constitution. In accordance with the theoretical explanations presented, the crafting of Good Living that has been scrutinised breaks free from the predominating strains, which have until now, limited or at least constrained its analysis.

The critical reading offered in the present work is not to be understood as a definitive or final analysis on Good Living. Rather, what this book has focused on accomplishing is reverting the theoretically void discussions that have surrounded Good Living since 2008. With particular exceptions, such as the work of Bretón (2017), Schavelzon (2015), Quijano (2011), Parga (2011), Recasens (2014), Walsh (2009) or Radcliffe (2015), Good Living has been engulfed by discussions wanting of theoretical development. This book has attempted to contribute to this critical literature on Good Living by developing an overarching explanation that knits together actors, policy, institutions, and law in the forging of an allegedly unique Ecuadorian occurrence. However, once this process has been completed questions regarding Good Living's origins and future are left unanswered. Firstly: is Good Living a uniquely Ecuadorian occurrence? Or is it part of broader regional transformations? Secondly: is Good Living legally enforceable in any way? Or is its framing as an empty signifier an insurmountable limitation towards legal enforceability? Thirdly: what does Good Living's predominant strains reflect in terms of the representation of alterity and the imagining of indigenous culture? Moreover, how do these representations limit or thwart transgressive politics? Let us begin our final analysis of Good Living by questioning the limits of crafting Good Living as a representation of alterity.

1 Crafting Good Living: from Speaking to Listening

A critical theory of Good Living moves beyond living well scholarship, proposing a constitutional principle that encapsulates the end product of a broader process of political, social, and economic events that unfolded throughout the critical juncture. Local and transnational in nature, the forces that converged to shape Good Living came from a multitude of places and spaces that are unaccounted for. This framing of Good Living's origins also plays a strategic role in calling into question the essentialised, romanticised, and more often than not, hyperreal representations of indigeneity that have been ingrained within the three predominating strains. The various ways hyperreal representations of indigeneity have become coupled within Indigenist or post-development readings of Buen Vivir and Living Well is well documented in Chapter 2. However, even statist interpretations of Buen Vivir mimic the nation-state building processes that were once utilised to negate Andean alterity (Escobar 2010, 28). As mentioned in Chapter 3, distinct processes of methodological nationalism sought to create a homogenising pattern for Ecuadorian society, a steamroller effect over difference that was spearheaded by the state. Through conflation of the nation-state with society, methodological nationalism claimed that territorial boundaries obliged citizens to share a common history, language, culture, and religion (Glick Schiller 2012, 524). Whilst focused on the nation-state, the homogenising undertones that engulf statist interpretations of Buen Vivir similarly seek to eliminate difference through cultural and political homogenisation. What can be induced from all three interpretations of Buen Vivir is that indigeneity, otherness or subaltern alterity plays a central role in framing the ways in which idealised interpretations of Living Well are to be developed or applied.

The transgressive politics that engulfed Ecuador during the critical juncture demanded new ways from which power could contain otherness. This book has pointed to targeted programs of intervention such as those conceived by the World Bank, deployed by NGOs, and executed by transnational agents operating in Ecuador. Programs like PRODEPINE, and their complicity with the myth of ethnodevelopment, sought to instill new forms of societal control upon transgressive political subjects. The attempt to coincide modernity, liberalism, and the "savage" crafted essentialised representations of indigeneity that sought to elevate the phantom figure of a pure Indian. Thus, indigeneity became an idealised representation of otherness that was crafted to coincide with the imaginaries of industrialised northern economies By linking communitarian relations, solidarity, and trust as marketable assets, otherness became contained within the hegemonic power of social capital and its articulation to world markets (Taussig 1993, 142). Faced with new and often transgressive forms of constructing the public sphere, eruptions of discursive democracy were contained by displacing their subaltern interlocutors. In this sense, not only was the subaltern's ability to speak thwarted but any possibility of hearing what the subaltern had been saying also silenced (Riach 2017).

Transgressive political demands were thus silenced as transnational and local narrators occupied the privileged positions of discourse formation. Programs of intervention such as PRODEPINE, the rise of social capital, the forging of ethnodevelopment, the importation of Bolivia's *Suma Qamaña's* by CONAIE, its reframing by Ecuadorian economists, the fashioning of an "alternative to development" model that was uniquely Ecuadorian and the inclusion of Buen Vivir as a constitutional principle, are all evidence of such displacement. Reframing of transgressive political demands under new theme programs of society such as social capital granted a new 'permission to narrate' which gradually disarmed transgressive political demands. Political agendas would thus shift from subaltern demands to the domestic and transnational elites that began to occupy policy construction spaces during the critical juncture (Spivak 1988, 283). What cannot go unnoticed in this process of privileged discourse formation is the innate complicity that existed between indigenous elites, academics, NGO workers, civil servants, and transnational actors in the forging of a new theme program of society first premised on social capital, then on ethnodevelopment and ultimately on Buen Vivir. Formation of an indigenous elite within CONAIE, deployment of international experts and bureaucrats, NGOs occupying policy spaces, penetration of multilateral development projects led by the World Bank and convulsive legislative reform during the critical juncture led to the emergence of a new discourse regarding rights to emerge (Bretón 2007; Schavelzon 2015, 147; Bowen 2011, 455).

This complicity by diverse "Orientalists"[1] forged essentialised notions of indigenous culture, simultaneously justifying market-orientated development projects whilst silencing demands for equality, justice or broader cultural rights. This complicity is best captured by Said (1977: 109) when he states:

> As momentous, generally important issues face the world—issues involving nuclear destruction, catastrophically scarce resources, unprecedented

---

1 Edward Said (1977, 19): The most readily accepted designation for Orientalism is an academic one, and indeed the label still serves in a number of academic institutions. Anyone who teaches, writes about, or researches the Orient—and this applies whether the person is an anthropologist, sociologist, historian, or philologist—either in its specific or its general aspects, is an Orientalist, and what he or she does is Orientalism. Compared with Oriental studies or area studies, it is true that the term Orientalism is less preferred by specialists today, both because it is too vague and general and because it connotes the high-handed executive attitude of nineteenth-century and early-twentieth-century European colonialism. Nevertheless, books are written and congresses held with "the Orient" as their main focus, with the Orientalist in his new or old guise as their main authority. The point is that even if it does not survive as it once did, Orientalism lives on academically through its doctrines and theses about the Orient and the Oriental.

human demands for equality, justice, and economic parity—popular caricatures of the Orient are exploited by politicians whose source of ideological supply is not only the half-literate technocrat but the superliterate Orientalist. The legendary Arabists in the State Department warn of Arab plans to take over the world. The perfidious Chinese, half-naked Indians, and passive Muslims are described as vultures for "our" largesse and are damned when "we lose them" to communism, or to their unregenerate Oriental instincts: the difference is scarcely significant. These contemporary Orientalist attitudes flood the press and the popular mind. Arabs, for example, are thought of as camel-riding, terroristic, hook-nosed, venal lechers whose undeserved wealth is an affront to real civilization. Always there lurks the assumption that although the Western consumer belongs to a numerical minority, he is entitled either to own or to expend (or both) the majority of the world resources. Why? Because he, unlike the Oriental, is a true human being. No better instance exists today of what Anwar Abdel Malek calls "the hegemonism of possessing minorities" and anthropocentrism allied with Europocentrism: a white middle-class Westerner believes it his human prerogative not only to manage the nonwhite world but also to own it, just because by definition "it" is not quite as human as "we" are. There is no purer example than this of dehumanized thought. In a sense the limitations of Orientalism are, as I said earlier, the limitations that follow upon disregarding, essentializing, denuding the humanity of another culture, people, or geographical region.

Following Said's reflections on Orientalism, as well as Andolina et al.'s (2009: 54) comments on Andeanism, this book proposes that Buen Vivir, as it currently stands within either of its predominating strains, is the continuation of a broader process that has sought to picture the region and its cultures through a 'representation that portrays contemporary highland peasants as outside the flow of modern history' (Starn 1991, 64 quoted in Andolina et al. 2009). What this effectively translates into is a privileged discourse formation in which an oversimplified representation of Andean indigenous actors perpetuates the well-established patterns of racial projects that placed Indians outside of history and Western modernity often through negative connotations (Andolina et al. 2009, 55). Similarly, Said's remarks on Orientalism argued that discourses about the Middle East were usually 'based on East-West dualisms, in which people of the Orient appeared in Western narratives as cultural stereotypes in value-laden geographies' (Said 1978 quoted in Andolina et al. 2009, 54). In its current state, Buen Vivir is another portrayal of Andeanism or Orientalism, an essentialised representation of otherness that stereotypically frames culture in order to pacify possible transgressions against Western modernity and its economic projects. For such reasons, this book positions critical Good Living as a theoretical bedrock from which new analytical scopes may be defined.

Buen Vivir, through it's stereotypical framing, and its displacement of transgressive politics, is made evident throughout the critical juncture. Demands for territorial autonomy, self-determination and broader cultural rights had framed indigenous resistance between 1986 and 1992. However, between the mid-1990s and early 2000s, new agendas relating to ethnodevelopment and social capital overwhelmed these transgressive political demands. These shifts between policy demands are evident in the wording of Ecuador's 2008 Constitution as well as the CONAIE policies analysed in Chapter 3. Previous chapters have also presented detailed accounts of the conflictive and often opposing wording Ecuador's Constitution harbours. Whilst much attention focused on presenting and consolidating "alternative economic models" other more transgressive demands such as collective and cultural rights, although recognised in various sections of the constitution, underwent little to no progressive development. In fact, according to indigenous leader Mónica Chuji, Ecuador's 2008 Constitution even reduced or thwarted the progressive development of cultural rights that had been envisioned by indigenous leaders prior to the Constitutional Assembly (Interview 2017). Rather than taking on the challenge of further developing subaltern demands for territorial autonomy, self-determination or cultural rights, new agendas relating to post-development and environmental conservation enveloped constitutional debates.

Permission to narrate transgressive political demands was thus dislocated from the grass-roots civil society collectives that had defined Ecuadorian politics in the early stages of the critical juncture. Transgressive political agendas were now occupied by a surging indigenous elite, domestic and transnational NGO workers, newly consolidated political actors, as well as the overarching themes of society they envisioned. Alterity was now to be constructed by transnational development actors and a domestic bourgeois-nationalist elite (Spivak 1988, 283). Aided by an indigenous elite, which serviced domestic and transnational intellectuals interested in the voice of the Other, Good Living was first consolidated in social capital and later through ethnodevelopment (Spivak 1988, 284). Buen Vivr's crafting since 2008, and what has been said within either strain, although interesting, is not in itself as relevant as what it has refused to say (Spivak 1988, 286). Whilst Buen Vivir's predominant strains say much in relation to their particular interpretations, they do little to recover what cannot be said or heard by the subaltern. This journey of silence, that continues to entrap Buen Vivir, oscillates between subaltern demands towards a reimagining of the political sphere and the hegemonic articulation that links alterity to world markets.

Silencing of transgressive politics is in its essence the power of Buen Vivir as an empty signifier. Through the promotion of tamed representations of indigeneity that are aided by social capital, ethnodevelopment or Buen Vivir, the incisive demands of what was once Latin America's most organised indigenous movement has, at least for now, been silenced. This strategic silencing is what frames Buen Vivir and Living Well as an empty signifier, a discursivity that caters to all whilst giving to neither. Through the absorption of meaning that stems from a multiplicity of collective actors, and the indeterminacy of their respective signifieds within the empty signifier, Buen Vivir's ability to take on the demands of the many is endless. However, its inability to fix meaning, at least for now, makes it a mirage, something that is desired but forever unattainable. Moving beyond Buen Vivir's current framing as an empty signifier and repositioning it as an enforceable legal principle with local and regional effects, will be the focus of the remaining paragraphs. Through a shift in current approaches towards Living Well, the following sections not only seek to overcome Buen Vivir's current state as empty signifier but also recover, or at the very least reinstate, the demands that led to collective action during the critical juncture. Re-situating these demands seeks to measure the silences lurking within Buen Vivir, thereby acknowledging what it refuses to say within either of its three predominant strains (Spivak 1988, 286). This exercise obliges us not only to let the subaltern speak but to also listen to what he, she or they have to say (Riach 2017).

2   Exhaustion of the Rights Discourse

This section shifts the tone of discussion from the Buen Vivir-Living Well nexus to the Critical Good Living approach that has been developed throughout the book. In this sense, Critical Good Living offers a new, theoretically robust approach towards the critical juncture, allowing new discussions to engage with the events the led to the 2008 Constitution. The political and social transformations that engulfed Latin American constitution making in the second part of the twentieth century define the legal applicability of Good Living as a legal principle. Gargarella (2013) has adequately pointed out that as the Latin American Left transformed during the critical juncture, the political agendas it sought were also distanced from earlier objectives. More importantly however, is the fact that once it began to speak the language of liberal rights, it gradually distanced itself from broader social questions and grass-roots struggles. Through far-reaching demands that saw the expansion of social rights as the new political goal to be attained within liberal constitutions, more complex and substantive questions regarding inequality, discrimination or marginalisation were gradually displaced (Gargarella 2013, 130). Focus on the expansion of economic and social rights came as a paradox, as their incorporation, more often than not, did not equate to substantial reforms to the democratic Caesarism that had been so predominant within Latin American jurisdictions (Gargarella 2013, 88).

This effectively translated into a process of constitution making that did little to oppose the coloniality of power engrained in Latin American legal thinking (Rodríguez-Garavito 2011; Quijano 2013). Thus, Latin American constitutions, both old and new, in their substantive provisions, failed to dismantle the political geographies that perpetuate colonial forms of societal control. Inclusion of broader economic, social and cultural rights within Latin American Constitutions are thus constrained by the engrained forms of political and social power that turn rights into dormant legal clauses. In essence, dormant legal clauses persist due to the hyper-presidential constitutional systems on which they depend. These vertical systems of power are exemplified by the demands of a strong president who wields constitutional authority in order to constrain the current and future applicability of progressive rights. Hence the dogmatic or rights focused section of Ecuador's Constitution remained indifferent to its organic section, effectively leaving political branches to decide whether or not to comply with their corresponding constitutional mandates. In order to overcome such limitations, Good Living, as well as other human rights, must be assessed through new interpretative understandings that allow revision of competing rights. Moreover, these revisions must assess the legitimacy of public authorities limiting the realisation of progressive rights.

Hence expansive economic, social or cultural rights, as well as the inclusion of Good Living within Ecuador's 2008 Constitution, must be reviewed through constructivist understanding of rights. In this revisioning of rights they come to be understood as the end product of political struggle, ideals that are worth pursuing but are nevertheless at the mercy of imperfect human institutions (Travers 2010, 53). Imperfect in nature, these new societal ideals may be framed in such a way as to overcome the idealised or stereotypically framed understandings of Good Living as well as the limitations imposed by human institutions. One way of achieving this is through the framing of Good Living as a mandate of optimisation, a mechanism in which the problems faced by the application of rights are resolved through the judicial interpretation of constitutional principles (Alexy 2015). Good Living as a constitutional principle, which seeks optimisation, demands judicial organs to assess the constitutional legitimacy of constraining rights when they conflict with one another or when public authority illegitimately limits them (Alexy 2015). If any such limitation implies a useless, unnecessary or disproportionate restriction on human rights then it must in essence be precluded.

Framed in this fashion, Good Living becomes a constitutional principle yearning for a judicial interpretation that allows it to transcend the general assumptions that currently overwhelm it as an empty signifier. Once interpreted through an integrative theory of constitutional rights, one that may balance the proportionality of one right over another, Good Living transcends the simple juxtaposition that currently exists between competing interpretations (Alexy 2003). Through an integrative theory that analyses constitutional rights, the analytical, empirical and normative dimensions of constitutional principles may be adequately assessed (Alexy 2002, 13). As such, the basic concepts, institutional structures, empirical premises, causation, and applicability of Good Living in relation to other constitutional principles and legal doctrines may be scrutinised. Good Living, as a new dimension of rights within Ecuadorian and Latin American law, overcomes the ontological competing "world views" that entrap post-development, ecologist, Indigenist or statist strains. This critical approach, or constructivist revision of Good Living, states that as a right, it must be appreciated through realistic understandings that consider the political, material and interpretative difficulties inherent in the making or realising of human rights (Travers 2010).

In addition to the framing of Good Living as a mandate of optimisation, we introduce D'Souza's (2010, 55) comments regarding the "rights conundrum." What D'Souza argues is that as a discourse, human rights have all but exhausted themselves, losing their power to inspire the changes that may cement their corresponding enforceability. Inextricably tied to this exhaustion are the dualisms that stem from liberal theories regarding private property rights and the more expansive economic, social, and cultural rights that have been demanded by the Global South since the mid-twentieth century. The human rights discourse has thus become entangled in a circulatory logic that reflects onto itself without procuring avenues from which enforceability may be further scrutinised. D'Souza (2010) attributes this shortcoming to the disconnect that exists between rights and their sociality. What this translates into is that in order to take the rights conundrum seriously, human agency must consider the indirect coercion that is dictated by social institutions (Ci 2005, 243 quoted in D'Souza 2010). This shift in the reasoning of rights demands that attributions of power be taken seriously because 'a human society in which no attribution of power and hence no formation of subjectivity ever take place is not recognisably a human society' (Ci 2005, 245 quoted in D'Souza 2010). Hence, rights, and their interlinkage with human agency, must conceptualise the institutional constraints that impede their fulfillment or progression (D'Souza 2010). Rights, as well as human life, are thus dependent on social institutions and the powers they respectively wield. Once again, it is imperative that Good Living, as well as other human rights, be analysed in relation to the impediments they face within Latin America's hyper-presidential systems.

This book introduced Foucaultian governmentality to explain the various ways in which the state ceded control from the local to the supranational. This displacement of sovereign power towards multilateral instances such as the World Trade Organization or Inter-American Court of Human Rights, not only created new forms of graduated sovereignty but also punctured the exercise of power from which rights were either constrained or enhanced. The critical juncture effectively witnessed how the displaced power of the state allowed new political forces to consolidate through opposition to neoliberal reform. These new political forces crafted novel policy demands such as plurinationality, the rights of nature or Good Living. Once again, if the current hyper-presidential systems and institutions that are enacted within Ecuador's constitutional system limit the realisation of human rights, then new avenues from which power may be subverted are needed. For this reason, the changing mechanics in the exercise of power by the Ecuadorian state will be the centre of analysis for the remaining discussion. The following states two broad propositions. The first of which underlines that the forms of graduated sovereignty that consolidated during the critical juncture created puncture wounds within state power. These punctures to sovereign power opened the supranational spaces from which subaltern agency could question the institutional powers that limits or enacts rights. The second point is that throughout the critical juncture the expansion of rights, specifically economic, social, and cultural rights, were not a particularly Ecuadorian event. Rather, what is here proposed is that the critical juncture witnessed the expansion of economic, social, and cultural rights on international, regional and domestic theaters. This expansion simultaneously reflected regional demands towards the improvement of welfare services and collective rights but also the consolidation of domestic and supranational judicial review as an avenue through which stale forms of sovereign power could be overturned. To this effect, whilst recent scholarship has framed the emergence of Buen Vivir and Sumak Kawsay within the predominating framings of state-led development, Indigenism and post-development, the main objective of both this book and section, is to present a new analytical framework. Moving beyond Buen Vivir or Sumak Kawsay, this section analyses Good Living, as a form of collective well-being that is intrincably tied to the concept of human dignity.

Moreover, the analysis that follows frames Good Living within international, regional and domestic legal transformations that surpass its framing as an empty signifier, effectively christening it as a constitutional principle that is echoed in the collective demands of Ecuadorians and other Latin Americans. Building on the concept of a collective regional understanding of human dignity, Good Living becomes a benchmark for the realization of rights within the regions varied, yet similarly distressed, legal systems.

3 The Importation of Law: Local and International Influences

The enactment of Good Living as a form of collective human dignity, finds its point of incepetion within the novel forms of graduated sovereignty that were enacted by the Inter-American Court of Human Rights (IACtHR), domestic judicial review throughout the region and strategic litigation in different Latin American states. This processes of gradual legal transformation was partially made possible through the gradual importation of foreign legal concepts and judicial remedies. However, it also reflects the maturity of regional legal systems as they responded to the social, institutional and economic demands brought forth by a myriad of collectives that became engaged in politics and refom during the critical juncture.

Novel forms of importation of legal systems emerged during the critical juncture as the aftermath of the fall of the Berlin Wall redefined geopolitics. As Dupré (2003a) underlines, 'post-communist constitutions were largely drafted following Western models,' a similar set of institutional mimicking, legal transplants or cross fertilization had already taken root in Latin America since the end of colonial rule (Dupré 2003a, 48; Gargarella 2013, 65). Gorbachev's Perestroika released wide ranging forces on the international stage, effectively reshaping legal systems in multiple jurisdictions. As Linz and Stepan (1996 in Dupré 2003a, 47) commented on what they considered to be "international influences" leading post-communist transitions:

> When we place in comparative perspective the transitions in the Soviet Union and the ex-Warsaw Pact countries of East Central Europe (Poland, Hungary, Czechoslovakia, the German Democratic Republic, Romania and Bulgaria), one of their most distinctive qualities concerns the variable we call *international influence*. One of the editors of the classic four-volume study of the transitions in southern Europe and South America, Laurence Whitehead, argued that, 'in all peacetime cases considered here internal forces were of primary importance in determining the course and outcome of the transition attempt, and international factors only play a secondary role.'

Two primary points must be underlined, the first of which reinstates the relevance of local processes in choosing the type of model that is enforced when new legal institutions are selected, designed and set in place. Secondly, one cannot dismiss the relevance that "international influence" had on a specific juncture, the decisions made therein and the results that emerged from a specific chain of events. As Dupré (2003a, 49) correctly underlines, Western legal regimes have been exported to other jurisdictions, this of course considers the diametrically different circumstances that made the exportation of law possible in colonial settings and the process of importation that came with the fall of the Berlin Wall. Notwithstanding, the exportation and hence importation of law, requires the convergence of a multiplicity of actors such as international institutions and individual experts, leaving states to carry out a merely marginal role (Dupré 2003a, 49). Similar to what occurred in Ecuador during the critical juncture, policy spaces that had been zealously guarded by the state were soon occupied by transnational actors and their sponsoring institutions, as such the receding state became a primordial mechanism during the critical juncture, allowing new legal institutions such as Good Living, plurinationality and the rights of nature to be erected (Gargarella 2013, 179; Grijalva 2012, 57)

Chapters 3 and 4 pinpointed the multiple actors, agencies and institutions that came together in the crafting of Good Living. Internal processes such as the rise of a consolidated indigenous movement, economic turmoil, political scandal and institutional crises became crucial events in shaping the type of legal systems that were forged in 1978, 1998 and 2008. However, of significant influence are the so-called "international influences" that also descended upon Ecuador during the critical juncture. In a similar analysis to what occurred in Latin America, Dupré (2003a, 50) identified international institutions, NGOs and individual experts as defining figures when the new legal regimes of postcommunist countries were decided. Hyde-Price (1994 in Dupré 2003a, 49) had considered these same factors when he spoke of how 'external factors can facilitate this process of domestic political reform.' The widespread force of these external factors can cover a multiplicity of areas such as: improving parliamentary practice, promoting and monitoring human rights, supporting independent media, developing NGOs and representative structures, encouraging local democracy and participation, and finally promoting education and analysis (Dupré 2003a, 49).

As had occurred in Latin America during the critical juncture, the convergence of local politics with international institutions and actors, as well as their subsequent political and economic objectives, traced a new line of political discourse that was neither local nor foreign, ancient nor modern. This emergence of a new discourse, was the result of multiple local, regional and international forces coming together. During Ecuador's critical juncture local politics became fused with international institutions and actors. This complicity between actors and institutions is analysed in Chapter 4 as the IMF, World Bank, PRODEPEINE, Pachakutik, CONAIE and others, came together during the critical juncture to redefine Ecuador's political arena. One striking example in this complicity, are the ways in which policy, discourse and finally law adopted the concepts and prescriptions of transnational actors. As Bretón (2005, 52) adequately points out PRODEPEINE 'led to an apparent ethnogenesis throughout Ecuador, as new identities and adscriptions of indigenous peoples emerged in an effort to secure funding' through Second Tier Organizations, that had, for the sake of reaching deep into international wallets, reorganized, dismantled or mutated social organizational structures of Andean indigenous groups. Reorganization of indigenous groups through internationally sponsored Second Tier Organizations became a mechanism through which funding could be secured (Bretón 2005, 54). Local politics had thus, similarly to what Dupré mentions in regards to post-communist countries, fallen under the international influence of actors, institutions and their much needed resources.

Similar to what had occurred in post-communist Europe, local politics were in no way immune to outside influence, pressure or preference. In regards to Good Living as a legal principle, this confluence of the local with the supranational, reinstates the point that as a concept, Good Living is neither an ancient knowledge, a statist formula for development or a recipe for post-development (Hidalgo-Capitán and Cubillo-Guevara's 2014). It is the by-product of multiple events coming together in the crafting of law to attend social, political and economic demands in the times of crises that unravelled throughout the critical juncture. For these reasons, it has been argued in Chapter 3 and 4 that indigenous mobilization led civil society movements during the critical juncture by adapting its political discourse to meet the needs of local politics and international actors and institutions. This ultimately would lead to what we identify as Buen Vivir or Sumak Kawsay, an empty signifier that merged the projects, policies and demands of the local, foreign and contextual to gain political momentum. It does also however, in its representation of Buen Vivir or Sumak Kawsay, explain why it failed as a legal principle. The proposed transition of moving towards a conceptualization of Good Living as a form of collective human dignity does not however seek to answer its ontological origins or its corresponding caveats within other epistemological fields. The role of international actors and institutions intervening in Ecuador is pivotal in explaining the importation of law and the convergence of agents, institutions and legal systems. Through this process, one must also consider the relevant role constitution making and the expansion of international human rights instruments had on Latin America as a whole during the critical juncture (Gargarella 2015, 1537; Tushnet 2017, 128).

During the critical juncture, politicized ethnic cleavages, state retreat, changing citizenship, transnational governmentality and new forms of discursive democracy all played a part in redefining how Ecuador's political arena was shaped. Moreover, these internal and external factors were propelled by wider processes that had been redefining geopolitical institutions since the late 1970s. As Alston (et al. 2007, 926) comments, human rights became a primary issue for multilateral institutions such as the United Nations. From 1977 onwards, the UN General Assembly, through GA Res.32/127 endorsed 'a new approach of appealing to States in areas where regional agreements in the field of human rights do not yet exist to consider arrangements with a view to the establishment within their respective regions of suitable regional machinery for the promotion and protection of human rights' (Alston et al. 2007).

Latin America proved to be a fertile ground for the expansion, promotion and enforcement of the regional machinery intended to promote and protect human rights. The consolidation of a uniquely Latin American approach to human rights protection on a supranational and national level, contrasts with the diverging approaches these efforts encountered in other regions. As was mentioned in the Twenty-Eighth Report of the Commission to Study the Organization of Peace in 1980 (in Alston et al. 2007, 930), African, Asian and Eastern European states, for diverging reasons all opposed a regional promotion of human rights. However, Latin America took on an expansive approach towards human rights, perhaps as a result of the multiple human rights abuses the region experienced between 1960 and 1990 (Brands 2010). Possible conditions that made adoption of a regional human rights organization possible may be attributed to:

> (1) the existence of geographic, historical and cultural bonds among states of a particular region; (2) the fact that recommendations of a regional organization may meet less resistance than those of a global body; (3) the likelihood that the publicity about human rights will be wider and more effective; and (4) the fact that there is less possibility of 'general, compromise formulae,' which in global bodies are more likely to be based on 'considerations of political nature' (Alston et al. 2007: 930).

The birth and consolidation of the Inter-American Human Rights System reflects a process of regional promotion towards human rights instruments. Rather than a localized system resulting from rural or urban social settings, the

Inter-American system defies traditional power structures laid out throughout Latin America since the early republican era. For example, the ceding of state sovereignty in favor of supranational organs is an event that only occurred during the critical juncture. Institutions like the IACtHR or WTO, are international institutional arrangements that were made possible in a specific period of time. Political freedoms were awarded so long as economic liberties were expanded, creating regional constitutional arrangements that faced strong multilateral trade institutions and an increasingly authoritative human rights protection system (Gargarella 2013; Ginsburg 2010; Melish 2009). Unsurprisingly, supranational organisms redefined state power and hence the citizenship regimes they controlled. Graduated sovereignty and the complex Inter-American system from which it sprawned, incorporated the use of *Vida Digna* (Human Dignity), effectively merging with local concepts relating to collective well-being, particularly those regarding economic, social and cultural rights.

Graduated sovereignty of the Latin American kind, emerges from American Declaration on the Rights and Duties of Man and the American Convention, allowing the IACtHR and the Inter-American Commission of Human Rights to monitor the mechanisms and actions utilized by states towards the protection of human rights (Harris 1998 in Alston et al. 2007: 1027).

In what follows, we will focus on the role of the Inter-American Court of Human Rights (IACtHR) as its jurisprudence has focused on developing the concept of *Vida Digna* which will later be linked to the notion of Good Living that imprinted in Ecuador's 2008 Constitution. Selective focus on the IACtHR and not the Inter-American Commission of Human Rights is done so as to highlight the growing body of jurisprudence on *Vida Digna* published by the former. This of course should not act in detriment to the valuable and transcendent tasks executed by the Inter-American Commission of Human Rights, its country reports and the *in loco* visits it has conducted throughout Latin America since its inception (Melish 2009: 346).

4 From Human Dignity to *Vida Digna*

Prior to our engagement with the IACtHR's development of jurisprudence around *Vida Digna*, one must first address the conceptual origins from where it emerges. The focus of this book has been to pinpoint the legal origins of Good Living as a legal principle, in order to do so, it has been argued that its inscription into formal law is the result of local demands meeting international influences, which once combined created a new discourse of rights. Up to this point it has also been argued, that under Indigenist, post-development or state-centered analysis Buen Vivir and Sumak Kawsay reproduce an empty signifier that dilutes any one discourse by the influx of multiple contradicting discursivities. In this same sense, it has been argued that this combination of discursivities allowed heterogenous civil society groups to come together under a single objective of combating market-led reform. In so doing, the indigenous collective that had led civil society mobilization ceded demands in favour of more "inclusive" market-orientated policy agendas, effectively disregarding what had once been a platform based on collective rights and territorial autonomy. Such a framing is what must be overcomed in order to grant legal applicability to Good Living on the basis of collective human dignity.

However, the inclusion of Good Living as a constitutional principle in 2008 opens the door to other important legal and political analysis. As an empty signifier, Buen Vivir or Sumak Kawsay fail to encapsulate and enforce the demands of at least twenty years of civil society mobilization. Constitutional inscription or what Habermas (1996, 75) coined as "juridification," depicts the formal transformation of new areas of social interaction into written law. Representations of Good Living in the form of Buen Vivir or Sumak Kawsay, in its current state at least, fail to grasp the underlying social, political and economic demands that sparked civil society mobilization in Ecuador. This of course does not intend to discard analytical development of either two, but rather reframe the conversation around other conceptual frameworks. On a similar note, one must be aware of the English language usage of a concept that was coined in Spanish. The usage of Good Living, rather than Buen Vivir or Sumak Kawsay, is done so in order to facilitate clear distinction between the three. This must not however be intererpeted as a preference of one language over another, but as form of earmarking what is deemed relevant within the conversation. Hence, our current argument develops Good Living as a distinction from Buen Vivir or Sumak Kawsay, so as to afford it the conceptual space needed to further develop *Vida Digna* as a collective right.

Good Living became a legal principle due to the international influences that came together during the critical juncture, effectively conjoining local demands with transnational discourses related to human rights. To all effects, it was the discourse of human rights as an authoritative legal model, that propelled indigenous demands and mobilization in the first place (Anaya 2000, 47).

Good Living as a constitutional principle, as the juridification of social practice into written law, stems from both local and transnational experiences. As was previously mentioned, the importation and exportation of law has been a constant in the evolution of Latin American legal systems. The multiple crises that came about during the critical juncture, presented a fertile ground from which new legal models could be imported into Latin America and Ecuador. One such concept was the *Vida Digna* jurisprudence that permeates the work of the IACtHR. *Vida Digna* is closely related to discussions surrounding human dignity, originally coined by the German Constitutional Court under the notion of a "mother right" or *Muttergrundrecht,* human dignity is defined as right which gives birth to other rights (Dupré 2003a, 67). However, even in its authorship and elaboration of the right to human dignity, the German Constitutional Court "borrowed," "transplanted," "cross-fertilized" or "mimicked" the doctrinal developments previously coined by HC Nipperdy (1962 in Dupré 2003a, 67).

Of course, questions surrounding human dignity have long framed discussions in politics, philosophy or theology. As Lebech (2004, 2) accurately points out:

> We may talk about four stages in the development of the idea of human dignity. Each depends on a time-typical framework and exemplifies a logical possibility. Cicero may represent the cosmo-centric framework of Antiquity, which explains human dignity on the basis of nature (2). Thomas Aquinas represents the Middle Ages' Christo-centric framework, which explains human dignity in relation to Jesus Christ (3). Immanuel Kant can represent the logo-centric framework of Modernity, explaining human dignity as a tribute to reason (4). Whereas Mary Wollstonecraft, finally, represents the polis-centred framework of Post-Modernity, which explains human dignity in relation to social acceptability (5). Each of these ways of accounting for human dignity can be understood as a source of the idea as it appears in the Declaration of Human Rights. Frameworks change because patterns of social organization change (...) It is an empirico-systemic structure, consisting in a series of conventions defining a way of living with all its practical and theoretical problems (...).

Human dignity is thus identified, analysed and understood in the different historically based frameworks from which it emerges (Lebech 2004, 12). Human dignity, as a "mother right" was first developed by the German Constitutional Court on the back of previous doctrinal writings. The Hungarian Constitutional Court would later borrow or transplant the concept through its 1990 jurisprudence via Case 8/1990, inaugurating a 'long series of cases that were based on the imported right to human dignity.' Construction of human dignity under German influence, premised the Kantian principle that the essential quality of humanity is dignity (Dupré 2003a,70). A fundamental aspect of human dignity, as understood through a Kantian lens, emphasizes the importance of individual self-determination and autonomy, as exemplified by the Hungarian Constitutional Court's case 23/1990 (in Dupré 2003a, 72):

> The right to human dignity is not merely a declaration of a moral value. The concept that human dignity is a value a priori and beyond law, and is inaccessible by law in its entirety does not preclude this value from being regarded as the source of rights—as many international conventions and constitutions do by following natural law—or the law from requiring the respect of dignity or the transformation of some of its aspects into a real right ... We shall see that the right to human dignity will fulfil its function only if it is interpreted in unity with the individual person's right to life; if we leave this out of consideration, abstract dignity will allow treatment of a concrete individual as an object.

As will be evidenced in the following section, *Vida Digna* jurisprudence as developed by the IACtHR transcends this atomistic and individually focused re-enactment of human dignity. Whilst the Kantian origins of such a concept may lay far from Ecuador's rural Andes or Amazonian jungles, the legal innovation of transforming an individualistically focused right into an over-arching legal precedent, that seeks to remedy economic, social and cultural inequalities, thereby attending local demands for reform, requires further analysis. Tracing the origins of Good Living as a legal principle seeks to confirm its applicability within Ecuador's and possibly Latin America's legal systems. Therefore, a merger of Kantian and indigenous proposals should be welcomed if the end product attends demands that have long been forgotten. Notwithstanding the evident distance one concept has from the other. Hence the legal and conceptual innovation that follows the IACtHR's analysis is the development of a collective sphere of human dignity that is uniquely Latin American. An example of this is the construction of human dignity from a collective or group orientated focus within the rulings of the IACtHR's, regarding indigenous people's rights and the expansion of economic, social and cultural rights in favour of the general population.

5   Graduated Sovereignty and the Role of the IACtHR

Since the dawn of its first republics, Latin American constitutionalism has mirrored models of Euro-American modernity in an attempt to mimic the developments of the United States Constitution or the ideals of the First French

Republic (Whitehead 2012, 129). However, from the 1990s onwards an ever-growing constructivist interpretation of law and society has fought epistemic coloniality and the absenting of otherness (Rodriguez-Garavito 2011, 1678). Transformations to legal practice have steadily focused on the historic intra-group inequalities that underline race and class relations in Ecuador and Latin America (Abertyn 2013, 164). This shifting of gears within Latin America's legal practice has created what Abertyn defined as a 'Living Law,' a new form of legal reasoning that is responsive to the cultural and socio-economic conditions in which it is applied. Overcoming the limitations intrinsically conditioned within formalistic interpretations of law generated a transformative jurisprudence that was adamant on addressing the cultural and customary issues from which cultural diversity was either prevented or realised (Abertyn 2013,173). Latin American legal practice and the jurisprudence that has flowed from domestic and regional courts since the early 1990s, reflects an understanding of law that is responsive to the multicultural, pluralistic, and local interpretations needed for the securement of economic, social, and cultural rights. Constructivist interpretations therefore reinterpret the contextual and historical conditions that sustain or perpetuate unequal relations (Abertyn 2013, 80). Through pluralistic interpretations of progressive social struggles, such as those once led by Ecuador's indigenous movement, recognition of difference has allowed legal systems to incorporate subaltern demands within the mechanics of legal enforceability (Abertyn 2013,181).

Subaltern demands counter that the entrenched power differences have been historically prevalent in Latin America. These entrenched legal differences, based either on class or race, crafted a legal system that has been complicit in the perpetuation of inequality and racism (Fischer and O'Hara 2009, 2). However, since the 1990s, the progressive development of Latin American law has witnessed the expansion of a legal reasoning that is responsive to the demands of marginalised sectors of civil society such as indigenous people, peasants or the urban poor. On a regional level, the Inter-American Court of Human Rights (IACtHR) has spearheaded the push towards a reinterpretation of economic, social, and cultural rights. This "regional push" towards the securement of the so-called "second generation" rights have consolidated into what legal circles define as the Inter-American constitutionality block (Burgorgue-Larsen 2014, p. 17). In words of Ecuador's Constitutional Court, what this translates into is that the 2008 Constitution includes various referral clauses to diverse and particularly open principles and international treaties foreign to the national legislation (Corte Constitutional 2017, 133). Jurisprudential integration of international law into domestic decisions was, after the 2008 Constitution came into effect, through cases No. 004-14-SCN-CC and No. 0072-14-CN in which the Court defined the constitutionality block as the congregation of norms, that although not expressly defined within the formal norms of the Constitution, are still recognized and ranked as objectives for the state (Corte Constitutional 2017, 133). What this means is that on a region-wide basis there is an increasing uniform interpretation of social, economic, and cultural rights. This regional (re)interpretation of law, has brought social, economic, and cultural rights to gradually receive similar judicial treatment across the Latin America republics.

This phenomenon is not only attributable to the constitutional convergence through treaty ratification that is analysed by Elkins et al. (2013), but also due to the increased jurisdictional capabilities enacted by the IACtHR since the late 1990s. In addition to this regional push, Ecuador's 2008 Constitution expanded the applicability of human rights instruments and the jurisdictional powers of the IACtHR. For example, Article 417 of Ecuador's 2008 Constitution allows for the direct applicability of international human rights instruments when they are needed to secure the enforcement of social, economic, and cultural rights threatened by domestic policies or legislation. Moreover, Article 424 of Ecuador's Constitution orders that international human rights instruments, which grant more favourable rights than those locally dictated, should prevail when threatened by domestic legislation or the public policies of the state. This rights-based approach towards the possible abuses that may arise from the exercise of sovereign power is thus reflected on the supranational level via the IACtHR.

More to the point, the powers granted to the IACtHR allows it to revise the various ways in which Ecuadorian legislation or policy expands or contracts economic, social, and cultural rights in accordance with the wording of the American Convention on Human Rights (ACHR). This is exemplified in the IACtHR's jurisdictional capability of revising draft legislation within domestic legal systems, as well as its power to demand that member states reverse, modify or annul any such measure which acts in detriment to rights contained within the ACHR (Burgorgue-Larsen 2014, p. 5). Whilst the IACtHR's power exists on paper, it is limited by a member state's willingness to derogate or annul any such law or policy inconsistent with the Inter-American Human Rights system. Notwithstanding, the fact that such supranational judicial oversight exists, is in itself, an interesting avenue from which Good Living, as a progressive development of economic, social, and cultural rights may be further enhanced.

The power of the IACtHR, in regard to revising national policy and law, is exemplified in the case of the *Kichwa Indigenous Community of Sarayaku v Ecuador* (Sarayaku). In this case, presented by the Kichwa indigenous people of

Ecuador's Pastaza Province, the IACtHR found that lack of synchronicity between domestic legislation and the mandates of the ACHR had inevitably led to an unlawful limitation of collective rights and the subsequent international responsibility of the Ecuadorian state (Sarayaku, 125). In its sentencing, the IACtHR connected a plethora of Kichwa collective rights to the right to property, recognised by Article 21 of ACHR, effectively intertwining cultural identity with territorial rights and native title. Through the knitting of a legal doctrine that interweaved cultural rights with a collective right to property, the IACtHR determined that the Ecuadorian state had unfulfilled its international obligations towards indigenous peoples (Antkowiak 2014, 113). Historic in nature, this ruling obliged Ecuadorian authorities to meet the international law obligations that stemmed from the ACHR and other international human rights instruments.

In regard to the policy omissions of the Ecuadorian state, the same ruling determined that the state had allowed oil prospection to destroy caves, water sources, and underground rivers used by the Sarayaku community for sustenance (Sarayaku 105). These omissions had been compounded by the subsequent loss of trees and plants of significant cultural value to the Sarayaku community. Hence, the omissions of the Ecuadorian Government had not only destroyed spaces of cultural importance but also threatened the environmental resources from which the Sarayaku community sourced food and water. In all, what these violations amounted to was that the policies of the Ecuadorian state had effectively violated the economic, social, and cultural rights of the Sarayaku community. Actions and omissions of this nature made the Ecuadorian state internationally responsible for the destruction of territory and its effects on the provision of environmental resources needed by the Sarayaku community for their sustenance and survival (Sarayaku 127).

Sarayaku marks a turning point in the proceedings of the IACtHR. It was the first judicial process in which a delegation of the IACtHR visited the affected territory. Whilst this was made possible by the willingness of the Ecuadorian Government's acceptance of *in situ* inspections, its relevance to regional transformations towards economic, social, and cultural rights should not go unnoticed (Sarayaku, 21). In fact, the transformative power of supranational litigation and the jurisprudence of the IACtHR is evidenced in the acknowledgement of the Ecuadorian state's responsibility regarding violations to economic, social, and cultural rights. As was stated by then Secretary for Legal Affairs of the Presidency of Ecuador, Mr Alexis Mera (Sarayaku 23):

> ...the Government considers that the State is responsible for the events that occurred in 2003. I want this to be clearly stated and understood. The

Government recognizes its responsibility. Therefore, all the actions that occurred, the invasive measures, the actions of the armed forces, the acts against the destruction of the rivers, are all issues that we as a Government condemn, and believe that there is a right to reparation....

In its final judgement the IACtHR stated that Ecuador and other Latin American states are obliged to adopt measures, as well as legal guarantees, that discourage violations either by action or omission, to the conditions from which a decent life may be secured (Sarayaku 167). The IACtHR also stated that in light of Ecuador's Constitution being one of the most advanced in its provisions regarding the rights of Indigenous and Afro-Ecuadorian People's, the Ecuadorian state had a twofold obligation to secure collective rights (Sarayaku 168). One stemming from its international obligations and another from the provisions nestled within its own legal system. Sarayaku exemplifies the unique particularities that make-up the Inter-American Human Rights System, one which adopts a broad understanding of legal interpretations in an effort to correct the systemic deficiencies pertaining to economic, social and cultural rights. Furthermore, Sarayaku highlights the impact indigenous political mobilisation had on transforming domestic and regional institutions of law. In a timespan of some thirty years, Ecuador's indigenous peoples had secured political rights, consolidated a national confederation, influenced constitutional reforms, occupied prominent positions within the three branches of government and won an international lawsuit against the Ecuadorian state. These events are testament to the changing nature of Latin American and Ecuadorian law. Sarayaku underlines how local struggles by transgressive subalterns may escalate and effectively reverse the coloniality of power that has historically been entrenched within Latin American law and politics.

Additionally, it is important to point out that these progressive developments to Latin American law, although gradual in their impact, effectively create new avenues for constructivist formations of law. Once again, we turn to Sarayaku to underscore such developments. Whilst much of the Sarayaku ruling deals with the prior and informed consultations the state is obliged to carry out before public policies affect collective rights, the ruling is also evidence of new approaches towards legal rationale. In its Sarayaku judgement for example, the IACtHR stated that:

> 104. Regarding the impact on the Sarayaku territory, it was alleged, and the State did not contest, that in July 2003 the CGC had destroyed at least one site of special significance for the spiritual life of members of the

Sarayaku People on the land of Yachak Cesar Vargas. The facts were recorded by the First Notary of Puyo as follows: [...] At the place known as PINGULLU, a tree whose name is LISPUNGU, of approximately twenty meters in length and one meter in width was destroyed. [...] In the evening [...], we interviewed the elderly Shaman Cesar Vargas [...] who stated [...]: That oil company employees had entered his sacred forest in PINGULLU and had destroyed all the trees that existed there, particularly, the great tree of Lispungu, which has left him without the powers to obtain his medicine to cure the ailments of his children and relatives [...].

105. Similarly, the State has not contested the fact the company laid down seismic lines, set up seven heliports, destroyed caves, water sources and underground rivers needed to provide drinking water for the community; and cut down trees and plants of great environmental and cultural value, and used for subsistence food by the Sarayaku. In addition, the State has not contested the fact that landings by helicopters destroyed part of the so-called Wichu kachi Mountain, or "place of parrots," a site of great significance in the worldview of the Sarayaku People. The oil company's activities led to the sporadic suspension of the Sarayaku People's ancestral cultural rites and ceremonies, such as the Uyantsa, the most important festival held every February, and the seismic line passed near sacred sites used for ceremonies initiating young people into adulthood.

Recourse to the cosmovision of the Sarayaku indigenous people, comments regarding places of cultural or environmental importance, as well as the overall attention paid to culture and land, together reflect a new form of envisioning law that at the very least is intent on incorporating otherness into legal reasoning. Alterity, or the incorporation of otherness which is here presented, differs from the essentialised representations that engulf predominant strains of Good Living. Indigenous culture is thus no longer framed in accordance to the privileged discourses of the empty signifier but rather spoken by the subaltern. As regional law listens to subaltern demands, new forms of enacting legislation are gradually consolidated. Hence, these initial attempts at forging a human rights system, which is responsive to collective rights, is evidence of a regional judicial praxis that seeks to guarantee economic, social, and cultural rights. This securement, and its interpretations within regional legal systems, highlights a particularly regional approach towards economic, social, and cultural rights.

Through its supranational powers, the rulings of the IACtHR underscores the changing nature of sovereign power throughout the region. Its ability to influence policy decisions and legislative frameworks reflect the graduated sovereignty that was discussed in previous chapters. The critical juncture not only brought reforms to economic policy but also opened new spaces from which civil society could contest the actions, omissions, and abuses of the state. This is relevant to Good Living for two reasons. First of all, it accentuates the ability of domestic and regional courts in judicialising the enforcement of rights. What this means is that when and if, rights are not upheld within domestic tribunals, recourse to supranational jurisdictions, such as the IACtHR, will allow the enactment of remedies and guarantees that advance the protection rights. In addition to this, the second link between the Inter-American Human Rights System and Good Living is that through its interpretations new approaches towards the securement of rights may be mapped out. With regards to Good Living, these new approaches may aid in the consolidation of economic, social, and cultural rights. This consolidation is best exemplified in the *Vida Digna* jurisprudence of the IACtHR, which has been evolving since the late 1990s. To this jurisprudence we now turn.

6   The *Vida Digna* Jurisprudence of the Inter-American Court of Human Rights

This section in no way references the totality of jurisprudence that may be related to the *Vida Digna* reasonings forwarded by the IACtHR. What it does achieve, however, is creating a link between Good Living and the *Vida Digna* jurisprudence of the IACtHR. This interlinkage is of the upmost importance for the future applicability of Good Living as a constitutional principle. Thus, what this section seeks to lay out is that if Good Living is to overcome the state of empty signifier annexed to Buen Vivir and Sumak Kawsay, it must transcend the theoretically void discussions currently engulfing it. To this effect, what the present work proposes is that Good Living is the Ecuadorian representation of broader legal transformations that have taken place both within the IACtHR and the domestic tribunals of Colombia, Guatemala or Costa Rica. Hence, Good Living through this interlinkage, is able to transcend the post-development, ecologist, Indigenist, and statist framings that condemn it to the volatility of empty signifier.

Once viewed as part of broader regional processes, Good Living becomes framed within the progressive development of economic, social, and cultural rights enacted by the IACtHR and domestic tribunals. As part of the Inter-American Human Rights System, Good Living is able to fix its meaning within the discourse of human rights that has been gradually evolving throughout

Latin America. Fixation of meaning, via the language of the Inter-American Human Rights Systems, allows Good Living to escape the void of the empty signifier. The IACtHR's *Vida Digna* doctrine creates a legal reference point to which the broad reclamations that fuelled civil society mobilisation during the critical juncture may find their awaited responses. In a nut shell, the *Vida Digna* doctrine intertwines the right to life stated in the ACHR with the adequate provision and guarantees needed to secure economic, social, and cultural rights. The legal effect of intertwining the right to life with economic, social and cultural rights, is that the state, through its actions and omissions carries the responsibility of creating the necessary conditions through which its citizens may lead a dignified life. If one retraces the demands that fuelled civil society mobilisation throughout the critical juncture to the provision of basic social services, welfare, and the securement of cultural rights, then *Vida Digna* jurisprudence would be the legal systems response to such petitions.

The strength of the *Vida Digna* doctrine is substantiated on the right to life that underscores the legal reasoning that brought it into being. Once economic, social, and cultural rights were intertwined with the right to life, *Vida Digna* became what has been termed as a 'configurative principle of several rights' (Antkowiak 2014, 129); one that is interdependent, interconnected, and indivisible from the provision of water, health care, education, housing, and the preservation of cultural identity. *Vida Digna* jurisprudence therefore becomes the basis from which protections pertaining to social development, non-discrimination, lands, resources, and cultural integrity may incrementally be consolidated throughout Latin America (Antkowiak 2014, 114). In the words of the IACtHR during the case of *Myrna Mack Chang v Guatemala* (quoted in Hnitidou 2016, 11):

> ...the right to life plays a fundamental role in the American Convention because it is a prior condition for the realisation of other rights. When the right to life is not respected, all other rights lack meaning....

When compared with the progress made by the European Court of Human Rights (ECtHR) in similar areas, the IACtHR presents a far more developed legal reasoning in its assessment of economic, social and cultural rights. One such example may be extracted from the ECtHR judgement in *Pretty v UK*. In its ruling, the ECtHR stated that it is 'unconcerned with issues to do with the quality of living,' hence the application of socio-economic rights are constrained to rather closed settings (Hnitidou 2016, 12). For such reasons, the IACtHR plays a relevant role in the future applicability of Good Living, as its decisions regarding the right to life may bring forth significant improvements to marginalised peoples such as the poor, peasants, and African or Indigenous Ecuadorians (Hnitidou 2016).

The right to life, and the *Vida Digna* jurisprudence that it underlines, although limited in European contexts has been echoed in other jurisdictions. As Hnitidou (2016, 8) states:

> ...In relation to the right to life in dignity, certain domestic jurisdictions have taken decisions acknowledging it. For example, the Indian Supreme Court in Maneka Gandhi v. Union of India and Francis Coralie Mullin v. the Administrator, Union Territory of Delhi interpreted the right to life as a right "to live with human dignity," including certain socio-economic rights to the right to life...

Vida Digna jurisprudence, in its Latin American version, obliges member states of the ACHR to minimally guarantee the conditions necessary for people who find themselves in situations of risk or vulnerability, such as the poor or indigenous people, to achieve minimum standards of dignity (Pasqualucci 2008, 2). This legal concern towards safeguarding the socio-economic rights of the most vulnerable segments of society is also echoed in Ecuador's 2008 Constitution. Titled as the "Rights of priority persons and groups," Article 35 of Ecuador's Constitution determines that:

> Elderly persons, girls, children and adolescents, pregnant women, persons with disabilities, persons in prison and those who suffer from highly complex diseases shall receive priority and specialized care in the public and private sectors. The same priority care shall be received by persons in situations of risk, victims of domestic and sexual violence, child mistreatment, natural or manmade disasters. The State shall provide special protection to persons who are doubly vulnerable.

What this reflects about Ecuador's legal system is the mirroring effect of domestic and regional law. *Vida Digna*, Good Living, and priority groups all reflect the same domestic and regional preoccupation towards the safeguarding of basic rights needed to secure the essence of human dignity.

To this effect, the IACtHR has also determined that *Vida Digna* is inherently interdependent with the right to cultural integrity and self-determination of indigenous people (Antkowiak 2014, 138). For example, in the case of *Yakye Axa v Paraguay* (2005, 11), the IACtHR ruled that encroachment of indigenous lands by economic development projects had led to the destruction of an indelible part of the community's historic memory. Furthermore, when reviewing the multidimensional effects such violations had spurred, it highlighted that the destitute living conditions forced upon the Yakye Axa indigenous community had compounded chronic health issues prevalent within indigenous communities (*Yakye Axa v Paraguay* 2005, 50.97). Similarly, in *Xákmok Kásek v Paraguay*, the IACtHR highlighted its preoccupation towards the securement of water, food, health care, and education within indigenous communities. In its judgement, the Court found that the state had failed to secure the basic services needed to protect a specific group of individuals from the immediate, special, and real risks of precarious health conditions (Antkowiak 2014, 151).

Revision of the IACtHR *Vida Digna* jurisprudence allows us to make the following statements. First of all, legal preoccupation towards the securement of economic, social, and cultural rights is not a uniquely Ecuadorian phenomenon but a transformative rights agenda that has been evolving for some time within the American continent and elsewhere. Secondly, the recollection of jurisprudence here presented allows us to see similar patterns in other jurisdictions but also witness the institutional limitations progressive rights agendas face. Thirdly, Good Living, as a constitutional principle, requires further judicial interpretation in order to fulfil its role as configurative principle or optimisation maxim. Fourthly, once tied to the human rights discourse, Good Living becomes a signifier with fixed meaning, the discursivities of post-development, ecologist, Indigenist or statist interpretations are contained in order to accommodate the discourse of rights. In this discourse, Good Living loses its nature as empty signifier by fixating meaning within the Latin American human rights system. Intertwined with the legal reasonings that take place domestically and regionally, Good Living, through the Latin American constitutionality block, becomes a new principle wanting of judicial interpretation.

Finally, this section has allowed us to shed light on the predominant concerns that fuelled collective action throughout the critical juncture. To this effect, securement of ethnic minority rights, expansion of socio-economic rights, and the duty of care Latin American states have towards their citizens prominently stand out within such demands. However, a fundamental point that this section highlights is that Latin American law in its domestic and regional scope, has gradually subdued the dynamics of colonial power that implicitly or explicitly, playout throughout the American continent. Strategic forms of litigation, as well as novel drafting of constitutions and laws, have begun to question the states sovereign power, effectively redefining Latin American jurisdictions. However, the expansive nature of such dynamics, as well as the intersectionality it harbours with other academic disciplines, makes it a query that transcends the scope of this book. Whilst beyond the scope of this particular research, hopefully other scholars will take on this endeavour.

Notwithstanding such limitations, the following sections briefly highlights some of the regional approaches where such dynamics have played out. This birds-eye-view of Latin American law will hopefully serve as an initial blueprint from which future research may take-off.

7 Convergence of Rights: Domestic Approaches to Economic, Social and Cultural Rights

The following section presents a brief analysis of the changing dynamics Latin American law experienced during the critical juncture. It does not however represent a compendium of all possible decisions or processes that may be related to the jurisprudential development of the right to life, *Vida Digna* or other economic, social and cultural rights protections. Rather, it serves as the aforementioned "blueprint" from which future research may rely on. As will be presented shortly, Latin America has in many cases succeeded in expanding judicial guarantees towards cultural and socio-economic rights, whilst in others simply stridden towards minimal changes. The critical juncture witnessed Latin America's amendment or complete overhaul of its constitutional outlay. The incorporation of new rights has brought forth negative and positive constitutional clauses that have either expanded or redefined constitutional rights (González-Bertomeu and Gargarella 2016). Regional reforms have thus incorporated broad economic, social and cultural rights into their legislations with the expectation that an active judiciary would further expand, define and consolidate the guarantees such rights merit (Uprimny 2010, 1591). Domestic judicial review by member states spanning from obligations stemming from the ACHR demanded that domestic courts revise socio-economic provisions and their relation to cultural rights (Sayán 2011, 1836). This two-tiered system of rights protection, which is divided into the supranational and domestic arena, is what we shall christen as the "mirroring effect" of Latin American Human rights law. Since the early 1990s, public interest litigation before domestic and regional tribunals has brought forth an evolving judicial practice that consolidates the mirroring effect by extending the protections and guarantees derived from the ACHR (González-Bertomeu and Gargarella 2016).

Domestic judicial engagement with economic, social, and cultural rights in various Latin American jurisdictions was predominately concerned with reviewing the unwritten laws that condition distribution of resources and power (Bilchitz 2013, 54). In this effort, racial, gender, and class classifications were subjected to legal scrutiny, as well as the ways in which wealth, resources, and even minimal thresholds for survival had come to be determined (Bilchitz

2013). Such a revision was aided by the willingness Latin American states expressed towards the jurisdictional capabilities of the IACtHR. Acquiescence by national governments permitted the IACtHR to gradually increase its reach in countries like Mexico (CMDPDH 2015), Peru (Sayán 2011, 1840), Chile (Burgorgue-Larsen 2014, 8) and Ecuador (Caicedo 2010, 518).

This building of a mutually supporting system between the IACtHR and certain Latin American jurisdictions gradually redefined legal approaches towards socio-economic and cultural rights. Judicial review led activist tribunals, such as the Colombian Constitutional Court, to take a "hands-on" approach towards the revision of policymaking that constrained human rights (Bonilla Maldonado 2013; Lijphart 1999, 227). Judicial activism since the early 1990s, led the constitutional tribunals of Colombia, Costa Rica and Peru to become what some have termed as a 'constitutional and political organ' (Landa 2010, 104). Domestic constitutional regimes were thus transformed into a 'dynamic and fluid assemblage of institutions, actors and decisions' (Landa 2010, 101). Within this dynamic assemblage, the emergence of a living law sought to reinterpret the conditions that perpetuate unequal socio-economic relations (Abertyn 2013, 180). Aided by the new constitutional texts that emerged throughout the region since 1979, judicial revision of socio-economic inequality chose the language of rights to usher in crucial discussions regarding distributive claims (Mota Pardo and Urueña 2016, 231). In Colombia for example, this discussion was inaugurated by the constitutional reform of 1991 (Mota Pardo and Urueña 2016).

Colombia's Constitutional Court (CCC) pioneered the dismantling of procedural barriers preventing the fulfilment of economic, social, and cultural rights. In what the CCC came to label as an 'unconstitutional state of affairs,' judicial intervention reviewed 'widespread violations' to socio-economic rights through the implementation of 'unconstitutional practices' via state policies (T-025/04). Such violations, according to the CCC, evidenced a 'persistent social problem' that required 'the intervention of several entities' and the allocation of 'significant additional budgetary efforts' in order to remedy ongoing violations towards interdependent rights (Parra Vera 2016, 159). Similarly, Costa Rica's Constitutional Chamber's Decision 4621–13, in its revision of the provision of health services, defined that public health care providers could not cite lack of material resources as valid legal arguments through which obligations could be forfeited (Parra Vera 2016, 165).

In a similar reasoning, Peru's Constitutional Tribunal stated that the principle of solidarity embedded in the constitutional order mandates the state to intervene when 'socio-economic reality directly contravenes social justice' (Parra Vera 2016, 157). The constitutional interpretation behind the Peruvian tribunals judgement had analysed the right to access a pension as a minimal threshold from which one could not be deprived from (Landa 2010, 117). In its reasoning, the Peruvian Court had determined that economic, social, and cultural rights are subject to 'progressive development' and hence should be measured in accordance to their overall provision to the general population (*Cinco Pensionistas v Peru* 147). In a similar fashion, the Guatemalan Constitutional Court upheld the states responsibility in providing minimal social services. In its 2010 ruling,[2] the Guatemalan Constitutional Court stated that there was no legitimate excuse the state could forward to justify the regression of healthcare services (Parra Vera 2016, 153). Once more, it reinstated the obligation of the state to preserve and attain a minimum standard of service provision, especially when situations of extreme precariousness or poverty are prevalent amongst the population (Parra Vera 2016, 154).

As can be seen from the aforementioned examples, a regional body of law has gradually emerged as economic, social, and cultural rights have taken centre stage within legal proceedings. In addition to local developments, the IACtHR interpretation of human rights treaties, and their enforcement upon member states of the ACHR, has amplified the breadth of applicable mandates (Alston et al. 2007, 1030). Once reviewed as a systematic totality or a system that integrates local and regional actors, institutions, and decisions the expansive protection of economic, social, and cultural rights is no way a uniquely Ecuadorian event. The preceding paragraphs are evidence of a regional push towards securing the economic, social, and cultural rights that have been so elusive within Latin American jurisdictions. It is in this "rights-based push" that this book positions Good Living. Fuelled by the collective action, protest, and strategic politics that came about during the critical juncture, a rights-based approach is the regions collective response towards societal demands for health, education, housing, and other basic welfare services needed in the securement of human dignity. The *Vida Digna* jurisprudence of the IACtHR provides a starting point from which Good Living may be further theorised by Ecuador's Constitutional Court. However, constitutional adjudication in Ecuador need only look at neighbouring Colombia to guide itself in the enactment of economic, social, and cultural rights.

Whilst Good Living as a constitutional principle is indeed a unique Ecuadorian legal development, its intertwinement with rights such as water, health, education, and the environment inextricably link it to the progressive

---

2 Constitutional Court of Guatemala, File 2643–2008, August 16, 2010.

development of rights that has been taking place in Latin America since the early 1990s. Through this linkage, Good Living is able to transcend its current state of empty signifier, finding a new home within broader discussions that seek to analyse how rights are to be enforced through constructivist revisions of law. Good Living as a living law is therefore the next step that should be taken if it is to claim its rightful place as a constitutional principle that received the backing of 65 per cent of Ecuador's population.

8 Back to Basics: Recalibrating the "Engine Room of the Constitution"

Good Living was crafted into Ecuador's 2008 Constitution. Its birth as a constitutional principle serves as a reminder of the complex political struggles that engulfed Ecuador and Latin America during the critical juncture. Far from the ontological interpretations it has received since its birth as Buen Vivir and Sumak Kawsay, Good Living is part of a broader, we dare say uniquely Latin American, process of enforcing economic, social, and cultural rights. This consolidation of a Latin American approach towards socio-economic and cultural rights can be signalled out for its intent on listening to what the subaltern has been attempting to utter for some five hundred years. Good Living is thus merely Ecuador's response to the racial and class differentiators that have been so prevalent in the American continent. This of course includes the Anglophonic states of North America, each of which has traversed its own historical path in the securement or violation of these rights.

Good Living, as a crafted discourse that was included into Ecuador's 2008 Constitution, is thus situated within the wider human rights discourse that swept Latin American constitutionalism from 1979 onwards. As part of a unique discourse, it escapes the current volatility that has defined its usage as empty signifier. Accommodation of Good Living within broader discussions regarding the enforceability of human rights within domestic and regional courts creates new spaces of academic debate. These spaces however lay in direct juxtaposition to the Indigenist, post-development or statist strains that so many have eagerly attributed to Good Living in the form of Buen Vivir or Sumak Kawsay. Future research, undoubtedly in the field of law, must therefore ascertain the legal theories from which Good Living may be consolidated. Whilst this book has merely presented Good Living within regional and domestic discussions regarding the enforceability of economic, social, and cultural rights future academic inquiry should take upon the challenge of situating Good Living as a constitutional principle that is applicable under Ecuadorian law. Of particular interest in this matter will be the usage of

Ecuador's *Ley Orgánica de Garantías Jurisdiccionales y Control Constitucional* (Organic Law for Jurisdictional Guarantees and Constitutional Control), as it is wielded to force domestic tribunals to further enhance judicial interpretations of Good Living. This task demands that local legal professionals, both public and private, take on the role of judicial political activism, effectively forcing the legal system to look into itself and resolve the many social, political, and economic dilemmas that mere written law has proven incapable of resolving. Moreover, such judicial activism demands that more poignant questions be raised against the powers, both implicit and explicit, that limit the realisation of rights. To this effect, we once again turn to the writings of Gargarella (2013) to state that Good Living, much like the *Vida Digna* jurisprudence of the IACTHR, must begin to question the obligations a state has towards its citizens. This not only serves to secure the basic welfare services needed for human dignity but also begins to question the wielding of state power, as well as other sectors of society that enforce class and racial differentiators.

Latin America has been a prolific nurturer of human rights. Since 1917, the region has constantly expanded civil, political, economic, social, and cultural rights. Notwithstanding, such attention towards the paper birth of rights has, according to Gargarella (2013), left the engine room of the constitution unscathed. What this ultimately translates into is that the constitutional powers that enact democratic Caesarism through hyper-presidential systems, have for the most part been left unreformed and in the case of Ecuador's 2008 Constitution even strengthened (Gargarella 2013). Hence, the following steps for Ecuadorian and Latin American law more generally is to restrain the endless production of paper rights by consolidating those that already exist. As can been seen in the brief jurisprudential revision this chapter has presented, the legal tools to enact or enforce economic, social, and cultural rights already exist within Latin American law. What is now needed is the political will and civil society impetus of demanding their concretion within their respective legal domains. Generating judicial and institutional guarantees towards economic, social, and cultural rights will redefine the engine room of the constitution by confronting sovereign power with civil society demands. Such guarantees, demanded on the streets of Latin America by the most disenfranchised, marginalised, and discriminated sectors of society are the next step towards securing a dignified life for the general collective. Good Living is thus the crafting of protest into law, the demands of the many against the few. Its future enactment however, depends no longer on protest or revolution but on the coming together of Ecuadorian society as a whole; a collective endeavour that reforms the engine room of the constitution in such a way that the demands of the past become the rights of the present.

9 Conclusion

This book has explored the origins, effects, and future of Good Living. In so doing, it has traced the origins of Good Living to the convergence of politicised ethnic cleavages, state retreat, and changing citizenship regimes. Moreover, it has tied these converging events together through the theoretical insights imported from transnational governmentality and discursive democracy. When tracing the micro-foundations of power that made Good Living possible, this book has further poised that social capital first and ethnodevelopment later are the forbearers of its constitutional crafting as the empty signifier of Buen Vivir and Sumak Kawsay. Led by the transnational actors that were deployed in Ecuador during the critical juncture, social capital and ethnodevelopment gradually subverted the transgressive politics that had emerged as a response to neoliberal reform. However, their progressive deployment was enhanced and made possible by the complicity of a local intellectual elite that believed in speaking outside of capitalist systems. In due time transnational governmentalities, aided by domestic intellectuals, created a detached position of progressive false consciousness. What this ultimately translates into is that Buen Vivir and Sumak Kawsay, as were crafted into Ecuador's 2008 Constitution and later developed within the three predominate strains, reflects an elitist technocracy that is not only governed by the discourses that flow from NGOs and the international development community but which do very little to guarantee the exercise of rights.

Buen Vivir and Sumak Kawsay's origins within the processes of transnational governmentality, as well as their master framing as an empty signifier, turned them into a discursivity that was strategically utilised to avoid fixation of meaning seeking to oppose neoliberal reform and the predominating status quo. Proposals such as autonomy, self-determination, and territorial rights presented by a multiplicity of actors that came together through protest were gradually displaced in favour of social capital, entrepreneurism, and civic virtue. Finally, this book proposes that the future of Buen Vivir and Sumak Kawsay lays in its ability to transcend its usage as empty signifier by recovering the demands of protest that were displaced by social capital and ethnodevelopment. This recovery of a rights based concept can be enacted through the *Vida Digna* jurisprudence of the IACtHR and its framing of a collective human dignity. To do so, it has been proposed that Good Living is part of a broader Latin American process of consolidating economic, social, and cultural rights. Moreover, Good Living should draw from the IACtHR *Vida Digna* jurisprudence in order to consolidate itself as a constitutional principle that is interconnected to collective rights and the effective implementation of institutional and judicial mechanisms. Such interconnectivity should in time turn paper rights into enforceable legal guarantees.

Whilst this book has consolidated a new critical approach towards Good Living, future research should further enquire into some of the main topics that were covered in previous chapters. Anthropological research for example should revise the usages, if any, Buen Vivir or Sumak Kawsay has received within Ecuador's indigenous communities. Political economy on the other hand should question the influence post-development theories had in the forging of Ecuador's 2008 Constitution and whether their inclusion brought about any significant changes to macroeconomic policy. Legal studies should continue questioning how Good Living may be intertwined with other economic, social, and cultural rights. Whilst other avenues of academic enquiry may depart from the critical readings here presented, it suffices to say that at least for now, Good Living may take on new avenues of theoretical development, roads that in the future will hopefully revise the demands, ailments, occurrences, actions, institutions, agents, and decisions that came together in the crafting of Good Living in Ecuador's 2008 Constitution.

Bibliography

Abbott, Kenneth W. 1985. "The Trading Nation's Dilemma: The Functions of the Law of International Trade," *Harvard International Law Journal* 26: 501–03.
Abertyn, Catherine. 2013. "Cultural Diversity, 'Living Law,' and Women's Rights in South Africa." In *Constitutionalism of the Global South: The Activist Tribunals of India, South Africa, and Colombia*, edited by Daniel Bonilla Maldonado. Cambridge: Cambridge University Press.
Acción Ecológica. 2016. "El Festín Minero y el Proyecto Panantza San Carlos. Namkims Una Nueva Víctima de La Minería y Las Empresas Chinas en Ecuador." *Business and Human Rights Resource Centre*. (Accessed 18 April 2018) https://www.business-humanrights.org/es/ecuador-ind%C3%ADgenas-nankints-desalojados-a-la-fuerza-para-abrir-paso-a-minera-explorcobres-de-ecuacorriente-y-seis-shuar-criminalizados-por-otro-incidente-incluye-v%C3%ADdeo#c141106.
Acosta, Alberto. 2010. "El Buen Vivir en el Camino del Post-Desarrollo una Lectura Desde La Constitución de Montecristi." *Fes-Ildis* 9: 43.
Actualidad. 2012. "Chimborazo y Tres Provincias Amazónicas Tienen Mayor Porcentaje de Población Indígena." *Andes*. (Accessed 19 March 2018) https://www.andes.info.ec/es/noticias/actualidad/1/3068.
Actualidad. 2009. "La 'hora de Sixto' fue en 1993." *El Comercio*. Quito. (Accessed 15 May 2018) http://www.elcomercio.com/actualidad/hora-sixto-1993.html.
Albó, Xavier. 2004. "Ethnic Identity and Politics in the Central Andes." In *Politics in the Andes: Identity, Conflict Reform*, edited by Jo-Marie Burt and Philip Mauceri, 17–37. University of Pittsburgh Press.
Alexander, Robert J. 2007. *A History of Organized Labor in Peru and Ecuador*. Westport: Praeger.
Alexy, Robert. 2015. "Análisis de la 'Teoria de los Derechos Fundamentales' de Robert Alexy." *Ámbito Jurídico*. (Accessed 3 July 2018) https://www.ambitojuridico.com/noticias/administrativo-y-contratacion/analisis-de-teoria-de-los-derechos-fundamentales-de-robert.
Alexy, Robert. 2003. "Constitutional Rights, Balancing, and Rationality." *Ratio Juris* 16 (2). Oxford: Oxford University Press: 131–40.
Alexy, Robert. 2009. *A Theory of Constitutional Rights*. Oxford: Oxford University Press.
Alonso González, Pablo, and Alfredo Macías Vázquez. 2015. "An Ontological Turn in the Debate on Buen Vivir—Sumak Kawsay in Ecuador: Ideology, Knowledge, and the Common." *Latin American and Caribbean Ethnic Studies* 10 (3): 315–34.
Alston, Philip, Ryan Goodman, and Henry J. Steiner. 2007. *International Human Rights in Context: Law, Politics, Morals*. Oxford: Oxford University Press.

Altmann, Philipp. 2014. "El Sumak Kawsay y el Patrimonio Ecuatoriano." *HISTOIRE(S) de l'Amérique Latine* 10: 1–16.

Altmann, Philipp. 2017. "Sumak Kawsay as an Element of Local Decolonization in Ecuador." *Latin American Research Review* 52, no. 5: 749–59.

Altmann, Philipp. 2014. "Good Life as a Social Movement Proposal for Natural Resource Use: The Indigenous Movement in Ecuador." *The Journal of Sustainable Development* 12: 82–94.

Altmann, Philipp. 2015. "Studying Discourse Innovations: The Case of the Indigenous Movement in Ecuador." *Historical Social Research* 40 (3): 161–84.

Anaya, James. 2000. *Indigenous Peoples in International Law*. Oxford: Oxford University Press.

Andolina, Robert, Nina Laurie, and Sarah Radcliffe. 2009. *Indigenous Development in the Andes: Culture, Power, and Transnationalism*. Durham: Duke University Press.

Andolina, Robert, Sarah Radcliffe, and Nina Laurie. 2005. "Development and Culture: Transnational Identity Making in Bolivia." *Political Geography* 24, no. 6: 678–702.

Anghie, Antony. 2007. *Imperialism, Sovereignty and the Making of International Law*. Cambridge University Press.

Anthias, Penelope, and Sarah A. Radcliffe. 2013. "The Ethno-Environmental Fix and Its Limits: Indigenous Land Titling and the Production of Not-Quite-Neoliberal Natures in Bolivia." *Geoforum* 64: 257–69.

Antkowiak, Thomas M. 2014. "Rights, Resources, and Rhetoric: Indigenous Peoples and the Inter-American Court." *University of Pennsylvania Journal of International Law* 35, no. 113: 113–87.

Anton Sánchez, John. 2018. (Instituto de Altos Estudios Nacionales), interviewed by Carlos E. Gallegos-Anda, Quito, Pichincha, Ecuador, 23 January 2018, Personal Archives.

Aparicio, Juan Ricardo and Mario Blaser. 2008. "The 'Lettered City' and the Insurrection of Subjugated Knowledges in Latin America." *Anthropological Quarterly* 81, no. 1: 59–94.

Asamblea Nacional del Ecuador. 2008. Actas de la Asamblea Nacional Constituyente 2007–2008 From: 29 November 2007, Acta 001—24 October 2008, Acta 098–A.

Ávila Santamaría, Ramiro. 2017. (Universidad Andina Simón Bolívar), interviewed by Carlos E. Gallegos-Anda, Quito, Pichincha, Ecuador, 3 October 2017, Personal Archives.

Balch, Oliver. 2013. "Buen Vivir: The Social Philosophy Inspiring Movements in South America." *The Guardian*. (Accessed 24 April 2018) https://www.theguardian.com/sustainable-business/blog/buen-vivir-philosophy-south-america-eduardo-gudynas.

Baltzly, Dirk. 2019. "Stoicism." Stanford Encyclopedia of Philosophy. (Accessed 18 July 2019) https://plato.stanford.edu/cgi-bin/encyclopedia/archinfo.cgi?entry=stoicism.

Barbosa dos Santos, Fabio Luis. 2011. "Nuestra América y Sumak Kawsay: Utopías de Modernidad en el Capitalismo Dependiente." *Ecuador Debate* 84 1: 135–250.

Barton, John H., Judith L. Goldstein, Timothy E. Josling, and Richard H. Steinberg. 2006. *The Evolution of the Trade Regime: Politics, Law, and Economics of theol GATT and the WTO*. New Jersey: Princeton University Press.

Baxter, Hugh. 2011. *Habermas: The Discourse Theory of Law and Democracy*. Palo Alto: Stanford Law Books.

Beaulac, Stephane. 2004. "The Westphalian Model in Defining International Law: Challenge the Myth." *Australian Journal of Legal History* 9 (181): 1–31.

Beck, Scott H, Kenneth J Mijeski, and Meagan M Stark. 2011. "¿Qué Es Racismo?: Awareness of Racism and Discrimination in Ecuador." *Latin American Research Review* 46, no. 1: 102–25.

Becker, Marc, and Silvia Tutillo. 2009. *Historia Agraria y Social de Cayambe*. Quito: Abya Yala and FLACSO-Ecuador.

Becker, Marc. 2008. "Indigenous Nationalities in Ecuadorian Marxist Thought." *A Contracorriente: Revista de Historia Social y Literatura en América Latina* 5, no. 2: 1–46.

Becker, Marc. 2013. "The Stormy Relations between Rafael Correa and Social Movements in Ecuador." *Latin American Perspectives* 40, no. 3: 43–62.

Becker, Marc. 2008. *Indians and Leftists in the Making of Ecuador's Modern Indigenous Movement*. Durham: Duke University Press.

Becker, Marc. 2011. *Pachakutik: Indigenous Movements and Electoral Politics in Ecuador*. Lanham: Rowman and Littlefield.

Bedford, Kate. 2009. *Developing Partnerships: Gender, Sexuality and the Reformed World Bank*. Minneapolis: University of Minnesota Press.

Bell, Karen. 2018. "Green Economy or Living Well? Assessing Divergent Paradigms for Equitable Eco-Social Transition in South Korea and Bolivia." *Journal of Political Ecology* 23, no. 1: 71–92.

Benavides, Hugo. 2004. *Making Ecuadorian Histories: Four Centuries of Defining Power*. Austin: University of Texas Press.

Benford, Robert D., and David A. Snow. 2000. "Framing Processes and Social Movements: An Overview and Assessment." *Annual Review of Sociology* 26: 611–39.

Bennett, Andrew, and Jeffrey T. Checkel. 2012. "Process Tracing: Form Philosophical Roots to Best Practices." *Simons Papers in Security and Development*. Vancouver.

Bennett, Andrew, and Jeffrey T. Checkel. 2015. "Process Tracing: From Philosophical Roots to Best Practices." In *Process Tracing: From Metaphor to Analytic Tool*, edited by Andrew Bennett and Jeffrey T. Checkel, 3–38. Cambridge: Cambridge University Press.

Bilchitz, David. 2013. "Constitutionalism, the Global South and Economic Justice." In *Constitutionalism of the Global South: The Activist Tribunals of India, South Africa, and Colombia*, edited by Daniel Bonilla Maldonado, 410. New York: Cambridge University Press.

Billerbeck, Sarah B K Von. 2016. "Conclusion." *Whose Peace? Local Ownership and United Nations Peacekeeping*, July: 1–27.

Blaug, Ricardo. 1996. "New Theories of Discursive Democracy: A User's Guide." *Philosophy and Social Criticism* 22, no. 1: 49–80.

Bonilla Maldonado, Daniel. 2013. "Introduction: Toward a Constitutionalism of the Global South." In *Constitutionalism of the Global South: The Activist Tribunals of India, South Africa, and Colombia*, edited by Daniel Bonilla Maldonado. New York: Cambridge University Press.

Bonilla Maldonado, Daniel. 2013. "Self-Government and Cultural Identity: The Colombian Constitutional Court and the Right of Cultural Minorities to Prior Consultation." In *Constitutionalism of the Global South: The Activist Tribunals of India, South Africa, and Colombia*, edited by Daniel Bonilla Maldonado, 243–90. New York: Cambridge University Press.

Bourdieu, Pierre. 1987. "The Force of Law: Toward a Sociology of the Juridical Field." *Hastings Law Journal* 38: 805–53.

Bowen, James D. 2011. "Multicultural Market Democracy: Elites and Indigenous Movements in Contemporary Ecuador." *Journal of Latin American Studies* 43, no. 3: 451–83.

Brands, Hal. 2010. *Latin America's Cold War*. Cambridge-Massachusetts: Harvard University Press.

Bretón Solo De Zaldívar, Víctor. 2008. "From Agrarian Reform to Ethnodevelopment in the Highlands of Ecuador." *Journal of Agrarian Change* 8, no. 4: 583–617.

Bretón Solo De Zaldívar, Víctor. 2007. "On Ethnofagic Neo-Indigenism: The Prodepeine Experience or the Limits of Neoliberal Multiculturalism." *Iconos, Revista de Ciencias Sociales*, FLACSO-Ecuador 29, no. Septiembre: 95–104.

Bretón Solo De Zaldívar, Víctor. 2015. "Tempest in the Andes? Part 2: Peasant Organization and Development Agencies in Cotopaxi (Ecuador)." Journal of Agrarian Change 15, no. 2: 179–200.

Bretón Solo de Zaldívar, Víctor. 2017. "Three Divergent Understandings of *Buen Vivir* in the Ecuador of the Citizens' Revolution." *Latin American and Caribbean Ethnic Studies* 12, no. 2: 188–98.

Bretón Solo De Zaldívar, Víctor. 2001. *Cooperación al Desarrollo y Demandas Étnicas en los Andes Ecuatorianos. Ensayos Sobre Indigenismo, Desarrollo Rural y Neoindigenismo*. Quito: FLACSO-Ecuador and Universitat de Lleida Giedem.

Bretón Solo de Zaldívar, Víctor. 2005. *Capital Social y Etnodesarrollo en los Andes*. Quito: Centro Andino de Acción Popular.

Bretón Solo De Zaldívar, Víctor. 2010. "Reforma Agraria, Desarrollo Rural y Etnicidad en los Andes Septentrionales (1960–2005)." In *Estado, Movimientos Sociales y Soberanía*

Alimentaria en América Latina: ¿Hacia un Cambio de Paradigma Agrario?, edited by Jordi Gascon and Xavier Montagut, 43–76. Quito: Flacso-Icaria Editorial-Xarxa Consum Solidari.

Bretón, Víctor, David Cortez, and Fernando García. 2014. "In Search of Sumak Kawsay: Introduction to the Dossier." *Iconos Revista de Ciencias Sociales*, FLACSO-Ecuador 18 no.1: 9–24.

Briones, Claudia. 2006. "Questioning State Geographies of Inclusion in Argentina: The Cultural Politics of Organizations with Mapuche Leadership and Philosophy." In *Cultural Agency in the Andes*, edited by Doris Sommer, 248–78. Durham: Duke University Press.

Broad, Robin, and Julia Fischer-Mackey. 2017. "From Extractivism towards Buen Vivir: Mining Policy as an Indicator of a New Development Paradigm Prioritising the Environment." *Third World Quarterly* 38, no. 6: 1327–49.

Brown, Dana. 2017. "Ecuador's 'Citizen Revolution.'" *The Next System Project*. (Accessed 2 February 2018) https://thenextsystem.org/learn/stories/ecuadors-citizen-revolution.

Brysk, Alison. 1994. "Acting Globally: Indian Rights and International Politics in Latin America." In *Indigenous Peoples and Democracy in Latin America*, edited by Donna Lee Van Cott, 29–54. New York: The Inter-American Dialogue.

Burchell, Graham. 1991. "Peculiar Interests: Civil Society and Governing 'The System of Natural Liberty.'" In *The Foucault Effect: Studies in Governmentality. With Two Lectures by and an Interview with Michel Foucault*, edited by Graham Burchell, Colin Gordon, and Peter Miller, 119–51. Hertfordshire: Harvester Wheatsheaf, 1991.

Burgorgue-Larsen, Laurence. 2014. "La Corte Interamericana de los Derechos Humanos como Tribunal Constitucional." *Vol. 22. Working Papers on European Law and Regional Integration*.

Burt, Jo-Marie, and Philip Mauceri. 2004. "Conclusion." In *Politics in the Andes: Identity, Conflict Reform*, edited by Jo-Marie Burt and Philip Mauceri, 269–79. Pittsburgh: University of Pittsburgh Press.

Business Correspondent. 2010. "El Código de Finanzas Alteró la Cuenta de Gastos." *El Comercio*. (Accessed 4 January 2018) http://www.elcomercio.com/actualidad/negocios/codigo-finanzas-altero-cuenta-gastos.html.

Caicedo, Danilo. 2010. "El Bloque de Constitucionalidad en el Ecuador. Derechos Humanos Mas Allá de la Constitución." *In Teoría y Practica de la Justicia Constitucional*, edited by Claudia Escobar García. Quito: Ministerio de Justicia y Derechos Humanos.

Calisto Friant, Martin, and John Langmore. 2015. "The Buen Vivir: A Policy to Survive the Anthropocene?" *Global Policy* 6, no. 1: 64–71.

Camapaña, Joffre. 2016. "Fernando Villavicencio Habría Creado Cuentas de Correo Falsas a Nombre de Empresario Enrique Cadena Para Acusarlo de Enriquecimiento,

Denuncia Abogado Joffre Campaña." *Ecuadorinmediato.* (Accessed 14 March 2018) http://www.ecuadorinmediato.com/index.php?module=Noticias&func=news_user_view&id=2818809028

Cançado Trinidade, Antonio Augusto. 2003. "The Developing Case Law of The Inter-American Court of Human Rights." *Human Rights Law Review* 3, no. 1: 1–25.

Caplan, Karen. 2009. "Indigenous Citizenship: Liberalism, Political Participation, and Ethnic Identity in Post-Independence Oaxaca and Yucatán." In *Imperial Subjects: Race and Identity in Colonial Latin America*, edited by A. Fischer and M.D. O'Hara. Durham: Duke University Press.

Capoccia, Giovanni, and Daniel Kelemen. 2007. "The Study of Critical Junctures." *World Politics* 59 (April): 341–69.

Caria, Sara, and Rafael Domínguez. 2016. "Ecuador's Buen Vivir." *Latin American Perspectives* 43, no. 1: 18–33.

Carrasco Vintimilla, Adrian. 1988. "Los Proyectos Políticos en el Ecuador y la Conformación del Estado Moderno." In *Estado, Política y Democracia en el Ecuador*, edited by Adrian Carrasco Vintimilla, Patricio Moncayo, Amparo Méndez Carrión, Rafael Quntero Lopez, Petronio Espinosa Ramón, Daniel Granda Arciniega, and Malva Espinoza, 9–50. Quito: Editorial El Conejo.

Casas, Tanya. 2014. "Transcending the Coloniality of Development: Moving Beyond Human/Nature Hierarchies." *American Behavioural Scientist* 58 (1): 30–52.

Cassidy, Brendan. 2006. "Whose Law, Which Discourse." In *Social Theory and Legal Politics*, edited by Gary Wickham, 24–40. Sydney: El Faro.

Cepeda Espinosa, Manuel José. 2017. (Universidad de los Andes), interviewed by Carlos E. Gallegos-Anda, Bogotá D.C., Colombia, 18 April 2017, Personal Archives.

Cepeda-Espinosa, Manuel José. 2011. "Transcript: Social and Economic Rights and the Colombian Constitutional Court." *Texas Law Review* 89 (1699): 1699–1705.

Cepeda, Fernando. 2017. (Universidad de los Andes), interviewed by Carlos E. Gallegos-Anda, Bogotá D.C., Colombia, 17 April, Personal Archives.

Cepek, Michael. 2012. "The Loss of Oil: Constituting Disaster in Amazonian Ecuador." *Journal of Latin American and Caribbean Anthropology* 17, no. 3: 393–412.

Cepek, Michael. 2012. *A Future for Amazonia: Randy Borman and Cofán Environmental Politics.* Austin: University of Texas Press.

Cerny, Philip G. 1997. "Paradoxes of the Competition State: The Dynamics of Political Globalization." *Government and Opposition* 32 (2): 251–74.

Chávez Galindo, Ana María, and Francisco Rodríguez Hernández. 1998. "El Programa de Solidaridad y la Organización Comunitaria en el Estado de Morelos." *Estudios Demográficos y Urbanos* 13, no. 2: 379–405.

Choudhry, Sujit. 2008. *Constitutional Design for Divided Societies: Integration or Accommodation?* Oxford: Oxford University Press.

Chuji, Mónica. 2017. (Sarayaku Indigenous Leader/Former Constitutional Assembly Representative), interviewed by Carlos E. Gallegos-Anda, Quito, Pichincha, Ecuador, (SKYPE Interview), 10 October, Personal Archives.

Cochrane, Regina. 2014. "Climate Change, Buen Vivir, and the Dialectic of Enlightenment: Toward a Feminist Critical Philosophy of Climate Justice." *Hypatia* 29, no. 3: 576–98.

Cohen, Jean L. 2012. *Globalization and Sovereignty*. Cambridge: Cambridge University Press.

Collier, David. 2008. "Case Selection, Case Studies and Causal Inference." *Newsletter of the American Political Science Association Organised Section for Qualitative and Multi-Method Research* 6 No.2: 1–16.

Collier, David. 2011. "Understanding Process Tracing." *The American Political Association Annual Meeting* 44 No. 4: 823–30.

Collier, Ruth Berins, and David Collier. 2002. *Shaping the Political Arena: Critical Junctures, the Labour Movement and Regime Dynamics in Latin America*. Notre Dame: University of Notre Dame Press.

Collins, Jennifer. 2004. "Ecuador's Indigenous Movement and the Rise of Pachakutik." In *Politics in the Andes: Identity, Conflict Reform*, edited by Jo-Marie Burt and Philip Mauceri, 38–58. Pittsburgh: University of Pittsburgh Press.

Comunicados. 2015. 'México debe cumplir Sentencia de la Corte Intermaericana de Derechos Humanos sobre Caso Radilla Pacheco' *Comisión Mexicana de Defensa y Promoción de los Derechos Humanos*, 16 June. (Accessed 2 March 2017). http://cmdpdh.org/2015/06/mexico-debe-cumplir-sentencia-de-la-corte-interamericana-de-derechos-humanos-sobre-caso-radilla-pacheco/.

Conaghan, Catherine M., James M. Malloy, and Luis A. Abugattas. 1990. "Business and the 'Boys': The Politics of Neoliberalism in the Central Andes." *Latin American Research Review* 25, no. 2: 3–30.

Confederación de Nacionalidades Indígenas del Ecuador. 1994. *"Proyecto Político de La CONAIE—1994."* Quito: Consejo de Gobierno de la CONAIE.

Constitution of the Republic of Ecuador. 2008. Legislative Decree 0, Official Registry 449, 20 October.

Constitution of the State of Ecuador. 1830. 23 September 1830. Quito, Ecuador.

Constitutional Court of Colombia. Judgment T–025/04. Magistrate: Manuel José Cepeda Espinosa. Bogotá D.C., 22 January, 2004.

Constitutional Court of Guatemala. 201. File 2643–2008, August 16. Guatemala.

Contini, Rina Manuela, and Antonio Maturo. 2012. "Multiethnic Societies: Citizenship? Citizenships and Intercultural Education." In *Citizenship: Practices, Types and Challenges*, edited by Dexter Petty and Vlay MacFarland, 131–41. New York: Nova Science Publishers.

Cook, Justin W., and Piert Tönurist. 2018. "From Transactional to Strategic: Systems Approaches to Public Service Challenges." (Accessed 1 June 2018). https://www.oecd.org/media/oecdorg/satellitesites/opsi/contents/images/h2020_systemsthinking-fin.pdf.

Corral, Fabian. 2009. "Teoria de La Felicidad." *El Comercio*. July 29. http://www.elcomercio.com/actualidad/teoria-felicidad.html.

Corte Constitucional del Ecuador para el Periodo de Transición. 2010 [Sentencia Corte Constitucional del Ecuador para el Periodo de Transición. 2010 [Sentencia No. 001-10-SIN-CC].

Crisis Económica y Financiera. 2001. "Ecuador Decretó la Muerte del Sucre y Dolarizó su Economía." *El Clarín*. September 9. (Accessed 7 April 2018) http://www.clarin.com/ediciones-anteriores/ecuador-decreto-muerte-sucre-dolarizo-economia_0_rJ6YxcxoFl.html.

Cuadra, Fernando De. 2015. "Buen Vivir: ¿Una Auténtica Alternativa Post-Capitalista?" *Polis* 40.

Cubillo-Guevara, Ana Patricia, and Antonio Luis Hidalgo-Capitán. 2016. "El Sumak Kawsay Genuino Como Fenómeno Social Amazónico Ecuatoriano." *OBETS. Revista de Ciencias Sociales* 10, no. 2: 301–33.

Cueva, Agustín. 2008. *Entre la Ira y la Esperanza y Otros Ensayos de Crítica Latinoamericana*. Edited by Alejandro Moreano. Buenos Aires: CLACSO.

Cuvi, Juan. "Yasuni y Buen Vivir." *El Comercio*. 2010. (Accessed 3 March 2018) http://www.elcomercio.com/opinion/yasuni-y-buen-vivir.html.

D'Souza, Radha. 2010. "The 'Rights' Conundrum: Poverty of Philosophy amidst Poverty." In *Rights in Context: Law and Justice in Late Modern Society*, edited by Reza Banakar, 55–71. Oxon: Routledge.

Darian-Smith, Eve. 2013. "Postcolonial Theories of Law." In *Law and Social Theory*, edited by Reza Banakar and Max Travers, 247–64. Oxford: Hart Publishing.

Dávalos, Pablo. 2017. (Pontificia Universidad Católica del Ecuador/Former Vice-Minister of Finance), interviewed by Carlos E. Gallegos-Anda, Quito, Pichincha, Ecuador, 14 November, Personal Archives.

Dávalos, Pablo, and Veronica Albuja. 2013. "Ecuador: Extractivist Dynamics, Politics and Discourse." In *The New Extractivism: A Post-Neoliberal Development Model or Imperialism*, edited by Henry Veltmeyer and James Petras, 144–71. London: Zed Books.

Dávalos, Pablo. 2003. "FMI y Banco Mundial: La Estrategia Perfecta." *América Latina en Movimiento*. (Accessed 4 May 2018) https://www.alainet.org/es/active/4613.

Dávalos, Pablo. 2014. *Alianza PAIS o la Reinvención del Poder Siete Ensayos sobre el Pos neoliberalismo en el Ecuador*. Bogotá: Ediciones desde Abajo.

Deflem, Mathieu. 2013. "The Legal Theory of Jürgen Habermas: Between the Philosophy and the Sociology of Law." In *Law and Social Theory*, edited by Reza Banakar and Max Travers, Second, 75–90. Oxford: Hart Publishing.

Della Porta, Donatella. 2008. "Comparative Analysis: Case-Oriented versus Variable-Oriented Research." In *Case Studies and Process Tracing: Theories and Practices*, edited by Donatella Della Porta and Michael Keating, 198–223. Cambridge: Cambridge University Press.

Della Porta, Donatella. 2009. *Democracy in Social Movements*. New York: Palgrave Macmillan.

Della Porta, Donatella. 2015. *Social Movements in Times of Austerity Bringing Capitalism Back into Protest Analysis*. Cambridge: Polity.

Diaz-Cayeros, Alberto, and Megaloni. Beatriz. 2003. "The Politics of Spending, Part II—the Programa Nacional de Solidaridad (PRONASOL) in Mexico." Vol. 1. Washington D.C. (Accessed 1 March 2018) http://documents.worldbank.org/curated/en/529521468773406296/The-politics-of-public-spending-part-II-the-Programa-Nacional-de-Solidaridad-PRONASOL-in-Mexico.

Domjahn, Thomas M. 2013. "What (If Anything) Can Developing Countries Learn from South Korea?" *Asian Culture and History* 5, no. 2: 16–24.

Dressel, Björn, and Marco Bünte. 2014. "Constitutional Politics in Southeast Asia: From Contestation to Constitutionalism?" *Contemporary Southeast Asia* 36 (1): 1.

Dryzek, John S. 2000. *Deliberative Democracy and Beyond: Liberals, Critics, Contestations*. Oxford: Oxford University Press.

Dupré, Catherine. 2003a. "Importing Human Dignity from German Law." In *Importing the Law in Post-Communist Transitions: The Hungarian Constitutional Court and the Right to Human Dignity*, 65–86. London: Hart Publishing.

Dupré, Catherine. 2003b. "Instrumentalising the Model." In *Importing the Law in Post-Communist Transitions: The Hungarian Constitutional Court and the Right to Human Dignity*, 105–28. London: Hart Publishing.

Dupré, Catherine. 2003c. "The Importation of Law." In *The Lancet*, 207: 1156–57. London: Hart Publishing.

Dupré, Catherine. 2003d. "Imported Law: Between Natural Law and Globalisation." In *Importing the Law in Post-Communist Transitions: The Hungarian Constitutional Court and the Right to Human Dignity*, 157–76. London: Hart Publishing.

Dussel, Enrique. 2009. "A New Age in the History of Philosophy: The World Dialogue between Philosophical Traditions." *Philosophy and Social Criticism* 35 (5): 499–516.

Eaton, Kent. 2013. "Recentralization and the Left Turn in Latin America: Diverging Outcomes in Bolivia, Ecuador, and Venezuela Comparative." *Comparative Political Studies* xx (x): 1–28.

Elkins, Z. 2005. "On Waves, Clusters, and Diffusion: A Conceptual Framework." *The ANNALS of the American Academy of Political and Social Science* 598, no. 1: 33–51.

Elkins, Zachary and John Side. 2007. "Can Institutions Build Unity in Multiethnic States?" *American Political Science Review* 101 No.4: 693–708.

Elkins, Zachary, Tom Ginsburg, and Beth Simmons. 2013. "Getting to Rights: Treaty Ratification, Constitutional Convergence, and Human Rights Practice." *434. Public Law and Legal Theory Working Paper*. University of Chicago.

Elkins, Zachary, Tom Ginsburg, and James Melton. 2009. *Endurance of National Constitutions*. Cambridge. Cambridge: Cambridge University Press.

Ellner, Steve. 2013. "Latin America's Radical Left in Power: Complexities and Challenges in the Twenty-First Century." *Latin American Perspectives* 40 (3): 5–25.

Escobal, Javier, and Carmen Ponce. 2003. "Innovaciones en la Lucha Contra la Pobreza Rural: Potencialidades y Limitaciones." In *La Pobreza Rural en América Latina: Lecciones para una Reorientación de las Políticas*, 41–48. Santiago: CEPAL/FAO/RIMISP.

Escobar, Arturo. 2000. "After Nature: Steps to Antiessentialist Political Ecology.'" *Current Anthropology* 40 No. 1: 1–30.

Escobar, Arturo. 2010. "Latin America At a Crossroads." *Cultural Studies* 24 No. 1: 1–65.

Escobar, Arturo. 2012. *Encountering Development: The Making and Unmaking of the Third World*. Princeton University Press.

Escobar, Germán, Xim: ena Milicevic F., and Julio Berdegué. 2003. "Chile: La Comuna de Portezuelo." In *La Pobreza Rural en América Latina: Lecciones para una Reorientación de las Políticas*, 105–24. Santiago: CEPAL/FAO/RIMISP.

Espinosa, Cristina. 2013. "The Riddle of Leaving the Oil in the Soil-Ecuador's Yasuní-ITT Project from a Discourse Perspective." *Forest Policy and Economics* 36: 27–36.

Estermann, Josef. 2012. "Crisis Civilizatoria y Vivir Bien Crisis Civilizatoria y Vivir Bien." *Polis Revista Lationamericana* 33: 1–22.

Executive Decree 1372. 2004. Official Registry of Ecuador 278 of 20 February. Creates the National Secretary for Planning and Development.

Executive Decree 725. 2011. Official Registry of Ecuador 433 of 25 April: Dispositions for the Organization of the Executive.

Faber, Daniel. 2005. "Building a Transnational Environmental Justice Movement: Obstacles and Opportunities in the Age of Globalization." In *Coalitions Across Borders: Transnational Protest and The Neoliberal Order*, edited by Joe Bandy and Jackie Smith, 43–70. Maryland: Rowman and Littlefield.

Fabricant, Nicole. 2013. "Good Living for Whom? Bolivia's Climate Justice Movement and the Limitations of Indigenous Cosmovisions." *Latin American and Caribbean Ethnic Studies* 8, no. 2: 159–78.

Falleti, Tulia G. 2016. "Process Tracing of Extensive and Intensive Processes." *New Political Economy 3467* (March). Taylor and Francis: 1–8.

Falleti, Tulia. 2010. Decentralisation and Subnational Politics in Latin America. Political Science. Cambridge University Press.

Fernandez, Albert Noguera. 2012. "What Do We Mean When We Talk about 'Critical Constitutionalism'? Some Reflections on the New Latin American Constitutions."

In *New Constitutionalism in Latin America: Promises and Practices*, edited by Almut Schilling-Vacaflor and Detlef Nolte, 99–118. Oxon: Ashgate Publishing.

Fernández, Blanca, Liliana Pardo, and Katherine Salamanca. 2014. "El Buen Vivir en Ecuador: ¿Marketing Político o Proyecto en Disputa? Un Dialogo con Alberto Acosta." *Revista de Ciencias Sociales*, FLACSO-Ecuador 18 No. 1: 101–17.

Ferrajoli, Luigi. 2010. "Igualdad y Diferencia." In *Igualdad y No Discriminación: El Reto de la Diversidad*, edited by Danilo Caicedo Tapia and Angélica Porras Velasco, 155–82. Quito: Ministerio de Justicia y Derechos Humanos.

Ferrer Mac-Gregor, Eduardo, Fabiola Martinez Ramirez, and Giovanni A. Figueroa Mejia. 2014. *Diccionario de Derecho Procesal Constitucional y Convencional*. Edited by Eduardo Ferrer Mac-Gregor, Fabiola Martinez Ramirez, and Giovanni A. Figueroa Mejia. Mexico D.F.: Poder Judicial de la Federación, UNAM, Instituto de Investigaciones Jurídicas.

Fine, Ben. 2001. "The Social Capital of the World Bank." In *Development Policy in the Twenty-First Century Beyond the Post-Washington Consensus*, edited by Ben Fine, Costas Lapavitsas, and Jonathan Pincus, 136–47. London: Routledge.

Fischer, Andrew and M.D. O'Hara. 2009. "Racial Identities and Their Interpreters in Colonial Latin America." In *Imperial Subjects: Race and Identity in Colonial Latin America*, edited by Andrew Fischer and Matthew O'Hara, 1–38. Duke University Press.

Fishkin, James S. 2011. *When the People Speak: Deliberative Democracy and Public Consultation*. Oxford: Oxford University Press.

Fitz-Henry, Erin. 2012. "The Natural Contract: From Lévi-Strauss to the Ecuadorian Constitutional Court." *Oceania* 82: 264–77.

Foucault, Michel. 1972. *The Archaeology of Knowledge and the Discourse on Language*. New York: Pantheon.

Foucault, Michel. 1991. "Governmentality." In *Studies in Governmentality*, edited by Graham Burchell, Colin Gordon, and Peter Miller, 87–104. Hertfordshire: Harvester Wheatsheaf.

Foucault, Michel. 1991. "Politics and the Study of Discourse." In *The Foucault Effect: Studies in Governmentality*, edited by Graham Burchell, Colin Gordon, and Peter Miller, 53–72. Hertfordshire: Harvester Wheatsheaf.

Foucault, Michel. 1991. "Questions of Method." In *the Foucault Effect: Studies in Governmentality. With Two Lectures by and an Interview with Michel Foucault*, edited by Graham Burchell, Colin Gordon, and Peter Miller, 73–87. Hertfordshire: Harvester Wheatsheaf.

Foucault, Michel. 1994. "The Subject and Power." In *Power: Essential Works of Foucault 1954–1984*, edited by James D. Faubion, 326–49. London: Penguin Books

Foucault, Michel. 2007. *Security, Territory, Population: Lectures at the College de France 1977–1978*. Edited by Michel Senellart. New York: Palgrave Macmillan.

Foucault, Michel. 2008. *The Birth of Biopolitics: Lectures at the College de France 1978–79*. Edited by Michel Senellart. Vol. 16. Palgrave Macmillan.

Friedman, Milton. 1970. The social responsibility of business is to increase its profits. *New York Times Magazine*.

Frost, T. 2015. "The Dispositif between Foucault and Agamben." *Law, Culture and the Humanities*: 1–21.

Fukuyama, Francis. 2016. "Social Capital, Civil Society and Development Social Capital, Civil Society and Development." *Third World Quarterly* 22 No. 1: 7–20.

Galindo, Alvaro. 2012. "Ecuador." In *Latin American Investment Protections: Comparative Perspectives on Laws, Treaties, and Disputes for Investors, States and Counsel*, edited by Jonathan C. Hamilton, Omar E. Garcia-Bolivar, and Hernando Otero, 245–92. Leiden: Martinus Nijhoff Publishers.

Gallegos-Anda, Carlos E. 2009. "Perspectivas Sobre Justicia Indígena en la Jurisprudencia Anglosajona: Casos Paradigmáticos de Estados Unidos, Nueva Zelanda y Canadá." In *Derechos Ancestrales: Justicia en Contextos Plurinacionales*, edited by Carlos Espinosa Gallegos-Anda and Danilo Caicedo Tapia. Quito: Ministerio de Justicia y Derechos Humanos.

Gallegos-Anda, Carlos E. 2017. "Good Living as a Living Law." *Australian Journal of Indigenous Education*, Special Edition: 1–11.

Gamu, Jonathan, Philippe Le Billon, and Samuel Spiegel. 2015. "Extractive Industries and Poverty: A Review of Recent Findings and Linkage Mechanisms." *Extractive Industries and Society* 2, no. 1: 162–76.

García-Sayán, Diego. 2011. "The Inter-American Court and Constitutionalism in Latin America." *Texas Law Review* 89 (1835): 1835–62.

García, Fernando. 2017. (Anthropology, FLACSO-Ecuador), interviewed by Carlos E. Gallegos-Anda, Quito, Pichincha, Ecuador, 6 November, Personal Archives.

García, Helena Alviar. 2011. "The Unending Quest for Land: The Tale of Broken Constitutional Promises." *Texas Law Review* 89 (1895): 1895–1914.

Gardbaum, Stephen. 2010. "A Democratic Defence of Constitutional Balancing." *Law and Ethics of Human Rights* 4, no. 1: 78–106.

Gargarella, Roberto. 2012. "Law and Social Protests." *Criminal Law and Philosophy* 6 No. 2: 131–48.

Gargarella, Roberto. 2013. *Latin American Constitutionalism, 1810–2010: The Engine Room of the Constitution*. New York: Oxford University Press.

Gargarella, Roberto. 2015. "Grafting Social Rights onto Hostile Constitutions." *Texas Law Review* 89 (1537).

Gasper, Des. 1997. "Sen's Capability Approach and Nussbaum's Capabilities Ethic." *Journal of International Development* 9 (2): 281–302.

Gasper, Des. 2004. *From Economism to Human Development*. Edinburgh: Edinburgh University Press.

GATT 1994: General Agreement on Tariffs and Trade 1994, Apr. 15, 1994, Marrakesh Agreement Establishing the World Trade Organization, Annex 1A, 1867 U.N.T.S. 187, 33 I.L.M. 1153 (1994).

Georgetown University. 2009. "Republic of Ecuador: Chronology of Presidents," *Political Database of the Americas*. (Accessed 8 June 2017): http://pdba.georgetown.edu/Executive/Ecuador/pres.html.

Gerlach, Allen. 2003. *Indians, Oil, and Politics: A Recent History of Ecuador*. Delaware: Scholarly Resources Inc.

Gilbert, Jeremie. 2007 *Indigenous Peoples' Land Rights Under International Law*. New York: Transnational Publishers.

Ginsburg, Tom. 2010. "Constitutional Specificity, Unwritten Understandings and Constitutional Agreement." 330. *Public Law and Legal Theory Working Paper*. University of Chicago.

Giovannini, Michela. 2015. "Indigenous Community Enterprises in Chiapas: A Vehicle for Buen Vivir?" *Community Development Journal* 50, no. 1: 71–87.

Glick Schiller, Nina. 2012. "Situating Identities: Towards an Identities Studies without Binaries of Difference." *Identities* 19 (4): 520–32.

Go, Julian. 2007. "A Globalizing Constitutionalism? Views from the Postcolony, 1945–2000." In *International Comparative Social Studies: Constitutionalism and Political Reconstruction*, edited by Said Amir Arjomand, 1st ed., 89–114. Brill Academic Publishers.

Goldoni, Marco. 2012. "Two Internal Critiques of Political Constitutionalism." *International Journal of Constitutional Law* 10, no. 4: 926–49.

Goodwin, Geoff. 2016. "The Quest to Bring Land under Social and Political Control: Land Reform Struggles of the Past and Present in Ecuador." *Journal of Agrarian Change*: 1–23.

Gordon, Colin. 1991. "Governmental Rationality: An Introduction." In *Studies in Governmentality*, edited by Graham Burchell, Colin Gordon, and Peter Miller, 1–52. Hertfordshire: Harvester Wheatsheaf.

Griffiths, Anne. 2013. "Reviewing Legal Pluralism." In *Law and Social Theory*, edited by Reza Banakar and Max Travers, Second, 269–86. Oxford and Portland: Hart Publishing.

Grijalva Jiménez, Agustín. 2012. *Constitucionalismo en Ecuador*. Quito: Corte Constitucional para el Periodo de Transición.

Grijalva, Wilson. 2008. *Breve Historia Bancaria del Ecuador*. Quito: Corporación Editora Nacional.

Grindle, Merilee. 2016. "Democracy and Clientelism: How Uneasy a Relationship?" *Latin American Research Review* 51, no. 3: 241–49.

Grosfoguel, Ramon. 2013. "The Epistemic Decolonial Turn: Beyond Political-Economy Paradigms." In *Globalization and the Decolonial Option*, edited by Walter D. Mignolo and Arturo Escobar, 65–77. New York: Routledge.

Grovogui, Siba N. 2014. "To the Orphaned, Dispossessed and Illegitimate Children: Human Rights Beyond Republican and Liberal Traditions." *Indigenous Journal Global Legal Studies* 18 No.14: 41–63.

Gualinga, Carlos Viteri. 2002. "Indigenous Vision of Development in the Amazon," *Polis*: 1–6.

Guardiola, Jorge, and Fernando Garcia-Quero. 2014. "Buen Vivir (Living Well) in Ecuador: Community and Environmental Satisfaction without Household Material Prosperity?" *Ecological Economics* 107: 177–84.

Gudynas, Eduardo. 2009. "La Ecología Política del Giro Biocéntrico en la Nueva Constitución de Ecuador." *Revista de Estudios Sociales* 32: 34–47.

Guerrero, Andrés. 1994. *Los Oligarcas del Cacao: Ensayo sobre la Acumulación*. Quito: El Conejo.

Guha, Ramachandra. 1997. "El Ambientalismo Estadounidense y la Preservación de la Naturaleza: Una Critica Tercer-Mundista." *Ecologismos* 14: 33–46.

Guridi Aldano, Luis, Yolanda Jubeto Ruiz, and Unai Villalba Eguiluz. 2015. "Aportaciones de la Economía Social y Solidaria en el Camino hacia el Sumak Kawsay (Buen Vivir) en Ecuador: Algunas Aclaraciones Conceptuales." *Observatorio de Economía Social Solidaria y Popular*.

Habermas, Jürgen. 1996. *Contributions to a Discourse Theory of Law and Democracy Jurgen Habermas*. Cambridge-Massachusetts: MIT Press.

Hale, Charles R. 2002. "Does Multiculturalism Menace? Governance, Cultural Rights and the Politics of Identity in Guatemala." *Journal of Latin American Studies* 34 No. 3: 485–524.

Hall, Stuart. 1984. "The State in Question." In *The Idea of the Modern State*, edited by Gregor McLennan, David Held, and Stuart Hall, 1–28. Milton Keynes: Open University Press.

Hamilton, Jonathan C., Omar E. Garcia-Bolivar, and Hernando Otero. 2012. "Latin American Arbitration and Investment Protections." In *Latin American Investment Protections: Comparative Perspectives on Laws, Treaties, and Disputes for Investors, States and Counsel*, edited by Jonathan C. Hamilton, Omar E. Garcia-Bolivar, and Hernando Otero, 1–3. Leiden: Martinus Nijhoff Publishers.

Harding, Timothy F. 2003. "Dependency: Nationalism and the State in Latin America." In *Development in Theory and Practice: Latin American Perspectives in the Classroom*, edited by Roland H. Chilcote, 61–66. Maryland: Rowman and Littlefield.

Haroon, Siddique. 2018. "Ecuador Referendum Endorses New Socialist Constitution." *The Guardian*. (Accessed 2 April 2018) https://www.theguardian.com/global/2008/sep/29/ecuador.

Harris, Angela P. 2013. "Critical Race Theory." In *Law and Social Theory*, edited by Reza Banakar and Max Travers, Second, 147–61. Oxford: Hart Publishing.

Harris, David. 2011. *Cases and Materials on International Law*. London: Thomson Reuters.

Harvey, David. 2005. *A Brief History of Neoliberalism*. Oxford: Oxford University Press.

Helmke, Gretchen, and Jeffrey K. Staton. 2011. "The Puzzling Judicial Politics of Latin America." In *Courts in Latin America*, edited by Gretchen Helmke and Julio Rios-Figueroa, 306–31. Cambridge: Cambridge University Press.

Helmke, Gretchen. 2017. *Institutions on the Edge: The Origins of Inter-Branch Crises in Latin America*. Cambridge: Cambridge University Press.

Hendrik, Wagenaarm. 2011. *Meaning in Action: Interpretation and Dialogue in Policy Analysis*. London: Routledge.

Hey, Jeanne A.K. 1995. *Theories of Dependent Foreign Policy and the Case of Ecuador in the 1980s*. Athens: Ohio University Press.

Hidalgo-Capitán, Antonio Luis, and Ana Patricia Cubillo-Guevara. 2014. "Seis debates abiertos sobre el sumak kawsay" *Iconos Revista de Ciencias Sociales* 48: 25–40.

Hnitidou, Ekaterini Katerina. 2016. *Beyond the Right to Life: The Right to Live in Dignity in the European Convention on Human Rights*. Lund University.

Holland, Dorothy, Gretchen Fox, and Vinci Daro. 2008. "Social Movements and Collective Identity: A Decentred, Dialogic View." *Anthropological Notebooks* 81, no. 1: 95–126.

Hollenstein, Patric. 2009. *La Reproducción de la Dominación Racial: Experiencias de una Familia Indígena en Quito*. Quito: Abya Yala and FLACSO Ecuador.

Houtart, Francois. 2011. "El Concepto de Sumak Kausay (Buen Vivir) y su Correspondencia con el Bien Común de La Humanidad." *Ecuador Debate* 84, 1: 57–76.

Huanacuni, Fernando. 2010. "'El Buen Vivir de Los Pueblos Indígenas Andinos.' Todo Está Interconectado, Interrelacinado y Es Interependiente." (Accessed February 7, 2017). http://www.alainet.org/es/active/36060.

Hudson, Wayne. 2008. "Fables of Sovereignty." In *Re-Envisioning Sovereignty: The End of Westphalia?* edited by Trudy Jacobsen, Sampford. Charles, and Ramesh Thakr, 19–32. Hampshire: Ashgate Publishing Group.

Hunt, Alan, and Gary Wickham. 1994. *Foucault and Law: Towards a Sociology of Law and Governance*. Boulder: Pluto Press.

Ibañez Langolis, J.M. 1985. *Teología de la Liberación y Lucha de Clases*. Madrid: Ediciones Palabra.

Indigenous and Tribal Peoples Convention. 1989. (No. 169), 27 June (entry into force 5 September 1991.

Ingram, Gregory K., Nils Fostvedt, Kyle Peters R., Gita Gopal, Ridley Nelson, Patrick Grasso, and Laurie Effron. 2003. *Aplicación de La Directriz Operacional 4.20 Sobre Poblaciones Indígenas: Evaluación de Los Resultados*. World Bank, Washington D.C.

Inter–American Court of Human Rights, 2003. *Case of the "Five Pensioners" v. Peru*. Judgement, February 28.

Inter–American Court of Human Rights. 2012. Case of the *Kichwa Indigenous People of Sarayaku v. Ecuador*. Judgment, June 27.

Inter-American Court of Human Rights. 2010. *Case of the Xákmok Kásek Indigenous Community v. Paraguay*. Judgement, August 24.

Inter-American Court of Human Rights. 2005. *Case of the Yakye Axa Indigenous Community v. Paraguay*. Judgement, June 17.

Inwagen, Peter van, and Sullivan Meghan. 2018. "Metaphysics." Stanford Encyclopedia of Philosophy. https://plato.stanford.edu/cgi-bin/encyclopedia/archinfo.cgi?entry=metaphysics.

Isaacs, Anita. 1993. *Military Rule and Transition in Ecuador*. London: St Antony's/McMillian Series.

Iturralde, Manuel. 2013. "Access to Constitutional Justice in Colombia: Opportunities and Challenges for Social and Political Change." In *Constitutionalism of the Global South: The Activist Tribunals of India, South Africa, and Colombia*, edited by Daniel Bonilla Maldonado. New York: Cambridge University Press.

Janvry, Alain de, and Elisabeth Sadoulet. 2003. "Nuevos Enfoques del Desarrollo Rural en América Latina." In *La Pobreza Rural en America Latina: Lecciones para una Reorientacion de las Politicas*, 59–78. Santiago: CEPAL/FAO/RIMISP.

Jarquin, Edmundo, and Koldo Echebarria. 2007. "The Role of the State and Politics in Latin American Development (1950–2005)." In *Democracies in Development: Politics and Reform in Latin America*, edited by J. Mark Payne, Daniel Zovatto G., and Mercedes Mateo Diaz. Washington D.C.: Inter-American Development Bank.

Javier, Escobal, and Carmen Ponce. 2003. "Síntesis de los Estudios de Caso." In *La Pobreza Rural en América Latina: Lecciones para una Reorientación de las Políticas*, 17–22. Santiago: CEPAL/FAO/RIMISP.

Jokisch, Brad D. 2014. "Ecuador: From Mass Emigration to Return Migration?" *Migration Information Source*. Washington D.C., (Accessed 6 December 2014). http://www.migrationpolicy.org/article/ecuador-mass-emigration-return-migration

Kitschelt, Herbert. 1986. "Four Theories of Public Policy Making and Fast Breeder Reactor Development." *International Organization* 40, no. 1: 65–104.

Kostakopolou, Dora. 2008. *The Cartography of Citizenship*. Cambridge: Cambridge University Press.

Kymlicka, Will, and Wayne Norman. 2003. "Citizenship in Culturally Diverse Societies: Issues, Contexts and Concepts." In *Citizenship in Diverse Societies*, 1–44. Oxford: Oxford University Press.

Kymlicka, Will. 1994. *Multicultural Citizenship*. Oxford: Oxford University Press.

Laclau, Ernesto; Mouffe, Chantal. 1985. *Hegemony and Socialist Strategy Towards a Radical Democratic Politics*. London: Verso.

Laclau, Ernesto. 1996. *Emancipation(s)*. London: Verso.

Lalander, R, and J Cuestas. 2017. "Sumak Kawsay y Buen Vivir en Ecuador." *Conocimientos Ancestrales y Procesos de Desarrollo* 18, December: 215–27.

Landa, Cesar. 2010. "Los Precedentes Constitucionales. El Caso del Perú" In *Teoría y Practica de La Justicia Constitucional*, edited by Claudia Escobar García, 97–149. Quito: Ministerio de Justicia y Derechos Humanos.

Larrea, Carlos, and Lavinia Warnars. 2009. "Ecuador's Yasuni-ITT Initiative: Avoiding Emissions by Keeping Petroleum Underground." *Energy for Sustainable Development* 13, no. 3: 219–23.

Larrea, Carlos, and Liisa L North. 1997. "Ecuador: Adjustment Policy Impacts on Truncated Development and Democratisation." *Third World Quarterly* 18 (5): 913–34.

Larrea, Carlos, Malva Espinosa, and Paola Sylva Charvet. 1987. *El Banano en el Ecuador: Transnacionales, Modernizacion y Subdesarrollo*. Quito: Corporación Editora Nacional.

Laurie, Nina, Robert Andolina, and Sarah Radcliffe. 2005. "Ethnodevelopment: Social Movements, Creating Experts and Professionalising Indigenous Knowledge in Ecuador." *Antipode* 37, no. 3: 470–95.

Laus Armingeon, Karolina Milewicz, Simone Peter and Anne Peters. 2011 "The Constitutionalisation of International Trade Law," In *The Prospects of International Trade Regulation: From Fragmentation to Coherence*, edited by Thomas Cottier and Panagiotis Delimatsis, 69–86, Cambridge: Cambridge University Press.

Law, John. 2004. *After Method: Mess in Social Science Research*. London: Routledge.

Lebech, By Mette, and Faculty Philosophy. 2004. "What Is Human Dignity?" *Maynooth Philosophical Papers*, no. 2: 59–69.

Lemaitre, Julieta. 2010. "Fetichismo Legal: Derecho, Violencia y Movimientos Sociales En Colombia." In *Teoría y Practica de la Justicia Constitucional*, edited by Claudia Escobar García, 23–45. Quito: Ministerio de Justicia y Derechos Humanos.

Levi, Margaret. 1996. "Social and Unsocial Capital: A Review Essay of Robert Putnam's Making Democracy Work." *Politics and Society* 24 (1): 45–55.

Levitsky, Steven, and James Loxton. 2013. "Populism and Competitive Authoritarianism in the Andes." *Democratization* 20 No. 1: 107–36.

Levitsky, Steven, and Lucan Way. 2002. "The Rise of Competitive Authoritarianism." *Journal of Democracy* 13, no. 2: 51–65.

Lewis, Colin M. 2008. "El Estado y el Desarrollo Económico." In *Historia General de América Latina VIII: América Latina Desde 1930*, edited by Marco Palacios and Gregorio Weinberg, 253–92. UNESCO/Editorial Trotta.

Ley Orgánica de Garantías Jurisdiccionales y Control Constitucional. 2009. Ley 0, Registro Oficial, Suplemento 52 de 22 de Octubre de 2009.

Li, Tania Murray. 2007. "Governmentality." *Anthropologica* 49 (2): 275–81.

Lichterman, Paul. 2006. "Social Capital or Group Style? Rescuing Tocqueville's Insights on Civic Engagement." *Theory and Society*. Vol. 35.

Lijphart, Arend. 1971. "Comparative Politics and the Comparative Method." The American Political Science Review 65 No. 3: 682–93.
Lijphart, Arend. 2012. *Patterns of Democracy: Government Forms and Performance in Thirty-Sex Countries*. New Haven: Yale University Press.
Lind, Amy. 2005. *Gendered Paradoxes: Women's Movements, State Restructuring, and Global Development in Ecuador*. University Park: The Pennsylvania State University Press.
Lixinski, Lucas. 2010. "Constitutionalism and the Other: Multiculturalism and Indigeneity in Selected Latin American Countries." *Anuario Iberamericano de Justica Constitutcional* 14: 235–66.
Llásag, Raúl. 2012. "Movimiento Indígena del Ecuador a Partir del Siglo XX: Visibilizando el Resurgir, sus Avances y Retrocesos." In *Justicia Indígena, Plurinacionalidad e Interculturalidad en Ecuador*, edited by S. Boaventura de Sousa and A. Grijalva, 85–157. Quito: Abya Yala and Fundación Rosa Luxemburg.
Lucero, José Antonio. 2006. "Representing 'Real Indians': The Challenges of Indigenous Authenticity and Strategic Constructivism in Ecuador and Bolivia." *Latin American Research Review* 41, no. 2: 31–56.
Mahoney, James. 2000. "Path Dependence in Historical Sociology." Theory and Society 29 (4): 507–48.
Mandato Constituyente. 2007. *No. 1*. Ecuador: Asamblea Constituyente. (Accessed 1 April 2018) http://www.superley.ec/pdf/mandatos/01.pdf.
Mansilla, Hugo Celso Felipe. 2011. "Ideologías Oficiales Sobre el Medio Ambiente en Bolivia y sus Aspectos Problemáticos." *Ecuador Debate* 84: 89–105.
Marcuse, Herbert. 1972. *A Study on Authority*. London: Verso.
Martien, van Nieuwkoop, and Uquillas Jorge E. 2000. "Defining Ethnodevelopment in Operational Terms: Lessons from the Ecuador Indigenous and Afro-Ecuadoran Peoples Development Project." *Latin America and Caribbean Region Sustainable Development Working Paper*. Washington D.C.
McAdam, Doug. 1982. *Political Process and the Development of Black Insurgency, 1930–1970*. Chicago: Chicago University Press.
McAdam, Doug. 1999. *Political Process and the Development of Black Insurgency 1930–1970*. Chicago: The University of Chicago Press.
McMichael, Philip. 2005. "Globalization." In *The Handbook of Political Sociology*, edited by Thomas Janoski, 577–606. Cambridge: Cambridge University Press.
McMichael, Philip. 2010. "Changing the Subject of Development." In *Contesting Development: Critical Struggles for Social Change*, edited by Philip McMichael, 1–15. New York: Routledge.
McNevin, Anne. 2011. *Contesting Citizenship: Irregular Migrants and New Frontiers of the Political*. New York: Columbia University Press.

Medina, Javier. 2001. "Suma Qamaña." *Gestión Pública Intercultural*. Vol. 8.

Mehmet, Ozay. 1995. *Westernizing the Third World: The Eurocentrity of Economic Development Theories*. London: Routledge.

Mejía-Acosta, Andres. 2006. "Crafting Legislative Ghost Coalitions in Ecuador: Informal Institutions and Economic Reform in an Unlikely Case." In *Informal Institutions and Democracy: Lessons from Latin America*, edited by Gretchen Helmke and Steven Levitsky, 69–86. Baltimore: The Johns Hopkins University Press.

Melish, Tara J. 2009. "The Inter-American Court of Human Rights: beyond Progresivity." In *Social Rights Jurisprudence: Emerging Trends in International and Comparative Law*, edited by Malcolm Langford, 372–408. Cambridge: Cambridge University Press.

Merino, Roger. 2016. "An Alternative to 'alternative Development'?: Buen Vivir and Human Development in Andean Countries." Oxford Development Studies 44, no. 3: 271–86.

Mignolo, Walter D. 2013. "Delinking: The Rhetoric of Modernity, the Logic of Coloniality and the Grammar of de-Coloniality." In *Globalisation and the Decolonial Option*, edited by Walter D. Mignolo and Arturo Escobar, 303–68. New York: Routledge.

Mijeski, Kenneth J., and Scott H. Beck. 2011. *Pachakutik and the Rise and Decline of the Ecuadorian Indigenous Movement*. Vol. 51. Ohio: Ohio University Press.

Miller, Russel A. 2006. "Collective Discursive Democracy as the Indigenous Right to Self-Determination." *Indian Law Review* 31, no. 341: 341–72.

Ministerio Coordinador de Desarrollo Social. 2016. "Listado de Nacionalidades y Pueblos Indígenas Del Ecuador." *Sistema de Indicadores Sociales del Ecuador*.

Ministerio de Relaciones Exteriores y Movilidad Humana. 2019. "Ecuador y Corea ratifican los avances en sus relaciones bilaterales," *Ministerio de Relaciones Exteriores y Movilidad Humana* (Accessed 1 August 2019) https://www.cancilleria.gob.ec/ecuador-y-corea-ratifican-los-avances-en-sus-relaciones-bilaterales/.

Ministerio de Relaciones Exteriores y Movilidad Humana. 2013. "Legislación y Normativa sobre Extranjeros en Ecuador," *Ministerio de Relaciones Exteriores y Movilidad Humana*, (Accessed 1 August 2019) https://www.cancilleria.gob.ec/wp-content/uploads/2013/04/legislacion_y_normativa_extranjeros_en_ecuador.pdf.

Mitchell, Timothy. 2013. *Rule of Experts: Egypt, Techno-Politics, Modernity*. Berkeley: University of California Press.

Moncayo, Patricio. 1988. "Evolución Del Estado En El Ecuador." In *Estado, Política y Democracia en el Ecuador*, edited by Adrian Carrasco Vintimilla, Patricio Moncayo, Amparo Mendez Carrión, Rafael Quintero López, Petronio Espinosa Ramón, Daniel Granda Arciniega, and Malva Espinoza, 51–82. Quito: El Conejo.

Monni, Salvatore, and Massimo Pallottino. 2016. "A New Agenda for International Development Cooperation: Lessons Learnt from the Buen Vivir Experience." Development (Palgrave) 58 (1). Nature Publishing Group: 49–57.

Montalvo, Tania L. 2013. "De Solidaridad a La Cruzada Contra el Hambre." *Expansion.* http://expansion.mx/nacional/2013/01/22/cruzada-nacional-contra-el-hambre-2013.

Montaña Pinto, Juan. 2009. "La Autonomía Jurídica y Jurisdiccional en Colombia." In Derechos Ancestrales: Justicia en Contextos Plurinacionales, edited by Carlos Espinosa Gallegos-Anda and Danilo Caicedo Tapia, 251–97. Quito: Ministerio de Justicia y Derechos Humanos.

Montaña, Juan. 2010. "La Interpretación Constitucional: Variaciones de un Tema Inconcluso." In *Teoría y Practica de la Justicia Constitucional*, edited by Claudia Escobar, 719–60. Quito: Ministerio de Justicia y Derechos Humanos.

Morely, Samuel A. 2003. "Estudios de Caso de Programas de Lucha Contra la Pobreza En América Latina." In *La Pobreza Rural En América Latina: Lecciones Para Una Reorientación de Las Políticas*, 23–40. Santiago: CEPAL/FAO/RIMISP.

Morgan, Kimberly J. 2016. "Process Tracing and the Causal Identification Revolution." *New Political Economy* 3467 (July). Taylor and Francis: 1–4.

Morton, Adam David. 2007. *Unravelling Gramsci.* Ann Arbor: Pluto Press.

Mota Pardo, Mariana, and Rene Uruena. 2016. "Economic Regulation and Judicial Review." In *The Latin American Casebook: Courts, Constitution, and Rights*, edited by Juan F. Gonzalez-Bertomeu and Roberto Gargarella, 227–47. London: Routledge.

Mouffe, Chantal. 2005. "For an Agnostic Public Sphere." In *Radical Democracy: Politics between Abundance and Lack*, edited by Lars Toner and Lasse Thomassen, 123–32. Manchester: Manchester University Press.

Naranjo Chiriboga, Marco. 2004. "Dos Décadas Perdidas: Los Ochenta y los Noventa." *Cuestiones Económicas* 20, no. 1: 224–50.

National Secretary for Planning and Development. 2009. "Plan Nacional para el Buen Vivir 2009–2013." SENPLADES, Quito.

Nederveen Pieterse. 2009. *Development Theory: Deconstructions/Reconstructions.* London: Sage Publications Ltd.

Negretto, Gabriel L. 2011."Shifting Constitutional Design in Latin America: A Two-Level Explanation." *Texas Law Review* 89 No. 1777: 1777–1805.

Negretto, Gabriel L. 2015. *La Política del Cambio Constitucional en América Latina.* Toluca: Fondo de Cultura Económica.

Negretto, Gabriel L. 2015. *La Política del Cambio Constitucional en América Latina.* Toluca: Fondo de Cultura Económica.

Negretto, Gabriel. 2013. *Making Constitutions. Presidents, Parties and Institutional Choice in Latin America.* Cambridge: Cambridge University Press.

Nelms, Taylor C. 2015. "'The Problem of Delimitation': Parataxis, Bureaucracy, and Ecuador's Popular and Solidarity Economy." Journal of the Royal Anthropological Institute 21 No. 1: 106–26.

Nobles, Richard, and David Schiff. 2013. *Observing Law Through Systems Theory*. Oxford: Hart Publishing.

North, Liisa L. 2004. "State Building, State Dismantling and Financial Crisis in Ecuador." In *Politics in the Andes: Identity, Conflict Reform*, edited by Jo-Marie Burt and Philip Mauceri, 187–206. Pittsburgh: University of Pittsburgh Press.

North, Liisa L., and Ricardo Grinspun. 2016. "Neo-Extractivism and the New Latin American Developmentalism: The Missing Piece of Rural Transformation." *Third World Quarterly* 6597 (April): 1–22.

Novo, Carmen Martínez. 2014. "Managing Diversity in Postneoliberal Ecuador." *Journal of Latin American and Caribbean Anthropology* 19, no. 1: 103–25.

Oatley, Thomas. 2016. *International Political Economy*. New York: Routledge.

Observatiorio de las PyME-UASB. "Cotizaciones de las Monedas 1990–2009." *Universidad Andina Simon Bolívar*, 2009. (Accessed 14 May 2018) http://www.uasb.edu.ec/UserFiles/381/File/COTIZACIONESDELASMONEDAS1990-2009___.pdf.

Office of the Secretary-General of the OECD. 2008. "OECD Benchmark Definition of Foreign Direct Investment."

Organización de Estados Americanos. 2009. "Derechos de los Pueblos Indígenas y Tribales sobre sus Tierras Ancestrales y Recursos Naturales: Normas y Jurisprudencia del Sistema Interamericano de Derechos Humanos." Vol. 56/09.

Organization of American States (OAS) 1969. *American Convention on Human Rights*, "Pact of San Jose," Costa Rica, 22 November 1969 (entry into force 18 July 1978).

Orile, Melissa A. 2004. "Taylor and Feminism: From Recognition of Identity to a Politics of the Good." In *Charles Taylor*, edited by Ruth Abbey, 140–66. Cambridge: Cambridge University Press.

Ospina, Pablo. 2017. (Universidad Andina Simón Bolívar), interviewed by Carlos E. Gallegos-Anda, Quito, Pichincha, Ecuador, 10 October, Personal Archives.

Osvaldo, Hurtado. 1977. *El Poder Político en el Ecuador*. Quito: Pontifica Universidad Católica del Ecuador.

Oviedo Freire, Atawallpa. 2014. "Ruptura de Dos Paradigmas." In *Bifurcación del Buen Vivir y el Sumak Kawsay*, edited by Atawallpa Freire Oviedo, 139–224. Quito: Sumak.

Pachano, Simón. 1996. *Democracia Sin Sociedad*. Quito: ILDIS.

Pallares, Amalia. 2002. *Peasant Struggle and Indian Resistance: The Ecuadorian Andes in the Late Twentieth Century*. Norman: University of Oklahoma Press.

Palmeter, David, and Stanimir A. Alexandrov. 2002. "Inducing Compliance in WTO dispute Settlement," in *The Political Economy of International Trade Law: Essays in*

Honor of Robert E. Hudec, edited by Daniel L.M. Kennedy and James D. Southwick, 646–67. Cambridge: Cambridge University Press.

Parra-Varea, Oscar. 2016. "The Protection of Social Rights." In *The Latin American Casebook: Courts, Constitution, and Rights*, edited by Juan F. Gonzalez Bertomeu and Roberto Gargarella, 147–71. New York: Routledge.

Pasqualucci, Jo M. 2008. "The Right to a Dignified Life (Vida Digna): The Integration of Economic and Social Rights with Civil and Political Rights in the Inter-American Human Rights System." *Hastings Int'l and Comp. L. Rev.* 1, no. 31: 1–33.

Perreault, Thomas. 2003. "Social Capital, Development, and Indigenous Politics in Ecuadorian Amazonia." *Geographical Review* 93, no. 3: 329–49.

Pesantes Salgado, Hernán. 2008. "El Proceso Constituyente del Ecuador: Algunas Reflexiones." *Revista IIDH*: 263–84.

Petras, James. 2008. "Social Movements and Alliance-Building in Latin America." *Journal of Peasant Studies* 35, no. 3: 476–528.

Political Constitution of the Republic of Ecuador. 1998. Legislative Decree 000, Official Registry 1, 11 August.

Ponce León, Fernando. 2016. "Good Living Contributions to the Theory of a Just Society." *Estado and Comunes* 2: 73–87.

Portes, Alejandro. 1998. "Social Capital: Its Origins and Applications in Modern Sociology." *Annual Review of Sociology* 24, no. 1: 1–24.

Pozo, Mauricio. 2007. "Finanzas: del Sucre Devaluado al Dólar." *Hoy en la Historia 25 Años*. Quito, October.

Prashad, Vijay. 2012. *The Poorer Nations: A Possible History of the Global South*. London: Verso.

Procacci, Giovanna. 1991. "Social Economy and the Government of Poverty." In *The Foucault Effect: Studies in Governmentality. With Two Lectures By and an Interview with Michel Foucault*, edited by Graham Burchell, Colin Gordon, and Peter Miller, 151–68. Hertfordshire: Harvester Wheatsheaf.

Puente, Diego. 2016. "Fernando Villavicencio y Cléver Jiménez Otra Vez Pueden Ir a La Cárcel." *El Comercio*. (Accessed 2 Febrary 2018) http://www.elcomercio.com/actualidad/fernandovillavicencio-cleverjimenez-justicia-ecuador-carcel.html.

Quade, E.S. 1972. "The Systems Approach and Public Policy." Santa Monica. (Accessed 21 April 2018) https://www.rand.org/pubs/papers/P4860.html.

Quick, Joe, and James T. Spartz. 2018. "On the Pursuit of Good Living in Highland Ecuador: Critical Indigenous Discourses of Sumak Kawsay." *Latin American Research Review* 53, no. 4: 757–69.

Quijano, Aníbal. 2011. "'Bien Vivir': Entre el 'desarrollo' y la Des/colonialidad del Poder." *Ecuador Debate* 84 1: 77–88.

Quijano, Aníbal. 2013. "Coloniality and Modernity/Rationality." In Globalization and the Decolonial Option, edited by Walter D. Mignolo and Arturo Escobar, 22–33. New York: Routledge.

Quintero López, Rafael. 1988. "La Democracia Ecuatoriana Sititada." In *Estado, Política y Democracia en el Ecuador*, edited by Adrian Carrasco Vintimilla, Patricio Moncayo, Amparo Mendez Carrión, Rafael Quntero López, Petronio Espinosa Ramón, Daniel Granda Arciniega, and Malva Espinoza, 141–65. Quito: Editorial El Conejo.

Quintero, Rafael, and Erika Silva. 1998. *Ecuador: Una Nación en Ciernes*. Quito: Abya Yala.

Radcliffe, Sarah A. 2015. "Development Alternatives." *Development and Change* 46 No.4: 855–74.

Radcliffe, Sarah A. 2012. "Geoforum Development for a Postneoliberal Era? Sumak Kawsay, Living Well and the Limits to Decolonisation in Ecuador." *Geoforum* 43 (2). Elsevier Ltd: 240–49.

Radcliffe, Sarah A. 2015. *Dilemmas of Difference: Indigenous Women and the Limits of Postcolonial Development Policy*. Durham: Duke University Press.

Radcliffe, Sarah A., Nina Laurie, and Robert Andolina. 2004. "The Transnationalization of Gender and Reimagining Andean Indigenous Development." *Development Cultures: New Environments, New Realities, New Strategies—Special Issue* 29, no. 2: 387–416.

Radcliffe, Sarah, and Nina Laurie. 2006. "Culture and Development in a Globalizing World: Geographies, Actors and Paradigms." *Routledge* 17, no. 1: 156–58.

Radcliffe, Sarah, and Sallie Westwood. 1996. *Remaking the Nation: Identity and Politics in Latin America*. London: Routledge.

Rajagopal, Balakrishnan. 2003. *International Law from Below: Development, Social Movements, and Third World Resistance*. Vol. 6. Cambridge-Massachusetts: Cambridge University Press.

Ralf, Michaels. 2013. "Globalisation and Law: Law Beyond the State." In *Law and Social Theory*, edited by Reza Banakar and Max Travers, Second, 287–304. Oxford and Portland: Hart Publishing.

Rama, Angel. 1984. *The Lettered City*. Hanover: Ediciones del Norte.

Ramírez, Rene, Fernando Martin, Julio Oleas, Diego Martinez, and Analia Minteguiaga. 2008. *Igualmente Pobres, Desigualmente Ricos*. Edited by Rene Ramirez. Quito: United Nations Development Programme.

Ramírez, René. 2010. "La Transición Ecuatoriana hacia el Buen Vivir." In *Sumak Kawsay/ Buen Vivir y Cambios Civilizatorios*, edited by Eduardo Tamayo and Veronica Leon Burch, 125–41. Quito: FEDAEPS.

Ramírez, Silvina, and Nahuel Maisley. 2016. "The Protection of the Rights of Indigenous Peoples." In T*he Latin American Casebook: Courts, Constitution, and Rights*, edited by Juan Gonzalez Bertomeu and Roberto Gargarella, 189–209. New York: Routledge.

Ramos, Alcida. 1994. "The Hyperreal Indian." *Critique of Anthropology* 14: 153–71.

Rask Madsen, Mikael, and Yves Dezalay. 2013. "Pierre Bourdieu's Sociology of Law." In *Law and Social Theory*, edited by Reza Banakar and Max Travers, 111–28. Oxford: Hart Publishing.

Rawls, John. 1995. "Political Liberalism: Reply to Habermas." *The Journal of Philosophy* 92 (3): 132–80.

Reardon, Thomas. 2003. "Desafíos de la Lucha Contra la Pobreza Rural en la Economía Globalizada de América Latina: Instituciones, Mercados y Proyectos." In *La Pobreza Rural En America Latina: Lecciones Para Una Reorientacion de Las Políticas*, 79–104. Santiago: CEPAL/FAO/RIMISP.

Recasens, Andreu Viola. 2914. "Discursos 'pachamamistas' versus Políticas Desarrollistas: El Debate sobre el Sumak Kawsay en los Andes." *Revista Iconos* 48, Jan.: 55–72.

Redacción. 2015. "Manuela Picq Dejó Ecuador Pero Asegura Que Vovlerá." *El Universo*. (Accessed 16 June 2018) http://www.eluniverso.com/noticias/2015/08/21/nota/5078381/manuela-picq-dejara-ecuador-esta-tarde.

Rescasens, Andreu Viola. 2014. "'Pachamamista' Discourses versus Development Policies: The Debate over Sumak Kawsay in the Andes." *Revista Iconos* 48, no. Enero (2014): 55–72.

Reuters. 2016. 'Asamblea aprobó el presupuesto de $29.835 millones para 2016,' El Universo (Accessed 22 February 2017), http://www.eluniverso.com/noticias/2015/11/24/nota/5260278/asamblea-aprobo-presupuesto-29835-millones-2016.

Riach, Graham. 2017. *Can the Subaltern Speak?* London: Macat International.

Rice, Roberta. 2012. *The New Politics of Protest: Indigenous Mobilization in Latin America's Neoliberal Era*. Arizona: University of Arizona Press.

Risse, Thomas. 2013. "Transnational Actors and World Politics." In *Hand Book of International Relations*, edited by Walter Carlsnaes, Thomas Risse, and Beth A. Simmons, 426–52. London: Sage.

Roberts, Kenneth M. 2015. "Populism, Political Mobilizations, and Crises of Political Representation." In *The Promises and Perils of Populism: Global Perspectives*, edited by Carlos de la Torre, 140–58. Lexington: University Press of Kentucky.

Rodriguez-Garavito, Cesar. 2011. "Beyond the Courtroom: The Impact of Judicial Activism on Socio-economic Rights in Latin America." *Texas Law Review* 89 (1669): 1669–98.

Rohlfing, Ingo. 2012. *Case Studies and Causal Inference: An Integrative Framework*. Basingstoke: Palgrave Macmillan.

Roitman, Karem. 2008. "Longos' and Cholos: Ethnic and Racial Discrimination among Mestizos in Ecuador." 58. *CRISE Working Paper*. Oxford.

Rootes, Christopher. 2005. "A Limited Transnationalization? The British Environmental Movement." In *Transnational Protest and Global Activism: Peoples, Passion, and Power*, edited by Donatella della Portaand Sidney Tarrow, 21–45. Maryland: Rowman and Littlefield.

Roseo Muñoz, Ana Belén and Geovanny Tipnaluisa. 2019. "20 Grandes Casos de Corrupción Están en Proceso en Ecuador," *El Comercio*. (Accessed 17 July 2019) https://www.elcomercio.com/actualidad/grandes-casos-corrupcion-ecuador-correismo.html.

Ross, Michael. 2012. The Oil Curse: How Petroleum Wealth Shapes the Development of Nations. New Jersey: Princeton University Press.

Rössel, Jörg. 2012. "Methodological Nationalism." In *Encyclopedia of Global Studies*, edited by Helmut K. Anheier and Mark Juergensmeyer, 1152–53. Los Angeles: Sage.

Rudel, Thomas K., Diane Bates, and Rafael Machinguiashi. 2002. "Ecologically Noble Amerindians? Cattle Ranching and Cash Cropping among Shuar and Colonists in Ecuador." *Latin American Studies Association* 37 No. 1: 144–59.

Ruttenberg, Tara. 2013. "Wellbeing Economics and Buen Vivir: Development Alternatives for Inclusive Human Security." *PRAXIS The Fletcher Journal of Human Security* XXVIII: 68–93.

Sabetti, Filippo. 1996. "Path Dependency and Civic Culture: Some Lessons from Italy About Interpreting Social Experiments." *Politics and Society* 24 No.1: 19–44.

Said, Edward W. 1977. *Orientalism*. London: Penguin.

Salazar, Francisco Ignacio. 1830. Actas del Primer Congreso Constituyente del Ecuador. Quito: Constitutional Assembly.

Sánchez Parga, José. 2010. *El Movimiento Indígena Ecuatoriano: La Larga Ruta de la Comunidad al Partido*. Quito: Abya Yala and Universidad Politécnica Salesiana.

Sánchez Parga, José. 2011. "Discursos Retrovolucionarios: Sumak Kawsay, Derechos de la Naturaleza y Otros Pachamamismos." *Ecuador Debate* 84: 31–50.

Sánchez, Francisco. 2002. *¿Democracia No Lograda o Democracia Malograda? Un Análisis del Sistema Político del Ecuador: 1979–2002*. FLACSO—Ecuador.

Sanin Restrepo, Ricardo. 2012. *Teoría Crítica Constitucional 2: Del Existencialismo Popular a La Verdad de la Democracia*. Quito: Corte Constitucional del Ecuador.

Santos, Boaventura de Sousa. 2002. *Toward a New Legal Common Sense: Law, Globalization, and Emancipation*. Cambridge University Press.

Santos, Boaventura de Sousa. 2014. *Epistemologies of the South: Justice Against Epistemicide*. London: Paradigm Publishers.

Sartori, Giovanni. 2005. *Parties and Party Systems: A Framework for Analysis*. Colchester: ECPR Press.

Sawyer, Suzana, and Edmund Terence Gómez. 2012. "Transnational Governmentality in the Context of Resource Extraction." in *The Politics of Resource Extraction: Indigenous Peoples, Multinational Corporation and the State*, edited by Suzana Sawyer and Edmund Terence Gomez, 1–9. Hampshire: Palgrave Macmillan.

Sawyer, Suzana. 2004. *Crude Chronicles: Indigenous Politics, Multinational Oil, and Neoliberalism in Ecuador*. Durham: Duke University Press.

Sayán, Diego García. 2011. "The Inter-American Court and Constitutionalism in Latin America." *Texas Law Review* 89 No.1835: 1835—62.

Schavelzon, Salvador. 2015. *Plurinacionalidad y Vivir Bien/Buen Vivir: Dos Conceptos Leídos desde Bolivia y Ecuador Post-Constituyentes*. Quito: Abya Yala.

Schejtman, Alexander, and Soledad Parada. 2003. "Los Programas Nacionales de Alivio de la Pobreza Rural: El Enfoque Consensual y sus Limitaciones." In *La Pobreza Rural en América Latina: Lecciones para una Reorientación de las Políticas*, 51–58. Santiago: CEPAL/FAO/RIMISP.

Schild, Veronica. 1998. "Market Citizenship and the 'New Democracies': The Ambiguous Legacies of Contemporary Chilean Women's Movements." *Social Politics* 5, no. 2: 232–49.

Schiwy, Freya. 2013. "Decolonization, and the Question of Subjectivity: Gender, Race and Binary Thinking." In *Globalization and the Decolonial Option*, edited by Walter D. Mignolo and Arturo Escobar, 125–49. New York.

Schneider, Sergio. 2014. "Agricultura Familiar en Latinoamérica Continuidades, Transformaciones y Controversias." www.flacsoandes.edu.ec.

Scholte, Jan Aart. 2008. "Civil Society and Sovereignty in a Post-Statist Circumstance." In *Re-Envisioning Sovereignty: The End of Westphalia?* edited by Trudy Jacobsen, Charles Sampford, and Ramesh Thakur, 331–48. Hampshire: Ashgate Publishing Group.

Schöneberg, Julia Maria. 2017. "NGO Partnerships in Haiti: Clashes of Discourse and Reality." *Third World Quarterly*: 1–17.

Schwartz, Warren F. and Alan O. Sykes. 2002. 'The Economics Structure of Renegotiation and Dispute Resolution in the WTO/GATT System' *John M. Olin Law and Economics Working Paper No. 143*.

Scott, John. 2014. "Buddhism." A Dictionary of Sociology. (Accessed 7 July 2019) https://www-oxfordreference com.virtual.anu.edu.au/view/10.1093/acref/9780199683581.001.0001/acref-9780199683581.

Scott, John. 2014. *A Dictionary of Sociology*. Oxford: Oxford University Press.

Seawright, Jason, and John Gerring. 2011. "Case Selection Techniques Case Study Research Options." *Political Research Quarterly* 61 (2): 294–308.

Sebastian, Thomas. 2007. 'World Trade Organization Remedies and the Assessment of Proportionality: Equivalence and Appropriateness,' *Harvard International Law Journal* 48:338–41

Secretaría Técnica Jurisdiccional Corte Constitucional del Ecuador. 2017. *Desarrollo Jurisprudencial de la Primera Corte Constitucional (Noviembre 2012–Noviembre 2015)*. Edited by Alfredo Ruiz Guzmán, Pamela Juliana Aguirre Castro, and Dayana Fernanda Ávila Benavidez. Quito: Corte Constitucional del Ecuador.

Seguridad. 2019. "20 grandes casos de corrupción están en proceso en Ecuador." *El Comercio*. (Accessed 2 April 2018) https://www.elcomercio.com/actualidad/grandes-casos-corrupcion-ecuador-correismo.html.

Selverston-Scher, Melina. 2001. *Ethnopolitics in Ecuador: Indigenous Rights and the Strengthening of Democracy*. Boulder: Lynne Rienner Publishers Inc.

SENESCYT. 2012. "Expediente de Creación de la Universidad Yachay." Quito. https://www.yachay.gob.ec/empresas/ http://www.yachay.gob.ec/expediente-universidad-yachay/.

Sesso Rojas, María Jimena. 2009. *El Proyecto Multipropósito Baba: Disputas Sobre Desarrollo y Sustentabilidad*. FLACSO.

Séverine, Deneulin. 2012. "Justice and Deliberation about the Good Life: The Contribution of Latin American Buen Vivir Social Movements to the Idea of Justice." *Bath Papers in International Development and Wellbeing*. Bath.

Shelton, Dinah. 2011. "Introduction." In *International Law and Domestic Legal Systems: Incorporation, Transformation, and Persuasion*, edited by Dinah Shelton, 1–22. Oxford: Oxford Scholarship Online.

Shilliam, Robbie. 2015. *The Black Pacific: Anti-Colonial Struggles and Oceanic Connections*. London: Bloomsbury Publishing.

Shurr, Caroline. 2013. *Performing Politics, Making Space: A Visual Ethnography of Political Change in Ecuador*. Stuttgart: Franz Steiner Verlag.

Sieder, Rachel, and Anna Barrera Vivero. 2017. "Legalizing Indigenous Self-Determination: Autonomy and *Buen Vivir* in Latin America." *The Journal of Latin American and Caribbean Anthropology* 22, no. 1: 9–26.

Silva Portero, Carolina. 2008. "¿Qué Es el Buen Vivir en la Constitución?" In *La Constitución del 2008 en el Contexto Andino: Análisis desde la Doctrina y el Derecho Comparado*, edited by Ramiro Ávila Santamaría, 111–55. Quito: Ministerio de Justicia y Derechos Humanos.

Skocpol, Theda. 1996. "'Unravelling from Above.'" *The American Prospect* 25: 20–25.

Smith, Jackie. 2005. "Globalization and Transnational Social Movement Organizations." In *Social Movements and Organization Theory*, edited by Gerlad F. Davis, Doug McAdam, William RIchard, Scott Mayer, and Nathan Zald, 226–48. Cambridge: Cambridge University Press.

Smith, Lionel D. 1997. *The Law of Tracing*. Oxford: Clarendon Press.

Sociedad. 2015. "Yasunidos Denunciarán en CIDH Casos de Pueblos No Contactados." *El Comercio*. (Accessed 2 April 2018) http://www.larepublica.ec/blog/socie

dad/2015/10/13/yasunidos-denunciaran-en-cidh-casos-de-pueblos-no-contactados/.

Soifer, Hillel David. 2015. *State Building in Latin America*. New York: Cambridge University Press.

Sosa, César. 2016. "Cuando Ecuador Perdió la Brújula del Modelo Coreano," *El Comercio*. (Accessed 8 July 2019) https://especiales.elcomercio.com/planeta-ideas/ideas/21-feb-2016/ecuador-modelo-coredelsur-tecnologia-mercados.

Spedding Pallet, Alison. 2010. "'Suma Qamaña' ¿kamsañ Muni? (¿Qué Quiere Decir 'Vivir Bien'?)." *Fe y Pueblo* 17: 4–39.

Spivak, Gayatari Chakravorty. 1988. "Can the Subaltern Speak?" In *Marxism and the Interpretation of Culture*, edited by Cary Nelson and Lawrence Grossberg, 24–28. London: Macmillan.

Stefanoni, Pablo. 2012. "¿Y quién no querría vivir bien"? Encrucijadas del proceso de cambio boliviano" en *Cuadernos del Pensamiento Crítico Latinoamericano N° 53*. CLACSO, mayo. Publicado en La Jornada de México, Página 12 de Argentina y Le Monde Diplomatique de Bolivia, Chile y España.

Supreme Court of Costa Rica. 2013. Constitutional Chamber, Decision 4621–13, April 13.

Szlablowski, David. 2007. *Transnational Law and Local Struggles: Mining, Communities and the World Bank*. Oxford and Portland: Hart Publishing.

Tarrow, Sidney G. 1994. *Power in Movement: Social Movements and Contentious Politics*. Cambridge: Cambridge University Press.

Tarrow, Sidney. 2005. *The New Transnational Activism. The New Transnational Activism*. Cambridge: Cambridge University Press.

Taussig, Michael. 1993. *Mimesis and Alterity: A Particular History of the Senses*. New York: Routledge.

Távarez, David. 2009. "Legally Indian: Inquisitorial Readings of Indigenous Identity in New Spain." In *Imperial Subjects: Race and Identity in Colonial Latin America*, edited by A. Fischer and M.D. O'Hara, 81–101. Durham: Duke University Press.

Taylor, Charles. 1989. *Sources of The Self: The Making of the Modern Identity*. Cambridge-Massachusetts: Harvard University Press.

The Economist. 2010. "Picking Winners, Saving Losers." *The Economist* (Accessed 17 February 2017) http://www.economist.com/node/16741043.

Tilly, Charles. 1978. *From Mobilization to Revolution*. New York: McGraw-Hill.

Torre, Carlos de la, and Steve Striffler. 2009. *The Ecuador Reader: History, Culture, Politics*. Edited by Carlos de la Torre and Steve Striffler. Duke University Press.

Torre, Carlos de la. 2013. "El Tecnopopulismo de Rafael Correa: ¿Es Compatible el Carisma con la Tecnocracia?" *Latin American Research Review* 48 No. 1: 24–43.

Torre, Carlos de la. 2006. "Ethnic Movements and Citizenship in Ecuador." *Latin American Research Review* 41 (2): 247–59.

Torre, Carlos de la. 2010. "Rafael Correa." In *Populist Seduction in Latin America*, (2nd) ed. Athens: Ohio University Press.

Torres Eguiño, Mario. 2012. *Suma Qamaña y Desarrollo*. Edited by S.J. Medina and Yampara. La Paz: Garra Azul.

Trampusch, Christine, and Bruno Palier. 2016."Between X and Y: How Process Tracing Contributes to Opening the Black Box of Causality." *New Political Economy* 3467 April: 1–18.

Travers, Max. 2010. "A Sociological Critique of Rights." In *Rights in Context: Law and Justice in Late Modern Society*, edited by Reza Banakar, 41–55. Ashgate Publishing Limited.

Tushnet, Mark. 2017. "The New 'Bolivarian' Constitutions: A Textual Analysis." In *Comparative Constitutional Law in Latin America*, edited by Rosalind Dixon and Tom Ginsburg, 126–53. Cheltenham: Edward Elgar Publishing.

UN General Assembly. 2007. *United Nations Declaration on the Rights of Indigenous Peoples: resolution / adopted by the General Assembly*, 2 October, A/RES/61/295.

Unceta, Koldo. 2014. *Desarrollo, Postcrecimiento y Buen Vivir*. Quito: Abya Yala.

Unidad de Noticias. 2016. "Gobierno Notifica la Disolución de Acción Ecológica." *El Comercio*. Unidad de Noticias. (Accessed 23 April 2018) http://www.elcomercio.com/actualidad/gobierno-notificacion-disolucion-accionecologica-panantza.html.

Uprimny, Rodrigo. 2010. "Recent Transformation of Constitutional Law in Latin America: Trends and Challenges." *Texas Law Review* 89: 1587–1609.

Uquillas, Alfredo. 2008. "El Modelo Económico Industrial en el Ecuador." *Observatorio de la Economia Lationamericana*, no. 104: 1–43.

Vallejo, María Cristina, Rafael Burbano, Fander Falconí, and Carlos Larrea. 2015. "Leaving Oil Underground in Ecuador: The Yasuní-ITT Initiative from a Multi-Criteria Perspective." *Ecological Economics* 109: 175–85.

Van Cott, Donna Lee. 1994. "Indigenous Peoples and Democracy: Issues for Policymakers." In *Indigenous Peoples and Democracy in Latin America*, edited by Donna Lee Van Cott, 1–28. New York: The Inter-American Dialogue.

Van Cott, Donna Lee. 2005. *From Movements to Parties in Latin America: The Evolution of Ethnic Politics*. Cambridge: Cambridge University Press.

Van Cott, Donna Lee. 2008. *Radical Democracy in the Andes*. Cambridge: Cambridge University Press.

van Teijlingen, Karolien, and Barbara Hogenboom. 2016. "Debating Alternative Development at the Mining Frontier: *Buen Vivir* and the Conflict around El Mirador Mine in Ecuador." *Journal of Developing Societies* 32, no. 4: 382–420.

Vanhulst, Julien, and Adrian E. Beling. 2014. "Buen Vivir: Emergent Discourse within or beyond Sustainable Development?" *Ecological Economics* 101: 54–63.

Vennensson, Pascal. 2008. "Case Studies and Process Tracing: Theories and Practices." In *Approaches and Methodologies in the Social Sciences: A Pluralist Perspective*, edited by Donatella Della Porta and Michael Keating, 223–39. Cambridge: Cambridge University Press.

Vera Arrata, Alfredo. 1993. *Los Papeles de la Deuda Externa: El Gran Atraco*. Quito: Abya Yala.

Verdesoto Custode, Luis. 2003. "Mestizaje y Ciudanía." *Democracia, Gobernabilidad y Cultura Política*. Edited by Felipe Burbano de Lara, 143–62. FLACSO-Ecuador.

Verdesoto Custode, Luis. 2005. *Instituciones y Gobernabilidad en el Ecuador: A un Cuarto de Siglo de Democracia*. Quito: Editorial Abya Yala.

Vicuña Izquierdo, Leonardo. 2004. *Neoliberalismo y Crisis: Política Económica del Ecuador*. Guayaquil: Casa de la Cultura Ecuatoriana.

Vicuña Izquierdo, Leonardo. 2007. *Endeudamiento Externo y Política Económica*. Quito: Banco del Estado.

Villalba, Unai. 2013. "Buen Vivir vs Development a Paradigm Shift in the Andes?" *Third World Quarterly* 6597, no. August: 1427–42.

Villavicencio, Arturo. 2016."Yachay: La Costosa Promesa Redentora." Plan v. (Accessed 22 February 2017) http://www.planv.com.ec/investigacion/investigacion/yachay-la-costosa-promesa-redentora.

Von Groddeck, Victoria, and Jan Oliver Schwarz. 2013. "Perceiving Megatrends as Empty Signifiers: A Discourse-Theoretical Interpretation of Trend Management." *Futures* 47: 28–37.

Waldmüller, Johannes. 2014. "Buen Vivir, Sumak Kawsay, 'Good Living': An Introduction and Overview." (Accessed 7 February 2017) http://www.alternautas.net/blog/2014/5/14/buen-vivir-sumak-kawsay-good-living-an-introduction-and-overview.

Waldner, David. 2012. "Process Tracing and Causal Mechanisms." *The Oxford Handbook of Philosophy of Social Science*, 65–84. Oxford: Oxford University Press.

Walsh, Catherine. 2007. "Shifting the Geopolitics of Critical Knowledge." *Cultural Studies* 21 No. 2: 224–39.

Walsh, Catherine. 2009. "The Plurinational and Intercultural State: Decolonization and State Re-Founding in Ecuador." *Culture (Special Issue)* 6: 65–84.

Weber, Heloise. 2015. 'Reproducing Inequalities through Development: The MDGs and the Politics of Method.' *Globalizations* 12 No.4: 660–76.

Weber, Heloise. 2002. "The Imposition of a Global Development Architecture: The Example of Microcredit." *Review of International Studies* 28 No. 3: 537–55.

Whitehead, Laurence. 2012. "Latin American Constitutionalism: Historical Development and Distinctive Traits." In *New Constitutionalism in Latin America: Promises and Practices*, edited by Detlef Nolte and Almut Schilling-Vacaflor, 126–60. Oxon: Ashgate Publishing Group.

Wickham, Gary. 2013. "Foucault and Law." In Law and Social Theory, edited by Reza Banakar and Max Travers, Second, 217–32. Oxford and Portland: Hart Publishing.

Widener, Patricia. 2011. *Oil Injustice: Resisting and Conceding a Pipeline in Ecuador.* Plymouth: Rowman and Littlefield.

Wolff, Jonas. 2012. "New Constitutions and the Transformation of Democracy in Bolivia and Ecuador." In *New Constitutionalism in Latin America: Promises and Practices*, edited by Almut Schilling-Vacaflor and Detlef Nolte, 183–200. Oxon: Ashgate Publishing Group.

World Bank. 2005. "Operation Manual OP 4.10—Indigenous Peoples." Washington D.C. (Accessed 14 May 2018) https://policies.worldbank.org/sites/ppf3/PPFDocuments/090224b0822f89d5.pdf.

World Bank. 2002. "Pertinencia Étnica del Proyecto De Asistencia Técnica Chile Solidario-Banco Mundial." Washington D.C. (Accessed 15 May 2018) http://documentos.bancomundial.org/curated/es/839981468769437587/Chile-Social-Protection-Technical-Assistance-Project-indigenous-peoples-plan.

World Bank. 2017. "Public Data." (Accessed 1 June 2018) https://www.google.com/publicdata/explore?ds=d5bncppjof8fq_&met_y=sp_pop_totl&idim=country:ECU:PER:BOL&hl=en&dl=en.

World Bank. 1996. *Ecuador Poverty Report*. Washington D.C.: World Bank.

World Bank. 2005. *Creating Fiscal Space for Poverty Reduction in Ecuador: A Fiscal Management and Public Expenditure Review*. Washington D.C.: World Bank and Inter-American Development Bank.

World Trade Organization. 2018. "The 128 Countries That Had Signed GATT by 1994," (Accessed 3 June 2018). https://www.wto.org/english/thewto_e/gattmem_e.htm.

Wullweber, Joscha. 2015. "Global Politics and Empty Signifiers: The Political Construction of High Technology." *Critical Policy Studies* 9, no. 1: 78–96.

Yates, Julian S., and Karen Bakker. 2013. "Debating the 'Post-Neoliberal Turn' in Latin America." *Progress in Human Geography* 38 No. 1: 62–90.

Young, Crawford. 1976. *The Politics of Cultural Pluralism*. Madison: University of Wisconsin Press.

Young, Iris Marion. 2001. "Activist Challenges to Deliberative Democracy." *Political Theory 5* October: 670–90.

Young, Iris Marion. 2001. "Equality of Whom? Social Groups and Judgements of Injustice." *The Journal of Political Philosophy* 9 No.2: 1–18.

Young, Iris Marion. 1989. "Polity and Group Difference: A Critique of the Ideal of Universal Citizenship." *Ethics* 99, no. 2: 250–74.

Zamosc, Leon. 2009. 'The Indian Movement and Political Democracy in Ecuador.' In *Latin American Democratic Transformations: Institutions, Actors, and Processes*, edited by William C. Smith, 271–96. Maiden: Wiley-Blackwell.

Index

Abbott, Kenneth 159
Abertyn, Catherine 229, 239
aborting 12, 197
absence
   selective 42
   strategic 41
abstentions 207
abstractions 15
   de-contextualised ontological 105
abuses 60, 234
   multiple human rights 224
   possible 230
academia 3, 12, 188
   legal 113
academic inquiry 33, 38, 40, 241
academics 5, 18, 33, 73, 78, 102, 204, 214
Acción Ecológica 40
accommodating 111
Accommodation of Good Living 241
accounts
   anthropological 25
   current 23
   ethnographic 39
   meticulous 9
   particular 15
   rich ethnographic 116
accumulation 119, 183, 203
accusations 105
ACHR 230–31, 235–36, 238, 240
Achuar indigenous 136
Acosta, Alberto 2, 4, 16, 73, 98–99, 101, 107, 132, 154, 162, 165, 181, 209
acquiescence, clear 119
Acta 78, 80, 91, 179
actions and omissions 231, 235
Activist Tribunals 239
actor-networks 43
actors
   collective 217
   external 41
   international 10, 20, 223
   intranational 223
   legitimate democratic 63
   local 64
   marginalised 211
   multiple 78, 100, 173, 222
   new 9–10, 19, 47, 195
   regional 240
   scattered 150
   social 43, 65, 82, 114, 172, 183
   social movement 29
   trans-national development 216
adaptation, subsequent 148
adaptive process 20
adding culture and stirring 175
adherence, new 156
administrations 54, 203
   colonial 120
   consecutive 127
   international 199
   local elite 123
   public 90, 95–96
   subsequent 127
administrative procedures 200, 206
advancement 19, 75, 94, 99, 107
   procedural 201
   technological 179, 181
Advancing Social Development policies 95
adversities 48
   economic 174
African Ecuadorians 211
Afro-Colombian groups 165
Afro Ecuadorian 49, 61–62, 114, 232
agency 29, 41, 105–6, 139, 173, 177, 182, 222
   galvanised political 42
   human 219
   international 169
   multilateral 117
   neo-utilitarian 107
   private 115
agenda 41, 180, 206–7
   broader socio-economic 41
   competing 130
   ethnic 138, 144
   ethnonationalist 135
   intellectual socio-economic 68
   inward-looking national development 20
   revolutionary 134
   sectorial 147
   social 68

INDEX 277

strategic 194
summit's 178
transformative rights 237
transgressive 191
agendas and actors 177
agent decisions 112
    particular 34
agent preferences 161
agents 9–10, 15, 26, 29, 37, 73, 149–50, 166,
    175, 178, 181–82, 195, 198, 201
    concrete social 204
    economic 62
    extra-constitutional 63
    individual 185
    legal 26
    political 166
    polymorphous ways 74
    transnational development 150
agrarian policy 39
agrarian reform 106, 115–16, 119
Agrarian Revolts 118
ailments 113, 144, 178, 188, 233, 244
    humanity's 181, 196
    previous policy 3
    structural societal 19
Albó, Xavier 40
Alexander, Robert 118–119
Algeria 124
allegations 16, 77
alliances 119, 131, 136, 142
    fluid discursive 177
allies 139
    former 141
    political 116
    potential 47
allocation 101, 239
Alonso González, Pablo 2
Alston, Philip 224–25, 240
alterity 83, 86, 102–3, 106, 164, 173, 180–81,
    195, 198, 204, 207, 212, 216, 233
    communal 82
    links 216
    political 194
alternativeness 99–100
    alleged 71
    novel 69
alternativeness masks 86
Altmann, Philip 25, 45, 70, 72, 74, 77, 138, 147,
    172

amalgamation 98, 102, 192
ama llula 72
ama quilla 72
ama shua 72
Amazon 15, 41, 48, 50–51, 56, 70, 114, 116, 119,
    132–33, 136, 147, 202–3, 205–6
Amazonian and Andean indigenous
    peoples 134–35
Amazonian indigenous community
    dynamics 116
Amazonian jungles 228
Amazonian lowlands 136
Amazonian oil fields 133
Amazonian regions 132
ambivalence 85, 173, 187, 197
    conceptual 181
    signified 190
    ulterior 187
American Convention on Human
    Rights 156, 230
Amin, Samir 176
anachronistic 163
Anaya, James 72, 132, 163, 226
ancestral Andean concept 1
ancestry 87
ancien régime 44
Andean 2, 83, 98, 101, 135, 138, 152–53
    equating 98
Andean alterity 213
Andean and Amazonian concept 71
Andean cohorts 142
Andean communities 105, 114, 153, 181
    rural indigenous 71
Andean Community 50
Andean conceptions 72
Andean cosmology 79, 81
Andean cultures 69, 72, 84, 103, 152
    hail 15
Andean elites 7
Andean faction of CONAIE 137
Andean Federación Ecuatoriana 133
Andean indigenous actors 215
Andean indigenous colonisers and
    Amazonian indigenous defending 119
Andean indigenous demands 119
Andean indigenous development 117
Andeanism 215
Andean nation 33, 128
Andean passport 50

Andean peoples   83, 87
Andean plains of Quito   136
Andean province   62
Andean representation in ethnodevelopment   105
Andean roots   84, 104
Andean system of life   81
Andean understandings of life   85
Andean villages   82, 84
Andes   9–10, 39, 41, 46, 48, 50, 82, 84–86, 90, 118–19, 123, 130, 132–34, 136, 176–77, 180, 184
Andolina, Robert   27, 32–33, 43, 47–48, 50–51, 55–56, 86–87, 104, 106, 148, 150, 152, 166, 168, 172, 176–78, 215
Anghie, Anthony   145
angle   185
　　new critical   76
Anglo-centric interpretations   99
Anglo-phonic states   241
Anglo-Saxon tradition   6
another world possible   12
antagonism, sharp   123
antecedent conditions aid   28
Anthias, Penelope   177
anthropocentrism   93, 99, 215
anthropologists   78, 214
anthropology   2, 9, 25–26, 41, 112, 114, 116
anti-establishment appeals   90
anti-feudal   120
anti-globalisation   101
anti-neoliberal   141
anti-oligarchic   120
anti-positivist explanations   105
antiquated notions   45
Antiquity   227
anti-statism   104
Antkowiak, Thomas   13, 158, 231, 235–37
Anton Sánchez, John   62
apparatus   62, 170–71
　　debilitated state   54
　　expansive state   37
appellatives   2, 85
　　unsubstantiated   97
applicability   3, 61, 116, 160, 218, 228, 230
　　direct   230
　　empirical   116
　　legal   6, 30, 209, 217, 226
application   103, 113, 119, 218, 235
　　formalistic   103
　　local   113
appointed President Alfredo Palacio   142
approaches
　　friendly   142, 180
　　grass-roots   177
　　guided   114
　　hands-on   239
　　highlight philosophical   9
　　innovated   108
　　innovative   175
　　mechanistic   22–24, 35–36
　　ontological   29
　　redefined legal   239
　　redefined rural development   114
　　regional   13, 233, 238
　　regional policy   169
　　rights-based   230, 240
　　robust   217
　　state-centered   112
　　substantive epistemological   113
　　systemic   22–23
Aquinas, Thomas   227
Arab plans   215
Arabs   215
Aramaic mannā   187
Araujo   131
arbitrariness   73
Archaeology of Knowledge   186
arena   167
　　altered political   124
　　convulsive political   10, 12, 19
　　domestic   238
　　domestic political   175
　　formed political   34
　　international human rights   110
　　national political   124
Argentina   11, 44, 71, 110, 158
Aristotle   146
Armingeon, Laus   159
Arosemena, Carlos Julio   119
arrangements   224
　　complex multilateral   159
　　creating regional constitutional   225
　　disappearing corporatist   175
　　political economic   167
articulated conflict-ridden demands   172

INDEX

articulation   56, 90, 172, 186, 189, 191–92, 194, 196, 198, 213
   correct   15
   mechanistic   188
articulatory power   188
   ethnodevelopment's   193
Asian Tigers   92
aspirations   17, 148, 150
   ontological   16
assemblage   171–72, 194
   dynamic   239
   theory-guided   25
assets   152, 174, 191
   flagship   152
   marketable   213
   new market   183
assimilation   86
assimilationist policies   119, 139
   expanding   121
associational hardware   176
associational involvement   183
Atamaint, Diana   205–7
atomised pluralism   128, 130
atomistic politics   46
atomized pluralism   128
attacking hunger   179
attributes   135, 189, 219
   political   163
attributions   68, 143, 219
austerity   77
Australia   163
authoritative analysis   8
authority   94, 126, 186, 205
   central mediating   64
   constitutional   94, 218
   indivisible jurisdictional   145
   political   59, 90
   presidential   94
   public   60, 211, 218
   the sole bearer of   96
   sovereign   153
autonomy   39, 45, 52, 123, 149, 163–64, 204, 210, 228, 243
   demanded   111
   discursive   41
   granted   134
   internal   45
   international human rights treaties favouring indigenous   110
   limiting national policy   159
   local   45, 133, 147
   national   159
   political   87, 133
autopoietic   12
Ávila, Santamaría, Ramiro   16
ayllu   15, 72
   llacta   72
   mama   72
ayllu camachic   72
   mama   72
Aymara indigenous   77
Aymara indigenous heritage   72
Aymara language in Bolivia   1
Aymara peoples of Bolivia   11
Azuay   151

backdrop   118
   empirical   109
   relevant   115
Bakker, Karen   31
Balch   11
Baltzly, Dirk   77
banana exports   123
bank, central   125
bank deposits   127
bank owners   126
banks   67, 125–26
   private   125
   run on the   127
Barbosa dos Santos, Fabio Luis   100–101
bargaining
   institutional   123
   institutional policy   131
   political   131
barriers, procedural   239
barter   79, 159
Barton, John   44
Baxter, Hugh   10
bearers   71, 104
Beck, Scott   1, 33, 41, 48–49, 103, 106, 111, 117, 124, 129, 131, 133–37, 140, 142–44
Becker, Marc   19, 28, 39, 46, 58, 104, 111, 116, 119, 132, 135–36, 138, 141–42, 144, 146–47
Bedford, Kate   19, 31, 43, 56, 149, 172, 177
beliefs   62–63, 143, 186, 203
   idiosyncratic   180
   normative   146
Beling, Adrian   77, 100–101

Bell, Karen   93
Benavides, Hugo   48, 121, 136
Benford, Robert   29, 190
Bennett, Andrew   22, 34–36
Berlin   16
Berlin Wall   9, 221–22
Bible   187
bibliography, specialized   115
Bilateral Investment Treaties   44
Bilchitz, David   238
bilingual literacy campaign   75
binaries   48, 82
   true or false   106
bio-centric   85
bio-centric development plan   78
biocentric environmentalism   18
bio-centrism   55, 101, 107
   strong   100
biodiverse hotspots   199
biodiversity   199–202
Biodiversity Commission   201
biopolitics   54, 145, 166–71, 182, 194
Biospherical egalitarianism   99
birds-eye-view   238
birth   6, 8, 34, 69, 104, 116, 133–34, 144, 155, 169, 198, 224, 227, 241–42
   constitutional   157
birth rate   145
Black Organizations   135
blatant reification   175
body politic   44
Bolívar   151
Bolivarian constitutions   67
Bolivarian democracies   90
Bolivia   1–2, 11, 38–39, 67, 71–72, 74, 76–79, 81, 86, 146, 173, 203
Bolivian and Ecuadorian constitutions   210
Bolivia's Suma Qamaña   9, 76–77, 214
Bonilla Maldonado, Daniel   136
borders   49, 120
   exceeded Ecuador's   11
boundaries   24, 117
   create the   34
   temporal   34, 36
   theoretical   112
Bourdieu, Pierre   62, 105, 182–83, 185
Bowen, James   214
branches   122, 128, 232
   judicial   129

legislative   19, 128, 131
   political   218
brand   6, 54, 61, 90, 118, 224
branding   85, 92
   technocratic populist   96
Brazil   1, 44, 104
breakdown   184
   democratic   133
breeding ground   177
   necessary   188
   optimal   58
   perfect   40
Bretón Solo de Zaldívar, Víctor   9–10, 25, 27, 56, 73, 86, 104–5, 114–15, 117–19, 132, 147, 150–52, 174–78, 184, 212, 214, 223
Briones, Claudia   175
broader legal transformations   234
brutal persistency   175
Bucaram presidency   140
Buddhism   77
Buen Vivir   1–2, 8, 11, 13, 70, 74–75, 196–97, 201–3, 209, 213–17, 220, 223, 226, 241, 244
   displaces   209
   entrap   216
   obtaining   201
   state-centered analysis   225
   term   71
Buen Vivir and neo-extractivism
   discredit   203
Buen Vivir and Sumak Kawsay   234, 241, 243
Buen Vivr's crafting   216
Bulgaria   221
bundle   52–53, 152, 189
bundling   54, 179, 191
bureaucrats   214
Burgorgue-Larsen, Laurence   157, 229–30, 239
Burki   149
Burt, Jo-Marie   40, 46
business   184
   private   181
Business and Human Rights   98

cabinet positions   142
cacao   118, 123
Caicedo, Danilo   239
calculation   171
Calisto Friant, Martin   72, 100

INDEX   281

Canada   163
Cañar   151–52
Cançado Trinidade, Antonio Augusto   157
Cancillería   50, 92
candidates, individual   140
capabilities   109, 146
    redefining citizen   146
    sovereign   122
    theory-building   168
    unique   185
    unlimited   99
    unprecedented   105
capital   69, 101, 182
    foreign   120, 126
    global   37
    new-found   185
    political   131, 137, 192
capital flows   44, 126
    private   125
capital goods   124
capitalise   41, 139, 153, 162, 167, 173
capitalism   16, 51, 61, 93, 96
    acceptable   96
    stakeholder   51–52, 175–76
    state-led socialist   97
capitalist   75, 92, 96, 98
capital lending   126
Capoccia, Giovanni   8, 37, 108
care
    priority   236
    specialized   236
caricatures, popular   214
Carlos Viteri Gualinga   2, 70, 79, 201
carve   145, 162
cascading effect   157–58
case-law, developing   157
cases inexistent   128
cases non-existent   133
case study   33–34, 36, 118, 199, 201
    in-depth   33
case study analysis   34
    in-depth   24
Cassidy, Brendan   73, 88
catalyst   27, 37–38
categories   26, 72, 128, 189
    circumscribed   48
    essentialised identity   87
    folk   87
    fourth   72–73

    implementing Sartori's   128
    legal   12, 26
    new   26
    ontological   77
    producing new   89
    social   170
Catholics   187
cauldron   48, 118
causal chains   23
causation   22, 219
caveats, corresponding   223
caves   231
    destroyed   233
Cayambe   151–52
cede   119, 173, 180
ceding   119, 160, 225
celebrations   129, 136
    protested state-sponsored   136
cement   6, 137, 219
census   118
    first agricultural   118
Central Andes   132
Central Ecuadorian Andes   84
Central Government   42–43, 202
central state authority   123
centre   62, 133, 160, 220
    gravitational   142
    modern urban   136
centre stage   170, 191, 240
centuries, mid-twentieth   121, 219
century writings   83
Cepeda-Espinosa, Manuel José   25
Cepek, Michael   10, 25, 104, 117, 152, 168, 180
ceremonies   233
Cerny, Philip   42, 106
chain   35
    interlocked   22
    reconstructed   42
    theory-guided   27
Chang, Myrna Mack   235
Changing citizenship   35, 53, 224
changing citizenship regimes   24, 27, 29,
    31–33, 36–37, 47–48, 51–52, 102, 106,
    108–9, 144, 147–48, 150, 160–61, 167–68,
    193, 211
charismatic appeal   183
chastising   87
    present   87
Checkel   22, 34–36

child mistreatment   236
children   78, 181, 233, 236
Chile   11, 62, 71, 175, 239
Chile's Programa Orígenes   174
Chile's women's movement   149
Chimborazo   84, 151
Chinese concept of Tao   1
Chinese immigration, prohibited   50
Cholango   85
Christ, Jesus   103, 227
christening   220
Christian contexts   187
Christian dogmas   134
Christo-centric framework   227
Chuji, Mónica   70, 80, 216
Cicero   227
circumscribed spatial clusters   155
citizen participation   69
    active   173
citizen petition   206
citizenry   47, 51, 54
    civil   29
    marginalised   41
    mobilised   32, 150
citizenry mobilisation   38, 190
citizenry's deprivation   13
citizens   3, 50–52, 61, 109, 148, 155–56, 235, 237, 242
    conscientious   179
    individual   148–49
    market-ready   152
    new social network savvy   150
    obliged   213
    senior   181
citizenship   48–50, 136, 146, 148–49, 153, 176
    contents of   110–11
    corporatist   147
    derogated conditional   146
    differentiated   139, 147
    idealised   146
    meta-ecological   102
    new form of   39, 148, 150
    redefined   49
    revised   147
citizenship categories   47
citizenship regimes   47–49, 51, 135, 144–46, 149–50, 225
    altered pre-existing   110

corporatist   147
defined   108, 167
designed   47
differentiated   144, 147
formed   150
neoliberal   146–47, 152
new   47, 145
new market-led   152
pre-existing   140, 146
prior   147
redefined   112, 155
redefined pre-existing   111
redefining of   148, 153
redesigning   50
shifting dynamics of   68, 149
subverted   31
underlined changing   164
utilised emerging   51
Citizenship regimes in Ecuador   48
citizens revolution   74, 202
citizen-state intermediation   58
citizen-state relations   1, 51, 66, 111, 159
    corroded   153
    defined   160
    ever-changing   67
    redefined   160
citizen-subject   56, 154, 175
    new   154
City of Knowledge   97
civic value   152
civic virtue   148–49, 152–53, 166, 176, 243
    consolidated   154
    market-based   153
    neoliberal   153
    new   148–49
civil servants   192, 214
civil society   29, 31, 43, 47, 49, 51, 53–55, 58–59, 64, 102, 104, 107, 131, 149–50, 167, 178, 184
civil society groups   3, 5, 18, 119, 195, 226
    disenfranchised   211
civil society mobilisations   3, 17, 47–48, 57–59, 140, 142
    boosted   109
    fuelled   235
    guided   157
    ignited   106
    transgressive   150

INDEX   283

civil society movements   223
civil society organisations   28, 42, 50, 55, 85,
    178, 180
  international   39
  multiple   191
class   65, 132, 229, 242
  particular   73
  urban middle   123
class agendas   142
class-based demands   144
  wider   40
class-based problematics   41
class classifications   238
class conflict   134
class dichotomies   134
class differentiators   241
classifications   68, 72, 84
  binary   84, 181
class relations   229
class struggle, merged   40
class struggles   135
cleavage   37
  generative   37–38, 41, 52–53,
    108
clientelistic handouts   46
clientelistic practices   54
  secured   51
closely-knit   28
closure   189
  self-referential   12
Clusters   23
coalitions   37, 128
  fragmented   130
  legislative   128
  secure stable   128
  unpopular multiparty   130
Cochrane, Regina   2
coercion   64, 122, 155, 169
  indirect   219
  political   131
coextensive   163
cognitive dissonance   46
Cohen, Jean   45
coherence   26, 69
cohesion   47, 62
  social   31, 63
cohesiveness   138
  sporadic   128

Cold War   120
Coleman   183, 185
collective action   43, 47, 58–60, 64, 66,
    99–100, 137, 140–41, 161, 167, 170, 188,
    190–92, 194–96, 209, 211, 217
  dismembered   197
  ethnic   168
  fuelled   59, 237
  particular forms of   190, 196
  shared   58
  wider   41
collective demands   10, 221
  transformed   164
collective rights   5, 45–46, 56, 62, 106, 110–11,
    135, 140, 190–91, 194, 202, 220, 226,
    231–33
  establishing   134
  pursued   9
  secure   232
  securing   163
collective rights agendas   170
collectives   58, 63, 221
  human   63
  transgender   211
collective sphere   228
colleges, electoral   60
Collier, David   1, 34, 36–38, 51,
    170
Collins, Jennifer   10, 137
collision   30, 45, 134, 170
collusion   125–26
  preeminent   127
  regulatory   127
Colombia   1, 44, 49, 71, 108, 158, 164, 234,
    239
  neighbouring   240
Colombian Constitutional Court   239
Colombia's Constitutional Court   239
colonial chronicles   86
coloniality   218, 232
  epistemic   229
colonial legacy   101
colonial rule   83, 221
Colonización   119
Colonization   119
Colta   151–52
Combating Poverty   77
commandeer   138, 140

commandeer nationwide protests 137
commodity 104
    intellectual 82
    marketable 136
commodity prices 1
commonplace 3, 91, 167, 204
communal 16, 195
    attacking 136
communal networks 191
    interconnect 148
communal practices 170
communal relations 170
communication 4, 12
    transjudicial 6, 8
communicative action 63
communism 9, 215
Communist Party 134
communitarian alterity 193
communitarian development models 96
communities 40, 75, 77–79, 82–84, 99–100, 105, 119, 163, 172, 176, 180, 183–84, 233, 236–37
    bustling 105
    cosmic 84
    distinct 163
    foreign legal 113
    given 149
    impoverished 176, 179
    international 148
    legal academic 113
    local 50, 55
    migrant 50
    monetised agricultural 132
    privileging 202
    religious 149
    self-organised 101
    transnational ngo 176
    transnational non-for-profit 176
community ancestors 81
community autonomy 39
community centric 11
community leaders 27
community networks 177, 185
community organisation 176
community organising structure 176
community participation 93, 174
community structures 180

competition 44–45
    free-for-all 147
    political 204
    political envisioned 44
complementarity 96
    human-nature 79
    subsequent theoretical 5
complements 22, 73, 122
completed questions 212
complexities 36, 60, 115, 117
complex networks setup 152
complex political struggles 241
complex processes 17, 21, 52, 160
complicity 130, 182, 190, 213–14, 223, 243
    innate 214
Comunas 15
Conaghan, Catherine 46, 168
CONAIE 13, 40–41, 84, 130, 134, 136–43, 181, 204, 214, 223
    birth of 28, 134
conceptions
    classic 144
    constitutionalize 210
    constructivist 12, 65
    limited 63, 163
    linear 23
    novel 112
    official state 136
    state-centered 163
    systematic 52
conceptual architecture 26
conceptual breadth 192
    universal 207
conceptual consistency 16
conceptual flaws 27
conceptual framework, guiding 115
conceptualisation 71, 82, 122
conceptualise 219
conceptualization 223
conceptual openness 77, 188
    unbounded 197
conceptual power struggle 204
conceptual rooting 105
concessions 130
concreteness 181, 192
Condemning 197
condition distribution 238

INDEX   285

conditions   60, 63, 120, 125–26, 128, 167, 169,
 171, 187, 192, 196, 200, 232, 236, 239
 historical   39, 58, 229
 necessary   18, 41, 133, 155, 169, 198, 235
 particular social   190
 political   9, 34, 37
 precarious health   237
 preferential market-access   43
 ripe   166, 192
 socio-economic   65, 137, 229
 spiritual   132, 203
 structural   48, 121–22, 166, 185
Confederation of Indigenous Nationalities of Ecuador   134
conflation   48, 95, 184, 213
conflicts   119, 128, 132, 152, 218
 ethnic   175
 fuelled political   168
 internal   142
confluence   26, 75, 223
conformation   63, 132, 196
conformity   63, 202
confrontation   129
 impeded   133
 political   120
 social   120
congregation   230
congress   61, 78–79, 119, 134, 139–40, 142, 214
 conservative controlled   140
 storming   141
congress woman, first   205
connection   79, 84, 104
consciousness   56
 intersubjective   54
 progressive false   243
Consejo   207
consensus   99
 reasonable   131
consent, informed   158
conservation   85, 172, 199
 environmental   4, 13, 78, 98, 107, 216
 planetary   80
 territorial   100
conservation groups   100
conservation policies   197
conservation projects   68
constituencies   139
 electoral   136

mobilized mass   90
 uniform   111
constituents   109
constitution
 liberal   217
 post-communist   221
constitutional adjudication   11, 240
constitutional articles   44, 90, 101, 164
Constitutional Assembly   68, 75, 78–80,
 88–89, 91, 106, 111, 130, 137, 140, 143,
 178–79, 193, 198
 appointed   143
constitutional convergence   18, 28, 111, 157,
 167, 230
 regional   28
Constitutional Court   206–7
 seated   200
Constitutional Court of Ecuador   205
Constitutional Court of Guatemala   240
Constitutional Court rule   206
constitutional framing   90
 new   1
constitutional General Duty   93
constitutional imbalance   94
constitutional inscription   3–5, 12, 21, 27–29,
 38, 69, 73, 80, 90, 102, 106, 113, 157, 226
constitutionalism, emerging   210
constitutional law   26, 90, 103, 174
constitutional magistrate   72
constitutional make-up   89, 128
 novel   61
Constitutional Mandate   143
constitutional outlay   238
constitutional powers   94, 242
 new-found   90
constitutional principle   3, 9–11, 13, 18, 21, 26,
 193, 196, 200–201, 212, 214, 218–20, 226,
 234, 237, 240–41, 243
constitutional ramifications   207
constitutional reform   5, 7, 14, 25, 44, 57, 61,
 67, 74, 108, 113, 130, 140, 143
 defined   13
 influenced   232
 necessary   130
constitutional reform in Ecuador   20, 67
constitutional reform processes   1
constitutional rights   6, 90, 92, 111, 148, 219
 redefined   238

constitutional scrutiny 90
constitutional shifts 210
Constitutional Table 78
constitutional text 3, 57, 62, 64
    approved 144
    first 146
    longest 1
    new 50, 239
constitutional tribunals 239
Constitution of Ecuador 68, 90, 92–93
construction 5, 16, 18, 21, 69, 76, 83, 87–88, 90–91, 96–98, 164, 168, 170, 180, 186, 189
    artificial 63
    constitutional 92
    democratic 91
    epistemological 83
    linear 22
    new 182
    popular 176
    scattered 81
    thematic 177, 186
    utopia under 2
constructions, ambivalent 174
constructive arguments, developing 87
constructivist conceptions of law and society 12, 65
constructivist formations 232
consultation process 206
consultations, informed 232
consumption 169
consumption patterns 101
containment 88, 139, 186
contempt 40, 59, 122, 143
contention 29, 46, 136, 167–68
    political 31, 198
contents, necessary 204
contestations 190, 204
contest neoliberal reforms 111
contests 3, 10, 17, 27–28, 58, 64, 75, 81, 83, 106–7, 197–98, 203, 232, 234
context 2, 13, 21, 28, 65, 67, 74, 113, 152, 186–87, 189, 197, 209
    economic 29, 89
    given 187–88
    legal 90
    national 197
    political 74
    rural 115
    spatiotemporal 161

contracts 126, 230
    making private 183
    modified public sector 142
contradictions 17, 70, 105, 178, 186, 195, 203
    clear 207
    manifest 85
control 10, 42, 54, 92, 133, 143, 168
    ceded 220
    exercised 52
    fleeting 141
    military 133
    removed state 42
    seized 110
    social 172
    societal 168, 170, 176, 182, 213, 218
Conventional proponents of deliberative democracy 61
Conventional theories on deliberative democracy focus 63
Convention on Human Rights 13
convergence 1, 7–8, 35, 37, 43, 46–47, 53, 58, 111, 155, 158, 160–62, 168, 222–23
    complex 20
    critical juncture's 139
    domestic 157
    regional 67
    systemic 22
    uncoordinated policy 155
Convergence of ghost coalitions 144
Convergence of NGOs in Latin America 105
convergence of politicised ethnic cleavages 68, 167, 243
converging forces 54, 108, 144, 156, 193
    necessary 15
converging occurrences 27, 33, 52, 109, 160, 211
converging power relations 166
convulsive legislative reform 214
Copenhagen Summit 95, 178, 181, 196
Coronel Lucio Gutiérrez 141
Coronel Lucio Gutiérrez's anti-system 141
corporatism 51, 66
corporatist policies 38–39, 167
corporatist practices 28, 31, 55, 121, 150
corporatist relationships 28
corporatist structures 58
Corral, Fabian 14
Correa, Rafael 91–92, 97, 143
    former President 91

INDEX 287

Correa Administration 88, 93, 200
corrupt public official syphoning 97
Corte Constitutional 7, 258, 229–30
cosmo-centric framework 227
cosmos 70, 77
cosmovision 9, 70, 75, 233
　cultural 72
　quotidian 75
Costa Rica 71, 156, 158, 234, 239
Costa Rica's Constitutional Chamber's
　　Decision 239
costs 125, 127
Cotacachi 79
Cotopaxi 151
coup 46, 141–42
Court 7, 12–13, 29, 61, 78, 156–58, 210, 230,
　　237
　domestic 199, 238
　national 7
　regional 8, 60, 229, 234, 241
creating idealised representations 173
creating indigenous elites 10
creating political opportunities 47
creation 40, 50, 63, 84, 110, 154, 190
　job 96
crises 59, 61, 83, 115, 122, 126, 128–29, 174, 223
　economic 50, 75, 113
　environmental 75
critical approach 161–62, 164–65, 168, 209,
　　219
　new 244
critical juncture 7–9, 14–15, 17–21, 27–29,
　　31–38, 47–67, 73–74, 86–88, 90–92, 98,
　　102–4, 106–9, 111–62, 166–69, 171–74,
　　177–78, 180–82, 184–86, 190–95, 198,
　　211–14, 216–17, 220–26, 234–35, 237–38,
　　240–41
critical juncture approach 36
Cuadra, Fernando de 4
Cuba 118
Cubillo-Guevara, Ana Patricia 1–2, 25–26,
　　68–69, 71–72, 102, 209, 223
Cuenca 151–52
cultural expressions 83, 138–39
cultural rights 6–7, 10, 12–13, 156, 158, 164,
　　173–74, 192, 194–95, 199, 216, 218–20,
　　225, 228–35, 237–44
cultural values 179, 231, 233
culture

　ancestral 184
　bridging 51
　local 82
　lost millenary 88
　merging 55
　national 121
currency de-valuations 126
currency fluctuations 124
current argument 226
current contractual arrangement 200
Czechoslovakia 221

Dávalos, Pablo 10, 38, 49, 84, 96, 125, 141,
　　168–69, 170
dealings
　legislative 136
　political 129, 142
debt 125–26
　private 125, 127
debt crisis 9, 43, 53, 169
　regional 1, 8, 37
　region's 38
debt relief 125
decentralisation 43, 45, 55, 79
　increased 44
decentralisation policies 123
decisions
　administrative 205
　binding 157
　clustered 155
　domestic 229
　interweaves 168
　judicial 90
　political 131, 207–8
　possible 238
　sovereign 145
Declaration of Human Rights 227
Declaration of Independence 3
Declaration of National Interest 200–202
Declare National Interest 202
decolonise 85
Decreto Ley 175
deficiencies 102, 197
　structural 121
　structural societal 179
　systemic 232
Deflem, Mathieu 10–11
degrees 4, 39, 41, 122, 129, 132–33
　lesser 39

dehumanized thought   215
de jure powers, generous   128
Delhi   236
deliberation   60–64, 81, 195, 204
  alternative forms of   64, 161
  limited forms of   61, 63
  new forms of   131, 195, 209
  participatory   63
deliberative democracy   32, 60–61, 63–65,
    131, 137, 161, 209, 211
  conventional   63
deliberative democracy focus   63
  new   110
  particular   192
  popular   7, 131
  radical   173
  regional   220
  transgressive   172, 175, 216
Della Porta, Donatella   31, 34, 108,
    135
demobilise   29, 54
democracies, modern   7
democracy   8, 31–32, 60–66, 75, 90–91, 109,
    129, 133, 138, 149, 204
  competitive   60
  discursive   59, 198, 209
  fragile   124
  judicial   63
  local   222
  participatory   60
  procedural   64
  radical   39
  social protest and discursive   57, 64
  transnational governmentalities and
    discursive   53
democratic institutions   123, 130
  formal   90
democratic interaction, making   204
democratic processes   159, 205
democratic renewal   176
democratic rule   1, 28, 146
democratic welfare states   10
democratize   179
Deneulin   98–99
dependency   178, 180
  resource   124, 180
  vertical   180
Dependency on transnational development
    resources   177

deployment   50, 148–50, 174–75, 179, 182, 187,
    214
  NGO policy   28
  progressive   243
  strategic   176, 182, 184
  strategic NGO   51
destruction   231–32, 236
  environmental   144
  nuclear   214
development   43, 68–69, 75, 77, 79, 82, 89,
    93–96, 99–101, 114–15, 152, 172–73, 175,
    195–96, 198, 203, 227–28
  doctrinal   158, 227
  human-scale   173
  industrial   97
  inward-looking   121
  local   240
  market-based   150
  national   90, 94, 121
  progressive   216, 229–30, 232, 234, 240
  state-centred   106
  urban   184
development agencies   64, 117, 167
  bilateral   28, 150, 178, 180
  international   42, 50, 65, 67, 77, 104, 149,
    171
  local   55
  multilateral   105, 117
development agendas   182
  social   180–81, 194, 196
developmental   88, 95, 134, 209
Developmental Good Living   96
developmentalism   92
  state-centric   98
developmental objectives   55
developmental policies   88, 99
  previous   38
developmental state, rich   51
development approach   11
  new   56
development architecture, global   43
Development Cooperation and Ethnic
    Demands   114
development discourse   184
development formula   70
development funds   176, 178, 180,
    184
development initiatives   174
  local   43

INDEX 289

development model 2
    alternative 84, 101
    alternative to 214
development paradigms 77, 114, 117–18
    new 107
    novel 95
    rural 115
    state-led vertical economic 98
development plans 89
development policies 33, 46, 69, 97, 176, 178
    based economic 175
    economic 93, 177
    industrial 92
    international 100
    previous inward-looking 124
    state-led 11
development policy prescriptions 180
development problems 121
development process 93
    national 202
development programs 154
    economic 104, 173
development projects 77, 104, 150–52, 184
    community-orientated 103
    economic 56, 93, 96, 175, 236
    failed 82
    justifying market-orientated 214
    localised NGO-led 55
    multilateral 214
development regime 46, 78, 103–4
development resources 182
    economic 56
development strategy 96
Dezalay 26, 73, 89, 183
Díaz Cayeros, Alberto 172–73
dichotomies 81–82, 99
dichotomous 190
Digna 19
dignity, abstract 228
discontent 48, 118
    fuelled popular 100
    political 118
discourse ambivalence 191
discourse analysis 197
discourse formation 162, 197, 213
    contested 212
    initial 154
    privileged 214–15

proto-conceptual 152
    strategic 4, 10, 57
discourse framing 179, 186
discourse fuses 5
discourses 4, 15–19, 25–26, 30, 55–56, 64–65,
        80–81, 85–86, 88–89, 91–92, 97–98, 100,
        102–5, 144, 163–64, 166, 186–91, 196–97,
        203–4, 210–11
    hegemonic 17, 64, 81, 177, 185, 187, 189, 191
    homogenising 187
    idealised 173
    legitimising 107
    multiple 14, 190
    new 57, 214, 222, 225
    new social capital 184
    ontological 24, 73, 106
    privileged 73, 187, 189, 233
    statist 95, 162
    strategic 4, 17, 181, 194
    subverted subaltern 150
    unique 190, 241
discrimination 48, 132, 139, 191, 217
    negative 132
    racial 58, 132–33
discursive 57, 171, 185
    homogenising 166
    strategic 195
discursive amplitude 181
discursive association 154
discursive construction 195
    new 20
discursive content 88
discursive democracy 27, 53, 57, 64–66, 102,
        106, 109, 111, 166, 193, 195, 199, 209–11, 213
discursivities 55, 103, 185, 187–89, 191,
        194–98, 203–4, 217, 226, 237, 243
displacement 39, 98, 159, 167, 214, 216, 220
dispositif 166, 168, 170–72, 182, 194
    consolidates Foucault's 170
    institutional 172
doctrines 113, 158, 214
    legal 219, 231
dollarisation 127, 141
domestic law 154
    harmonised 157
    redefined 153
Domjahn, Thomas 93
drinking water 233
    safe 179

Dryzek, John   27, 32, 51, 57, 61, 63–64, 106, 111, 131, 137
D'Souza, Radja   19, 219
dualisms   100, 219
   socio-political   86
Durán-Ballén government   137
Dussel, Enrique   12
Dutch Disease   124
dynamics   31, 67, 115, 237–38
   anti-natural   81
   complex   18, 39, 49, 52, 90
   institutional   37, 39, 48, 108, 116, 161
   political   108
   reinforcing   36
   shifting geopolitical   15
   shifting policy   7
   social   116, 164
   theorised   211

early stages   169, 216
early-twentieth-century   214
East Central Europe   221
Eastern Europe   110, 224
East-West dualisms   215
Eaton, Kent   18–19
eco-Andeanism   86
eco-biotic habitat   83
ecological alternatives   78
ecological connotations   101
ecological field worker   99
Ecological Inference Method   144
ecologist   5, 68–69, 74, 79, 98, 219, 234, 237
Ecologist and Post-developmental Good Living   98
ecologist/post-developmental   4, 161
ecology   83
   deep   98, 164
economic agendas   40, 57
   liberal   178
   neo-extractive   203
economic conditions   14, 37, 40, 111, 124–25
   deteriorated   127
   ever-worsening   28
   regional   1
economic development   44, 52, 56, 92–93, 96, 171, 173, 179, 181, 184, 188, 203
   accelerated   93
   alternative   182
   industrial export-orientated   93

   national   94
   secure   55
   state-centred   69
   state-led   95
Economic Development Majority Report   179
economic liberalisation   44, 46–47, 153–54, 157–58, 170
   enforced   159
economic meltdown   31, 37, 129
economic policy   19, 47, 56, 67, 143, 159–60, 234
   inward-directed   159
   inward-looking   92
   inward-orientated   122
economic processes   71, 73, 108, 116
economic reforms   31–32, 41–42, 56, 72, 108–9, 117, 130, 137, 140, 144, 167, 188
   generative cleavage of   38–39, 108
   merged   168
economics   101, 184–85
   associative   176
   laissez-faire   125
   orthodox   91
ecosophy   98
ecosphere   98, 102
   bio-centric   100
ECtHR (European Court of Human Rights)   235
ECtHR judgement   235
Ecuador
   and Latin America   6, 9, 12, 30, 38, 80, 109, 153, 208, 229
   by transnational agents   55
   citizenship   49
   Communist Party   134
   Constitution   2, 89, 101, 210
   courts   90
   developmental state   46
   Government   46, 88, 97, 125, 231
   neo-constitutionalism   6
   politics   8, 40–41, 46, 49, 80, 109, 117, 128–31, 138, 147, 161
   society   13, 188, 213, 242
   state   32, 43, 47, 67, 88, 134, 177, 220, 231–32
education   2, 13, 62, 91, 96, 121, 127, 157–58, 173–74, 179, 184, 235, 237, 240

INDEX   291

El Comercio   62, 91, 97–98, 120, 138, 142, 200,
    202, 205
elections   49, 128, 140–41
    competitive   60
    democratic   129
    popular   140
    presidential   68, 137
    regular   159
Electoral Code   207
Electoral Council   201
electricity outages   91, 137
elites   12, 123
    agro-banking   130
    agro-export   118, 125
    competitive enlightened   64
    deliberating   60
    domestic bourgeois-nationalist   216
    local   58
    national   102
    pressuring   119
El Telégrafo   141
El Universo   98
emancipation   17, 30, 89, 106, 150, 181
emancipatory agendas   178
empowerment   114–15, 150
empty signifier   166, 168, 181, 185–97, 199,
    203–4, 208, 212, 216–17, 219–20, 223, 226,
    233–35, 237, 241, 243
enforceability   3, 10, 21, 196, 219, 241
    corresponding   219
    legal   12, 20, 212, 229
    possible   20
    subsequent   3
    subsequent judicial   25
    surrounding Good Living's   3
enforcement   30, 111, 145–46, 167, 224, 230,
    234, 240
entrepreneurship   56, 152, 154, 184, 191,
    194
environment   2, 93, 100–101, 157, 184,
    240
    balanced   4, 202
    complex policy   46
    healthy   101
    macroeconomic   120–21
    right policy   126
environmental conservation movement   100
environmental degradation   3, 100, 200
environmentalists   58, 177, 181, 192

environmentally-protected areas   165
environmental politics   79, 100
    revitalised   79
environmental shift   100
envisioning   114, 171, 210
epistemological discursive strategy   106
epistemological fields   8–9, 26, 112,
    223
    multiple   113
epistemologies   12, 17, 83
    multiple   12
epochs   83, 132
equality   3, 48, 71, 75, 138, 214
    political   60
    securing   134
    securing economic   94
    social   4, 19, 191–92
Equifinality   36
equilibrium   74, 77, 80–81, 83
    collective   83
    ecological   74
equity   10
    economic   180
    social   68
era   31, 43, 170
    colonial   118
    early republican   225
    new   103, 120
    post-Washington consensus   149
    pre-democratic   28
    turbulent   1
Escobal, Javier   174
Escobar, Arturo   43, 101–2, 124, 213
Esmeraldas   62
Esping-Andersen   94
essentialised notions   87–88, 150, 152, 180,
    184
    representations   165, 197, 215, 233
Estermann, Josef   2, 9, 70, 164
estrangement   136, 139
ethnic cleavages   7, 38–40, 109, 117–18, 175,
    182
    converging forces of politicised   29, 37,
    160
ethnicity   38, 40–41, 56, 111, 114, 152, 182,
    184–85
    coupled   152
    fusing   56
Ethnicity and social capital   177

ethnic minorities   5, 17, 28–29, 63, 164, 192
    dispersed   104
    portrayed   184
ethnic platforms   115
ethnic politics   33, 45, 80, 144, 180
ethnic rights   171
    strong   135
ethnocultural demands   135
    interweaved   137
ethnodevelopment   56–57, 105, 115, 164, 166, 170–71, 173, 175, 177–80, 182, 184–95, 197, 214, 216–17, 243
    discourse of   105, 107, 177
    market-led   57
    market-orientated   66
    myth of   178, 213
ethnodevelopment agendas   196
ethnopolitics   39–40
    reviewed   42
Europe   44, 50, 127
    post-communist   223
    southern   221
European Court of Human Rights (ECtHR)   235
expenditures   91, 202
    budget   127
    mandated welfare   127
exploitation   99, 200–202
    expansive   97
    responsible   202
extraction   200
    natural resource   100
    possible   200
    rent   200
    stop oil   200

Faber, Daniel   104
failures   99–100, 110, 123, 149, 204
    final   204
    systemic   131
Falleti, Tulia   23–24, 33–34, 36, 52, 55, 123
Febres Cordero administration   125
feminists   5, 69, 144, 177, 188, 192
Fernández, Albert   16, 165
Ferrajoli, Luigi   139
Ferrer Mac-Gregor, Eduardo   21
financial meltdown   125
financial sector   125–27

Fischer, Andrew   229
Fishkin, James   60–61
fissures   137–38, 190
    internal   115
Floresmilo Simabaña   76
food   2, 13, 187, 237
    sourced   231
forces
    agricultural labour   121
    armed   120, 232
    articulate antagonistic   188
    emerging social   170
    enacted unleashed   44
    external   43, 140
    internal   221
    international   223
    overarching   211
    ranging   221
    unleash   44
foreign currency reserves   118, 121, 124–25
foreign debt   121–22, 124
    contracted   143
foreign debt servicing plans   125
foreign Direct Investment   97, 126
formulations   5, 14, 17, 20, 85, 152
    charged discursive   85
    disciplinary   169
    doctrinal   13
    international policy   43
    ontological   15
    state-led   88
    theoretical   13
Foucault, Michel   4, 26–27, 32, 54, 59, 106, 111, 145–46, 162, 168–71, 186–87
frames   8, 29, 57, 80, 113, 116–17, 168, 193, 195, 199, 208
    enacted   162
    international legal   111
    post-development Good Living   114
framing   21, 29, 41–42, 52, 78, 97, 100, 106, 122, 190, 192, 212–13, 220, 226
    political   40–41, 45
Francis Coralie Mullin   236
Frost, T.   25, 172
Fukuyama, Francis   170, 183

Gaia hypothesis   85
Galindo, Alvaro   10, 44, 174

INDEX 293

Gallegos-Anda, Carlos Espinosa 2, 65, 163
Gamu, Jonathan 124
Garantías Jurisdiccionales 242
García, Fernando 75, 84, 86, 165
García-Quero, Fernando 72
García-Sayán, Diego 10, 157
Gardbaum, Stephen 5–6
Gargarella, Roberto 25, 29–31, 37, 39, 44–45,
 55, 59–60, 89, 94, 131, 137, 156–57,
 217–18, 221–22, 224–25, 238, 242
Gasper, Des 125, 179
GATT 10, 43, 156, 158–59
GDP 125–27
 shrunken Ecuador's 125
gender 98, 115, 117, 184, 238
General Assembly 224
Gerlach, Allen 39, 117, 120–21, 123, 137, 141
German Constitutional Court 227
German Democratic Republic 221
Gerring, John 34
ghost coalitions 128–31, 136, 140, 144
 cost 140
Giddens, Anthony 43
Ginsburg, Tom 225
Giovannini, Michela 89
Glick Schiller, Nina 48, 95, 213
Global Alliance 77
globalisation 44, 49
 regarding 43
Global North 43–44, 114
Global South 19, 37, 43, 101, 113–14, 125, 219
goal 203
 new political 217
 possible aspirational 16
 ultimate 168
Goldoni, Marco 67
Good Living 1–21, 23–33, 35–107, 109, 111–18,
 144, 152–54, 157, 160–69, 171–209, 211–12,
 216–23, 225–26, 230, 233–37, 240–44
 analysis of 8, 11, 15, 17–18, 26, 29, 32, 34,
  73, 102, 112–13, 166, 168–69, 196
 applicability of 219, 234–35
 attainment of 93–94
 birth of 59, 108, 193
 constitutional inscription of 18, 31, 105
 crafting of 74, 111, 212, 222, 244
 critical strain of 74, 102, 163
 egalitarian redistribution statist 95

emergence of 8, 108, 114, 161
empty signifier of 160, 192, 196
frame 30, 76, 90, 204, 220
framing of 25, 71, 87, 106, 199, 218–19
origins of 34, 53, 155, 157, 162, 168, 193,
 209, 211, 228, 243
postmodern theory of 82
state-centred 97
strain of 68, 80, 85, 87–88, 96, 98–101,
 103, 180, 204
usage of 2, 78, 165, 196, 226
Gordon, Colin 54
governability 130
governance 31, 39, 42, 46, 52, 54–57, 59, 133,
 169–70, 172
 authoritative political 8
 democratic 110, 124, 143
 multilayered 145, 148
 technology of 56–57, 168
 strong central 9
governmentality 32, 42, 54–57, 59, 64–65,
 111, 146, 161, 164, 166, 168–70, 172
graduated sovereignty 145, 153, 155, 158–59,
 220–21, 225, 228, 234
 allocated 158
Gramsci, Antonio 189
grass-roots associational structures 176
Greco-Roman Hellenic 70
Grijalva Jiménez, Agustín 13, 127, 222
Grinspun, Ricardo 92, 119
growth 95
 annum 120
 economic 42, 93, 97
 impressive gdp 122
 market-led 152
 national 179
Gualinga, Carlos Viteri 2, 70–71, 75, 202–3,
 205, 208
 contrast 203
 guiding 208
Guamote 151–52
Guaranda 151–52
Guardiola, Jorge 72
Guatemala 158, 234–35, 240
Guatemalan Constitutional Court 240
Guayaquil 123
Gudynas, Eduardo 2, 98, 100, 107, 154, 162,
 164, 209

Guerrero, Andrés 118
guidance 168
Gutiérrez, Lucio 141–42

Habermas, Jürgen 12, 61, 63–65, 161, 195, 210, 226
habitus 62, 105
 apparatus of 182
 orchestrated 62
Hale, Charles 27, 32, 45, 55–56, 106, 119, 166, 173
Hamilton, Jonathan 44
Harding, Timothy 95
harmony 1, 70, 74, 77, 81, 97, 100, 202
 social 73
Harris, Angela P. 87, 225
Harvey, David 42, 44, 106
health care 158, 179, 235, 237
Healthier 91
hegemonic articulation 185, 189, 192, 197, 216
hegemonic project 82, 188–90, 192
Helmke, Gretchen 19, 27, 40, 59, 61, 94, 122–23, 128–29, 131
Hendrik, Wagenaarm 171
heterogeneity 113
Hidalgo-Capitán, Antonio Luis 4–5, 68–69, 71–72, 102, 223
Hikes 127
Hnitidou, Ekaterini Katerina 235–36
Hogenboom, Barbara 196–97
Holland 58
housing 2, 7, 13, 92, 96, 127, 158, 202, 235, 240
 dignified 7
 secure 157
 sovereign state 46
Houtart, Francois 2, 85, 100
Huanacuni, Fernando 2, 81
Hudson, Wayne 44–45
human dignity 208, 220–21, 225, 227–28, 236, 240, 242
 collective 221, 223, 226, 243
 construction of 227–28
 to live with 236
 surrounding 227
humanity 55, 77, 99, 181–82, 184, 197, 215, 227
human rights 10, 13, 19, 44–45, 48, 51, 110–11, 145, 148, 153–57, 173, 218–20, 222, 224–27, 230, 234, 241–42

 constrained 239
 guaranteed 28
 regarding international 157
 threatened basic 28
human rights adjudication, regarding 156
human rights-based development 51
human rights discourse 5–6, 8, 10, 51, 157, 167, 195, 199, 219, 226, 234, 237
human rights instruments 224, 230
 international 224, 230–31
human rights regimes 46–47
 international 110
human rights system 233, 237
 unified 111
human rights treaties 18, 50, 110, 157, 240
 inscribed international 5
 international 7, 110
Hungarian Constitutional Court 227
Hungary 8, 221
Hybridity 86
hyperinflation 126–27
hyper-presidential system 37, 89, 92, 128, 130, 198, 220, 242
 current 220

IACtHR (Inter-American Court of Human Rights) 6, 8, 12, 19, 45, 110, 156, 199, 220–21, 225–40, 242–43
Ibañez Langolis, J.M. 135
idealisation 4
 new 149
identity 40–41, 47, 81, 87, 95, 99, 106, 131–32, 134, 138–39, 177, 179, 188–90, 192
 cultural 13, 158, 231, 235
 denaturalise indigenous people's 86
identity constructions indigenous people, based 132
identity politics 5, 19, 38–40, 45, 49, 51, 55, 106, 132
 coupled 41
ideological 71–72, 180
Illapa 83
Imbabura 62, 151
Imbabura Province-Northern Ecuador 79
IMF 43, 124–26, 142, 169, 223
immiseration 58, 92, 171, 188
importation 124, 214, 221–22, 226
 gradual 221

imports 106, 152
  conceptual 98, 198
import substitution industrialisation 95
Incheon 93, 97
India 236
Indians 86–87, 104, 117, 213, 215
  blood 85
  generic 180
  half-naked 215
  perfect 87
  real 87, 180
Indian Supreme Court in Maneka Gandhi 236
Indigenist 5, 76, 85–86, 112, 162–63, 194–95, 209, 211, 213, 219, 225, 234, 237, 241
Indigenist and post-developmental discourses 81
Indigenist and post-development understandings of Good Living 115
Indigenist currents 197
Indigenist Good Living 72
Indigenist interpretations of Good Living 87
Indigenist Left's construction 87
Indigenist/Pachamama 4, 161
Indigenist strains 114
Indigenist strains of Good Living 16, 87, 193
Indigenist Sumak Kawsay 87
Indigenist understandings 114
indigenous 1, 5, 39–40, 45, 67, 69, 75, 78–80, 84, 86, 103–4, 114–15, 132–36, 151, 154, 203–4, 232
indigenous alterity 180
indigenous bourgeoise 84
indigenous claims 136
indigenous cohorts 133
indigenous communities 84, 88, 114, 116–17, 133–34, 147, 151–52, 154, 163, 166, 170, 174–75, 178, 205, 210, 237
  active 39
  demanded 176
  politicising 147
  pre-colonial 71
  reconstitute 176
  transformed Andean 176
indigenous communities monitoring oil activity 40
indigenous conception 89

indigenous cosmologies 70, 79, 87
indigenous demands 106–7, 117–18, 147, 180
  propelled 226
  supported 119
indigenous elite 84, 214, 216
  bureaucratic 198
  surging 216
indigenous enclaves 147
indigenous epistemologies 4, 14, 16, 72, 99
  recovered 18
  unique 82
indigenous leaders 15, 18, 72, 78, 118, 190, 205, 207, 216
indigenous mobilisation 9–10, 40, 88, 107, 111, 131, 190, 205, 223
indigenous movements 28, 38, 76, 103, 112, 115, 117, 137, 146, 167, 196, 205
indigenous nationalities 45, 70, 72, 133
  distinct 45, 48
  multiple 46
Indigenous Nationalities of Ecuador 134
indigenous networks 176
indigenous NGOs 104
indigenous ontology 205
indigenous organisations 88, 119, 134–36, 138, 173
  first transprovincial 133
indigenous peoples 31, 39, 41–42, 45–46, 49, 56, 58, 69–72, 82, 85–87, 98–99, 118–21, 132–35, 142, 144, 163–64, 177, 179, 204–6, 210–11, 236
indigenous politics 8, 39–41, 85, 114, 116–17, 141, 178
indigenous resistance 101, 180
inductive reasoning 34, 162, 168
inequality 58, 69, 75, 174, 229
  cultural 228
  historic 31, 38, 199
  historic intragroup 229
  structural 30, 118
inexistence 86
inflation 125, 127
Ingram, Gregory 177
institutions 5, 7–8, 15, 17, 20, 22–24, 57, 59, 61–63, 73–74, 86, 88, 129, 148–50, 153, 155–56, 168–69, 171–72, 222–23, 239–40
  academic 214
  bilateral development 173

institutions (Cont.)
    international financial   19, 86, 150
    mainstream development   173
    multilateral financial   169–70
    multinational   10
    redefining geopolitical   224
integration   133, 169, 196, 198–99
    diluted   198
    jurisprudential   229
intellectual elite   182, 190
    local   243
intellectuals   77, 79, 144, 150
    domestic   243
    mestizo   5, 72
    public   185
    trans-national   216
    urban   116, 136
Inter-American Commission of Human Rights   156, 225
Inter-American constitutionality block   229
Inter-American Court of Human Rights. *See* IACtHR
Inter-American Human Rights System   9, 156, 224, 230, 232, 234–35
Inter-American Human Rights System and Good Living   234
Inter-American Special Rapporteur on Freedom of Expression   60
interculturality   75, 80, 138
interest rates   126–27
International Criminal Court   45
International Labor Organization's Indigenous and Tribal Peoples Convention   45, 130
International Monetary Fund   1, 172
intervention   57, 105, 107, 150, 154, 166–67, 171–72, 174, 177–78, 184, 191–92, 194, 196, 198
    policies of   167, 179
    processes of   67, 88
    programs of   57, 104, 153, 166, 171–72, 174, 196, 198, 213
    societal   174
    targeted programs of   181, 213
interventionist state   27, 38, 46, 147–48, 150, 167
investments   44, 91, 149, 199, 202
    human capital   95
    productive   179

inward-looking economic development policies   121
Isaacs, Anita   19, 120
Italy   49, 149, 153

Janvry, Alain de   175
Japan   95
Jarquin, Edmundo   124–25
Jeju   97
Jokisch, Brad   49
Judeo-Christian beliefs   81
Judeo-Christian traditions   70
judicial accountability   124
Judicial Activism   239
judicial review   67, 90, 196, 220, 239
    domestic   221, 238
    expansive   13
    regional   111
judicial rules   63, 65
judiciary   59
    active   238
judiciary powers   61
    special   12
Jung's texts   83
juridical abstraction   10
juridical patrimony   157
juridification   7, 10, 12, 65, 89, 195, 226
jurisdictions   6, 18, 168, 222, 236–37
    civil law   21–22
    common law   21
    contentious   156
    domestic   44, 236
    international investment treaties ceding sovereign   9
    multiple   221
jurisprudence   156–58, 225, 227, 229, 231, 234, 237
    existing   200
    relevant   157
    solid   158
    transformative   229
jurisprudential   13
jurisprudential development   13, 18, 238
justice   13, 77, 99, 149, 154, 214
    environmental   199
    social   31, 137, 144, 239
juxtaposition   219
    direct   241

INDEX

Kant   227–28
Kapiszewski   90
Kayambi indigenous   205
Keal   145
Kelemen   8, 37, 108
Keller   172
Kennedy administration   119
Kichwa Indigenous Community of Sarayaku   72, 230–31
Kitschelt, Herbert   23
knowledge   93, 97, 113, 168, 171–72, 178, 182, 186, 194–95, 197
   ancient   223
   archaic   13–14
   disseminate   179
   local   106
   new   166
   political   185
   scientific   179
Kostakopolou, Dora   145–46
Kymlicka, Will   5, 55, 148–49

label   14, 29, 86, 97, 134, 203, 214, 239
   pejorative   85
labour   95, 132
   secure   92
Laclau, Ernesto   29, 168, 185, 187–90, 192, 194, 204, 207
land   13, 41, 62, 83, 100, 118, 120, 132–34, 136, 144, 157, 170, 233, 235
   ancestral   119
   arable   118
   collective   136
   communal   117, 137
   state-sponsored   134
   transforming communal   136
Landa, Cesar   239–40
land reform   115, 119, 132, 170
   long-awaited   119
   successful   136
   unsuccessful   132
land titles   119
   demanded   136
Langmore, John   100
language   6, 48, 51, 56, 70, 95, 152, 208, 210, 213, 217, 226, 235, 239
   common   72
Larrea, Carlos   94, 96–97, 168, 175, 199

Latacunga   151–52
Latin America   5–6, 12, 38–40, 42–43, 58, 77–78, 109–13, 117, 119–20, 147–48, 155–58, 163–64, 171–73, 175–76, 193–95, 220–22, 224–25, 228–30, 235, 241–42
Latin American approach   224, 241
Latin American Constitutions   218
Latin American Human rights law   238
Latin American jurisdictions   111, 167, 218, 238–40
Latin American states   19, 39, 42, 44–45, 47, 122, 157–58, 221, 232
Laurie, Nina   56, 117, 150, 152, 166, 172, 177–78
law
   changing dynamics Latin American   238
   constructivist conceptions of   12, 65, 229
   exportation of   222, 226
   importation of   5–6, 8, 221–23
   international human rights   45, 156–57
   WTO   159
Law of Agrarian Reform and Colonization   119
Lebech, Mette   227
legal institutions   8, 74
   international   153
   new   222
   permeated   210
   vertical   6
legal interpreters   62–63
legal precedent   210, 228
legal principle   1, 4, 8, 11, 16, 20, 29–30, 114, 116, 161, 164, 217, 223, 225–26, 228
   abstract   154
legal procedures   90
   corresponding   14
legal systems   12, 20, 38, 58, 111, 116, 143, 153, 221–23, 226, 228–29, 232, 236, 242
   domestic   110, 230
   regional   221, 233
legal theories   11, 241
legal transformations   9, 32, 71, 75, 164
   domestic   220
   unprecedented   67
legislation   1, 8, 50, 72, 119, 202, 230, 238
   domestic   5, 7, 157, 164, 230–31
legitimacy   6, 218
   constitutional   218
   democratic   43
   political   96

Lemaitre, Julieta 58
Levi-Strauss, Claude 186–87
Levitsky, Steven 90–91, 128
Lewis, Colin 96
liberalisation 148, 171
    constitutionalised market 130
    expansive 129
    financial 125, 130, 140
    market-led 155
    pro-economic 46
Liberation Theology 85, 103
Lichterman, Paul 184–85
Lijphart, Arend 106, 147, 239
Lind, Amy 19, 125, 168
Lixinski, Lucas 56
Llasag, Raúl 45, 87, 104, 119–20, 123, 130, 134, 137, 139–40, 142, 173
Lluco, Miguel 33
loan conditionalities 43
    sovereign 3
logics 22, 55, 104, 196
    circulatory 219
    contradictory 181
    disciplining 31, 57
    formal 74
    friendly 194
    intersecting 180
    linear 36
    market-based 166
Lovelock, James 85
Loxton, James 90–91, 128
Lucero, José Antonio 135
Luxembourg 110
Luxemburg, Rosa 190–91, 194

macroeconomic conditions 124, 129
    corroded 127
    fledgling 127
    reforms 37, 98, 170
Magaloni, Beatriz 172–73
Mahoney, James 36–37, 108
Mahuad, Jamil 50, 141
Mainwaring 43
Maisley, Nahuel 158
Malek, Anwar Abdel 215
management 54, 141, 145
    autonomous environmental 100
    inadequate policy 122

Mansilla, Hugo Celso Felipe 14, 73, 85, 103, 105
Maori 163
Mapuche 11, 175
Marcuse, Herbert 87, 96
marginalisation 48, 58, 132, 173, 197, 203, 217, 236
market 10, 42, 44, 51, 55–56, 79, 104, 142, 149–50, 173–75, 180, 184, 193–94, 203
    capitalist 82, 104
    expanding 174
    global 179, 184
    international 3, 126
    present 159
market-based citizenship 148
market fundamentalism 104, 182
    perpetuated 181
market-led reforms 10, 39, 58, 130, 226
    former adopted 57
Marxists 83, 98, 103
master frame 100, 181, 190
    new political 137, 139
    political 40, 107, 135, 140, 191–92
    proto-political 41
    shared collective action 190
    successful 144
    successful political 144
Mauceri, Philip 40, 46
Mauss, Marcel 186
McAdam, Doug 47, 58, 139–40
McKeown 22–23, 34
McMichael, Philip 42–43
McNevin, Anne 145
measures
    administrative 171
    collusive policy 141
    IMF austerity 143
    invasive 232
    market-led 137
    regressive 164
    retaliatory trade 160
mechanics 62, 229
mechanisms 50, 55, 88, 94, 164, 169, 173, 175, 189, 218, 223, 225
    articulatory 170, 172, 187, 190, 195, 198
    procedural 66, 177
    redistributive 94
Medina, Javier 2, 9, 76–78, 81–87, 107

INDEX 299

Mehmet, Ozay 42
Mejía-Acosta, Andres 19, 27, 40, 61, 94, 128–31, 136
Melish, Tara 225
Mera, Alexis 231
mercantilization 93
merger 115, 152–53, 185, 191, 228
Merino, Roger 72, 79, 96, 99
metanarratives 154, 179, 196
method
  deductive 23
  inductive 23, 209
  selected 20
methodology 20–23, 27, 32, 34–36, 108–9, 162
  selected 21, 23–24, 109, 162
Mexico 44, 136, 174–75, 239
Middle East 215
Mijeski, Kenneth 1, 19, 33, 41, 48–49, 83, 103, 106, 111, 117, 124, 129, 131, 133–37, 140, 142–44
military regimes 120–21, 123–24
Mill, J.S. 146
Miller, Russel 63
minorities 5, 215
  gendered 58
  numerical 215
Miskito 163
Mitchell, Timothy 172, 180
mobilisation 32, 41, 57, 131–32, 137, 139, 147, 150, 226
  citizen 58, 137
  conaie-led 41, 49
  nationwide 138, 140, 144
modernisation 1, 96–97, 106
  industrial 96
modernising logics 97
  previous 96
modernity 14–15, 79, 82, 86, 98, 100, 154, 195, 213, 227
  scripts of 153–55, 159–60
Monni, Salvatore 99–100
Montalvo, Tania 174
Morgan, Kimberly 108–9
Morton, Adan David 54, 56
Mota Pardo, Mariana 239
Mouffe, Chantal 29, 133, 168, 185, 187–90, 194
movements 31, 40, 76, 103, 142, 193

contradictory 190
deep ecology 98, 100
defining 36
environmental 85
environmental justice 104
ethnonationalist 133
new peasant 115
radical 103
multiculturalism 45, 51, 55–56, 144
  articulated neoliberal 184
  economic orientated 56
  liberal 55–56, 75, 140
Muslims 187
  passive 215

Naes, Arne 98
Naranjo 126–27
National Assembly 94, 200–202
National Development Plan 46, 68, 93–94
National Electoral Council of Ecuador 200, 205
National Plan for Good Living 68, 91, 93
natural resources 93, 97, 101, 133, 201–2
Navajo 163
Nederveen Pieterse, Jan 42, 51, 94–96, 173, 175–76, 179, 185
Negretto, Gabriel 113, 130–31
Negros 174
Nelms, Taylor 4
neoliberalism 42–43, 116, 150, 177, 179, 192, 194
  social 55–56, 66
neoliberal reforms 114, 136, 166, 168, 175, 184, 188, 190–93, 196, 198, 220, 243
neo-structuralism 42
neo-utilitarianism 105
networks 10, 25, 88, 95, 101, 105, 107, 149–50, 155, 168, 170, 172, 176, 182–83
  clientelistic 94
  social 101, 149, 152
  trans-national advocacy 43
New Zealand 71, 163
NGOs 28, 50, 55, 64–65, 67, 77–78, 85–86, 101, 103–5, 107, 115, 117, 149–50, 175–76, 178, 180, 184
  developing 222
  domestic 192
  foreign 55
  international 43, 167

NGOs (Cont.)
  local   200
  local environmental   40
  multinational   117
  transformed   178
Nicaragua   158
Nobles, Richard   90
Nordic countries   94, 106
norms   6, 12, 143, 149, 183, 230
  international human rights   154
  legal   72, 113
North, Liisa   41–42, 50, 92, 119, 124–25
Nuestra América   91N

OAS   156
Oatley, Thomas   121
obligations   157, 183, 239–40, 242
  international   231–32
  twofold   232
Observatorio PyME   126
OECD   22, 126
oil   117, 120–21, 123, 134, 200, 202–3
  interventionist   51
  multinational   39, 116
oil exports   120, 124, 133
  country's   127
  increased   124
oil revenues   38, 95, 124
ontology   2, 74, 84, 185, 102, 204
  marginalising   82
  millenary indigenous   55
OPEC   121
order   38–39, 44, 47, 65, 68, 76, 154, 170, 198, 209
  chronological   153
  constitutional   65, 239
  domestic legal   110
Organic Law for Jurisdictional Guarantees and Constitutional Control   242
organisations   41, 69, 80, 115, 134, 137, 151, 156, 200, 210, 224149
  international activist   40
  long-standing social   10
  multilateral   152
  radical ecologist   40
Orientalism   86, 214–15
origins   2–3, 11, 14, 19–20, 25, 30, 79, 81, 83, 103, 106, 115–16, 161, 164–65, 204, 209
  alleged   161
  alleged communitarian indigenous   95

  conceptual   204, 225
  discursive   76, 154, 193
  ethnic   115, 208
  genuine   25
  geographical   132
  legal   3, 76, 225
  ontological   2, 25–26, 72–73, 75, 223
  socio-historical   27
Orlie, Melissa   182
OSG   176
Ospina, Pablo   62, 79
Otavalo   84, 151–52
otherness   213, 215, 229, 233
outflows   126
  volatile capital   126
outsourcing   145
Oviedo Freire, Atawallpa   5, 9, 71–73, 81–83, 85–87, 107, 154, 162, 209

Pacari   72, 147
Pachacamac   83
Pachakutik   41, 48–49, 117, 130, 137, 139–40, 142–44, 223
  left   140
Pachamama   68, 71, 81
Pachano, Simón   128
Pachasofía   9, 70, 164
pacification   169
Palier   22–23, 34, 162
Pallares, Amalia   117, 132, 135, 147
Pallottino   99–100
Palmeter   159
Panama   71
Parada   174
paradigms
  alter-development   101
  civilizing   9
  cultural   98
  economic   8, 79, 98
  foreign   98
  new   81, 83, 102
  new ethical   100
  new socio-economic   79
  recreating indigenous   2
  rural   114
  universal   83
Paraguay   158, 236–37
Parga   85, 103, 163–64, 212

INDEX 301

Parra Vera, Oscar 158, 164, 239–40
parties 44, 131, 141, 171
 ethnic 143
 new 138
 traditional 130
party politics 131
 defining Ecuadorian 128
 elite-controlled 40
 squabbling 61
Pasqualucci, Jo 236
Pastaza province 9, 39, 133, 136, 152
path 36, 97, 205
 historical 241
peasants 5, 56, 58, 69, 102, 133, 135, 138, 177, 181, 188, 192, 229, 236
 contemporary highland 215
 mobilised Ecuador's 144
 non-indigenous 136
Permanent Commission of Biodiversity 201
Perreault, Thomas 136, 170, 172
Peru 38–39, 44, 49, 146, 158, 173, 239–40
Petras, James 134
Pichincha 151
plurinationality 70, 220, 222
pluriverse 12, 17
 trans-modern 12
Poland 221
policies 15, 17, 30–31, 39, 42, 46, 68, 71, 155, 168–69, 171–72, 174–75, 177, 188, 190, 193, 210, 212, 223, 230–31
 commercial 155–56
 macroeconomic 37, 170, 172, 244
 neo-extractivist 69
policy agendas 173, 192
 inclusive market-orientated 226
policy reform 129–30, 155, 195
 ghost coalitions enacting 130
 internal 47
 market-led 107
 market-orientated 191
 pass 131
 unpopular 136
political actors 29, 37, 46, 72, 90, 108, 111, 161
 consolidated 216
 new 57, 110
political agendas 40–41, 52–53, 55–56, 66, 78, 81, 88, 104, 107, 134, 136–39, 142, 214, 217
 transgressive 194, 198, 216

political arena 7, 9–10, 17, 31–32, 36, 38, 41–42, 51–53, 108, 110, 117–18, 130, 133, 142, 144, 146–47, 159, 223–24
political association, defined 147
political crises 111, 122, 129
 prolonged 129
political demands 31, 57, 88, 144, 173, 191, 194, 196, 198, 210
political economy 112, 114, 116, 244
 international 25
political elites 41, 84, 130, 139
 traditional 195
political forces 3, 40, 67, 136, 143
political leverage 33, 111, 192
 lost 58
 necessary 137
political mobilisation 33, 40, 131, 139, 154, 232
political opportunities 47, 58, 139–40, 182
 strategic 47
political participation 48–49, 158
 granted 49
 inclusive 69
 limited 9
 redefined 145
 reserved 146
 restricted 146
political parties 24, 39–41, 48, 84–85, 128–31
 conservative 141–42
 existing 49
 fragmented 46
 left-leaning 58, 192
 main 129
 traditional 130, 144
political processes 7, 17, 26, 106, 130, 150, 164, 186
political rights 41, 133, 146, 156
 secured 232
 universal 144
politicised ethnic cleavages 11–12, 24, 27, 29, 31–33, 36–38, 52, 57–58, 66, 68, 106, 108, 111, 144, 147–48, 160–61, 167–68, 170, 193, 211
Ponce 174
Ponce León, Fernando 2, 72
population control 88
populism 90
 irrational 95
Portes, Alejandro 182–83

Portugal 110
Post-2008 Ecuador 92, 152
Posta 205–6
post-communist countries 6, 222–23
post-development 11, 15–16, 98, 101, 112, 195, 197, 216, 220, 223, 225, 234, 237, 241
   entrap 219
Post-Modernity 227
post neoliberal order 92
poverty 13, 19, 48, 90, 92–93, 103, 105, 127, 170–76, 181, 183–84, 191, 194, 199, 203
   eradication of 3, 179
power 4, 6–7, 30, 47, 59–60, 62, 73, 89, 101–2, 141, 156–57, 165–66, 171–72, 181–83, 185–86, 195–98, 218–20, 230, 232–33, 242–43
   symbolic 89, 186
   transformative 231
power dynamics 53, 80, 89–90, 102, 106, 164, 173, 198
power relations 25–26, 73–74, 84, 89, 145, 167, 209
power structures 32, 67, 84, 90, 106
Pozo, Mauricio 127
Prashad, Vijay 175
praxis 99
   regional judicial 233
premises 36, 147, 178
   empirical 219
   market-based 150
   ontological 166
   state-centric 95
principles 3–4, 6, 9–10, 99, 144, 150, 159, 163–64, 206, 239
   configurative 13, 158, 235, 237
   core 179
   enforcing 48
   formal constitutional 7
   ground-breaking legal 89
   guiding 181–82
   justiciable constitutional 199
   new legal 65, 161
   normative 74
   open 229
   traditional 72
a priori existence 162
privatisations 3, 44, 104, 137, 185
   state-owned asset 140
   unconstitutional 130

Procacci, Giovanna 171
procedural restrictiveness 61
   liberal 63
process tracing 21–25, 34–36, 52–54, 57, 64, 162
   conventional 22, 35
   selected theory-guided 23
   standard 35
   theoretically-guided 167
productivism 176
profit motive 93
promotion 95, 104, 179, 203, 216, 224
   regional 224
promulgation 50
PRONASOL 174
property 15, 165, 231
   collective 158, 165
   private 44–45
property ownership 56
property rights 101
   private 46
   regarding private 219
protest 33, 58–60, 70, 118, 136, 139, 161, 178, 188, 191, 198, 210–11, 240, 242–43
Public choice theories 42
public sphere 31–32, 37, 64, 68, 96, 99, 110, 131, 137, 139, 193, 195, 198, 209–11, 213
Puente, Diego 98
Putnam, Robert 105, 149, 153, 183, 185
Puyo 134, 233

Quade, E.S. 22
Quichua 11, 136
Quietism 87
Quijano, Aníbal 73, 212, 218
Quito 118, 123, 136

race 65, 145, 229
   conflates 87
   regarding 87
racial projects 47, 86, 146, 215
   present 87
racism 38, 132, 144, 173, 188, 197, 229
   structural 31, 41, 58, 132
Radcliffe, Sarah 12, 46–47, 71, 73, 102, 106, 117, 132, 136, 150, 152, 172, 177–78, 212
Rajagopal, Balakrishnan 45–46, 178
Ramachadra 98

INDEX

Ramírez, Rene   73, 95–97, 107, 145, 154, 158, 162, 209
  former National Secretary   94
  former National Secretary René   88
  realist utopia   97
Ramos, Alcida   85, 87, 104, 180
rampant   128
Rask Madsen, Michael   26, 73, 89, 183
Rawls, John   61, 64–65, 131, 161, 195, 210
referendum   129, 137, 140, 200–201, 205–7
  constitutional   32
  national   1, 200–201, 205
Reformatory Law of Agrarian Reform and Colonization   119
reforms   9, 19, 24, 94, 101, 113, 118–19, 124, 133, 143, 170, 228, 234, 242
  anti-neoliberal   191, 196
  domestic political   111, 222
  economic structural   114
  electoral   49, 129, 137, 146, 211
  installed unprecedented   123
  land tenancy   170
  legal   58, 105, 111, 119, 148
  legislative   28, 130, 136
  neo-liberal   194
  radicalising   121
reformulation   140
Refugee Convention   50
reminisces   81, 83
representation   14, 47, 58–61, 65, 87, 106, 115, 139, 150, 204, 212, 215, 223
  abstract legal   195
  accuracy of   73
  assaulted   130
  constitutional   195
  cultural   15
  democratic   94
  dystopian hyperreal   87
  elite-based   64
  idealised   71, 153, 173, 213
  indirect   61
  mystical   86
representative structures   222
Republica   201
Rescasens, Andreu Viola   73, 85, 102–3, 150, 212
resources   5, 13, 40, 54, 90, 101, 158, 167–68, 183, 202, 223, 235, 238

economic   115, 180
embattled Ecuador's   124
endogenous   82
environmental   231
financial   126, 176, 180
human   183
potential   182
scarce   123, 214
Restrictive immigration policy   50
retreating state   24, 27, 31–32, 36, 42–43, 51, 106, 108, 110, 148, 160–61, 164, 167–68, 171, 175, 191, 193
  elusive or   122
revision   27–28, 30, 32, 72, 74, 76, 102–3, 149–50, 160, 181, 190, 218, 237, 239
  complete   116
revolution   242
  agrarian   96
  cultural   95
revolutionary mass identity   191–92, 194
  unitary   196
Riach, Graham   213, 217
Rice, Roberta   25, 27, 33, 41, 43, 47, 51, 58–59, 72, 133–35, 137, 139, 190, 192
rights   1, 4, 6–7, 11, 13, 19, 29, 31, 60–62, 67, 198, 202, 206–8, 210, 218–22, 225, 227–28, 230, 232, 234–44
  broader cultural   214, 216
  collective land   164
  competing   218
  economic   97, 108
  equal   49
  ethnic minority   237
  interdependent   239
  new   19, 25, 67, 238
  novel   26, 198
  social   158, 164, 217–18
  special   139, 210
  territorial   78–79, 134, 136, 231, 243
Riobamba   151–52
Rodríguez-Garavito, Cesar   12, 65, 174, 210, 218, 229
Rohlfing, Ingo   33–34
Roldos-Hurtado presidency   75, 124
Romania   221
Ross, Michael   124
Rössel, Jörg   95
ruling paradigms   100

rural Andes 9, 77, 151, 166, 176, 228
rural communities 75, 105, 133, 152–54, 170, 177, 198
  sustaining 149
Russia 126

Sadoulet, Elisabeth 175
Said, Edward 214
Sánchez, Francisco 46, 49, 128–29, 131
Sánchez-Parga, José 71, 73, 153
Sanin Restrepo, Ricardo 65
Santos, Boaventura de Sousa 100–101
Sarayaku 204, 230–33
Sartori, Giovanni 25, 46, 128, 147
Sawyer, Suzana 9, 19, 25, 27, 32, 39–40, 51, 55, 70, 104, 136–37, 139, 152, 168
Sayán, Diego 238–39
Schavelzon, Salvador 9, 68, 73, 78–79, 88, 94–96, 212, 214
Schiff, David 90
Schild, Veronica 56, 149–50, 166
Scholte, Jan Aart 43
Schöneberg, Julia Maria 172
Schwarz, Warren 186, 188–89
Seawright, Jason 34
Sebastian, Thomas 159
Second Tier Organisations 176, 223
sectors 69, 242
  discriminated 242
  industry 95
  marginalised 53, 229
  private 92, 236
  progressive 181
securement 45, 69, 105, 158, 171, 180, 229, 233–35, 237, 240–41
Segovia 46
self 102, 149, 209
Selverston-Scher, Melina 40, 70, 133, 135
service provision 240
  public 125
services 92, 95, 125, 159, 184, 200
  basic 13, 127, 158, 235, 237
Séverine, Deneulin 2, 13
Shelton, Dinah 110
Shilliam, Robbie 4
Shiwiar indigenous 136
Shuar Federation indigenous people 133, 205
Siddique 67

signifiers 187, 226, 237
  all-encompassing 191
  fixed 187
  multiple 181
  unique 192
Silva Portero, Carolina 4
Simbaña 95
Simmons, Beth 18, 154–55
Skocpol, Theda 25, 184
Smith, Jackie 21
Snow, David 29, 190
social capital 19, 51, 104–5, 114–15, 117, 148–50, 152–53, 166, 170–89, 191–96, 198, 213–14, 216–17, 243
  sources of 182, 184
social capital and ethnodevelopment 189–92, 195, 197, 243
social conflict 33, 37, 39, 54, 167
  defused 51, 122
  pacified 38
social development 17, 178–79, 181, 192, 199, 235
  granted 191
Social Development Summit 179
socialism 62, 69
  egalitarian republican 96
  installed creole market 130
socialist constitution 67
socialists 5, 68–69, 74, 83, 96, 133–34
social movements 11–12, 39–41, 45, 47, 64, 69, 78, 102, 131, 139, 167, 178
social protest 32, 56–61, 63–66, 127, 195, 198–99
  product of 65, 195
Soifer, Hillel 27, 46, 59, 109, 118, 122–23, 131
solidarity 1, 71, 82, 93, 101, 149–50, 154, 170, 182, 191, 193, 213, 239
  bounded 183
  forged network 43
  local 82
  pre-colonial millenary communal 101
  regarding 194
  social 150
solidarity networks 83, 191
  community-based 19
Solórzano, Carlos 141
Somers 104–5, 149, 153, 164, 176, 181–83, 185

INDEX 305

Somers, Margaret 181
Sosa, César 97
South Africa 110
South America 11, 42, 103, 221
South Central 183
South East Asia 93, 95
South Korea 92–93, 97
sovereignty 46, 51, 101, 110, 145, 155, 157
  absolute 44
  all-powerful 153
  bounded 144–45
  ceding 28, 44, 57
  central unitary 44
  classic notions of 147, 160
  domestic 58
  parliamentary 67
  popular 65
  receding 209
  strengthened 121
  territorial 55
  weakened 31, 167
Soviet Union 183, 221
Spain 49, 101, 110
Spartz, James 2
Specialized Permanent Commission on Biodiversity and Natural Resources 201–2
Spedding Pallet, Alison 74
Spill 120
Spivak, Gayatari Chakravorty 214, 216–17
state 28, 39, 41–42, 44–47, 49–52, 54–55, 57–58, 60, 62–64, 69–70, 74–75, 91–96, 109–11, 122, 124, 133, 144–45, 148–50, 153, 156, 159, 167, 220, 224–25, 230–37, 239–40
  all-powerful 154
  central 38, 122–23, 134
  contested 46
  current 199, 215, 217, 226, 241
  developmental 42
  elite-controlled 195
  elusive 127
  independent 163
  intercultural 62, 76
  intermediary 183
  monolithic 171
  multinational 140, 210
  national 76
  neutral 42
  pluricultural 130
  plurinational 62, 78, 84
  rogue 160
  unconstitutional 239
  weak 127, 139
statist 162–63, 193–95, 211
Statist Good Living 88, 91, 97
Stefanoni, Pablo 14
subaltern alterity 213
subaltern epistemologies 12
subjectivity 73, 219
  collective 46
submission 127, 189
subsidies 46, 121, 127
subsistence 7, 132
substantiation 47, 77–78
  theoretical 158
subversive discourses 188, 196
  multiple 166
subversive politics 174
  debilitated 198
Sucres 125
Sullivan, Meghan 77
Sumak Kawsay 1–2, 5, 11, 15–16, 62, 69–72, 75–76, 80–88, 196, 201, 203, 220, 223, 225–26, 234, 241, 243–44
  alleged power 83
  alternative epistemological 83
  essentialised 88
  framing of 82, 84
  genuine 2
  homogenous 71
  millenary 86
  referencing 86
  regarding 80
  sustainability 71
Suma Qamaña 1–2, 70, 74, 77–78, 81, 83–84, 203
Suma Qamaña in Ecuador 79
supranational agreements 159
supranational jurisdictions 157, 234
supranational jurisprudence 157
supranational organs 156, 158, 225
sustainable development 19, 90, 179
  demanded 138
Sweden 95

system   4, 12, 16, 59–60, 63, 170, 187, 197, 239–40
  authoritative human rights protection   225
  capitalist   243
  collapsing party   128
  country's party   46
  economic   82, 94, 101
  electoral   129–30
  financial   125, 141
  fragmented multi-party   128
  hyper-presidential constitutional   218
Systemic analysis   22
  qualitative   22
Szlablowski, David   1, 4

Tagaeri and Taromenane indigenous peoples   202, 205
Tariffs   43, 156
Tarrow   34–35, 47, 112, 135
Taussig   213
taxes, indirect   127
Taylor, Charles   15, 181, 197
technocratic governance   38, 54, 95
  state-centred   91
technologies   39, 95–96, 126
  deployed   170
  new   56
  state-led   54
technopopulism   19, 95
territorial autonomy   5, 9, 45, 52, 66, 72, 81, 88, 135, 140, 147, 170, 174, 191, 194, 216
  securing   135
  threatened   190
territories   45, 54, 72, 87, 111, 133–34, 145, 158, 163, 170, 204, 231
  transformed indigenous   85
Texaco   120
Thatcher, Margaret   46
theoretical framings   3, 21, 24, 32, 53–54, 57, 73, 106, 109, 161, 168
theoretical promiscuity   105, 153, 176, 181, 185
theories   13, 17, 23–24, 82, 103, 113, 116, 121, 149, 159, 162, 164, 211
  critical   64, 85, 212
  democratic   57, 59
  new   99–100, 149
  post-colonial   25
  post-modern constructivist   69

two-dimensional   28
theory-guided process tracing   23–29, 32–36, 52–54, 66, 76, 108–9, 111–13, 116, 118, 162, 168, 193, 211–12
Tibanlombo   126
Tilly, Charles   47
Torre   1, 9, 19, 37, 83, 91, 95
trade, Carlos de la   21, 43–44, 156, 184
  fair   79
trade liberalisation   41, 125, 154–55, 159
  adopted   3
Trampusch, Christine   22–23, 34, 162
transformation   7, 15, 26, 42, 51, 54, 63, 66, 104, 108, 120, 164, 171, 228–29
  political   8, 41, 106–7
  post-colonial   103
  social   30, 106–7, 217
transgressive politics   57–58, 86, 88, 168, 172, 180–81, 184, 187–89, 191, 193, 195–96, 198, 212–13, 216
  master framing of   166, 185
  new form of   31, 175, 184
  pacified   166
transgressive politics Good Living   30
transnational   8–10, 19, 50–51, 54–55, 64–65, 67, 85, 104, 145, 150, 167, 192, 195, 212–13
transnational actors   28, 58, 64–65, 153–55, 171, 193, 209, 214, 222–23, 243
transnational agendas   178
transnational agents   19, 55, 85, 148, 150, 169–71, 213
transnational capital   134, 197
transnational citizens   49, 51
transnational community   153
  multi-ethnic   150
transnational conservation projects   85
transnational democracy   51, 64
transnational development   181, 185
transnational development resources   177
transnational discourses   184, 226
transnational elites   214
transnational engagement   52
transnational entities   159
transnational form   168
transnational governance   55
transnational governmentalities   53–57, 66, 74, 104–7, 109, 148, 160, 167–68, 170, 177, 193–94, 224, 243
transnational interconnectedness   82

transnational networks 40, 50, 66, 153
transnational NGOs 10, 150, 180
Travers, Max 218–19
treaties 110, 153, 155
   international 229
treaty ratification 44, 230
   international 18, 111
   regional human rights 45
Tribal Peoples Convention 45, 130
Tunupa 83
turmoil 118
   economic 107, 122, 124, 222
   financial 28
   managing macroeconomic 127
   political 33
Tushnet, Mark 67, 111, 224
Tutillo, Silvia 118–19, 133–34

Unai 84, 99
Unceta, Koldo 100
United Nations 178–79, 224
universal citizenship 49–50, 61, 146
   principle of 49–50
Uprimny, Rodrigo 37, 67, 210, 238
Uquillas, Alfredo 177
Uyantsa 233

vacuum 29
   contextual 28
   theoretical 148
Valencia 126–27
Vallejo, María Cristina 200
Van Cott, Donna Lee 9, 25, 33, 37–38, 40, 59, 61, 70, 104, 133, 135–36, 140–41
Vanhulst, Julien 77, 100–101, 203
van Inwagen, Peter 77
van Nieuwkoop, Martien 177
Van Teijilingen, Karolien 196–97
Vargas, Antonio 141
Vázquez, Alfredo Macías 2, 14, 69, 72–73, 87, 106, 165
Veltmeyer, Henry 134
Venezuela 1, 67, 124, 173
Verdesoto, Luis 146, 207
Vicuña 120–21, 124–27
Vida Digna 13, 29, 158, 199, 225–28, 234–36, 238, 240, 242–43
Vietnam 118
Villalba, Unai 101, 164

Villavicencio, Arturo 97
Viola 86
violence 58, 122, 134, 183–84
   epistemic 80
   exclusionary 83
   sexual 236
voting rights 110
vulnerability 236
   deepened 126
   economic 48

Waldmüller, Johannes 2, 72–73
Waldner, David 21–22, 28, 34, 36, 108–9
Walsh, Catherine 212
Warnars, Lavinia 199
Washington 46, 180
water 2–3, 13, 158, 174, 231, 235, 237, 240
wealth 3, 119, 203, 238
   distribution 4, 68, 118
Weber, Heloise 43, 177
weighing 138, 164
welfare 3, 94, 172, 235
wellbeing 13, 29, 59, 89, 93, 105, 169–71
   social 92
   social questions 169
   threatened human 179
Westwood 46–47, 71, 136
Whitehead, Laurence 221, 229
Whitten 121
Wichu kachi Mountain 233
Wickham, Gary 4, 57, 86
Widener, Patricia 40
Wiraxucha 83
Wollstonecraft, Mary 227
women 58, 78, 181, 211
World Bank 43, 48, 51, 104–5, 117, 124–27, 149–50, 152, 167, 169, 172, 174, 176–77, 181, 183–84
world markets 105, 170, 213, 216
World Trade Organization 9, 43, 155, 220
Wotipka 145, 154
WTO 43–44, 55, 158–59, 225
Wullweber, Joscha 187, 189

Xákmok Kásek 237

Yachak Cesar Vargas 233
yachay 97
Yachay City of Knowledge 97

Yakye Axa   236–37
Yampara   74
Yashar   19, 25, 27, 32–33, 37–39, 41, 47, 51, 104, 106, 110–11, 117, 119, 121, 128, 132–35, 145–47
Yasuindos Collective   207
Yasuní   199–201, 205
   regarding   200–201
Yasunidos Collective   205, 207

Yasuni Initiative   200–201, 205
Yasuní National Park   199–200
Yasuní referendum   205
Yates, Julian   31

Zamosc, Leon   142
Zapatista mobilisations   136
Zapatista revolt   175

www.ingramcontent.com/pod-product-compliance
Lightning Source LLC
Chambersburg PA
CBHW070909030426
42336CB00014BA/2345